KU-413-598

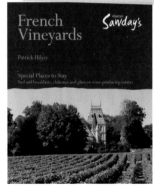

Alastair
Sawday's

Special Places
to Stay

French Châteaux
& Hotels

"Sawday unearths the
most beguiling châteaux,
auberges and hotels."
The Daily Telegraph

ipa

French
Vineyards

Alastair **Sawday's**

Patrick Hilyer

Special Places to Stay
Bed and breakfasts, châteaux and gîtes on wine-producing estates

Alastair
Sawday's

Special Places
to Stay

French
Self-catering

"Like listening to
recommendations from
trusted family friends."
Living France Magazine

Edited in Nicola Crosse

Go Slow France

Alastair **Sawday's**

Alastair Sawday
with Ann Cooke-Yarborough

Special places to stay, slow travel and slow food

Foreword
by Jean-Christophe Novelli

Alastair
Sawday's

Special Places to Stay

Twelfth edition
Copyright © 2011 Alastair Sawday
Publishing Co. Ltd
Published in 2011
ISBN-13: 978-1-906136-40-6

Alastair Sawday Publishing Co. Ltd,
The Old Farmyard, Yanley Lane,
Long Ashton, Bristol BS41 9LR, UK
Tel: +44 (0)1275 395430
Email: info@sawdays.co.uk
Web: www.sawdays.co.uk

The Globe Pequot Press,
P. O. Box 480, Guilford,
Connecticut 06437, USA
Tel: +1 203 458 4500
Email: info@globepequot.com
Web: www.globepequot.com

All rights reserved. No part of this publication may be
used other than for the purpose for which it is intended
nor may any part be reproduced, or transmitted, in any
form or by any means, electronically or mechanically,
including photocopying, recording or any information
storage or retrieval system, without prior written
permission from the publisher. Requests for
permission should be addressed to: Alastair Sawday
Publishing in the UK; or The Globe Pequot Press in
North America.

A catalogue record for this book is available from the
British Library. This publication is not included under
licences issued by the Copyright Agency. No part of
this publication may be used in any form of advertising,
sales promotion or publicity.

Alastair Sawday has asserted his right to be identified
as the author of this work.

Series Editor Alastair Sawday
Editor Angharad Barnes
Assistant to Editor Joanna Vitkovitch
Editorial Director Annie Shillito
Writing Alex Baker, Angharad Barnes,
Jo Boissevain, Ann Cooke-Yarborough,
Monica Guy
Inspections Katie Anderson, Rose Angas,
Richard & Linda Armspach, Angharad
Barnes, Isabelle Browne, Ann Cooke-
Yarborough, Jill Coyle, Penny Dinwiddie,
John & Jane Edwards, Georgina Gabriel,
Diana Harris-Sawday, Rosie Jackson,
Susan Luraschi, Annie Shillito, Victoria
Thomas, Elizabeth Yates
Thank you to those people who did an
inspection or two.
Accounts Bridget Bishop, Amy Lancastle
Sales & Marketing & PR Rob Richardson,
Sarah Bolton, Lisa Walklin, Helen Beilby
Web & IT Dominic Oakley, Chris Banks,
Phil Clarke, Nicole Deleon, Paul Nattress,
Mike Peake, Russell Wilkinson

And thanks to Ann Cooke-Yarborough
for her invaluable support.

*We have made every effort to ensure the accuracy
of the information in this book at the time
of going to press. However, we cannot accept
any responsibility for any loss, injury or
inconvenience resulting from the use of
information contained therein.*

Production: The Content Works
www.thecontentworks.com
Maps: Maidenhead Cartographic Services
Printing: Butler, Tanner & Dennis, Frome
UK distribution: Penguin UK, London

Cover photo credits
1. Red Cover/Di Lewis 2. Red Cover/Christopher Drake 3. Loupe Images/Chris Tubbs

Alastair

Sawday's

Special Places
to Stay

French
Bed & Breakfast

4 Contents

5

interesting of all [their] guests," and are clearly rejecting the marketing schemes that deliver individuals who have no notion of the spirit of 'chambres d'hôtes'.

If you are a fervent believer in, and lover of, French bed and breakfast, don't let the bureaucrats kill it off. Many owners are saying that the authorities require registration, declaration, taxation and lengths of concomitant endless red tape. Their response? They might simply close down. France will be left with little but business-minded managers of euro-regulated guest houses and boutique hotels. I paint a dire picture, but in ten years' time it could well look like this.

French tourism has taken a battering over the last two crisis years, though more visitors still go there than to any other European country. Rather like a beautiful old statue, France is worth seeing however weathered she is. She has lost none of her beauty, none of her special charm; all she needs is for us to show our appreciation by going there and not worshipping the false gods of long-distance holidays.

Our B&B owners are standing up to the storm. They still, bless them, think of our readers as "the most civilised and

My own favourite memory of a French B&B this year is this. My wife, Em, having breakfast on the rather dishevelled and pet-strewn lawn of our B&B, found herself having to manipulate her coffee cup around the vast dog that draped itself over her lap. Its back feet were on the ground, and so were its front feet. I was more amused than she was, but it was all part of the fun, and the sort of experience rarely available through Novotel — le 'café-au-chien'.

Alastair Sawday

Photo left: Tom Germain
Photo right: Maison Coutin, entry 615 (Lesley Chalmers)

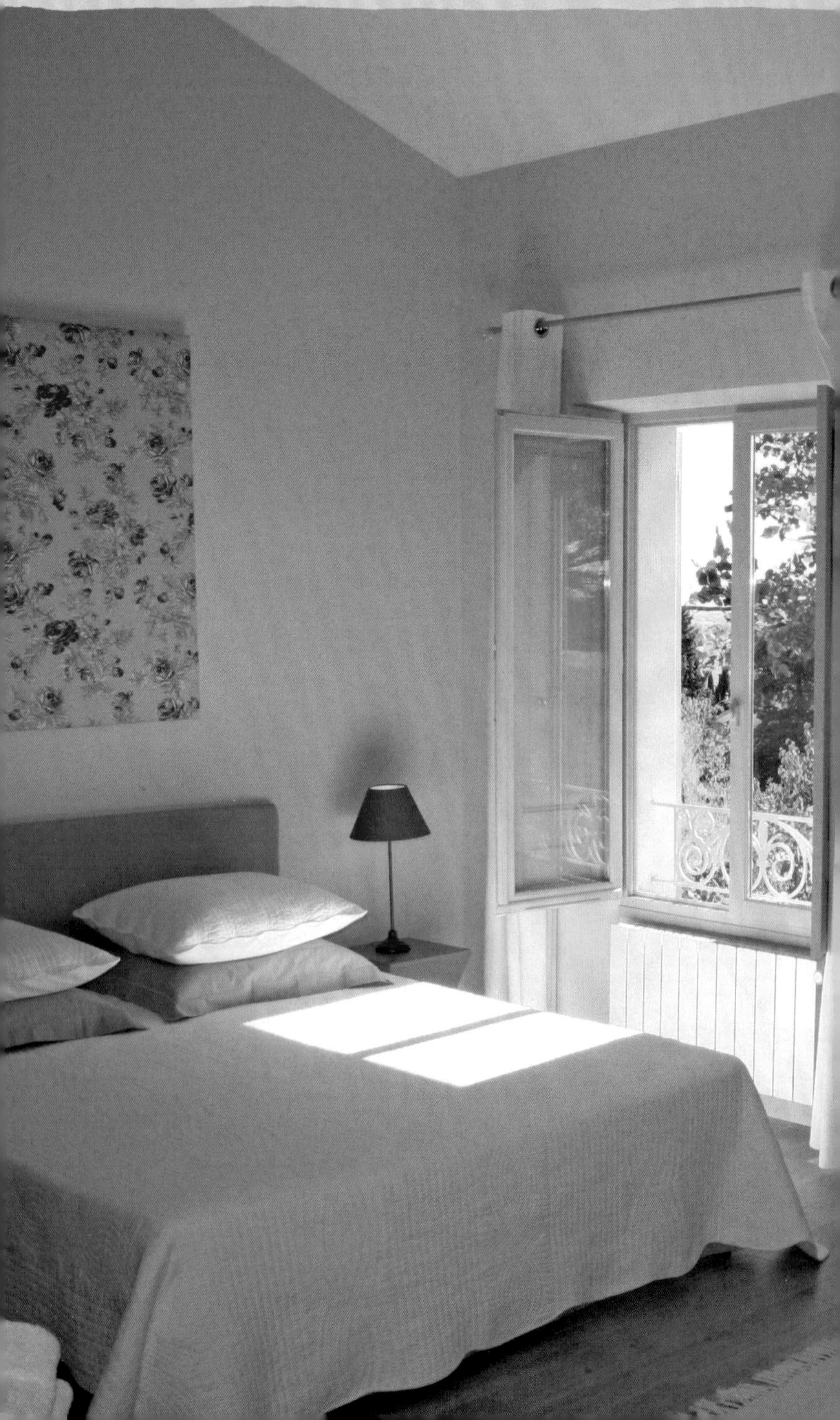

For many years Alastair Sawday Publishing has been 'greening' the business in different ways. Our aim is to reduce our environmental footprint as far as possible – with almost everything we do we have the environmental implications in mind. (We once claimed to be the world's first carbon-neutral publishing company, but are now wary of such claims.) In recognition of our efforts we won a Business Commitment to the Environment Award in 2005, and in 2006 a Queen's Award for Enterprise in the Sustainable Development category. In that year Alastair was voted ITN's 'Eco Hero'.

We have created our own eco-offices by converting former barns to create a low-emissions building. Through a variety of innovative and energy-saving techniques this has reduced our carbon emissions by 35%.

But becoming 'green' is a journey and, although we began long before most companies, we still have a long way to go.

In 2008 we won the Independent Publishers Guild Environmental Award. The judging panel were effusive in their praise, stating: "With green issues currently at the forefront of publishers' minds, Alastair Sawday Publishing was singled out in this category as a model for all independents to follow. Its efforts to reduce waste in its office and supply chain have reduced the company's environmental impact, and it works closely with staff to identify more areas of improvement. Here is a publisher who lives and breathes green. Alastair Sawday has all the right principles and is clearly committed to improving its practice further."

Our Fragile Earth series is a growing collection of campaigning books about the environment. Highlighting the perilous state of the world yet offering imaginative and radical solutions and some intriguing facts, these books will make you weep and smile. They will keep you up to date and well armed for the battle with apathy.

THE QUEEN'S AWARDS
FOR ENTERPRISE:
SUSTAINABLE DEVELOPMENT
2006

Photo left: La Rougeanne, entry 582
Photo right: Tom Germain

The buildings

Beautiful as they were, our old offices leaked heat, used electricity to heat water and rooms, flooded spaces with light to illuminate one person, and were not ours to alter.

So in 2005 we created our own eco-offices by converting some old barns to create a low-emissions building. Heating and lighting the building, which houses over 30 employees, now produces only 0.28 tonnes of carbon dioxide per year. Not bad when you compare this with the 6 tonnes emitted by the average UK household. We achieved this through a variety of innovative and energy-saving building techniques, described below.

Insulation We went to great lengths to ensure that very little heat will escape, by:
- laying insulating board 90mm thick immediately under the roof tiles and on the floor
- lining the whole of the inside of the building with plastic sheeting to ensure air-tightness
- fixing further insulation underneath the roof and between the rafters
- fixing insulated plaster-board to add another layer of insulation.

All this means we are insulated for the Arctic, and almost totally air-tight.

Heating We installed a wood-pellet boiler from Austria, in order to be largely fossil-fuel free. The pellets are made from compressed sawdust, a waste product from timber mills that work only with sustainably managed forests. The heat is conveyed by water to all corners of the building via an under-floor system.

Water We installed a 6000-litre tank to collect rainwater from the roofs. This is pumped back, via an ultra-violet filter, to the lavatories, showers and basins. There are two solar thermal panels on the roof providing heat to the one (massively insulated) hot-water cylinder.

Lighting We have a carefully planned mix of low-energy lighting: task lighting and up-lighting. We also installed three sun-pipes – polished aluminium tubes that reflect the outside light down to chosen areas of the building.

Electricity All our electricity has long come from the Good Energy Company and is 100% renewable.

Materials Virtually all materials are non-toxic or natural. Our carpets, for example, are made from (80%) Herdwick sheep-wool from National Trust farms in the Lake District.

Doors and windows Outside doors and new windows are wooden, double-glazed, beautifully constructed in Norway. Old windows have been double-glazed.

We have a building we are proud of, and architects and designers are fascinated by. But best of all, we are now in a better position to encourage our owners and readers to take sustainability more seriously.

Photo: Tom Germain

What we do

Besides moving the business to a low-carbon building, the company works in a number of ways to reduce its overall environmental footprint:

- all office travel is logged as part of a carbon sequestration programme, and money for compensatory tree-planting is dispatched to SCAD in India for a tree-planting and development project
- we avoid flying and take the train for business trips wherever possible; when we have to fly, we 'double offset'
- car-sharing and the use of a company pool car are part of company policy; recycled cooking oil is used in one car and LPG in the other
- organic and Fair Trade basic provisions are used in the staff kitchen and organic food is provided by the company at all in-house events
- green cleaning products are used throughout the office
- all kitchen waste is composted and used on the office organic allotment.

Our total 'operational' carbon footprint (including travel to and from work, plus all our trips to visit our Special Places to Stay) is just over 17 tonnes per year. We have come a long way, but we would like to get this figure as close to zero as possible.

When, two years ago, we sang the praises of travelling by train to France, little did we know that the train was to be the saviour of many a traveller in 2010. Stranded far from home by the ash spewing from the erupting Icelandic volcano, hundreds of those who were quick enough to find a seat on a train discovered a modernised, highly efficient form of travel they scarcely knew; many swore never to fly to France again. Other visitors, however, were trapped at home and could not even leave this island to take up their bookings, making the volcano a harsh blow for those French owners who had already been feeling the bite of the recession and the pound's freefall against the euro. Faced with all these obstacles, the number of British people holidaying abroad has hit a record low over the past couple of years.

Luckily, chambres d'hôtes owners remain optimistic for the future, hoping the British will realise that they absolutely need to replenish their spirits with French food and wine, stunning landscapes and, of course, the people they have come to love. To entice their lesser-spotted Anglo-Saxon friends back, French owners are definitely casting around for those extra special crumbs, hoping to attract them especially for mid-week stays and the shoulder seasons. They love their regions, their villages, their history, and they yearn for travellers to stay more than one night and take the time to discover those hidden delights. With a wine-tasting here, an introduction to flamenco there, a yurt just for you somewhere else, a truffle-hunting expedition in the autumn... venture back to France again, and find out for yourselves.

With planes everywhere grounded by the ash cloud, we got a glimpse of what a future without air travel might feel like. How refreshing it was to have skies free of jet trails for the first time in years! With train travel being the fastest and cheapest way for many people to reach their already-booked holiday destinations, the arrival of the traincation ('vacation by train') was heralded – and not just for eco-geek reasons of carbon emission efficiency. More and more of us are beginning to wonder why we should hurtle headlong into yet another airport experience when we have the choice of a slower and more soul-nourishing way to travel. Watching the gradual changing of the landscape becomes as much a part of the holiday as the place where you end up - spiced with a dash of schadenfreüde

Photo: Château de Termes, entry 484

when you think of the poor wretches facing hours in airports entangled in a host of security measures. One of our own team recently swapped plane for train. Florence, former co-editor of this very guide, set off overland to China and Vietnam, travelling through eastern Europe and Siberia, scaling a temperature change of seventy degrees. Crossing the earth this way is a deeper, more meaningful way of travelling; it brings a better understanding and connection with a place and its people, and stores up memories of real smells, sights and weather felt on the skin rather than a collection of distilled aerial views from a porthole thousands of feet high.

B&B owners continue to take lighter steps through the environment to reduce their carbon footprints. You'll find new places trying to be as self-sufficient as they can with solar powered everything and natural pest control. They care deeply about their food and its sourcing and offer superb organic produce straight from their potagers. They'll send you in the right direction for local cheese-, bread- and cider-makers – or they may produce these delights themselves. And treehouses, gypsy caravans and yurts are popping up all over the place.

Around thirty of the places in this guide also feature in our *Go Slow France*, a large format, beautifully illustrated, in-depth guide to some fifty special places whose owners are going the extra mile to protect the environment, its biodiversity and its vital food-producing capacity, to grow and cook natural, organic and, as far as possible, local food, to be part of the local community and live their lives at its simple best. Their stories are inspiring and we are proud to be publishing them. If you do make the journey by train, there are plenty of owners who will pick you up from the station. It's easy to take a bike if you pre-book, no dismantling required: with Eurostar you can check it in an hour before you go and pick it up the other end – magic! If not, borrow or hire a bike while you're there and head off on bike trails from your doorstep.

However you choose to get there, when you arrive with the Sawday seal you'll be welcomed more warmly than ever: you have been missed for the last two years.

Angharad Barnes

Photo: Le Couradou, entry 592

It's simple. There are no rules, no boxes to tick. We choose places that we like and are fiercely subjective in our choices. We also recognise that one person's idea of special is not necessarily someone else's so there is a huge variety of places, and prices, in the book. Those who are familiar with our Special Places series know that we look for comfort, originality, authenticity, and reject the insincere, the anonymous and the banal. The way guests are treated comes as high on our list as the setting, the architecture, the atmosphere and the food.

Inspections

We visit every place in the guide to get a feel for how both house and owner tick.

We don't take a clipboard and we don't have a list of what is acceptable and what is not. Instead, we chat for an hour or so with the owner and look round - closely (it involves bouncing on beds, looking at linen, testing taps). It's all very informal, but it gives us an excellent idea of who would enjoy staying there and our aim is to match places and guests. If the visit happens to be the last of the day, we sometimes stay the night. Once in the book, properties are re-inspected every three to four years so that we can keep things fresh and accurate.

Feedback

In between inspections we rely on feedback from our army of readers, as

Photo: Le Jas du Boeuf, entry 627

well as from staff members who are encouraged to visit properties across the series. This feedback is invaluable to us and we always follow up on comments. So do tell us whether your stay has been a joy or not, if the atmosphere was great or stuffy, the owners cheery or bored. The accuracy of the book depends on what you, and our inspectors, tell us.

A lot of the new entries in each edition are recommended by our readers, so keep telling us about new places you've discovered too. Please use the forms on our website at www.sawdays.co.uk, or later in this book (p. 409).

However, please do not tell us if the bedside light was broken, or the shower head was scummy. Tell the owner, immediately, and get them to do something about it. Most owners are more than happy to correct problems and will bend over backwards to help. Far better than bottling it up and then writing to us a week later!

Subscriptions

Owners pay to appear in this guide. Their fee goes towards the high costs of inspecting, of producing an all-colour book and of maintaining our website. We only include places that we like and find special for one reason or another, so it is not possible for anyone to buy their way onto these pages. Nor is it possible for the owner to write their own description. We will say if the bedrooms are small, or if a main road is near. We do our best to avoid misleading people.

Photo: La Verrerie, entry 308

Disclaimer

We make no claims to pure objectivity in choosing these places. They are here simply because we like them. Our opinions and tastes are ours alone and this book is a statement of them; we hope you will share them. We have done our utmost to get our facts right but apologise unreservedly for any mistakes that may have crept in.

You should know that we don't check such things as fire regulations, swimming pool security or any other laws with which owners of properties receiving paying guests should comply. This is the responsibility of the owners.

Finding the right place for you

All these places are special in one way or another. All have been visited and then written about honestly so that you can decide for yourselves which will suit you. Those of you who swear by Sawday's books trust our write-ups precisely because we don't have a blanket standard; we include places simply because we like them. But we all have different priorities, so do read the descriptions carefully and pick out the places where you will be comfortable. If something is particularly important to you then check when you book: a simple question or two can avoid misunderstandings.

Maps

Each property is flagged with its entry number on the maps at the front. These maps are a great starting point for planning your trip, but please don't use them as anything other than a general guide – use a decent road map for real navigation. Most places will send you detailed instructions once you have booked your stay.

Ethical Collection

We're always keen to draw attention to owners who are striving to have a positive impact on the world, so you'll notice that some entries are flagged as being part of our "Ethical Collection." These places are working hard to reduce their environmental footprint, making significant contributions to their local community, or are passionate about serving local or organic food. Owners have had to fill in a very detailed questionnaire before becoming part of this Collection – read more on page 410.

Photo left: La Parare, entry 685
Photo right: Un Ciel à Paris, entry 121

Map 7   33

©Maidenhead Cartographic, 2011

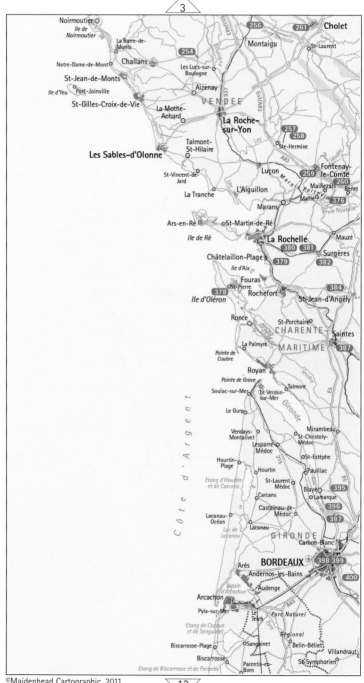

©Maidenhead Cartographic, 2011

Map 9   35

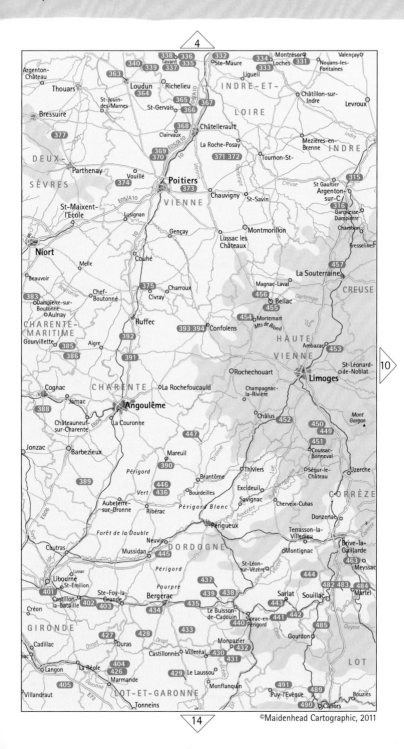

©Maidenhead Cartographic, 2011

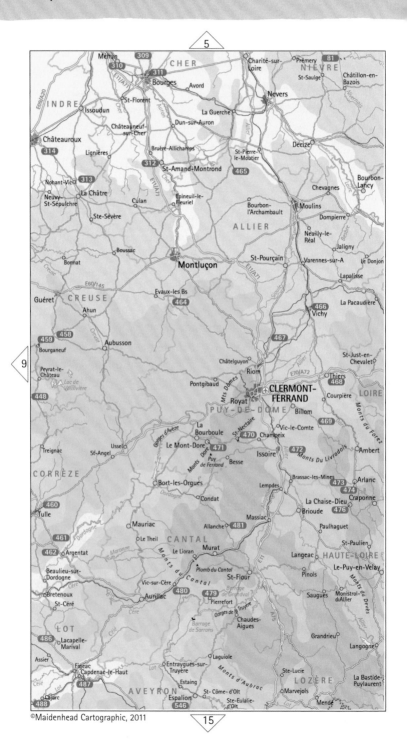

©Maidenhead Cartographic, 2011

Map 11   37

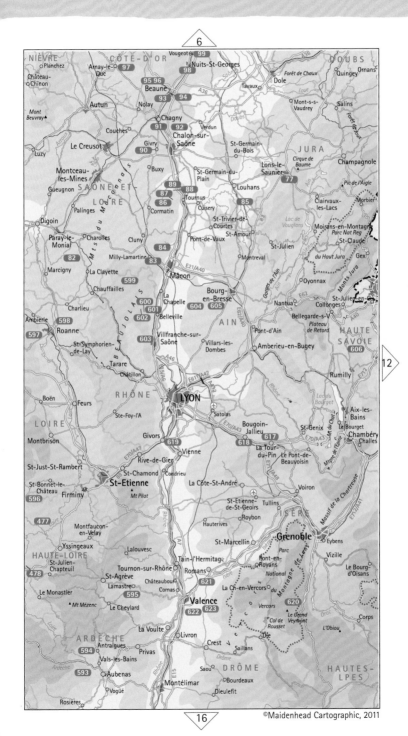

©Maidenhead Cartographic, 2011

©Maidenhead Cartographic, 2011

Map 13   39

©Maidenhead Cartographic, 2011

©Maidenhead Cartographic, 2011

Map 15   41

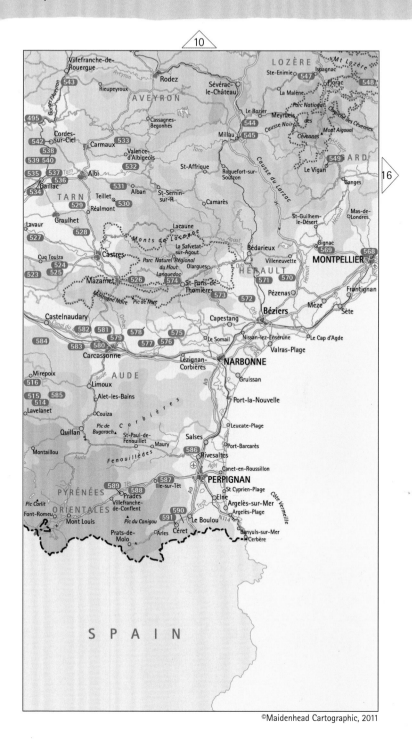

©Maidenhead Cartographic, 2011

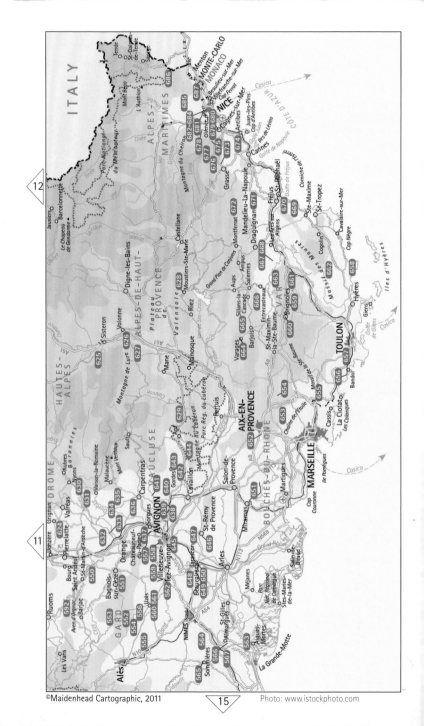

©Maidenhead Cartographic, 2011

Photo: www.istockphoto.com

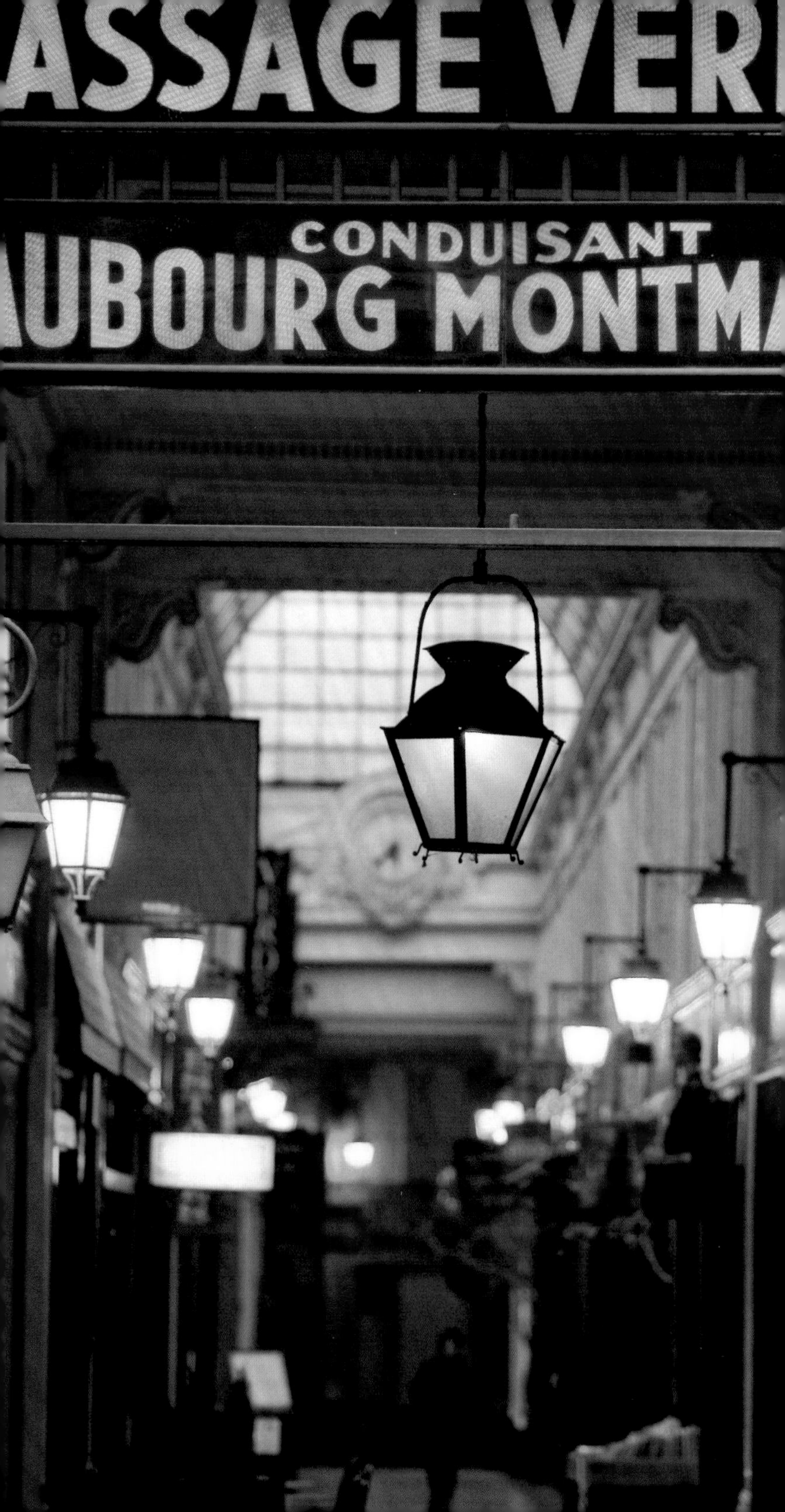
ASSAGE VER
CONDUISANT
UBOURG MONTM

The North • Picardy

Photo: www.istockphoto.com

Picardy

Maison Warlop

In serene country, a dazzling house whose hill-shaped roof becomes a timbered vault way above swathes of natural stone floor. The Picardy sky pours in and fills the vast minimally furnished living space and your hostess shows pleasure at your amazement… then serves you elegant food and intelligent conversation. Bedrooms are pure and peaceful: white walls, patches of colour, crazy-paved floors, excellent beds and design-conscious bathrooms, 1930s antiques and touches of fun. Civilised seclusion… and a beautiful neo-gothic church (built in 1930) next door, to which Martine has the key. *Cookery courses & 'French culture' stays.*

Price	€65-€118.
Rooms	3: 2 twins/doubles, 1 family room for 4.
Meals	Dinner with wine, €26-€28.
Closed	Rarely.
Directions	From A1 exit 13 on D1029 for St Quentin; in Villers Carbonnel, right at r'bout D1017 for 5km to Fresnes Mazancourt; 1st right after village sign, house next to church.

Martine Warlop
Maison Warlop,
1 rue Génermont,
80320 Fresnes Mazancourt, Somme
Tel   +33 (0)3 22 85 49 49
Email martine.warlop@wanadoo.fr
Web   www.maison-warlop.com

Entry 37   Map 5

Picardy

Château d'Omiécourt

On a working estate, Omiécourt is a proudly grand 19th-century château and elegant family house (the Thézys have four teenage children), with tall slender windows and some really old trees. Friendly if formal, communicative and smiling, your hosts have worked hugely to restore their inheritance and create gracious French château guest rooms, each with an ornate fireplace, each named for a different period. In an outbuilding near the two pools is a neat and cosy apartment with sloping ceilings; there's a 'boutique', too, of pretty things. A house of goodwill where you will be very comfortable. *Min. two nights July/August.*

Price	€105-€145. Extra bed €25.
Rooms	5: 3 doubles, 1 family room, 1 suite for 3.
Meals	Restaurants 12km.
Closed	Rarely.
Directions	From A1 south for Paris; exit 13 onto D1029 for St Quentin; in Villers Carbonnel right at lights D1017 for 9km to Omiécourt; right in village, château on right.

Dominique & Véronique de Thézy
Château d'Omiécourt,
80320 Omiécourt,
Somme
Tel   +33 (0)3 22 83 01 75
Email contact@chateau-omiecourt.com
Web   www.chateau-omiecourt.com

Entry 38   Map 5

La Gaxottière

The high walls guard a secret garden, a goldfish pond, lots of intriguing mementos and a blithe, animated hostess – a retired chemist who loves her dogs, travelling and contact with visitors. In the old house, the two mellow, beamed, fireplace'd rooms for breakfasts are brimful of old pieces and personal collections; two bedrooms have log fires and bathrooms are old-fashioned. Madame lives in the brilliantly converted barn; all is harmony and warmth among the antiques. Drink it all in with this great soul's talk of France and the world. Sleep in peace, wake to the dawn chorus and breakfast in the sunshine.

Château de St Vincent

An enchantment for garden lovers who want real, old château style, non-plush living. Madame is still repairing her 200-year-old family home and her garden, her great love, complete with stream and island, is a work of art. The house is elegantly well-worn, you breakfast in a handsomely oak-panelled room hung with colourful antique plates, and sleep in 2.1 metre-long antique sleigh beds. The second bedroom is simpler, and the washing arrangements, with continental bath, are not American standard. But Madame's passion for house and garden should convince you. *Children over ten welcome.*

Price	€50-€60. Single €40.
Rooms	3: 1 double, 1 twin, 1 single.
Meals	Dinner with wine, €20.
Closed	Rarely.
Directions	A1 exit 10; N31 for Compiègne 4km, 1st right after 1st r'bout onto small lane for Jaux; 1st right to Varanval, over hill. House on right opp. château gates.

Price	€110.
Rooms	1 twin. Children's room available.
Meals	Auberge 4km.
Closed	Mid-October to mid-May.
Directions	From Senlis D330 for Borest & Nanteuil for 8km; right at cemetery; 1st right; across Place du Tissard towards big farm; left Rue de la Ferme; gates at bottom, No. 1.

Françoise Gaxotte
La Gaxottière,
363 rue du Champ du Mont,
Hameau de Varanval,
60880 Jaux, Oise
Tel   +33 (0)3 44 83 22 41
Email   lagaxottiere@sfr.fr

Hélène Merlotti
Château de St Vincent,
1 rue Élisabeth Roussel,
60300 Borest, Oise
Tel   +33 (0)3 44 54 21 52

Entry 39   Map 5

Entry 40   Map 5

Picardy

Le Château de Fosseuse

Your tall windows look over the great park fading away to wooded hillside (with railway); beneath your feet are 16th-century bricks. A monumental staircase ushers you up to big, canopied, glorious-viewed bedrooms that are château-worthy but not posh; behind the panelling of one is a secret staircase. Your hosts are a fascinating, cultured marriage of exquisite French manners and Irish warmth who labour on to save their family home and genuinely enjoy sharing it. Antique rugs line the hall's walls; gumboots for guests (all sizes) wait by the door; Michelin stars are a very short drive.

Price	€80. Suite €100–€156.
Rooms	3: 2 doubles, 1 suite for 2-4.
Meals	Restaurant 2km.
Closed	Christmas.
Directions	From A16 exit 13 for Esches D923; in Fosseuse, château gate on right at traffic lights.

Shirley & Jean-Louis Marro
Le Château de Fosseuse,
60540 Fosseuse,
Oise
Tel   +33 (0)3 44 08 47 66
Email   chateau.fosseuse@wanadoo.fr
Web   www.chateau-de-fosseuse.com

Entry 41   Map 5

Picardy

Le Clos

The sprucest of farmhouses, whitewashed and Normandy-beamed, sits in its lush secret garden, reached via a door in the wall. Indoors, you find a remarkably fresh, open-plan and modernised interior, with a comfortable sitting room to share. Your bedroom above the garage is spacious, neat, uncluttered and warm; the bedding is the best, the shower room spotless and modern with coloured towels. Dine with your informative hosts by the old farm fireplace on *tarte aux pommes du jardin*. Philippe, the chef, receives much praise. Chantal, a retired teacher, keeps you gentle company. A peaceful spot, close to Paris.

Ethical Collection: Food.
See page 410 for details.

Price	€58. €70 for 3.
Rooms	2 family rooms for 2-3.
Meals	Dinner with wine, €25.
Closed	Rarely.
Directions	From A16 exit 13 for Gisors & Chaumont en Vexin approx. 20km; after Fleury left to Fay les Étangs; 2nd left; house on left.

Philippe & Chantal Vermeire
Le Clos,
3 rue du Chêne Noir,
60240 Fay les Étangs, Oise
Tel   +33 (0)3 44 49 92 38
Email   philippe.vermeire@wanadoo.fr
Web   www.leclosdefay.com

Entry 42   Map 5

Picardy

Fosse-Valle

Everything in this smart old house is beautifully done, from the immaculately smooth white bedlinen to the delicious little sauna in the wooden garden cabin. Since moving here four years ago and starting B&B, Pascale has devoted her enthusiasm and flair to her guests. She and her husband, who works in Beauvais, love chatting to their visitors over dinner, served on a pretty cloth with antique cutlery. Full of good advice, they know the area well. Bedrooms are classic-handsome in the main house and romantic-cosy in the adorable garden cottage, every detail refined with a personal touch. Light-hearted and welcoming.

Price	€140.
Rooms	2: 1 double. Cottage: 1 double.
Meals	Dinner €35.
Closed	Mid-December to January.
Directions	From Dieppe D915 to Gisors; D10 for Vernon, left to Dangu; thro' village, over river, 1st right to Boury en V.; thro' Boury for Vaudancourt; 2nd last house on right, white iron gates.

Pascale Ravé
Fosse-Valle,
5 route de Vaudancourt,
60240 Boury en Vexin, Oise

Mobile +33 (0)6 23 05 03 72
Email pascale.rave@fossevalle.fr
Web www.fossevalle.fr

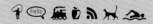

Entry 43   Map 5

Picardy

Les Chambres de l'Abbaye

Chloé and her artist husband have the most unusual, delightful house in a village with a fine Cistercian abbey. You are free to roam a series of beautiful rooms downstairs, read a book in the pale blue formal salon, visit Jean-François' studio: his striking, exciting pictures decorate the rooms, too. The suite is on the first floor, the two others higher up; all are fresh, immaculate, groomed like a French lady. You eat well and much is homemade, including walnut wine and liqueur from their own trees; walk it off round the partly unmanicured garden with its summerhouse and pond. It's a pleasure to stay here.

Ethical Collection: Food.
See page 410 for details.

Price	€85-€90. €115 for 3.
Rooms	3: 2 doubles, 1 family suite for 3.
Meals	Dinner with wine, €27.
Closed	Christmas.
Directions	From A16 exit 15 to Beauvais; N31 for Rouen, 25km; left to St Germer de Fly centre; entrance on left down hill just before church.

Chloé Comte
Les Chambres de l'Abbaye,
2 rue Michel Greuet,
60850 St Germer de Fly, Oise

Tel +33 (0)3 44 81 98 38
Email comte.resa@free.fr
Web www.chambres-abbaye.com

Entry 44   Map 5

Les Jardins du Vidamé

In beautiful 17th-century Gerberoy (records go back to 923 AD), this venerable place, Ben's family home, has real age and oodles of ancient charm in a multitude of timbers, cobbles and bricks where untamed roses ramble and wisteria wends its way. Bedroom walls are intensely French-floral; photographs, prints and mellow water-colours talk from the past; add a heavy carved bedstead, the odd bit of mahogany, and the atmosphere is of another period. Even the bathroom looks 1920s. Your delightful young hosts, busy with young children and tea room, will happily chat and may share their family-cluttered living room.

Domaine de Montaigu

This inviting 18th-century house in lovely countryside is run with aplomb by two delightful, gentlemanly hosts. Welcoming, comfortable, with a small sauna and an outdoor pool, it feels like a small hotel. Montaigu's history is reflected in five antique-furnished, frilled and furbelowed rooms in pure French style, while 'Colette' flaunts an extraordinary 1950s collector's set of mirror-fronted furniture. In the dining room, where breakfast is served, a long table is set about with Louis XVI chairs, sideboards heave with glassware and tassels drip from a satin-velvet sofa. Shamelessly flamboyant!

Price	€70. €125 for 3, €140 for 4.
Rooms	1 family suite.
Meals	Dinner €20. Wine by the glass €3-€7. Tea room/restaurant in outbuilding.
Closed	December-February.
Directions	From Beauvais D901 & D133 to Gerberoy. In village square, left of arched building Rue Henri Le Sidaner, up hill, 1st left Impasse du Vidamé; entrance on right.

Price	€85-€100.
Rooms	5: 4 doubles, 1 suite for 4.
Meals	Restaurant 1.6km.
Closed	Rarely.
Directions	From A1 exit 9 to Compiègne; bypass town on N31 for Soissons. 5km after Jauzy right D943 to Le Soulier (don't take 1st turning to Ambleny). Signed to Domaine.

Céline & Ben Guilloux
Les Jardins du Vidamé,
4 impasse du Vidamé,
60380 Gerberoy, Oise
Tel   +33 (0)3 44 82 45 32
Email   infolesjardinsduvidame@orange.fr
Web   www.les-jardins-du-vidame.com

Philippe de Reyer
Domaine de Montaigu,
16 rue de Montaigu,
02290 Ambleny, Aisne
Tel   +33 (0)3 23 74 06 62
Mobile   +33 (0)6 12 14 62 52
Email   info@domainedemontaigu.com
Web   www.domainedemontaigu.com

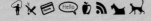

Entry 45   Map 5

Entry 46   Map 5

Picardy

Ferme de Ressons

Ressons is home to a warm, dynamic, intelligent couple who, after a hard day's work running this big farm (Jean-Paul) or being an architect (Valérie) and tending three children, will ply you in apparently leisurely fashion with champagne, excellent dinner and conversation; they also hunt. The deeply carved Henri III furniture is an admirable family heirloom; bedrooms are colour-coordinated, views roll for miles and sharing facilities seems easy. A house of comfort and relaxed good manners, whose decoration and accessories reflect the owners' travels. *Fishing in small lake.*

Price	€50–€60.
Rooms	5: 1 double, 1 twin, each with bath, sharing wc; 2 doubles, 1 twin, sharing bath & 2 wcs.
Meals	Dinner €19. Wine €14; champagne €18.
Closed	Rarely.
Directions	From Fismes D967 for Fère en Tardenois & Château Thierry 4km. Don't go to Mont St Martin cont. 800m beyond turning; white house on left.

	Valérie & Jean-Paul Ferry
	Ferme de Ressons,
	02220 Mont St Martin,
	Aisne
Tel	+33 (0)3 23 74 71 00
Email	ferryressons@orange.fr

Entry 47   Map 5

Picardy

La Quincy

The old family home, faded and weary, timeless and romantic, is well loved and lived in by this charming, natural and quietly elegant couple. Corridors cluttered with books, magazines and traces of family life lead to an octagonal tower, its great double room and child's room across the landing imaginatively set in the space. A fine antique bed on a fine polished floor, charming chintz, erratic plumbing and two parkland views will enchant you. Shrubs hug the feet of the delicious 'troubadour' château, the garden slips into meadow, summer breakfast and dinner (good wine, book ahead) are in the orangery. Special.

Price	€62.
Rooms	1 family suite for 3.
Meals	Occasional dinner with wine, €20.
Closed	Rarely.
Directions	From A26 exit 13 for Laon; Laon bypass for Soissons; N2 approx. 18km; exit Nanteuil la Fosse; thro' Nanteuil for La Quincy; château on right outside village.

	Jacques & Marie-Catherine Cornu-Langy
	La Quincy,
	02880 Nanteuil la Fosse, Aisne
Tel	+33 (0)3 23 54 67 76
Email	la.quincy@yahoo.fr

Entry 48   Map 5

Picardy

Domaine de l'Étang

The village on one side, the expansive estate on the other, the 18th-century wine-grower's house in between. There's a civilised mood: Monsieur so well-mannered and breakfast served with silver and fine china in the comfortably elegant guest living room. Wake to church-spire and rooftop views in rooms with soft comfort where, under sloping ceilings, French toile de Jouy is as inviting as English chintz (your hosts spent two years in England). Bathrooms are frilled and pretty. Shrubs hug the hem of the house, a pool is sunk into the lawn behind and Laon trumpets one of France's first gothic cathedrals.

Price	€60–€68.
Rooms	3: 1 double, 1 twin; 1 double with separate bath.
Meals	Restaurant 100m.
Closed	Rarely.
Directions	A26 exit 13 for Soissons; after r'bout right to Mons en Laonnois, Clacy & Thierret; from centre of Mons cross flyover; right after 30m. Ring mobile on arrival in village.

	Monsieur & Madame Woillez
	Domaine de l'Étang,
	2 rue St Martin,
	02000 Mons en Laonnois, Aisne
Tel	+33 (0)3 23 24 44 52
Mobile	+33 (0)6 26 62 36 41
Email	gitemons@sfr.fr
Web	www.domainedeletang.fr

Entry 49   Map 5

Picardy

Le Clos

Genuine country hospitality and cooking are yours in the big old house. Madame is kindly and direct; Monsieur is the communicator (mainly in French), knows his local history and loves the hunting horn. His 300-year-old family house is cosily unposh: floral curtains, French-papered walls, original wainscotting, funny old prints in bedrooms, comforting clutter in the vast living room, posters in the corridors. The master bedroom is superb, others are simple and fine; one has a ship's shower room, all look onto green pastures. And there's a pretty lake for picnics across the narrow road. *Sawday self-catering also.*

Price	€50–€60.
Rooms	4: 2 doubles, 1 twin, 1 suite for 5 (1 triple, 1 twin).
Meals	Dinner with wine, €22.50. Restaurant in village.
Closed	Mid-October to mid-March, except by arrangement.
Directions	From A26 E17 exit 13 on N2 for Laon; 2nd left; D516 to Bruyères 7km; left D967 for Fismes; house on left entering Chérêt.

	Michel & Monique Simonnot
	Le Clos,
	02860 Chérêt,
	Aisne
Tel	+33 (0)3 23 24 80 64
Email	leclos.cheret@club-internet.fr
Web	www.lecloscheret.com

Entry 50   Map 5

Picardy

La Commanderie

Up here on the hill, not easy to find, is a Templar hamlet and a millennium of history: an enclosed farmyard, a ruined medieval chapel framing the sunrise, a tithe barn with leaping oak timbers – and this modern house. José-Marie, an unhurried grandmother of generous spirit, loves the history, harvests her orchards and vegetables, and welcomes genuinely. Bedrooms are in plain, dated farm style but open the window and you fall into the view that soars away on all sides of the hill, even to Laon cathedral. Homely, authentic and simple, with lived-in plumbing and great value – most readers love it.

Price	€50–€55.
Rooms	3: 1 double, 2 family suites.
Meals	Occasional dinner with wine, €17. Restaurants 10km.
Closed	Last week of October–February, except by arrangement.
Directions	From Calais A26 exit 12 to Crécy sur Serre; D35 to Pont à Bucy; 1st left; D26 right for La Ferté Chevresis 4km; small lane left up hill. Drive thro' farm on left. Signs.

	José-Marie Carette
	La Commanderie,
	Catillon du Temple,
	02270 Nouvion et Catillon, Aisne
Tel	+33 (0)3 23 56 51 28
Mobile	+33 (0)6 82 33 22 64
Email	carette.jm@wanadoo.fr
Web	www.gite-templier-laon.com

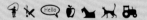

Photo: Lesley Chalmers

Paris – Île de France

Photo: www.istockphoto.com

Paris - Île de France

Le Logis d'Arnières

Wonderfully preserved in authentic 1920s style: a high-windowed, fully panelled dining room with extraordinary dressers; and fabulous bathroom fittings. It is exuberantly sober and shapely with Versailles parquet and fine fireplaces as well. Tae, from Chile, uses her fine sense of style and colour to bond these antiques with richly baroque Chinese chairs and lots of South American pieces and paintings. Claude is as articulately enthusiastic as she: a fabulous couple. Quiet spot, vast natural garden, joyous hosts, resident horses, gentle labradors, swings… beautiful breakfasts set you up for Chartres, Paris, Versailles.

Price	€80. €120 for 4.
Rooms	2 suites for 5.
Meals	Restaurant 200m.
Closed	Rarely.
Directions	From Paris A10 exit 10 to toll gate, right after toll; right again on D27 to St Cyr; continue for Arpajon; 1st house on left.

Claude & Tae Dabasse
Le Logis d'Arnières,
1 rue du Pont-Rué,
91410 St Cyr sous Dourdan, Essonne
Tel   +33 (0)1 64 59 14 89
Email   taedabasse@free.fr
Web   www.dabasse.com/arniere

Entry 109   Map 5

Paris - Île de France

Ferme de Vert St Père

Cereals and beets grow in wide fields and show-jumpers add elegance to the fine landscape. A generous farm courtyard surrounded by very lovely warm stone buildings encloses peace and a genuine welcome from young hosts and labradors alike, here where Monsieur's family has come hunting for 200 years. Find family furniture (the 1900s ensemble is most intriguing) and planked floors in beautiful bedrooms, immaculate mod cons and a super breakfast area for guests in a beamy outbuilding with open fire, sofa, kitchen and TV. Utter peace, a remote setting, and a Michelin-rated auberge in the village.

Price	€65. Apartments €100.
Rooms	1 + 2: 1 family room for 3. 2 apartments for 4.
Meals	Restaurant in village, 1.5km.
Closed	Christmas.
Directions	From A5 exit 15 on N36 for Meaux, 200m; 2nd right to Crisenoy after TGV bridge, thro' village for Tennis/Salle des Fêtes; 1.5km to farm.

Philippe & Jeanne Mauban
Ferme de Vert St Père,
77390 Crisenoy,
Seine-et-Marne
Tel   +33 (0)1 64 38 83 51
Mobile   +33 (0)6 71 63 31 36
Email   mauban.vert@wanadoo.fr
Web   vert.saint.pere.free.fr

Entry 110   Map 5

Le Clos de la Rose

For seekers of garden peace, for champagne and architecture buffs (vineyards and historic Provins nearby), this gorgeous green retreat from crazed Paris – cool, quiet, stylishly homely – has been restored with fine respect for 200-year-old origins: limewash, timbers, country antiques, a gathering of books. Charming Brendan (he's Irish) and gentle, organised Véronique have a lovely family and, amazingly, time to chat over aperitifs. Bedrooms have pretty colours, antique linen and patchwork charm, the adorable cottage (with kitchen) is ideal for a longer stay. Don't miss dinner, hot or cold: you choose. *Ask about champagne tours.*

Le Moulin de St Martin

Agnès is gentle, with artistic flair, Bernard is gregarious, charming, convivial: together they have created a delectable B&B. The old mill is on an island encircled by Corot's Grand Morin river; lovely old willows lap the water, the pretty villages of Le Voulangis and Crécy lie beyond. A warm sober elegance prevails: there are 17th-century floorboards topped by oriental rugs; Asian antiques and art in gilt frames; cherry-red toile and snowy bed linen; terraces for summer views; log fires for nights in. Disneyland Paris, a world away, may a short drive but, above all, fine châteaux beckon. *Minimum two nights.*

Price	€75-€159.
Rooms	2 + 1: 2 doubles. Cottage for 2-3.
Meals	Breakfast €11. Dinner €29. Wine €19-€30. Champagne €31. Restaurant 5-minute drive.
Closed	Rarely.
Directions	A4 exit 18 to La Ferté sous Jouarre; D407 for Montmirail; thro' wood to Montapeine (6km from r'bout in La Ferté); D68 for St Ouen; 1.8 km right; 400m to gate.

Price	€75-€85.
Rooms	2: 1 double, 1 twin/double.
Meals	Dinner €28. Wine €18.
Closed	Rarely.
Directions	From Paris A4 for Metz, exit 16 for Crécy; 3rd lights right; through Crécy for Voulangis & Tigeaux. Leaving Crécy left, Le Moulin 200m, signed. Ring bell.

Véronique & Brendan Culligan
Le Clos de la Rose,
11 rue de la Source, L'Hermitière,
77750 St Cyr sur Morin, Seine-et-Marne
Tel +33 (0)1 60 44 81 04
Mobile +33 (0)6 82 56 10 54
Email resa@clos-de-la-rose.com
Web www.clos-de-la-rose.com

Bernard & Agnès Gourbaud
Le Moulin de St Martin,
7 rue de St Martin, Voulangis,
77580 Crécy la Chapelle, Seine-et-Marne
Tel +33 (0)1 64 63 69 90
Email moulindesaintmartin@orange.fr

Entry 111   Map 5

Entry 112   Map 5

Paris - Île de France

Châtelet district

You will meet a most civilised couple – she bubbly and interested, he quietly studious, a university professor – in their very personal, gently refined apartment where original timbers divide the living room and two friendly cats proclaim the cosiness. It is beautifully done and eminently French, like a warm soft nest, with antiques, lots of greenery, interesting art. Mona loves her guests and is full of interesting tips: the Seine and historic Paris are at the end of the road. Your attractive, compact guest quarters are nicely private with good storage space, pretty quilts and lots of light. *Minimum two nights.*

Price	€95.
Rooms	1 twin.
Meals	Restaurants nearby.
Closed	Summer holidays.
Directions	Lift to 3rd floor. Metro: Châtelet (1, 4, 7, 11, 14), Pont Neuf (7). RER: Châtelet les Halles. Parking: Conforama car park, via Rue du Pont Neuf then Rue Boucher.

	Mona Pierrot Châtelet district, 75001 Paris
Tel	+33 (0)1 42 36 50 65
Email	pierrot-jean@orange.fr

Entry 113   Map 5

Paris - Île de France

Bonne Nuit Paris

Absolute Paris, 300 years old but not grand, beams galore and modern comforts, independent rooms and a warm family welcome, little streets, friendly markets: this is real privilege. Charming, intelligent Jean-Luc serves his own honey, Denise's jams and fresh baguettes in their generous, rambling living room. Guest rooms are on the floor below. Each has a fun-lovingly colourful shower room, a lot of quirk (the last word in creative basins) and an appealing mix of old woodwork and contemporary prints. Simplicity, panache and personality, real attention and service are the hallmarks: you will feel well cared for.

Price	€135-€250. Extra person €75.
Rooms	3: 2 doubles, 1 triple.
Meals	Restaurants within walking distance.
Closed	Rarely.
Directions	Metro: République (2, 3, 5, 8, 11). Buses: 20, 46, 56, 65, 75. Parking: 3 car parks, €50 for 3 days.

	Denise & Jean-Luc Marchand Bonne Nuit Paris, 63 rue Charlot, 75003 Paris
Tel	+33 (0)1 42 71 83 56
Mobile	+33 (0)6 72 35 90 75
Email	jean.luc@bonne-nuit-paris.com
Web	www.bonne-nuit-paris.com

Entry 114   Map 5

Paris - Île de France

Notre Dame district

At the end of the street are the Seine and the glory of Notre Dame. In a grand old building, up a number of 17th-century stairs, the unaffected tall-windowed rooms look down to peace in a little garden. The low-mezzanined family room has a bathroom off the internal landing where a simple breakfast is laid beside the spiral stair. Upstairs, the second, smaller room has the bed in the corner and a fresh décor. Madame is polyglot, active and eager to help when she is available; she leaves breakfast ready if she has to go out. She and her daughter appreciate the variety of contact guests bring.

Price	€85–€135.
Rooms	2: 1 double; 1 quadruple with separate bath.
Meals	Continental breakfast left ready if owner has to go out.
Closed	Rarely.
Directions	Metro: Maubert-Mutualité (10). RER: St Michel. Parking: Book ahead.

Brigitte Chatignoux
Notre Dame district,
75005 Paris

Tel +33 (0)1 43 25 27 20
Email brichati@hotmail.com

Entry 115   Map 5

Paris - Île de France

10 rue Las Cases

In a provincial-quiet city street, classy dressed stone outside, intelligence, sobriety and style inside. Madame takes you into her vast, serene apartment: no modern gadgets or curly antiques, just a few good pieces, much space, and light-flooded parquet floors. Beyond the dining room, your cosy buff bedroom gives onto a big, silent, arcaded courtyard. Your hosts have lived all over the world, and Madame, as quiet and genuine as her surroundings, now enjoys her country garden near Chartres and the company of like-minded visitors – she is worth getting to know. *Two or more nights preferred.*

Price	€85.
Rooms	1 twin/double.
Meals	Restaurants within walking distance.
Closed	Rarely.
Directions	Discuss door code before arrival. Lift to 2nd floor. Metro: Solférino (12), Assemblée Nationale (12), Invalides (8). Parking: Invalides.

Élisabeth Marchal
10 rue Las Cases,
75007 Paris

Tel +33 (0)1 47 05 70 21

Entry 116   Map 5

Paris - Île de France

1 rue Lamennais

Even the air feels quietly elegant. Soisick uses no frills, just good things old and new: the sense of peace is palpable (nothing to do with double glazing). Her flat turns away from the rowdy Champs-Élysées towards classy St Honoré: ask this gentle Parisian for advice about great little restaurants – or anything Parisian. The simple generous bedroom has size and interest – an unusual inlaid table is set off by white bedcovers – and leads to a dressing room fit for a star and your tasteful white and grey bathroom. With three windows, parquet floor and its mix of antique and modern, the living room is another charmer.

Paris - Île de France

Côté Montmartre

Walk in and touch an 1890s heart: floral inlay on the stairs, stained-glass windows behind the lift. On the top landing, a curly bench greets you. Young and quietly smiling, Isabelle leads you to her personality-filled living room, a harmony of family antiques and 20th-century design, and a gift of a view: old Paris crookedly climbing to the Sacré Cœur. Breakfast may be on the flowering balcony, perhaps with fat cat Jules. Your big white (no-smoking) bedroom off the landing is modern and new-bedded in peaceful rooftop seclusion; the shower room a contemporary jewel. Interesting, cultured, cosmopolitan people, too.

Price	€90.
Rooms	1 twin/double.
Meals	Restaurants nearby.
Closed	Rarely.
Directions	Metro: George V (1), Charles de Gaulle-Étoile (1, 2, 6). Buses: 22, 30, 31, 52, 73, 92, 93, Balabus. Parking: Étoile.

Price	€130–€150. Child bed €30.
Rooms	1 double.
Meals	Restaurants nearby.
Closed	Rarely.
Directions	Metro: Trinité (12), Pigalle (2, 12). RER: Auber. Buses: 26, 43, 67, 68, 73, 81, 85.

	Soisick Guérineau
	1 rue Lamennais,
	75008 Paris
Tel	+33 (0)1 40 39 04 38
Email	soisick.guerineau@wanadoo.fr

	Isabelle & Jacques Bravo
	Côté Montmartre,
	11 bis rue Jean Baptiste Pigalle,
	75009 Paris
Tel	+33 (0)1 43 54 33 09
Mobile	+33 (0)6 14 56 62 62
Email	isabelle.c.b@free.fr
Web	www.cotemontmartre.com

Entry 117   Map 5

Entry 118   Map 5

Paris - Île de France

B&B Guénot

A garden! In Paris! A restful corner and quiet, well-travelled hosts with their ten-year-old son greet you after a day of cultural excitements. The architect-renovated apartment, a delight of clever design, embraces their private garden. All rooms turn towards the greenery, including your charming compact bedroom with its timber floor, large oil painting and wonderful bathroom. Once through the door that leads off the red-leather sitting room, you are in this intimate space, enjoying a lovely wide window onto bird twitter. A generous continental breakfast – and you're ready for more museum fare.

Paris - Île de France

Les Jardins de Marie

A big modern block and a fine old-style French welcome. Ground-floor rooms look out to communal gardens where birds sing among the lilac; the Bois de Vincennes is a walk away. Marie loves having guests and welcomes you easily to her cheerful family living room. Gérard was a biscuit engraver: the engraver's tables will intrigue you, as will the metal biscuit moulds turned into lamps. Pretty, colourful, comfortable bed-rooms give onto the peaceful back garden. Walk the leafy Coulée Verte – the old railway line – to Bastille, ride the 87 bus for an almost-free view of Paris sights, return to the quiet garden. *Two minutes from metro.*

Price	€100-€110.
Rooms	1 double.
Meals	Restaurants within walking distance.
Closed	Rarely.
Directions	Metro: Nation (1, 2, 6, 9), Rue des Boulets (9). RER: Nation. Buses: 26, 56, 57, 86.

Price	€90.
Rooms	3: 1 double with separate shower & wc; 1 twin/double, 1 family room for 3, sharing separate bathroom.
Meals	Restaurants nearby.
Closed	Rarely.
Directions	Metro: Michel Bizot (8). RER: Gare de Lyon. Buses: 46, 87.

Anne-Lise Valadon
B&B Guénot,
4 passage Guénot,
75011 Paris
Tel   +33 (0)1 42 74 23 84
Mobile   +33 (0)6 22 34 34 53
Email   anne-lise.valadon@wanadoo.fr
Web   www.bb-guenot.com

Marie-Hélène Chanat
Les Jardins de Marie,
46 rue de Fécamp,
75012 Paris
Tel   +33 (0)1 40 19 06 40
Email   g.chanat@voila.fr
Web   www.aparisbnb.com

Entry 119   Map 5

Entry 120   Map 5

Paris - Île de France

Un Ciel à Paris

For 30 years they brought up three children, taught primary kids, played the piano (Lyne), and cooked divinely (Philippe), unaware of hidden beauty overhead: the fabulous trompe-l'œil ceiling ('sky in Paris') discovered by sheer chance in 2009. Soft, warm, cocoon-like bedrooms, beautifully decorated, lightly furnished, give onto trees and a rustic house; marble-tiled shower rooms are perfect. Loving their new life as B&B hosts in this gently elegant flat where striking modern art sets off family antiques, Philippe and Lyne will give you insider advice and share their passions for art, opera and Paris. *Over eights welcome.*

Price	€140–€150. Extra bed €40.
Rooms	2 doubles. Extra bed on mezzanine.
Meals	Dinner with wine, €60.
Closed	Rarely.
Directions	Metro: Gobelins (7). RER: Port Royal. Bus: 27, 47, 83, 91. Batobus: Jardin des Plantes.

Lyne & Philippe Dumas
Un Ciel à Paris,
3 bd Arago,
75013 Paris

Tel	+33 (0)1 43 36 18 46
Mobile	+33 (0)6 69 73 37 26
Email	phildumas@noos.fr
Web	www.uncielaparis.fr

Entry 121 Map 5

Paris - Île de France

Montparnasse district

A little house in a quiet alley behind Montparnasse? It's not a dream and Janine, a live-wire cinema journalist who has lived in Canada, welcomes B&B guests to her pretty wood-ceilinged kitchen/diner; she's a night bird so DIY breakfast will be laid for you. The square bedroom across the book-lined hall, a pleasing mix of warm fabrics, honeycomb tiles, old chest and contemporary art, has a good new pine bathroom. In summer, rent the whole flat, its richly French sitting room with art, antiques and music, its adorable central patio, superbly rich second bedroom and bathroom. *Minimum two nights.*

Price	B&B €70 for 2. Self-catering €950–€1,000 per week.
Rooms	1 double. For self-caterers: 2 doubles, 2 bathrooms.
Meals	Restaurants nearby.
Closed	B&B October–June. Self-catering July–September.
Directions	Metro: Gaîté (13). RER: Denfert-Rochereau. Buses: 28, 58.

Janine Euvrard
Montparnasse district,
75014 Paris

Tel	+33 (0)1 43 27 19 43
Email	janine.euvrard@orange.fr

Entry 122 Map 5

Paris - Île de France

Montparnasse district

Filled with books, paintings and objects from around the world, the Monbrisons' intimate little flat is old and fascinating. Lively American Cynthia, an art-lover, and quintessentially French Christian, knowledgeable about history, wine and cattle-breeding, offer great hospitality, thoughtful conversation, and may take you to historical landmarks. Their guest room, quiet and snug, has a king-size bed and a good bathroom with views of trees. Twice a week, the open market brings the real food of France to your street; shops, cafés and restaurants abound; you can walk to the Luxembourg Gardens.

Paris - Île de France

Les Toits de Paris

The attic-level flat, the guest room opposite and the most courteous young owners (with baby Marius) are all of a lovely piece: modest, quiet, clothed in gentle earthy colours, natural materials and discreet manners. You will feel instantly at ease in this cultured atmosphere. Across the landing, your quiet and intimate room has a super-comfy bed, a convertible sofa and a darling little writing desk beneath the sloping beams; the beautiful bathroom has everything. Walk round 'the village', discover its quirky little shops, its restaurants for all tastes and budgets – then head for the riches of central Paris. *3rd floor, no lift.*

Price	€90.
Rooms	1 twin/double.
Meals	Occasional dinner with wine, €25. Restaurants nearby.
Closed	August.
Directions	Metro: Edgar Quinet (6), Montparnasse (4, 6, 12, 13).

Price	€120.
Rooms	1 double & single sofabed.
Meals	Restaurants nearby.
Closed	Rarely.
Directions	Metro: Commerce (8), Émile Zola (10), Convention (12). RER: Javel. Buses: 62, 70, 80, 88.

Christian & Cynthia de Monbrison
Montparnasse district,
75014 Paris

Tel	+33 (0)1 43 35 20 87
Mobile	+33 (0)6 27 20 74 44

Matthieu & Sophie de Montenay
Les Toits de Paris,
25 rue de l'Abbé Groult,
75015 Paris

Email	resa@chambrehotesparis.fr
Web	www.chambrehotesparis.fr

Paris - Île de France

11 rue de Siam

A vivacious photographer, Anne has her eyrie up a small private stair in the upper-class peace of charming Passy. Here, she lays breakfast for you in a pretty kitchen with the perfect night-and-day Eiffel Tower view. In your elegant, atmospheric suite (where sitting and sleeping sections connect) are Asian artefacts and family antiques, a chic and fragrant bathroom, a window to the quiet white courtyard. Prints, photographs, a piano, gorgeous books on art… all superb illustrations of Anne's interests and fascinating travellers tales. And she's full of insights into what's on in Paris. *German & Italian spoken.*

Price	€100–€110. Extra person €20.
Rooms	1 suite for 2-3, sharing bathroom.
Meals	Restaurants within walking distance.
Closed	Rarely.
Directions	Metro: Rue de la Pompe (9). RER: Henri Martin. Buses: 63, 52.

Anne de Henning
11 rue de Siam,
75116 Paris

Tel +33 (0)1 45 04 50 06
Email dehenni@club-internet.fr

Entry 125   Map 5

Paris - Île de France

Studio Amélie

In Montmartre village, between busty boulevard and pure-white Sacré Cœur, barrister Valérie and her architect husband offer a super-chic and ideally autonomous studio off their charming, pot-planted and cobbled courtyard with your bistro table and chairs. A bed dressed in delicate red against white walls, an antique oval dining table, a pine-and-steel gem of a corner kitchen, a generous shower, a mirror framed in red. Valérie's discreet decorative flourishes speak for her calm, positive personality and her interest in other lands. A delicious Paris hideaway you can call your own. *Minimum three nights.*

Price	€100; €650 per week.
Rooms	1 studio for 2 & kitchenette.
Meals	Breakfast not included. Guest kitchen. Restaurants nearby.
Closed	Rarely.
Directions	Metro: Anvers Sacré Coeur (2), Abbesses (12). Metro/RER: Gare du Nord. Buses: 30, 54, 85. Parking: Rue Feutrier.

Valérie Zuber
Studio Amélie,
75018 Paris

Mobile +33 (0)6 30 93 81 35
Email studiodamelie@wanadoo.fr
Web www.montmartre-eiffel.com

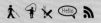

Entry 126   Map 5

Paris - Île de France

Au Sourire de Montmartre

A whole four-storey Paris building for this lovely young family and their guests is privilege indeed and you will happily climb to the top-floor living room to join them to breakfast copiously on homemade jams (yes, even in Paris) and mountain cheeses (Patrick comes from Chambéry). Ilhame has a Moroccan's natural gift for hospitality. Previously a school secretary, she loves her new 'job' and fits it into family life with intelligence and an easy smile. The smallish rooms, all different, all with good little shower rooms (one with a hammam) are done with clever use of space and quiet flair. All Paris is a scenic bus ride away.

Price	€135-€155. Extra mattress €25.
Rooms	5: 4 doubles, 1 twin.
Meals	Restaurants within walking distance.
Closed	Rarely.
Directions	Metro: Jules Joffrin (12). RER: Gare du Nord. Buses: 31, 60, 80, 85.

Ilhame Aurenty
Au Sourire de Montmartre,
64 rue du Mont Cenis,
75018 Paris

Email   contact@sourire-de-montmartre.com
Web   www.sourire-de-montmartre.com

Paris - Île de France

Belleville district

Sabine, artist and art therapist, "feeds people with colours". Jules makes the organic bread with a dazzling smile, and big, beautiful Taquin, his guide dog, loves people. Kindly and artistic, they live calmly in this bit of genuine old Paris between two tiny gardens and a tall house. The simple guest room, with good double bed and flame-covered sleigh-bed divan, a welcome tea-maker and an old-fashioned bathroom, shares a building with Sabine's studio. Healthfoody continental breakfast is in the cosy family room in the main house or outside under the birdsung tree. Such peace in Paris is rare. *Minimum two nights.*

Price	€75.
Rooms	1 family room for 3.
Meals	Restaurants within walking distance.
Closed	July/August.
Directions	Metro: Jourdain (11), Place des Fêtes (11). Buses: 26, 48, 60. Parking: Place des Fêtes.

Sabine & Jules Aïm
Belleville district,
75019 Paris

Tel   +33 (0)1 42 08 23 71
Email   jules.aim@free.fr

Paris - Île de France

Villa Mansart

Wind your way up the handsome staircase, nudge open the attic door. The guest sitting room has sunny walls and ethnic rugs. Slim, arched bedrooms are blue or vanilla-and-orange with family furniture and windows peeping over rooftops. Breakfast on fresh fruit and mini-pastries in an elegant dining room or on the terrace. Marble steps, rescued from a local demolition, sweep down to an immaculate peaceful garden curtained by trees. Your quietly affable, cultured hosts are proud to show you Sully Prudhomme's house and their modern art. Such calm, only 20 minutes from the centre of Paris. *Garage available.*

Price	€88. Triple €118.
Rooms	2: 1 double, 1 family room for 3. Extra single bed in sitting room.
Meals	Restaurants nearby.
Closed	Rarely.
Directions	From Paris A4 exit 5 to Pont de Nogent; at exit keep left, don't take tunnel; along viaduct; at 2nd lights under bridge; Av L. Rollin for Le Perreux centre; next lights straight on; 2nd left 200m.

Françoise Marcoz
Villa Mansart,
9 allée Victor Basch, 94170 Le Perreux
sur Marne, Val-de-Marne

Tel	+33 (0)1 48 72 91 88
Mobile	+33 (0)6 62 37 97 85
Email	villamansart@yahoo.fr
Web	www.villamansart.com

Entry 129   Map 5

Paris - Île de France

La Maison du Coteau

The climb is worth every puff: a hawk's eye view to the distant Eiffel Tower, and freedom in an unusual set-up. One of a delightful bunch of Burgundy-based owners will welcome you to this contemporary light-filled house, providing the wherewithal for you to do breakfast when you like among an intriguing mix of antique and modern, French and Asian pieces. The many-sofa'd salon opens wide to hillside garden and sky, front rooms have colour and light, the suite is snug for families, the penthouse is sheer delight. Use your own fridge and the communal kitchen for meals, borrow a DVD – great for families. *Direct train to Paris.*

Price	€138-€220. Weekly rates available.
Rooms	5: 2 doubles, 1 twin/double, 1 family suite, 1 penthouse for 2-4 (with kitchen & terrace).
Meals	Communal kitchen. Restaurant 200m.
Closed	Rarely.
Directions	From A6 exit Arcueil: plan on booking. RER B Arcueil-Cachan. Bus: 186 (Porte d'Italie).

Paris en Douce
La Maison du Coteau,
94230 Cachan
Val-de-Marne

Tel	+33 (0)3 80 49 60 04
Email	info@paris-en-douce.com
Web	www.paris-en-douce.com

Entry 130   Map 5

Paris - Île de France

Le Clos des Princes

Paris is 20 minutes by train, Versailles 15 by motorway. Here, behind wrought-iron gates in an elegant suburb, the French mansion sits in an exuberant town garden of pergolas, box bushes and mature trees. Your kind, attentive hosts – she an ex-English teacher, he with a passion for Sully-Prudhomme – may give you the poet/philosopher's two-room first-floor suite; he lived here in 1902. Polished floorboards, pretty prints, choice antiques, decorative perfume bottles by a claw-footed tub, all dance to the 19th-century theme. Breakfast unveils gorgeous porcelain and delicious homemade muffins and jams. Outstanding.

Price	€95–€110.
Rooms	1 suite for 2 with separate bath. Sofabed available for children.
Meals	Restaurant 400m.
Closed	Mid-July to August.
Directions	From Paris Périphérique, exit Porte d'Orléans onto N20; A86 after Bourg la Reine to Versailles; exit 28 for Châtenay Malabry; over Salvador Allende r'bout; right at 2nd r'bout; house on left.

Christine & Éric Duprez
Le Clos des Princes,
60 avenue Jean Jaurès, 92290 Châtenay
Malabry, Hauts-de-Seine

Tel +33 (0)1 46 61 94 49
Email ce.duprez@yahoo.com
Web www.leclosdesprinces.com

Entry 131   Map 5

Paris - Île de France

L'Orangerie

In a garden full of roses, behind the busy avenue that leads straight to the château, a mini Marie-Antoinette Trianon houses two little luxury flats. In each, arched windows light a pale living area where a modern plush sofa stands on new parquet flanked by Louis XV chairs. The bathroom is marble, the mezzanine bedroom generously comfortable and everything is brand new – except the antiques. One flat has a fuchsia-flashed colour scheme, the other is a sober taupe. Two couples can easily share the terrace, Madame delivers fresh viennoiseries for tomorrow's breakfast. Extraordinarily civilised. *Minimum two nights.*

Price	€135–€180.
Rooms	2 apartments for 2.
Meals	Restaurants 300m. Light supper available.
Closed	Rarely.
Directions	Paris A13 for Rouen 7km; exit 5 for Versailles Centre; left, then Bd Jardy; Bd du Général Pershing & Av. des États Unis, Av. de St Cloud, Av. Rockefeller, Av. de Paris. No. 37 on left.

Patricia White-Palacio
L'Orangerie,
37 avenue de Paris,
78000 Versailles, Yvelines

Tel +33 (0)9 53 61 07 57
Mobile +33 (0)6 82 42 81 39
Email mp.white@free.fr

Entry 132   Map 5

Paris - Île de France

7 rue Gustave Courbet

Behind the modest façade, on an upmarket housing estate, is a generous interior where Madame's paintings stand in pleasing contrast to elegant antiques and feminine furnishings. Picture windows let the garden in and the woods rise beyond. The larger guest room is soberly classic in blue, with a fur throw and big bathroom; the smaller one with skylight, books and bath across the landing is excellent value. Madame, charming and gracious, sings as well as she paints and enjoys cooking elegant regional dinners for attentive guests; she is very good company. Small, intimate, privileged, and so near Versailles.

Price	€55–€70.
Rooms	2: 1 double; 1 double with separate bath.
Meals	Dinner with wine, €20.
Closed	Rarely.
Directions	Paris A13 onto A12 for St Quentin en Yvelines; exit N12 for Dreux; exit to Plaisir Centre; 1st exit off r'bout for Plaisir Les Gâtines, 1st left for 400m; right into Domaine des Gâtines; consult roadside plan.

	Hélène Castelnau
	7 rue Gustave Courbet,
	Domaine des Gâtines,
	78370 Plaisir, Yvelines
Tel	+33 (0)1 30 54 05 15
Email	hcastelnau@club-internet.fr

Entry 133   Map 5

Paris - Île de France

Les Colombes

On the doorstep of Paris, in the grounds of a royal château, surrounded by quiet tree-lined residential avenues, it's a trot from an atmospheric racecourse, almost on the banks of the Seine, with forest walks, good restaurants, efficient trains to and from Paris, impeccable, harmonious rooms, table d'hôtes and a deeply pretty garden to relax in. What Les Colombes lacks in old stones it makes up for in a welcome steeped in traditional hospitality – and that includes generous breakfasts, home-grown fruit and veg at dinner – and glowing antiques. Courteous, caring French hosts and great value. *Paris 15 minutes by train.*

Price	€73–€83. Extra bed €30.
Rooms	3: 2 doubles, 1 twin.
Meals	Dinner with wine, €40.
Closed	Rarely.
Directions	A86 exit 2 onto D308 for Poissy 7km; enter Maisons Laffitte; 2nd exit at r'bout, Av François Mansart; Av Louvois; right Av le Nôtre; right Av Carnot; cont. Av Béranger.

	Irène & Jacques James
	Les Colombes,
	21 avenue Béranger,
	78600 Maisons Laffitte, Yvelines
Tel	+33 (0)1 39 62 82 48
Email	jacques.james@orange.fr
Web	perso.orange.fr/les-colombes

Entry 134   Map 5

Domaine des Basses Masures

The serene and beautiful Rambouillet forest encircles this hamlet and the house is a former stables; horses still graze in the field behind. Long, low and stone-fronted, cosily draped in Virginia creeper and wisteria, it was built in 1725. Madame, hospitable and easy-going, does B&B at one end; the gîte is at the other. The B&B bedrooms, one a twin, the other with a big double bed, are friendly and charming, with pretty paintings and mirrors on the walls. Come to walk or ride, or visit the cities and sights: Versailles is 20 minutes, Paris not much further. *Sawday self-catering also.*

À l'Ombre Bleue

Let the willows weep over the village pond; you go through the high gate into a sheltered paradise. The prettiest rooms have masses of old pieces, dolls, books, pictures to intrigue you, a chirruping garden with two rescue dogs to play with and the most caring hostess to provide an exceptional brunch. Have dinner too if you can (Catherine teaches cookery and sources locally: it's delicious). The miniature garden house is a lovers' dream: tiny salon downstairs, bedroom sporting superb bath up. Fulsome towels, extras of all sorts; charming, chatty Catherine thinks of everything. *Paris 45 minutes by train.*

Price	€80-€90.
Rooms	2: 1 double, 1 twin.
Meals	Restaurant 2km.
Closed	Rarely.
Directions	Directions on booking.

Price	€65-€85.
Rooms	3: 1 double, 1 twin. Garden house: 1 double.
Meals	Dinner with wine, €22. Light supper €14.
Closed	Rarely.
Directions	Paris A13 exit 8 on A12; 1st exit N12 W 35km; left D983 16km to Faverolles; left D152/80 for Gazeran 5km; right D71 to stop sign; right; gate opp. village pond.

Mme Walburg de Vernisy
Domaine des Basses Masures,
13 rue des Basses Masures,
78125 Poigny la Forêt, Yvelines
Tel   +33 (0)1 34 84 73 44
Email   domainebassesmasures@wanadoo.fr
Web   www.domaine-des-basses-masures.com

Catherine Forget-Pépin
À l'Ombre Bleue,
22 rue de la Mare, Les Pâtis,
78125 Mittainville, Yvelines
Tel   +33 (0)1 34 85 04 73
Email   catherine@alombrebleue.fr
Web   www.alombrebleue.fr

Entry 135   Map 5

Entry 136   Map 5

Paris - Île de France

Château d'Hazeville

Utterly original, a meld of brimming creativity and scholarship, this place dazzles. Your artist host uses his fine château-farm, dated 1400s to 1600s, as a living show of his talents: huge abstract paintings, hand-painted plates and tiles, a stunning 'Egyptian' reception room (and loos!). The old stables house hi-tech artisans, the gardens are spacious and beautiful, with long lush views. Guest rooms in the courtyard dovecote are deeply luxurious; generous breakfasts come on china hand-painted by Monsieur; he also knows the secret treasures of the Vexin. *Over sevens welcome. Hot-air ballooning possible.*

Price	€135.
Rooms	2: 1 double, 1 twin.
Meals	Restaurants 5km.
Closed	Weekdays & school term time.
Directions	From Rouen N14 for Paris; 20km before Pontoise, at Magny en Vexin, right D983 to Arthies; left D81 thro' Enfer; château on left.

Guy & Monique Deneck
Château d'Hazeville,
95420 Wy dit Joli Village,
Val-d'Oise
Tel   +33 (0)1 34 67 06 17

Entry 137   Map 5

Paris - Ile de France

La Ferme de Bouchemont

Renovated with boldness, style and plenty of charm, this lofty farmhouse reflects the creative talents of its French/Spanish jewellery designer owners. Rooms blend traditional features — tiled floors, aged beams, brick alcoves — with neo-classical and contemporary furnishings. The guest entrance leads to an airy breakfast room — off which a pretty terraced garden — and stairs to a bedroom of soft, country-house elegance. Up again — wow! A dramatic bedroom in coffee and cream: très chic. Gorgeous bathrooms, generous breakfasts, discreet hosts. A stylish gem deep in the country. *Minimum two nights July/August.*

Price	€100.
Rooms	2 suites.
Meals	Dinner with wine, €35.
Closed	Rarely.
Directions	Chartres N10 to Rambouillet 24km; left to St Symphorien le Château then for Château d'Esclimont; pass château gate; immed. left for 400m to Bouchemont; house on left opp. pond.

Maria Calderon & Didier Thébaud
La Ferme de Bouchemont,
11 rue de la Remarde, 28700 St Symphorien le Château, Eure-et-Loir
Tel   +33 (0)2 37 90 97 18
Mobile   +33 (0)6 08 58 13 68
Email   il.etait.une.fois@wanadoo.fr
Web   www.la-ferme-de-bouchemont.com

Entry 138   Map 5

Paris - Ile de France

Château de Jonvilliers

Delightful hosts: Virginie beautifully French, Richard a gentle Europeanised American, and their two sons. Down a wooded drive and set in a big leafy garden, the family house has tall windows, fine proportions and the air of a properly lived-in château: elegance and deep armchairs by the marble fireplace under crystal chandeliers. The top floor has been converted into five good rooms with sound-proofing, big beds, masses of hot water, rich, bright colour schemes... and just the right amount of family memorabilia: oils, engravings, lamps, old dishes. It feels easy, intelligent and fun.

Price	€85-€95.
Rooms	5: 4 doubles, 1 triple.
Meals	Restaurants 5km.
Closed	Rarely.
Directions	A11 exit Ablis on N10 for Chartres. At Essars, right to St Symphorien, Bleury & Ecrosnes; right & immed. left to Jonvilliers, 2.5km. White château gates straight ahead.

Virginie & Richard Thompson
Château de Jonvilliers,
17 rue Lucien Petit-Jonvilliers,
28320 Ecrosnes, Eure-et-Loir
Tel +33 (0)2 37 31 41 26
Email info@jonvilliers.com
Web www.jonvilliers.com

Entry 139 Map 5

Paris - Ile de France

Les Chandelles

At the end of a pretty village, a converted farmhouse behind high gates. Jean-Marc teaches golf to all ages and levels, Catherine is full of advice for visitors. They, their son and two big sloppy dogs receive you with alacrity in the old beamed kitchen then send you up steep, in part slippery barn stairs to simple white rooms where patches of bright colour punctuate the space. The two newer rooms, bigger, higher (yet more steep stairs) and more luxurious in fabric and fitting, are aimed at families, and there's a wood-clad sitting room for guests, its sofa spread with an African throw. *Golfing holidays.*

Price	€65-€85. Family room €115-€150.
Rooms	4: 2 doubles, 2 family rooms.
Meals	Kitchen available on request. Restaurants in Nogent le Roi & Maintenon.
Closed	Rarely.
Directions	From Paris A13, A12, N12, exit Gambais for Nogent le Roi. Entering Coulombs, left at lights for Chandelles; left at x-roads 1.5km; house on right.

Catherine & Jean-Marc Simon
Les Chandelles,
19 rue des Sablons, Chandelles,
28130 Villiers le Morhier, Eure-et-Loir
Tel +33 (0)2 37 82 71 59
Email info@chandelles-golf.com
Web www.chandelles-golf.com

Entry 140 Map 4

Normandy

Photo: www.istockphoto.com

Normandy

Manoir de Beaumont

In the old hunting lodge for guests, a vast, boar- and stag's-headed dayroom with log fire, chandelier and bedrooms above – ideal for parties. In the main house (charming, heavily wallpapered, colourful) is the handsome Jouy'd room for four. From the very lovely garden are hilltop views. Monsieur manages the Port and is a mine of local knowledge; Madame tends house, garden and guests, masterfully. Proud of their region, naturally generous, elegant, poised, they are keen to advise on explorations: nature, hiking, historical visits… Legend has it that Queen Victoria 'stopped' at this very gracious house.

Price	€51–€59.
Rooms	3: 1 double, 1 quadruple, 1 suite.
Meals	Restaurant 2km.
Closed	Rarely.
Directions	From Eu D49 E for Incheville 5km; before Ponts & Marais right for Forest of Eu & Rte de Beaumont 3km; manoir 200m on right after Ferme de Beaumont (signs).

Catherine & Jean-Marie Demarquet
Manoir de Beaumont,
76260 Eu,
Seine-Maritime
Tel +33 (0)2 35 50 91 91
Email catherine@demarquet.eu
Web www.demarquet.eu

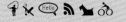

Entry 141 Map 1

Normandy

Le Clos Mélise

In a charming village on the edge of a green, a dear little cottage in a big sloping garden. Madame is a quietly spoken, welcoming and attentive hostess, keeps a spotless and pretty house, and joyfully paints with oils; her love of colour is reflected inside and out. The attic bedroom up a steep staircase may be small but is delightfully cosy; the other two, one large, one small, are on the ground floor of an adjacent wing, each with a door to the garden. Walls are white and fabric is toile de Jouy, floorboards are polished, fluffy towels are tied with bright bows, breakfasts are delicious – especially the yogurt gâteau!

Ethical Collection: Environment.
See page 410 for details.

Price	€52.
Rooms	3 doubles.
Meals	Restaurant in village.
Closed	Rarely.
Directions	From Le Tréport D925 for Dieppe 15km; in Biville sur Mer right Rue de l'Église; No. 14 faces you in middle of fork in road.

Marie-José Klaes
Le Clos Mélise,
14 rue de l'Église,
76630 Biville sur Mer, Seine-Maritime
Tel +33 (0)2 35 83 14 71
Mobile +33 (0)6 79 71 07 68
Email closmelise@wanadoo.fr
Web closmelise.monsite.orange.fr

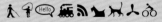

Entry 142 Map 1

Normandy

St Mare

A fresh modern house under a steep slate roof in a lush green sanctuary; it could not be more tranquil. The garden really is lovely and worth a wander – a tailored lawn, a mass of colour, huge banks of rhododendrons for which the village is renowned (three of its gardens are open to the public). Claudine runs home and B&B with effortless efficiency and gives you homemade brioches for breakfast; smiling Remi leads you to guest quarters in a freshly wood-clad house reached via stepping stones through the laurels. Bedrooms are comfortable, sunny, spotless, shining and utterly peaceful – two are big enough to lounge in.

Price	€75–€120.
Rooms	3: 1 suite for 2, 1 suite for 2 & kitchenette, 1 suite for 4.
Meals	Restaurants 20-minute walk.
Closed	Rarely.
Directions	From Dieppe D75 to Varengeville sur Mer 8km; 1st left after entering village onto Chemin des Petites Bruyères; house on left.

	Claudine Goubet
	St Mare, Le Quesnot, Chemin de Petites Bruyères, 76119 Varengeville sur Mer, Seine-Maritime
Tel	+33 (0)2 35 85 99 28
Mobile	+33 (0)6 18 92 28 20
Email	claudine.goubet@chsaintmare.com
Web	www.chsaintmare.com

Entry 143   Map 4

Normandy

Château Le Bourg

Silk bedspreads and scatter cushions, soaps, colognes and fresh roses... and Leonora's mix of English mahogany and French fabrics is as refined as her dinners. Having finished the soberly elegant bedrooms – one with boudoir touches – of her grand 19th-century mansion, she is turning her attention to the garden: it will undoubtedly delight. An intelligent hostess and fine cook, she is both entertaining and generous, handles house parties for celebrations and has a mass of books for you to browse on your return from walking the old railway line or exploring the cliffs. *Sawday self-catering also.*

Price	€85–€100.
Rooms	2 doubles.
Meals	Dinner with wine, €25–€70.
Closed	Rarely.
Directions	A16 from Calais exit 23 to A28, exit 6 to Londinières. left D12 8km to Bures en Bray. House opposite church, with high iron gates between red & white brick pillars.

	Leonora Macleod
	Château Le Bourg, 27 Grande Rue, 76660 Bures en Bray, Seine-Maritime
Tel	+33 (0)2 35 94 09 35
Email	leonora.macleod@wanadoo.fr

Entry 144   Map 4

Normandy

Les Glycines

Close to coast and ferry, in a quiet village in undulating farmland, a wisteria-hugged, red-brick house with gregarious bilingual hosts. Inside, a sitting room with sofa, wood-burner, books, DVDs; outside, a large lawn and sweet sheltered alcove for reading and dreaming. It's intimate: just two bedrooms, one sky-lit and country-pretty, one wallowing in fine fabrics and green views; awake to fresh fruit and croissants. Jenny and Christopher, who've lived in France for ten years, point you to walks, bike rides, cheese makers, cider farms... auberge meals in Londinières and gourmet offerings in Rouen.

Price	€65.
Rooms	2 doubles.
Meals	Restaurants 8km.
Closed	Rarely.
Directions	A28 exit 7 for Neufchâtel Nord; left D928 to Ménonval; D36 thro' Fesques onto D97 to Lucy. House on left at end of village.

Christopher & Jenny Laws
Les Glycines,
19 rue de la Houssaye-Béranger,
76270 Lucy, Seine-Maritime

Tel   +33 (0)2 35 93 12 45
Mobile +33 (0)6 47 59 21 41
Email   kpylaws@orange.fr

✗ Hello 🔊

Normandy

23 Grand Rue

Peter loves his wines (he was in the trade), Madeleine is energetic and vivacious, both welcome you generously at their 'maison bourgeoise' on the edge of a château village. Set back from the road behind fence and clipped hedge are four cosy classically furnished bedrooms: books and fresh flowers, immaculate duvets, smart French furniture, a calvados nightcap on the landing. Shower rooms are small and beautifully tiled. There's a conservatory for breakfast, a front room for relaxing and, at a table dressed with silver, French dinners are served. Dieppe, Rouen, Honfleur: all are wonderfully close.

Price	€50-€75.
Rooms	4: 2 doubles, 1 twin; 1 triple with separate bath.
Meals	Dinner with wine, €25.
Closed	Rarely.
Directions	A28 exit 9 to Neufchâtel en Bray; D1 Dieppe to Mesnières en Bray. Through village, tall cream house on left after village centre, 150m after café.

Peter & Madeleine Mitchell
23 Grand Rue,
76270 Mesnières en Bray,
Seine-Maritime

Tel   +33 (0)2 32 97 06 31
Email   info@23grandrue.com
Web   www.23grandrue.com

✗ Hello 🐾 🔊

Normandy

La Charretterie

A delicious 18th-century working farmhouse, in the family for three generations. Views sail over pastures, cows and gorgeous garden: clumps of lavender, exuberant roses, weathered teak, hazes of flowers. The Prévosts are a courteously friendly pair whose efficiency shines. Expect fresh, harmonious and beamy bedrooms, one under the eaves, the other down, and two shower rooms immaculately dotted with mosaics and fresh flowers. No sitting room but a big breakfast room, warm, woody and inviting, its long table spread with homemade breads, brioche, yogurts and jams. A super stopover on the way to the coast.

Price	€60-€70.
Rooms	2: 1 double, 1 quadruple.
Meals	Restaurants 3km.
Closed	Rarely.
Directions	From Dieppe D927 for Rouen; exit Bacqueville en Caux onto D149 for Bacqueville, 2km; right, then immed. left into Rue du Pavé; over 3 x-roads, on for 800m. House behind farmyard entrance.

Corinne & Arnaud Prévost
La Charretterie,
4 rue du Tilleul, 76730 Pierreville,
Seine-Maritime

Tel	+33 (0)2 35 04 26 45
Email	arnaud.prevost@cegetel.net
Web	charretterie.perso.sfr.fr

Entry 147   Map 4

Normandy

Le Clos du Gui Nel

Brace yourself for the last lap home or, better still, unwind in this leafy Norman oasis, neatly set between Dieppe and Le Havre. Welsh cobs graze in the lee of a little Norman church by the immaculately restored farmhouse. A deep pitched roof caps the attractive timbered façade, the stout oak doors and the high windows. No sitting room but fresh, charming, ground-floor rooms with their own entrance. If up and about early you may meet Etienne, a doctor, as he dashes off to work, or chat to Catherine about her beloved ponies as you breakfast on French pastries in the handsome dining room.

Price	€78.
Rooms	2 doubles.
Meals	Restaurant 2km.
Closed	Rarely.
Directions	From Dieppe D925 to Veules les Roses; D142 to Fontaine le Dun; D89 for Canville les Deux Églises: do not go into Bourville; entrance on right by small church back from road.

Catherine & Étienne Stevens
Le Clos du Gui Nel,
4 rue de Canville, 76740 Bourville,
Seine-Maritime

Tel	+33 (0)2 35 57 02 31
Mobile	+33 (0)6 70 55 26 39
Email	contact@gui-nel.com
Web	www.gui-nel.com

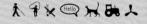

Entry 148   Map 4

Normandy

Le Clos du Vivier

The lush garden shelters fantails, ducks, bantams, sleek cats and a phenomenal variety of shrubs and flowering plants. While Monsieur works in town, Madame tends all this, and her guests, with respect for everyone's privacy; she also offers guidance on hiking, and there's tennis and fishing nearby. She is an intelligent, active and graceful person, her bedrooms, some under sloping ceilings, are cosily colourful, her bathrooms big and luxurious, her breakfast richly varied. After a jaunt, you can read their books, relax among their lovely antiques or make tea in their breakfast room. The cliffs at Étretat are 20 minutes away.

Price	€100–€120.
Rooms	3: 1 twin/double, 1 triple, 1 suite for 5.
Meals	Restaurants in Valmont, 1km.
Closed	Rarely.
Directions	From Dieppe D925 W for Fécamp 60km; left D17 to Valmont centre; left D150 for Ourville 1.2km; right Chemin du Vivier; house 2nd entrance on right (No. 4), signed 'Fleur de Soleil'.

	Dominique Cachera & François Gréverie
	Le Clos du Vivier,
	4-6 chemin du Vivier, 76540 Valmont,
	Seine-Maritime
Tel	+33 (0)2 35 29 90 95
Email	le.clos.du.vivier@wanadoo.fr
Web	www.leclosduvivier.com

Normandy

Manoir de la Rue Verte

The 300-year-old house stands in a classic, poplar-sheltered farmyard, its worn old stones and bricks, and less worn flints, bearing witness to its age – as does some timberwork inside. Otherwise it has been fairly deeply modernised, and filled with knick knacks and paddywhacks from everywhere. The long lace-clothed breakfast table before the winter fire is most welcoming, as are your retired farmer hosts. Madame was born here, has a winning smile and loves to talk (French only). Her pleasant rooms are in simple rural style; the only sounds are the occasional lowing of the herd and the shushing of the poplars.

Price	€50.
Rooms	4: 1 double, 1 triple; 2 doubles sharing shower & wc.
Meals	Auberge 1km, restaurant 4km.
Closed	Rarely.
Directions	From Dieppe N27 for Rouen 29km; right N29 through Yerville, cont. 4.5km; left D20 to Motteville; right to Flamanville. 21 rue Verte behind church. Farm 300m on left; signed.

	Yves & Béatrice Quevilly Baret
	Manoir de la Rue Verte,
	21 rue Verte, 76970 Flamanville,
	Seine-Maritime
Tel	+33 (0)2 35 96 81 27

Normandy

Vignacourt

From the smart jolly bathrooms to the towels for the pool, Vignacourt is sophisticated, civilised and presided over by Alix, a gentle, charming hostess. She lives with her youngest daughter in this imposing 19th-century house on the outskirts of Rouen. You will find a pool with white-lacquered loungers, a salon in resolutely modern style, a white dining table for beautiful breakfasts and, in the fine limestone stables, three immaculate guest rooms with orangery-style windows and a private entrance each. Delight in opera and architecture in Rouen, visit cheese makers and cider farms in the countryside. A treat.

Price	€120.
Rooms	3: 2 doubles, 1 twin.
Meals	Restaurant 500m.
Closed	Rarely.
Directions	From A28 exit 13 for Isneauville; right at stop sign; 300m after leaving village, house on left behind high wooden gates.

Alix d'Argentre
Vignacourt,
2871 route de Neufchâtel,
76230 Isneauville, Seine-Maritime

Mobile	+33 (0)6 22 27 77 20
Email	alix@vignacourt.com
Web	www.vignacourt.com

Entry 151   Map 4

Normandy

Chambres avec Vue

The elegant black door hides a light, stylish interior with soul-lifting views across old Rouen to the spires of the cathedral. Dominique, a cultured hostess full of energy and enthusiasm, has a flair for decoration – as her paintings, coverings and contemporary and country furniture declare. Oriental rugs on parquet floors, French windows to balcony and garden, bedrooms brimful of interest. Nothing standard, nothing too studied, a very personal home and leisurely breakfasts promising delicious surprises. The house's hillside position in this attractive suburb is equally special. Such value! *Covered garage space for one car.*

Price	€60.
Rooms	3 doubles.
Meals	Restaurant 1km.
Closed	October-November.
Directions	In Rouen follow Gare SNCF signs; Rue Rochefoucault right of station; left Rue des Champs des Oiseaux; over 2 traffic lights into Rue Vigné; fork left Rue Hénault; black door on left.

Dominique Gogny
Chambres avec Vue,
22 rue Hénault,
76130 Mont St Aignan, Seine-Maritim

Tel	+33 (0)2 35 70 26 95
Mobile	+33 (0)6 62 42 26 95
Email	chambreavecvue@online.fr
Web	chambreavecvue.online.fr

Entry 152   Map 4

Normandy

Le Clos Jouvenet

From your bath you gaze upon the cathedral spire. It is a privilege to stay in these refined city surroundings, safely inside a serene walled garden above the towers of Rouen. The garden is as elegantly uncomplicated as the house and its Belgian owners, the décor classic sophisticated French to suit the gentle proportions: there are pretty pictures and prints, lots of books, handsome antique furniture and breakfast is served in the kitchen, warmed by slate and oak. Madame is charming, Monsieur enjoys guests too, and you wake to birdsong and church bells. *Priority to two nights at weekends & high season.*

Price	€100–€120.
Rooms	4: 2 doubles, 2 twins/doubles.
Meals	Restaurants within walking distance.
Closed	Mid-December to mid-January.
Directions	From SNCF station Bd de L'Yser for Boulogne / Amiens; left Route Neufchâtel same direction; 1st right Rue du Champ du Pardon then Rue Jouvenet; left at lights; 2nd right.

Catherine de Witte
Le Clos Jouvenet,
42 rue Hyacinthe Langlois,
76000 Rouen, Seine-Maritime
Tel +33 (0)2 35 89 80 66
Email catherinedewitte@sfr.fr
Web www.leclosjouvenet.com

Normandy

Manoir de Captot

Gracious living is declared at the pillared gates, the drive curves through horse pastures to a serene 18th-century mansion, the forest behind may ring with the stag's call, the heads of his kin abound. The fine classic French interior is peacefully formal: gorgeous primrose-yellow dining room with an oval mahogany table for breakfast feasts, a collection-filled drawing room, a beautiful high first-floor bedroom with the right curly antiques and pink Jouy draperies. Michèle cherishes her mansion and resembles it: gently friendly with impeccable manners. Rouen, ten minutes away, has heaps of lovely restaurants.

Price	€85–€95.
Rooms	3: 1 suite for 2-3, 2 doubles.
Meals	Restaurants in Rouen, 10-minute drive.
Closed	Rarely.
Directions	From Rouen D982; north side of river Seine west 3km to Canteleu on left; D351 for Sahurs; entrance on right 900m after church, big iron gates.

Michèle Desrez
Manoir de Captot,
42 route de Sahurs,
76380 Canteleu, Seine-Maritime
Tel +33 (0)2 35 36 00 04
Email captot76@yahoo.fr
Web www.captot.com

Normandy

Le Brécy

Jérôme has happy childhood holiday memories of this elegant 17th-century manor house; he and delightful Patricia moved to join *grand-mère* who had been living here alone for years. A long path flanked by willows leads down to the Seine: perfect (when not mud-bound!) for an evening stroll. One suite is on the ground floor, in classically French coral and cream, its windows opening to a walled garden; the second, equally refined, is in the attic. Breakfast is when you fancy: brioches, walnuts, fresh fruit in a pretty green-panelled room. Ask Patricia about the Abbey and walks to its gardens. A charming rural paradise.

Ethical Collection: Environment.
See page 410 for details.

Price	€82-€95.
Rooms	2: 1 suite for 2, 1 suite for 3 & study.
Meals	Restaurant in village.
Closed	Rarely.
Directions	From Paris A13 exit 24 'Maison Brulée'; ferry from La Bouille Bac to Sahurs; left for St Martin de Boscherville; after Quevillon, 2nd left for Le Brécy; signed.

Jérôme & Patricia Lanquest
Le Brécy,
72 route du Brécy, 76840 St Martin
de Boscherville, Seine-Maritime
Tel +33 (0)2 35 32 69 92
Email lebrecy@sfr.fr
Web lebrecy.perso.sfr.fr

Entry 155   Map 4

Normandy

Le Moulin Auguérard

The bedrooms are pretty, the building is lofty, the owners are charming and attentive. Nadine works in marketing, Guy is a happy just-retired full-time host. There's a a ground-floor sitting room with an open fire, a cosy feel and a staircase curving up to one of the family's bedrooms above – and the guest double with its seagrass floor and pretty antique bed. On the second floor is the much bigger triple: stripped boards, elegant fireplace, soaring views. (Note: between the floors is an independent flat that the owners plan to buy.) The garden is whimsical, the village is delightful and the mill race flows by.

Price	€60-€70.
Rooms	2: 1 double, 1 triple.
Meals	Restaurant 600m.
Closed	Rarely.
Directions	From Beauvais D981 to Gisors; right by château for St Denis; at St Paër right D17 into St Denis. Thro' village, house at far end; entrance on right after public gardens.

Nadine & Guy Masurier
Le Moulin Auguérard,
46 rue Guérard,
27140 St Denis le Ferment, Eure
Tel +33 (0)2 32 27 09 62
Mobile +33 (0)6 70 29 02 13
Email lemoulinauguerard@orange.fr
Web www.lemoulinauguerard.com

Entry 156   Map 5

Normandy

La Lévrière

The garden laps at the river bank where moorhens nest; trout swim, birds chirrup, deer pop by – it's the dreamiest village setting. Madame is charming and takes everything (including escapee horses) in her stride and her young family love it when guests come to stay. Breakfast is at a grey-painted table with crimson plexiglass chairs; garden loungers are a temptation to stay. Bedrooms are across the way, two in the granary, one up, one down, the third in the immaculate coach house attic with a fine garden view. Creamy walls, sweeping floors, rafters, toile de Jouy, fresh flowers… stay a long while.

Price	€80.
Rooms	3: 1 triple, 1 suite for 3, 1 suite for 4.
Meals	Auberge opposite.
Closed	Rarely.
Directions	From Beauvais D981 to Gisors; right by château for St Denis; at St Paër right D17 into St Denis; house on right, signed.

Sandrine & Pascal Gravier
La Lévrière,
24 rue Guérard,
27140 St Denis le Ferment, Eure

Tel	+33 (0)2 32 27 04 78
Mobile	+33 (0)6 79 43 92 77
Email	contact@normandyrooms.com
Web	www.normandyrooms.com

Entry 157   Map 5

Normandy

La Buissonnière

A farmhouse in a village setting, oozing charm and graceful living: stepped roof, pale façades, country-style shutters and wonderful interior dimensions. A large arched bay window lets in light and looks out onto a deep-terraced garden with a water feature, box, lavender and wild patches. Three rightly-named, 1920s-style rooms, Blanche, Lune and Chine, are modern of fixture, generous of linen, fluffy of duvet; around the house, artefacts and curios catch the eye. A refined living room bares its beams above a chequered tile floor; here you will relax over fine breakfasts with your friendly, cosmopolitan hosts. Sheer delight.

Price	€65-€85.
Rooms	3: 1 double, 1 triple, 1 family room for 3.
Meals	Restaurant 3km.
Closed	Rarely.
Directions	From Vernon, left to Dangu; right D146 thro' Bordeaux St Clair to St Rémy; right D4 for 2km, left to Bus St Rémy.

Laurent Bonnet
La Buissonnière,
19 rue du Valcorbon,
27630 Bus St Rémy, Eure

Tel	+33 (0)2 32 52 33 09
Mobile	+33 (0)6 83 26 08 55
Email	jacob-bonnet@wanadoo.fr
Web	la-buissonniere.over-blog.com

Entry 158   Map 5

Normandy

La Réserve

You will like Valérie, lively mother of four, the moment she opens the door to her quietly refined house. After breakfast, you will want to stay for ever: a feast for eye and palate, home-grown eggs and jams, cake of the day, cheese, cold meats and… a fruit kebab; tongues loosen, friendships bud. Outside, soft limewash walls stand among lavender-edged lawns and orchards, kindly Flaubert the Leonberger ambles, cows graze; inside are grey woodwork and gorgeous rooms, superb beds, handsome rugs on parquet floors, modern sculptures and fine antiques. Monet's ineffable gardens are just down the hill. Exceptional.

Ethical Collection: Environment.
See page 410 for details.

Price	€130-€160. Extra bed €40. Whole house available.
Rooms	6: 2 doubles, 4 twins/doubles.
Meals	Restaurants 1km.
Closed	November-March, except by arrangement.
Directions	From A13 exit 16 to Giverny; first left Rue Claude Monet; pass church, 1st left Rue Blanche Hoschedé Monet/Chemin du Grand Val 1km; left and follow signs 800m to house.

Valérie & François Jouyet
La Réserve,
27620 Giverny,
Eure

Tel	+33 (0)2 32 21 99 09
Email	mlreserve@gmail.com
Web	www.giverny-lareserve.com

Entry 159   Map 4

Normandy

Clos de Mondétour

Tiny church to one side, lazy river behind, views to weeping willows and majestic limes – the house oozes grace and tranquillity. Grégoire and Aude have created a calm, charming atmosphere inside: this is a family home. Lofty, light-drenched bedrooms with polished floorboards, antiques and monogrammed bed linen are beautifully refined; bathrooms are light and luxurious. The living area, with a striking tiled floor and bold colours, is a restful space in which to settle in front of a log fire – or enjoy a special breakfast among fresh flowers and family silver. Aude's horses graze in the meadow behind.

Price	€80-€140.
Rooms	3: 1 double, 1 twin, 1 family suite.
Meals	Restaurants nearby.
Closed	Rarely.
Directions	A13 to Paris, exit 17 for Gaillon; D31 to Auteuil Authouillet; main street in village left to Chambray D836; D63 for 2km to Fontaine. Entrance next to phone box.

Aude Jeanson
Clos de Mondétour,
17 rue de la Poste,
27120 Fontaine sous Jouy, Eure

Tel	+33 (0)2 32 36 68 79
Mobile	+33 (0)6 71 13 11 57
Email	aude.jeanson@closdemondetour.com
Web	www.closdemondetour.com

Entry 160   Map 4

Normandy

L'Aulnaie

Michel and Éliane have invested natural good taste in their restoration of this lovely 19th-century farmhouse in a particularly pretty village. Guests share a self-contained part of the house with its own dayroom and breakfast area – there's lots of space to settle in – with books, music and open fire. Bedrooms are gentle, beautiful, fresh, with Jouy-print fabrics, plain walls and honey-coloured floors. Enthusiastic, charming Éliane is an amateur painter and inspired gardener, pointing out the rich and the rare; lawns sweep down to a stream that meanders beneath high wooded cliffs. Such value!

Price	€75.
Rooms	2: 1 double, 1 twin.
Meals	Restaurants nearby.
Closed	Rarely.
Directions	A13 exit 16 for Cocherel; after 10km to Chambray; left at monument 100m; left to Fontaine sous Jouy. In centre right Rue de l'Ancienne Forge 800m; Rue de l'Aulnaie on right.

Éliane & Michel Philippe
L'Aulnaie,
29 rue de l'Aulnaie,
27120 Fontaine sous Jouy, Eure

Tel	+33 (0)2 32 36 89 05
Mobile	+33 (0)6 03 30 55 99
Email	emi.philippe@worldonline.fr
Web	chambre-fontaine.chez-alice.fr

Normandy

Manoir Les Perdrix

The young, hands-on owners of Les Perdrix are full of infectious enthusiasm for their enterprise: running a themed, welcoming, upmarket B&B. Food tastings, painting courses, walking weekends – they can do it all! In the throes of serious restoration, the old house has an intimate dining room for tasty breakfasts and jolly dinners, a cavernous reception room and comfortable bedrooms off a winding second-floor corridor: thick duvets and pretty linen, coordinated fabrics and polished floors, shower gels and plush bathrooms. The run-around garden – great for kids – is within earshot of the road to Verneuil.

Price	€80–€95. Extra person €20.
Rooms	5: 4 twins/doubles, 1 family suite for 4.
Meals	Dinner with wine, €15–€27.
Closed	Rarely.
Directions	From Paris A13 for Versailles & Rouen to A12; N12 to Dreux; approx. 25km after Dreux do not take 1st or 2nd exits for Tillières, but next right, signed. Left at fork for entrance.

Christine Vandemoortele
Manoir Les Perdrix,
Les Marnières,
27570 Tillières sur Avre, Eure

Mobile	+33 (0)6 21 21 08 52
Email	postmaster@manoirlesperdrix.fr
Web	www.normandy-guest-house.com

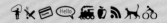

Normandy

Les Granges Ménillonnes

An active farm until 1950, it sits beside a pretty garden in the prettiest countryside in the Eure valley, 20 minutes from Monet's gardens at Giverny, midway between Rouen and Paris. In converted outbuildings, big comfortable bedrooms, one with a balcony, furnished with warm colours, honeyed floorboards and country quilts beneath a riot of beams overlook cobbled paths, tumbling hydrangeas, lily pond and loungers that beckon you to doze over a book — though excellent walking abounds. Chantal and Michel, dynamic hosts, serve brilliant meals in the dining room and drinks in the salon bar — and run a proper farm shop.

Normandy

Clair Matin

Handsomely carved Colombian furniture, strong colours, interesting prints — not what you expect to find at an 18th-century manor with a Norman-cottage face and an unexpected turret. Your kind and very lovely Franco-Spanish hosts raised five children in South America before renovating their French home. Bedrooms, not huge, are solidly comfortable, bathrooms are immaculate and, at the huge Andean cedar breakfast table, you will find fresh breads, homemade jams and good conversation. Jean-Pierre is a passionate gardener and his plantations burst with every kind of shrub and flower: stunning! *Watch children in garden.*

Price	€70.
Rooms	5: 2 doubles, 1 twin, 1 suite for 4, 1 suite for 7.
Meals	Dinner with wine, €24.
Closed	Rarely.
Directions	A16 to Rouen, A13 for Paris exit 17 (Gaillon) D316 to Autheuil-Authouillet; left D836 thro' Chambray & Cocherel to Ménilles; right Rue Grand'Cour. House on left at fork.

Price	€60-€75. €90-€100 for 4.
Rooms	3: 1 double, 1 family room, 1 suite.
Meals	Auberges 6km.
Closed	Rarely.
Directions	From A13 exit 17; D316 for Évreux through Autheuil, St Vigor & up hill 11km; right to Reuilly; house on road, 200m past Mairie on right.

Michel & Chantal Marchand
Les Granges Ménillonnes,
2 rue Grand'Cour,
27120 Ménilles, Eure

Tel +33 (0)2 32 26 45 86
Mobile +33 (0)6 70 46 87 57
Email contact@lesgranges27.com
Web www.lesgranges27.com

Jean-Pierre & Amaia Trevisani
Clair Matin,
19 rue de l'Église,
27930 Reuilly, Eure

Tel +33 (0)2 32 34 71 47
Email bienvenue@clair-matin.com
Web www.clair-matin.com

Normandy

La Londe

The big beautiful garden flows down to the river Eure – what a setting – and the old farmhouse and yesteryear buildings are as neat as new pins. Delightful Madeleine devotes herself to home and guests and bedrooms are neat, clean, pretty, sober and relaxing; the double's French windows open to the garden, the perfect small suite sits under the eaves. Expect antique lace, silver snuff boxes, a kitchen/salon for guests and very delicious breakfasts with garden views. A form of perfection in a privileged and peaceful spot: woods and water for walking, canoeing, fishing; Giverny – or Rouen – a half-hour drive.

Price	€57–€62.
Rooms	2: 1 double, 1 suite for 3.
Meals	Guest kitchen. Restaurants 5km.
Closed	Rarely.
Directions	A13 exit 19 for Louviers & Évreux; 2nd exit N154 to Acquigny; D71 thro' Heudreville for Cailly to La Londe; left; house on right.

Madeleine & Bernard Gossent
La Londe,
4 sente de l'Abreuvoir,
27400 Heudreville sur Eure, Eure

Tel	+33 (0)2 32 40 36 89
Mobile	+33 (0)6 89 38 36 59
Email	madeleine.gossent@online.fr
Web	www.lalonde.online.fr

Normandy

Manoir de la Boissière

Madame cooks great Norman dishes with home-grown ingredients served on good china. She has been doing B&B for years, is well-organised and still enjoys meeting new people when she's not too busy. Guest quarters, independent of the house, have pretty, traditional rooms, good bedding and excellent shower rooms. Sympathetically restored 15th-century farm buildings, carefully chosen furniture – some tenderly hand-painted – and ducks and swans on the lovely pond add character. Near the motorway yet utterly peaceful – though courting peacocks in spring/summer may wake you.

Price	€62. Triple €75.
Rooms	5: 2 doubles, 1 twin, 1 triple, 1 family room for 3 (with kitchenette).
Meals	Dinner with cider, €25. Guest kitchen.
Closed	Rarely.
Directions	From Rouen N15 for Paris 40km; at Gaillon right D10 for La Croix St Leufroy approx. 7km; in La Boissaye, Chambres d'Hôtes signs.

Clotilde & Gérard Sénécal
Manoir de la Boissière,
Hameau la Boissaye,
27490 La Croix St Leufroy, Eure

Tel	+33 (0)2 32 67 70 85
Email	chambreslaboissiere@wanadoo.fr
Web	www.chambres-giteslaboissiere.com

Normandy

Au Vieux Logis

They are full of character and terribly French, this artist owner and her crooked house marked by the slings and arrows of 500 years: wonky floorboards, bathrooms among the beams, old-fashioned floral bedrooms and a sensuous garden full of old favourites: lilac and honeysuckle, luscious shrubs and fruit trees. Set in the middle of the village, the quiet old house has an atmosphere that inspires ease and rest. (Saint-Exupéry, author of the *Le Petit Prince* and a friend of Madame's father, stayed here.) Madame, a good, generous soul, was once an antique dealer so breakfast is served on old silver.

Price	€48-€96.
Rooms	4: 2 doubles, 1 triple, 1 quadruple.
Meals	Dinner €17. Wine €15.
Closed	Rarely.
Directions	A13 exit 19 to Louviers; D313 for Elbeuf 11km; left D60 to St Didier des Bois. House with white iron gate opp. church.

Annick Auzoux
Au Vieux Logis,
27370 St Didier des Bois,
Eure
Tel   +33 (0)2 32 50 60 93
Email levieuxlogis5@orange.fr
Web   www.levieuxlogis.fr

Normandy

Manoir d'Hermos

The sedately old-French bedrooms with good antiques and satin touches are up the grand old staircase of this 16th-century house where brick and sandstone sit in peace by birdy orchard, pastoral meadows and spreading lake. Madame is a most welcoming hostess, full of spontaneous smiles, who puts flowers everywhere and whose family has owned the house for 100 years. She also organises big parties (not when B&B guests are here), serves good breakfasts and brunches at one table and keeps four gentle donkeys. The orchards produce cider and trees are being planted to Napoleonic plans discovered in the archives.

Price	€59-€80. Triple €78-€99. Quadruple €118.
Rooms	2: 1 triple, 1 quadruple.
Meals	Restaurants 2km.
Closed	Rarely.
Directions	From A13, A28 exit 13. D438 on left for 400m, right D92; on for 1km, signed.

Béatrice & Patrice Noël-Windsor
Manoir d'Hermos,
27800 St Éloi de Fourques,
Eure
Tel   +33 (0)2 32 35 51 32
Email contact@hermos.fr
Web   www.hermos.fr

Normandy

Les Clématites

An enchanting *maison de maître*, one of several that housed the nimble-fingered ribbon weavers, with the bonus of fine table d'hôtes. Hidden amid the fields of the Normandy plains, it stands in a dream of a garden, overgrown here, brought to heel there, flanked by a majestic walnut and age-old pears, filled with shrub roses; the odd forgotten bench adds to the Flaubertian charm. Inside, Marie-Hélène, bright-eyed and eager, has used Jouy cloth and elegant colours to dress the country-French bedrooms that fill the first floor. These ex-Parisian hosts are courteous, considerate, truly endearing.

Price	€68.
Rooms	3: 1 double, 1 twin, 1 triple.
Meals	Light supper with wine, €17. Occasional dinner with wine, €28.
Closed	Rarely.
Directions	From Évreux D613 for Lisieux 50km; entering Duranville right D41 for St Aubin de Scellon 2.5km; drive on right.

**Marie-Hélène François &
Hughes de Morchoven**
Les Clématites, Hameau de la Charterie,
27230 St Aubin de Scellon, Eure

Tel	+33 (0)2 32 45 46 52
Mobile	+33 (0)6 20 39 08 63
Email	la.charterie@orange.fr
Web	monsite.orange.fr/la.charterie

Entry 169   Map 4

Normandy

Les Hauts Vents

Corine, a farmer's daughter, was born nearby and is cheerfully passionate about the area and its rural heritage. Her bewitching garden – where, Monet-style, a bridge spans the lily pond – is listed as a protected bird sanctuary. The house is long, low and typical Normandy. Two of the bedrooms are on the first floor of a converted outbuilding, all are painted in joyous colours and are freshly, modestly furnished. Breakfast is in the family's conservatory where musical instruments jostle with collections of plants, teapots and Russian dolls. Camargue horses and a donkey graze in the paddock. An enchanting place.

Ethical Collection: Food.
See page 410 for details.

Price	€67. Extra person €15.
Rooms	1 double.
Meals	Dinner with wine, €25. Light supper €15.
Closed	Rarely.
Directions	From Rouen A13 for Caen exit 2; N175 to Pont-Audemer; D810 for Bernay; 1km before Lieurey, right to Les Hauts Vents, 1st right Chemin du Seureur, 1st entrance on left, No. 60.

Corine Angevin
Les Hauts Vents,
27560 Lieurey,
Eure

Tel	+33 (0)2 32 57 99 27
Email	corine.angevin@free.fr
Web	leshautsvents.free.fr

Entry 170   Map 4

Normandy

Le Coquerel

Jean-Marc brims with ideas for your stay and love for his garden, modern art and long divine dinners with guests. He has turned the old cottage, surrounded by soft pastures, into a country gem in a flower-exuberant garden. Inside, a mix of the sober, the frivolous, the cultured and the kitsch: old and modern pieces, rustic revival and leather, paintings and brocante. Bedrooms stand out in their uncomplicated good taste, bathrooms are irreproachable, but it's your host who makes the place: duck in cider, strawberry soup and laughter, butterflies alighting on the table at breakfast. *Unfenced water.*

Price	€58–€70. Triple €75. Family room €85.
Rooms	5: 1 double, 1 twin, 1 triple, 2 family rooms.
Meals	Dinner with wine, €25. Picnic available.
Closed	Rarely.
Directions	From Pont Audemer D810 for Bernay 12km; right through St Siméon; up hill for Selles; house on left at top.

	Jean-Marc Drumel Le Coquerel, 27560 St Siméon, Eure
Tel	+33 (0)2 32 56 56 08
Email	coquerel127@nordnet.fr
Web	www.chambredhoteducoquerel.com

Entry 171   Map 4

Normandy

Les Aubépines

That lovely timber frame embraces a heart-warming antique clutter spread over original bricks, beams, tiles and carved family furniture. Guests share this marvellous space as family; Madame cooks with delight (maybe over the open fire), does excellent table d'hôtes and tends the intimate paradise of her garden whence views glide over forested hills; Monsieur smiles, charms – and mends everything. The delicious bedrooms are subtly lit by dormer windows, country-furnished, pastel-hued and comfortably bathroomed; the suite has steep rafters. Enchanting – they deserve a medal! *Minimum two nights.*

Price	€65–€70.
Rooms	3: 2 twins/doubles, 1 suite for 4.
Meals	Dinner with wine, €25.
Closed	October–February, except by arrangement.
Directions	From Paris A13 exit 26 for Pont Audemer D89; at 'Médine' r'bout. on for Évreux & Appeville Annebault 4km; left immed. after Les Marettes sign, follow Chambres d'Hôtes signs.

	Françoise & Yves Closson Maze Les Aubépines, Aux Chauffourniers, 27290 Appeville dit Annebault, Eure
Tel	+33 (0)2 32 56 14 25
Mobile	+33 (0)6 72 26 18 59
Email	clossonmaze@orange.fr
Web	pagesperso-orange.fr/lesaubepines

Entry 172   Map 4

Normandy

Les Sources Bleues

A privileged setting on the banks of the Seine just below Rouen: once every four years the great armada comes sailing by. The garden (old trees, long grasses, the odd goat, sheep and pig) is 50m from the water's edge and there are binoculars for bird-watching. This Panda (WWF) house is for guests only: the owner lives next door. Bedrooms may be in need of a lick of paint but are old-fashioned and charming, the family rooms are squeezed into the attic. There are beams and panelling and windows onto that stunning view, a kitchen/diner, a surprisingly fancy sitting room. Monsieur cooks, expertly, or you can do it yourself.

Price	€58-€70. €80 for 4.
Rooms	4: 2 quadruples, 2 suites for 3.
Meals	Dinner €20. Wine €12-€15; cider €5. Kitchen available.
Closed	Rarely.
Directions	From Pont Audemer D139 NE for 10km to Bourneville & D139 to Aizier. There, left at Mairie for Vieux Port, D95; on right.

Yves Laurent
Les Sources Bleues,
Le Bourg, 27500 Aizier,
Eure
Tel   +33 (0)2 32 57 26 68
Mobile +33 (0)6 80 62 84 31
Web   www.les-sources-bleues.com

Normandy

Le Moulin

You will warm to this couple who, whatever they turn their hand to – once farm and DIY store, now garden and chambres d'hôtes – turn it to perfection. The lovely half-timbered mill, operating from 1769 to 1965, is in working order stilll; ask Monsieur to give you a demo. Two neat, comfortable and immaculate bedrooms have carpeting or polished boards, gentle hues and dormer windows, and views of the oh-so-pretty garden; bliss to fall asleep to the sound of trickling water. Courteous and kind are the owners, bucolic is the setting. There's gourmet dining in Conteville, and a sweet, simple restaurant up the road.

Price	€68. Suite €75. €90 for 3.
Rooms	2: 1 double, 1 family suite for 3.
Meals	Restaurant 2km.
Closed	Rarely.
Directions	From Le Havre exit Tancarville; N178 10km; 1st right to Foulbec, signed.

Mme Derouet
Le Moulin,
27210 Foulbec,
Eure
Tel   +33 (0)2 32 56 55 25
Email   raymond.derouet@free.fr

Normandy

La Petite Folie

Two townhouses doubling as havens from the artistic bustle of Honfleur. Built for a sea captain in the 1830s, one displays grand mansarde windows, while its more modest 14th-century neighbour houses two self-catering apartments. American Penny married French Thierry, together they created lavish bedrooms, each an enchanting mix of handsome bedsteads, plump duvets, lacquered armchairs and mahogany chests. The garden is a neatly planted square of charm, its focal point a summerhouse with a Byzantine flourish and belvedere views out to sea. A charming small hotel. *Min. two nights. Not suitable for under 12s (except for one apt).*

Price	€135-€150. Apartments €175-€195. Prices per night.
Rooms	5 + 3: 4 doubles, 1 twin. 3 apartments: 2 for 2, 1 for 4.
Meals	Breakfast to apartments on request. Restaurants nearby.
Closed	Mid-January to mid-February.
Directions	A13 exit A29 Honfleur; towards centre then 'Naturospace'. Over bridge, to Rue Haute; road forks, keep right. 100m, on right, green shutters.

Penny & Thierry Vincent
La Petite Folie,
44 rue Haute,
14600 Honfleur, Calvados

Mobile	+33 (0)6 74 39 46 46
Email	info@lapetitefolie-honfleur.com
Web	www.lapetitefolie-honfleur.com

Entry 175 Map 4

Normandy

Au Grey d'Honfleur

There's a secret, fairytale look to this pair of tall narrow houses in a quiet cobbled backstreet. You don't quite know what to expect but you'll be enchanted by the sense of being somewhere rare and special. Stairs and steps in all directions link the little rooms; age-old beams and sloping ceilings contrast with imaginative décor and perfect modern luxury. Josette, a globe-trotting lawyer, knows a thing or two about what's required of a guest bedroom… Looking down over the haphazard roofs of medieval Honfleur, the formal, delightful, miniature terraced garden and fountain, add to the delight. One of the loveliest. *Min. two nights.*

Price	€110-€145.
Rooms	2 doubles.
Meals	Restaurants within walking distance.
Closed	Rarely.
Directions	From fountain r'bout at entrance to town, ahead to Bassin; left onto Rue de la République, 2nd right to Rue de Près, left to Rue de la Foulerie, left again to Rue de la Bavole. No. 11 on left; car park 50m.

Josette Roudaut
Au Grey d'Honfleur,
11 rue de la Bavole,
14600 Honfleur, Calvados

Email	info@augrey-honfleur.com
Web	www.augrey-honfleur.com

Entry 176 Map 4

Normandy

La Cour Ste Catherine

Through the Norman gateway into the sun-drenched courtyard; Liliane and history embrace you. The building was first a convent, then fishermen's cottages, later a *ciderie*. Now this historic quarter is a conservation area and all has been properly restored. Breakfast viennoiseries are served in the huge beamed room where the apples were once pressed; sip a summery aperitif in the courtyard with fellow guests. Bedrooms are sunny, airy, impeccable, contemporary, one in the hayloft with its own outside stair. There's a small sitting room for guests and Honfleur at your feet; your charming hosts know the town intimately.

Ethical Collection: Environment.
See page 410 for details.

Price	€80-€100. Extra bed €25.
Rooms	5: 2 doubles, 2 twins/doubles, 1 family suite.
Meals	Restaurants nearby.
Closed	Rarely.
Directions	In Honfleur, from Ste Catherine church for Hôtel Maison de Lucie; after hotel 1st left; left again. Signed.

Liliane & Antoine Giaglis
La Cour Ste Catherine,
74 rue du Puits,
14600 Honfleur, Calvados
Tel   +33 (0)2 31 89 42 40
Email   coursaintecatherine@orange.fr
Web   www.coursaintecatherine.com

Entry 177   Map 4

Normandy

La Cerisée

In glamorous, horsey Deauville, a wee garden cottage all to yourselves: pink and grey kitchen/living room downstairs, airy blond bedroom up. It's a cosy, uncomplicated and imaginative mix of new-simple and antique-reclaimed – plus Isabelle's beautiful driftwood art. She is elegantly informal and stores her raw materials in the flowery patio that you share with her and Alain. Breakfast is DIY – fresh ingredients delivered to the door – but if you prefer she will happily provide in her own pretty kitchen/diner. Deauville bursts with beaches, bicycle outings, markets and luscious seafood. Great value in a fascinating area.

Price	€110-€130.
Rooms	Cottage for 2.
Meals	Restaurants 50m.
Closed	Rarely.
Directions	From Deauville railway station for Centre Ville; right Quai de la Marine, past Hôtel Ibis, 3rd on left Rue du Général Leclerc. House on left after 1st x-roads.

Isabelle Laratte
La Cerisée,
15 rue du Général Leclerc,
14800 Deauville, Calvados
Tel   +33 (0)2 31 81 18 29
Email   la.cerisee@wanadoo.fr
Web   chambre-hotes-deauville.com

Entry 178   Map 4

Normandy

La Longère

There are two stars in this show: the whirl-wind Fabienne who decorates everything from tables to crockery and delivers breakfast feasts (a party every morning!), and the seductively long, low, half-timbered 17th-century farmhouse. Fabienne and her as-generous husband throw open their home and sheltered garden, join you for dinner and perhaps drinks on the terrace; she also happily babysits. Smallish rooms are pretty with quilts and hand-painted furniture, tiles or polished floorboards; children will love the hideaway mezzanine in the family suite. An endearing hostess, and beaches five minutes away. *Min. two nights at weekends.*

Price	€75–€140.
Rooms	4: 2 doubles. Wing: 1 family room for 4, 1 family suite for 5.
Meals	Dinner with wine, €28. Restaurant 300m.
Closed	Rarely.
Directions	A13 exit for Deauville-Trouville to Canapville; 1.3km after village, lane on left; 3rd house on right.

Fabienne Fillion
La Longère,
Chemin de la Libération,
14800 Bonneville sur Touques, Calvados
Tel +33 (0)2 31 64 10 29
Mobile +33 (0)6 08 04 38 52
Email fafillion@wanadoo.fr
Web www.lalongerenormandie.com

Entry 179   Map 4

Normandy

Maison d'hôtes les Vikings

Markets, casino and fashionable arty beaches are 15 minutes away yet you're far enough from the crowds to relax in peace. Sheltered from the road by shrubby residential lushness, the 1930s villa is deliciously eccentric with its wisteria-matching timbers and bits of stained glass. Likeable and quietly smiling, Jacky is the artist (he and Christophe are in retail). His driftwood and pebble creations bring the beach indoors, deckchair stripes enhance the theme, strong colours and period furniture anchor it in the smallish bedrooms. Pretty bathrooms, too. Is there crumble for breakfast? *Minimum two nights (three July/Aug).*

Price	€99–€119.
Rooms	3: 2 doubles, 1 twin/double.
Meals	Restaurants 1km.
Closed	Mid-January to mid-February.
Directions	A13 exit Deauville/Trouville to Pont l'Évêque; thro' town centre for Caen; 1st left after Mairie D48 for Coquainvilliers 800m; house on right.

Jacky & Christophe Advielle
Maison d'hôtes les Vikings,
15 av de la Libération,
14130 Pont l'Évêque, Calvados
Tel +33 (0)2 31 64 14 44
Email contact@lesvikings.fr
Web www.lesvikings.fr

Entry 180   Map 4

Normandy

La Baronnière

The Baron moved on but left a half-timbered glory of a manor house, expanses of grass dotted with apple trees, a stream-fed lake, sheep in a nearby pasture – enchanting. Geese gabble, birds triumph, children rejoice (dens in trees, games on lawns, bikes). Christine, who's English, loves caring for the old house and chatting with guests; her French husband cooks beautiful meals served in the pretty conservatory. The room in the old pantry has a Louis XIV bed on old honeycomb tiles, the other is up an outside staircase in the handsome timbered barn. *Unfenced water. Min. 2 nights. Telephone bookings only. Sawday self-catering also.*

Price	€90.
Rooms	2 doubles.
Meals	Dinner with wine, €50-€60.
Closed	Rarely.
Directions	From Liseux N13 for Evreux; D145 at Thiberville to La Chapelle Hareng. Follow signs; do not go into Cordebugle.

Christine Gilliatt-Fleury
La Baronnière,
14100 Cordebugle,
Calvados
Tel   +33 (0)2 32 46 41 74
Email   labaronniere@wanadoo.fr
Web   labaronniere.com

Entry 181   Map 4

Normandy

Manoir de Cantepie

It may have a make-believe face, among the smooth green curves of racehorse country, but it is genuine early 1600s and astonishing from all sides. Inside, an astounding dining room, resplendently carved, panelled and painted, serves for tasty organic breakfasts. Bedrooms, all amazing value, have a sunny feel, and are delightful: one with white-painted beams and green toile de Jouy, another in yellows, a third with a glorious valley view. Madame, a beautiful Swedish lady, made the curtains and covers. She and her husband are well-travelled, polyglot and cultured: they make their B&B doubly special.

Price	€75.
Rooms	3 doubles.
Meals	Restaurant 1km.
Closed	Mid-November to February.
Directions	From Caen N13 for Lisieux 25km; at Carrefour St Jean D50 (virtually straight on) for Cambremer; 5km from junc., house on right; signed.

Christine & Arnauld Gherrak
Manoir de Cantepie,
Le Cadran, 14340 Cambremer,
Calvados
Tel   +33 (0)2 31 62 87 27
Email   c.gherrak@dbmail.com

Entry 182   Map 4

Normandy

La Ferme de l'Oudon

With infectious enjoyment, Dany has rescued this old house, blending designer modern with atmospheric ancient and creating an exciting yet serene haven of well-being. Patrick is a great decorator. Come and chat in the kitchen conservatory, mingle with this lively couple, admire the organic potager. The honeymoon-perfect Lavoir suite over the lily pond has fireplace and flat screen, trendy shower and corkscrew stairs up to a sunken bed. The other two have just as much personality. Bathrooms are excellent with careful detail and colour splashes. Taste, panache, generosity. *Sawday self-catering also. Hammam spa.*

Ethical Collection: Environment & Food.
See page 410 for details.

Price	€130–€195.
Rooms	4: 1 double, 3 suites.
Meals	Dinner €45. Wine €12–€20. Restaurants 2km.
Closed	January.
Directions	A13 exit 29a for La Haie Tondue; D16 to Carrefour St Jean; N13 for Crèvecoeur 3km; D16 to St Pierre sur Dives then D40 to Berville. La Ferme at last x-roads, on left.

	Patrick & Dany Vesque
	La Ferme de l'Oudon,
	12 route d'Écots,
	14170 Berville l'Oudon, Calvados
Tel	+33 (0)2 31 20 77 96
Mobile	+33 (0)6 11 72 91 59
Email	contact@fermedeloudon.com
Web	www.fermedeloudon.com

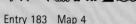

Entry 183   Map 4

Normandy

Ferme de la Ruette

The gates glide open to a gravelled sweep and a tree'd lawn framed by mellow cider-farm buildings. Elegant, compassionate Isabelle looks after house, garden, guests – and rescue cats and horses – with warmth and charm; Philippe, a friendly GP, fills the game larder. The barn houses two bedrooms, a delightful family suite under the rafters (up a steep private stair) and a cosy guest sitting room with a bar. Rooms have pretty striped wallpapers, seagrass floors and elegant Louis XV-style chairs, quirky *objets* on shelves and in crannies, beds dressed with white heirloom spreads. Vivacious, bustling Caen is an easy drive.

Price	€60–€80. Extra bed €10.
Rooms	3: 2 doubles; 1 family suite for 4 (with kitchenette).
Meals	Restaurant 5km.
Closed	Rarely.
Directions	From Caen ring road exit 13; N158 for Falaise 13km; left D132A to Cauvicourt; right opp. church, follow Chemin Haussé to end of lane.

	Isabelle & Philippe Cayé
	Ferme de la Ruette,
	5 chemin Haussé,
	14190 Cauvicourt, Calvados
Tel	+33 (0)2 31 78 11 82
Mobile	+33 (0)6 28 26 22 61
Email	laruette@gmail.com
Web	www.fermedelaruette.fr

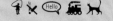

Entry 184   Map 4

Normandy

Normandy

Château des Riffets

The square-set château stands handsome still as the park recovers from the 1999 storm: they lost 2,300 trees. Admire yourself in myriad mirrors, luxuriate in a jacuzzi, bare your chest to a rain shower, play the piano, and lie at last in an antique bed in one of the great, cherished bedrooms. Monsieur is a former psychologist, gracious Madame was an English teacher, and a fine breakfast is served at one big table. Take a stroll in the 30-acre wooded park, hire a nearby horse or a canoe, hone your carriage-driving skills. Period ceilings, tapestries and furniture make Riffets a stunning château experience.

Le Gaudin

Shooting through the centre of this 18th-century farmhouse is a chimney of 4,500 bricks. Clive knows: he built it! Every feature conveys space, age and the care and creativity of your British hosts. Exposed stone walls; an old manger, now a wine rack; Denise's upholstered coffee table; a dolls' house in the sunny breakfast room, and the long table at which guests gather for Clive's superb dinners. Sophisticated bedrooms, delighting in hand-sewn fabrics, are a fanfare of colours. Pilgrims to Mont St Michel once filled their bottles at the stream in the wooded grounds; many attractions are close. No wonder people return.

Price	€120-€170.
Rooms	4: 2 doubles, 2 suites.
Meals	Restaurant 1km.
Closed	Rarely.
Directions	From Caen N158 for Falaise; at La Jalousie, right D23; right D235 just before Bretteville; signed.

Price	€70-€90.
Rooms	4 doubles.
Meals	Dinner with wine, €30.
Closed	January-March.
Directions	Caen ring road exit 9 onto A84; exit 43 for Aunay sur Odon; through Aunay, D6 to Thury Harcourt. 4km on left.

	Anne-Marie & Alain Cantel
	Château des Riffets,
	14680 Bretteville sur Laize,
	Calvados
Tel	+33 (0)2 31 23 53 21
Mobile	+33 (0)6 14 09 74 93
Email	chateau.riffets@wanadoo.fr
Web	www.chateau-des-riffets.com

	Clive & Denise Canvin
	Le Gaudin, Route d'Aunay,
	14260 Campandré Valcongrain,
	Calvados
Tel	+33 (0)2 31 73 88 70
Email	legaudin14@yahoo.co.uk
Web	www.legaudin.co.uk

Entry 185   Map 4

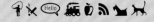

Entry 186   Map 4

Normandy

Le Clos St Bernard

The second farmhouse to be built in the village, it was named, 400 years later, in honour of the family dog. Madame loves her house, its history, her family and her guests, and delights in concocting Norman breakfasts of *tergoule*, crêpes, fresh juices, rice pudding. Bedrooms have tiled floors, pretty bedcovers, interesting antiques; showers have embroidered towels and the bedroom/salon under the eaves is worth the climb. There's a big guest dining salon (with kitchenette where the hens once lived) that opens to a garden terraced against salt breezes. Charming, great value. *Min. two nights. Sawday self-catering also.*

Ethical Collection: Environment.
See page 400 for details.

Price	€65.
Rooms	3: 2 doubles, 1 twin.
Meals	Guest kitchenette. Restaurant in village.
Closed	Mid-November to mid-March.
Directions	From Caen ring road N; exit 5 for Douvres Délivrande then Courseulles sur Mer (21km total); at r'bout left D35 to Reviers; over r'bout; 1st left Rue de l'Église; house at top of road.

Nicole Vandon
Le Clos St Bernard,
36 rue de l'Église,
14470 Reviers, Calvados

Tel	+33 (0)2 31 37 87 82
Email	leclosbernard@orange.fr
Web	www.leclosbernard.com

Normandy

La Malposte

It's just plain lovely, this little group of stone buildings with wooden footbridge over the rushing river, trees and flowers and hens. There's the age-old converted mill for the family and the hunting lodge for guests, where Madame's talented decoration marries nostalgic past (antiques, old prints, photographs) and designer-hued present. A spiral stair winds to a sitting/dining room with guest kitchen and homemade preserves (superb fig jam); sun pours into the room at the top. Woods for nut-gathering, beaches nearby, table tennis and that playful stream. Your hosts are sweet and love having families. *Unfenced water.*

Price	€78.
Rooms	3: 1 double; 1 double, 1 twin, sharing shower & wc.
Meals	Guest kitchen. Restaurants 2km.
Closed	Rarely.
Directions	From Ouistreham D35 through Douvres & Tailleville; over D404; right at r'bout entering Reviers; 2nd Chambres d'Hôtes on left.

Patricia & Jean-Michel Blanlot
La Malposte,
15 rue des Moulins,
14470 Reviers, Calvados

Tel	+33 (0)2 31 37 51 29
Email	jean-michel.blanlot@wanadoo.fr
Web	www.lamalposte.com

Normandy

Le Mas Normand

A fun place, warm and colourful. Mylène is a live wire, Christian quieter, both are sociable, informal and attentive. They've done a great job on their lovely 18th-century house: old stonework and beams, modern showers, a modern-rustic style, Provençal fabrics and soaps from Mylène's native Drôme. Bedrooms are sheer delight: the sunny double on the ground floor, the charming suites across the yard, one with an *armoire de mariage*, the new family room a big cosy comfy eco caravan. Christian is a trained chef: good food is guaranteed. Ducks, geese and hens roam, the beach is at the end of the lane. Special.

Price	€70. Suites €90-€140. Gypsy caravan €90-€140.
Rooms	4: 1 double, 2 suites for 2-4, gypsy caravan for 2-4.
Meals	Dinner with wine, €45-€50.
Closed	Rarely.
Directions	From Caen D7 for Douvres 8km; left D404 5km; D79 to Courseulles sur Mer; D514 to Ver sur Mer; at village entrance 1st left Ave. Provence; 1st right; 1st left, at end on right.

Christian Mériel & Mylène Gilles
Le Mas Normand,
8 impasse de la Rivière,
14114 Ver sur Mer, Calvados
Tel   +33 (0)2 31 21 97 75
Email   lemasnormand@wanadoo.fr
Web   www.lemasnormand.com

Entry 189   Map 4

Normandy

Le Manoir de Basly

In the comfortingly walled luxury of an old stone manor and well-kept antiques, this is a place of classic French refinement where you are received by gracious, friendly hosts who enjoy sharing their lifelong knowledge of their region. In the main house: two faultlessly elegant bedrooms – original stones and timbers, draped beds, delicate muslin, stitched cotton, rich brocade in soft colours – and the guests' living room. On the ground floor of the tiny cottage, the cherry on the cake: a sweet pale bedroom, more lovely furniture, a welcoming sitting area and… a wee terrace of its own. A naturally sophisticated welcome.

Price	€90-€130.
Rooms	2: 1 twin, 1 suite for 4.
Meals	Restaurants nearby.
Closed	Rarely.
Directions	Caen ring road exit 5, D7 for Douvres la Délivrande 10km; at r'bout left D404 to Courseulles sur Mer; 2nd left to Basly. In village opp. Canadian memorial; tall blue gates.

Monique Casset
Le Manoir de Basly,
2 route de Courseulles,
14610 Basly, Calvados
Tel   +33 (0)2 31 80 12 08
Mobile +33 (0)6 61 13 12 08
Email   lemanoirdebasly@wanadoo.fr
Web   lemanoirdebasly.ifrance.com

Entry 190   Map 4

Normandy

Manoir des Doyens

The lovely old house of golden stone is the warmly natural home of interesting people: an extrovert military historian who runs battlefield tours, and his gentle lady. Rosemary goes the extra mile for guests and serves her own jams for breakfast. Stone stairs lead to old-fashioned, comfortably casual guest rooms and good, clean bathrooms; the courtyard houses visiting grandchildren's swings, slide, rabbits and games room; the family sitting room is shared and there are always interesting people to chat to over breakfast or a calvados. A 15-minute walk from town but all you hear is the honk of the goose!

Price	€55.
Rooms	3 triples.
Meals	Restaurants 1km.
Closed	Rarely.
Directions	From N13 exit 37 for Bayeux & St Lô; for Bayeux; 2nd left; right at T-junc. Signed St Loup Hors & Chambres d'Hôtes.

Lt Col & Mrs Chilcott
Manoir des Doyens,
St Loup Hors,
14400 Bayeux, Calvados
Tel +33 (0)2 31 22 39 09
Email michaeljohn.chilcott@sfr.fr

Entry 191   Map 4

Normandy

Les Glycines

This lovely couple, she softly spoken and twinkling, he jovial, talkative and exceedingly French, have retired from farming and moved into the heart of Bayeux. You can glimpse the cathedral spires from their house; it was once part of the old bishop's palace. Beyond the gates and the wisteria, the door opens onto a lofty beamed living room rejoicing in good antiques and a monumental fireplace; through another is the kitchen. Up the ancient stone stair are pretty guest rooms – immaculate bedding, pastel-tiled showers – that look quietly over a pocket-handkerchief garden. Delicious breakfasts, history all around, and no need for a car!

Price	€65.
Rooms	3: 2 doubles, 1 family room.
Meals	Restaurant 50m.
Closed	Rarely.
Directions	From Caen N13 to Bayeux; head for Gare SNCF; right after traffic lights; over 1st x-roads & traffic lights, park on left; house 50m on right, signed.

Louis & Annick Fauvel
Les Glycines,
13 rue aux Coqs,
14400 Bayeux, Calvados
Tel +33 (0)2 31 22 52 32

Entry 192   Map 4

Normandy

Clos de Bellefontaine

Come to be pampered and effortlessly spoiled at this elegant townhouse, a ten-minute stroll from the famous Tapestry. Bedrooms are chic and gracious with choice antiques, colours are mocha and white, floors polished parquet or seagrass. Choose the top floor for snugness and charm, the first floor for grandeur and space. With a walled garden and two handsome ground-floor salons – antiques, family photographs, help-yourself refreshments – to lounge around in; you won't miss home. Carole's breakfasts, with homemade tarts, fruit compotes and cheeses, are the highlight of the stay.

Price	€95-€130.
Rooms	2: 1 double, 1 twin.
Meals	Restaurants nearby.
Closed	Rarely.
Directions	Caen ring road N13 for Cherbourg exit 36 to Bayeux. Left at 1st r'bout Bd Montgomery 200m; 1st right; house on left behind tall black iron gates. Don't confuse with Château de Bellefontaine.

Carole & Jérôme Mallet
Clos de Bellefontaine,
6 rue de Bellefontaine,
14400 Bayeux, Calvados
Mobile +33 (0)6 81 42 24 81
Email clos.bellefontaine@wanadoo.fr
Web clos.bellefontaine.monsite.wanadoo.fr

Entry 193   Map 4

Normandy

La Suhardière

Up the drive, across the spotless (non-working!) farmyard to be met by a charming, smiling hostess who delights in gardening and cooking – dinner is a wonderful affair. Beyond the dinky little hall, the salon, with its high-backed chairs, dark farmhouse beams and profusion of white lace, is a good little spot for a quiet read. The big sunny bedrooms are cosily frilly with their country furniture, framed Millet reproductions and more lace; gentle morning views over the garden drop down to the pond where you may fish: the setting is delightful. Walkers will be happy in this pretty rolling countryside. *Small dogs welcome.*

Price	€55.
Rooms	2: 1 double, 1 family room for 3.
Meals	Dinner with wine, €22.
Closed	Rarely.
Directions	From Caen A13 for Cherbourg, exit Carpiquet (airport) & Caumont l'Éventé D9; 500m before Caumont, house signed left.

Alain & Françoise Petiton
La Suhardière,
14240 Livry,
Calvados
Tel +33 (0)2 31 77 51 02
Email petiton.alain@wanadoo.fr

Entry 194   Map 3

Normandy

Le Château

The château dates proudly from 1580. In the yard, now restored to tremendous shape and character as a garden area for guests, an ancient arched barn houses three beamy bedrooms (admire astounding roof timbers through a trap window). Just beyond the flowering stone steps, the fourth room is in a tiny cottage. These country-elegant rooms are beautiful in Jouy and stripes, restful and private. Madame is a vibrantly warm, well-read, eco-friendly person, who speaks good English, loves having guests and can discourse at fascinating length about the Vikings, the Inuit, the Dukes of Normandy...

Price	€70–€85.
Rooms	4: 2 doubles, 1 twin, 1 suite for 5.
Meals	Dinner with wine or cider, €35. Child €20. Restaurants nearby.
Closed	December to mid-January.
Directions	From Cherbourg N13; D514; exit for Grandcamp Maisy; cont. D514 for Vierville sur Mer; right after water tower (signed tennis club). House at end of lane, 400m.

Dominique Bernières
Le Château,
Chemin du Château,
14450 Grandcamp Maisy, Calvados
Tel +33 (0)2 31 22 66 22
Email marionbandb@wanadoo.fr
Web perso.wanadoo.fr/alain.marion/gbindex.html

Entry 195   Map 3

Normandy

L'Hermerel

Some sort of perfection? A round pigeon tower, a private chapel and lovely hosts complete the picture of this charming, partly 15th-century, fortified working farm. The lofty beamed rooms and vast fireplaces have been carefully restored and it all feels unpretentiously stylish with a friendly, relaxed atmosphere. Up the old worn stone stair of the interconnecting wing to green velvet armchairs, taffeta drapes and vases of wild flowers: these bedrooms have been decorated quite beautifully. Breakfasts of compotes, farm milk, special jams and breads, a walled garden to share and the sea a short walk away.

Price	€70.
Rooms	3: 1 twin/double, 1 family room, 1 suite.
Meals	Restaurants in Grandcamp Maisy.
Closed	November–March.
Directions	From Bayeux N13 west 30km, exit D514 to Osmanville & cont. for Grandcamp 4km; left D199a for Géfosse Fontenay 400m; follow signs on right.

François & Agnès Lemarié
L'Hermerel,
14230 Géfosse Fontenay,
Calvados
Tel +33 (0)2 31 22 64 12
Mobile +33 (0)6 79 44 58 24
Email hermerel@orange.fr
Web www.manoir-hermerel.com

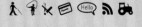

Entry 196   Map 3

Normandy

Ferme-Manoir de la Rivière

Breakfast by the massive fireplace may be oil lamp-lit on winter mornings in this 13th-century fortress of a dairy farm, with its ancient tithe barn and little watchtower. Isabelle is proud of her family home, its flagstones worn smooth with age, its high vaulted stone living-room ceiling, its second-floor rooms, one narrow with a shower in a tower, one with exposed beams and *ciel de lit* drapes. Her energy boundless, she is ever improving her rooms, gives you homemade brioche for breakfast and imaginative Norman cuisine – much supported by delightful Gérard. *Out-of-season cookery weekends. Sawday self-catering also.*

Ethical Collection: Environment & Food.
See page 410 for details.

Price	€60-€75.
Rooms	3: 1 double, 2 triples.
Meals	Dinner with cider or wine, €25.
Closed	Rarely.
Directions	From Bayeux N13 30km west; exit on D514 to Osmanville & on for Grandchamp, 5km; left for Géfosse Fontenay; house 800m on left before church.

Gérard & Isabelle Leharivel
Ferme-Manoir de la Rivière,
14230 Géfosse Fontenay,
Calvados

Tel   +33 (0)2 31 22 64 45
Mobile +33 (0)6 81 58 25 21
Email   leharivel@wanadoo.fr
Web   www.lemanoirdelariviere.net

Entry 197   Map 3

Normandy

La Fèvrerie

Your blithe, beautiful, energetic hostess is a delight. Her charming ex-farmer husband now breeds horses while she indulges her passion for interior decoration: her exquisite rooms are a festival of colours, textures, antiques and embroidered linen. It's a heart-warming experience to stay in this wonderful old Normandy farmhouse where the great granite hearth is always lit for breakfasts of superb local specialities served on elegant china; there is a richly-carved 'throne' at the head of the long table. A pretty garden behind, and a very special address, in sweet countryside a short drive from Barfleur.

Price	€72-€80.
Rooms	3 twins/doubles. Children's room available.
Meals	Restaurants 3km.
Closed	Rarely.
Directions	From Cherbourg D901; after Tocqueville right D10; 1st left.

Marie-France & Maurice Caillet
La Fèvrerie,
4 route d'Arville,
50760 Ste Geneviève, Manche

Tel   +33 (0)2 33 54 33 53
Mobile +33 (0)6 80 85 89 01
Email   lafevrerie@orange.fr
Web   www.lafevrerie.fr

Entry 198   Map 3

Normandy

Maison Duchevreuil

An urban treasure, an oasis on the built-up edge of bustling Cherbourg(nuns lived here until 1914). Plants and flowers tumble prettily over the edges of the narrow canal that feeds the pond with rainwater from 18th-century roofs. Wide stone steps lead to the delightful French-formal walled garden and a multitude of paths, trees, shrubs, and handsome furniture to relax into. Guest bedrooms in converted farm buildings are full of light and attractively dressed in striking colours and rug-strewn parquet: not fussy but classy. Like her house and garden, Madame is charming and elegant. *Minimum two nights in high season.*

Price	€100. Extra bed €20.
Rooms	2 suites for 2-4.
Meals	Restaurants 2km.
Closed	Rarely.
Directions	With Cherbourg railway station on right, head for Équeurdreville 2km; after tunnel left for Octeville 200m; at lights right to Val Abbé; 3rd right; archway end of road.

	Sophie Draber
	Maison Duchevreuil,
	36 avenue Duchevreuil,
	50120 Équeurdreville, Manche
Tel	+33 (0)2 33 01 33 10
Mobile	+33 (0)6 87 42 34 89
Email	contact@maisonduchevreuil.com
Web	www.maisonduchevreuil.com

Entry 199   Map 3

Normandy

Eudal de Bas

Old-fashioned hospitality in a modern house. You are just a mile from the oft glittering sea and Michel, who used to make submarines, has a passion for sailing. He and Éliane are hosts of the best sort; easy, friendly, helpful but not intrusive. His shipbuilding skill is evident: the attic space has been cleverly used to make two snug rooms with showers (one with a kitchenette); the landing is a pleasant sitting area. A brilliantly quiet position, simple décor, spotless rooms and Éliane will even rise early for dawn ferry-catchers. It's ideal for beach holidays and channel crossing alike.

Price	€52.
Rooms	2: 1 double; 1 triple & kitchenette.
Meals	Restaurants within 2km.
Closed	Rarely.
Directions	From Cherbourg D901 then D45 W 13km to Urville Nacqueville; 1st left by Hôtel Le Beau Rivage; up hill D22 for 2km; 2nd left; sign.

	Michel & Éliane Thomas
	Eudal de Bas,
	1 rue Escènes,
	50460 Urville Nacqueville, Manche
Tel	+33 (0)2 33 03 58 16
Email	thomas.eudal@wanadoo.fr
Web	pagesperso-orange.fr/gitethomas

Entry 200   Map 3

Normandy

Manoir St Jean

Standing near the Normandy coastal hiking path, the old stone manor looks proudly across the town and out to sea. Long retired from farming, the sociable Guérards welcome guests with courtesy. This is living in French genteel style, everything in its beautiful place, spotless and well-loved, and bedrooms and bathrooms simple. You are in quiet country, just 6km from the ferries; the very basic triple room with its outside entrance would be suitable for early ferry-catchers: Madame leaves a breakfast tray. Lovely gardens, great views, delicious breakfasts, genuine old-style French charm. *No arrivals before 6pm.*

Price	€60–€65.
Rooms	3: 1 double, 1 twin, 1 triple.
Meals	Restaurants 3km.
Closed	Rarely.
Directions	From Cherbourg D901 to Tourlaville & for St Pierre Église. Right at exit for Château Ravalet & St Jean; up hill to Centre Aéré, follow Chambres d'Hôtes signs.

	Mme Guérard
	Manoir St Jean,
	50110 Tourlaville,
	Manche
Tel	+33 (0)2 33 22 00 86

Entry 201   Map 3

Normandy

Bruce Castle

Live graciously – even if it's only for a stopover (Cherbourg is 15km away). The Fontanets are a charming and amusing couple and their 1914 neo-classical mansion is full of pretty antiques. From the restrained elegance of the hall a handsome white staircase sweeps up to big, serene bedrooms with garden and woodland views; oriental rugs and crystal chandeliers add another dash of luxury. Breakfast off white porcelain with antique silver cutlery in a charming dining room that doubles as a dayroom for guests. In the 20-acre grounds are the ruins of an 11th-century castle... to stay here is a huge treat.

Price	€100–€120.
Rooms	2 doubles.
Meals	Restaurant 8km.
Closed	Rarely.
Directions	From Cherbourg N13 for Valognes & Caen exit to D119, then D50 to Brix. Left just before church; entrance on left.

	Anne-Rose & Hugues Fontanet
	Bruce Castle,
	13 rue du Castel, 50700 Brix,
	Manche
Tel	+33 (0)2 33 41 99 62
Mobile	+33 (0)6 72 95 74 23
Email	bruce-castle@orange.fr
Web	www.bruce-castle.com

Entry 202   Map 3

Manoir de Bellauney

Even the smallest bathroom oozes atmosphere through its *œil de bœuf*. The youngest piece of this fascinating and venerably ancient house is over 400 years old; its predecessor stood on the site of a monastery, the fireplace in the lovely Medieval bedroom carries the coat of arms of the original owners. To furnish the rooms, your ex-farmer hosts hunted out carved *armoires de mariage*, lace canopies, footstools – and hung tapestry curtains at the windows. They share their energy enthusiastically between this wonderful house, its small dense garden, and their guests. Sheer comfort among warm old stones.

Brown Owl House

Philomena and Pierre – she Irish, he French – are generous, hospitable and fun and you pretty much get the run of their big, solid, 400-year-old farmhouse. The style is contemporary-formal and the atmosphere chatty, laid back and child-friendly. Philomena is a professionally trained cook: book 24 hours ahead and you will be treated to a delectable Anglo-French dinner. The living room, vast and open-plan, is part clear up to the rafters, part overlooked by an attractive mezzanine. The peaceful and immaculate bedrooms have honey-coloured floorboards and views over the immense garden and tree-lined fields. *Golf 20km.*

Price	€70-€100. €120 for 3.
Rooms	3: 1 double, 1 suite for 2, 1 suite for 2-3.
Meals	Restaurants 4km.
Closed	November-March.
Directions	On RN13 exit at Valognes; follow Route de Quettehou D902; house 3km after Valognes, No. 11.

Price	€70-€90.
Rooms	5: 1 family room; 3 doubles, 1 twin, sharing 2 baths.
Meals	Dinner with wine, €29.
Closed	Rarely.
Directions	N13 Cherbourg to Valognes then D2 for 8.5km; right D126 to Golleville. In village centre, right to Route du Château, entrance to No. 7 on left.

	Christiane & Jacques Allix-Desfauteaux Manoir de Bellauney, 50700 Tamerville, Manche
Tel	+33 (0)2 33 40 10 62
Email	bellauney@wanadoo.fr
Web	www.bellauney.com

	Philomena & Pierre Van der Linden Brown Owl House, 7 route du Château, Ferme de la Poissonnerie, 50390 Golleville, Manche
Tel	+33 (0)2 33 01 20 45
Email	contact@brown-owl-house.com
Web	www.brown-owl-house.com

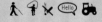

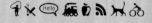

Normandy

Le Château

Gravel crunches as you sweep up to the imposing granite château on the Cherbourg peninsula. The beguiling fairytale turrets, Françoise's welcome and Bernard's collection of vintage horse-driven carriages (the whole family love horses) soon work their magic. External stone stairs lead to the red-velvet charm of the 'Chambre Château'; ancient chestnut stairs in the converted outbuilding lead to simple family rooms. In the morning, as you breakfast generously in a light-flooded, pink-panelled family dining room and sip your café au lait, you might like to nod a grateful 'merci' to Bernard's obliging Normandy cows.

Price	€80–€110.
Rooms	3: 1 double. Outbuilding: 1 double, 1 family suite for 4.
Meals	Restaurant 500m.
Closed	Rarely.
Directions	From Valognes D2 for St Sauveur le Vicomte; left onto D24, 3km; auberge Pont Cochon left before bridge. Driveway on left opp. church.

Françoise Lucas de Vallavieille
Le Château,
50700 Flottemanville Bocage,
Manche
Tel   +33 (0)2 33 40 29 02
Email   contact@chateau-flottemanville.com
Web   www.chateau-flottemanville.com

Entry 205   Map 3

Normandy

La Roque de Gouey

A fishing and sailing port and a bridge with 13 arches: a pretty place to stay. The enchanting *longère* is the home of two of our favourite owners: Madame, the same honest open character as ever and Monsieur, retired, who has time to spread his modest farmer's joviality. Your side of the house has its own entrance, dayroom and vast old fireplace where old beams and *tomettes* flourish. The bedrooms up the steepish outside stairs are small, with pretty bedcovers and antiques that are cherished, the ground-floor room is larger, and the breakfast tables sport flowery cloths. Brilliant value.

Price	€55. €70 for 3.
Rooms	4: 1 double, 1 twin, 1 family room for 3, 1 family suite for 5.
Meals	Guest kitchen. Restaurants 500m.
Closed	Rarely.
Directions	From St Sauveur le Vicomte D15 to Portbail; right just before church Rue R. Asselin; over old railway; house 250m on right.

Bernadette Vasselin
La Roque de Gouey,
Rue Gilles Poërier,
50580 Portbail, Manche
Tel   +33 (0)2 33 04 80 27
Email   vasselin.portbail@orange.fr

Entry 206   Map 3

Normandy

La Vimonderie

Sigrid's big country kitchen and crackling fire are the heart of this fine 18th-century granite house and you know instantly you are sharing her home: the built-in dresser carries pretty china, her pictures and ornaments bring interest to the salon and its Normandy fireplace, and she proudly tells how she rescued the superb elm staircase. A fascinating person, for years a potter in England, she has retired to France and vegetarian happiness. Bedrooms have colour and lace, unusual antiques and original beams. Five acres of garden mean plenty of space for children and grown-ups alike. Great value. *Minimum two nights.*

Price	€50.
Rooms	2 doubles.
Meals	Dinner with wine, from €18. Light supper from €10. Picnics from €5. Guest kitchen.
Closed	January/February.
Directions	From Carentan N174 to St Lô 13km; r'bout 1km before Cavigny, 3rd exit for Pont Hébert; over m'way; 2nd r'bout 2nd exit D377 for Cavigny; 3rd house on right.

	Sigrid Hamilton La Vimonderie, 50620 Cavigny, Manche
Tel	+33 (0)2 33 56 01 13
Mobile	+33 (0)6 59 21 48 07
Email	sigrid.hamilton@googlemail.com
Web	www.lavimonderie.com

Entry 207   Map 3

Normandy

1 St Léger

The totally French farmhouse, 19th-century without, rustic trad within, is colourful, neat, immaculate. One room is pink-flavoured, the other blue, each with bits of crochet, a carved armoire (one *cherbourgeoise*, the other from St Lô) and a clean, compact shower room; the gloriously ostentatious blue bathroom is also yours for the asking – giant tub and plants rampaging. But most special of all is the charming, elegant Madame Lepoittevin, full of smiles and laughter, actively involved in a walking group in summer – why not join in? You can picnic in the pretty garden or cook your own on the barbecue.

Price	€42.
Rooms	2: 1 double; 1 double with separate wc.
Meals	Barbecue available. Restaurant 2km.
Closed	1st two weeks in March.
Directions	From St Lô D972 for Coutances, through St Gilles; house sign on left, 4km after St Gilles, on D972.

	Micheline Lepoittevin 1 St Léger, 50570 Quibou, Manche
Tel	+33 (0)2 33 57 18 41
Mobile	+33 (0)6 18 93 47 95
Email	rico123@hotmail.com

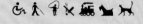

Entry 208   Map 3

Normandy

La Haute Gilberdière

Generous, artistic and young in spirit, the Champagnacs are a privilege to meet. Their 18th-century *longère* bathes in a floral wonderland: roses climb and tumble, narrow paths meander and a kitchen garden grows your breakfast – wander and revel or settle down in a shady spot. Inside, bedrooms are perfect with handsome antiques, pretty bed linen and polished floors, or modern with pale wood and bucolic views. The honey-coloured breakfast room is warmly contemporary in timber and exposed stone; Monsieur's bread comes warm from the oven served with homemade jams. Wonderful. *Minimum two nights.*

Price	€60-€120.
Rooms	2: 1 double. Barn: 1 family suite for 2-4.
Meals	Restaurants 5km.
Closed	November-March.
Directions	From Avranches D973 for Granville & Sartilly; left at end of village D61 for Carolles; 800m house on left.

Édith & Pierre Champagnac
La Haute Gilberdière,
50530 Sartilly,
Manche

Mobile	+33 (0)6 80 87 17 62
Email	champagnac@libertysurf.fr
Web	www.champagnac-farmhouse.com

Entry 209   Map 3

Normandy

6 rue du Château d'Eau

A lovely welcome awaits from hosts Maurice and Jeanne, for whom running B&B has been a long-held dream and entertaining guests is second nature. Maurice will take you on an oyster tour – Blainville calls itself oyster capital of France – and fill you in on local history and places of interest. Spoiling breakfasts overlooking the garden with jams and homemade brioche (Maurice used to be a baker) match spoiling comfort; iron-framed beds, lots to read, considered use of space and busy, pretty, classically French décor; a hand-painted jar here, a floral collage there. And a postcard-perfect coast a short walk away.

Price	€45.
Rooms	2: 1 double, 1 twin.
Meals	Restaurant 200m.
Closed	Rarely.
Directions	From Coutances D44 for Agon Coutainville; D244 to Blainville; follow road down hill, right before Tourist Office.

Jeanne & Maurice Posloux
6 rue du Château d'Eau,
50560 Blainville sur Mer,
Manche

Tel	+33 (0)2 33 45 34 13
Mobile	+33 (0)6 67 62 12 46

Entry 210   Map 3

Manoir de la Porte

A pepperpot turret to give a medieval flourish to the sturdy, creeper-dressed 16th-century manoir. There's a Japanese bridge to take you to the jungly island, a large and luscious garden, two bright, romantic top-floor bedrooms with old-fashioned bathrooms and a tempting sitting area; a fabulously ancient, tiled dining room with huge fireplace, a trio of tables and solid granite walls… the ingredients of rustic character are here. Add ethnic rugs dotted about, a pair of curly-toed Rajasthani slippers on the venerable stone stairs – and know that your friendly, chatty, ex-army hosts are great travellers.

Le Petit Manoir

You can walk to Mont St Michel in two hours – and glimpse it from the top of the stairs. The quietly courteous Gédouins keep cows and pigs; Jean is mayor; Annick, once a teacher, makes jams, crêpes and beautiful Breton breakfasts. The small rooms are in spotless French country style: no frills or soft touches, just a few little pictures on lightly patterned walls. In the courtyard are passionfruit and figs; two large cider presses brim with geraniums and the old stone bakery will charm you. All is rural peace in this tiny village by the marshes. *Minimum two nights.*

Price	€70-€85.
Rooms	2 family rooms for 3.
Meals	Dinner with wine, €21. Kitchen available.
Closed	Rarely.
Directions	Caen A84 for Rennes exit 36 to Villedieu les P.; thro' town; D975 for Avranches to Le Parc. Right at lights D39 to Ste Pience & D476 for Noirpalu 1.5km; at junc. D175 for Bourguenolles; house 400m on left.

Price	€40.
Rooms	2: 1 double, 1 twin.
Meals	Restaurants 500m.
Closed	Rarely.
Directions	From A84 exit 34 for Pontorson; after Précey right to Servon; right at church 500m; farm on left.

	Annick & Hervé Lagadec
	Manoir de la Porte,
	50870 Ste Pience,
	Manche
Tel	+33 (0)2 33 68 13 61
Email	manoir.de.la.porte@wanadoo.fr
Web	www.manoir-de-la-porte.com

	Annick, Jean & Valérie Gédouin
	Le Petit Manoir,
	21 rue de la Pierre du Tertre,
	50170 Servon, Manche
Tel	+33 (0)2 33 60 03 44
Email	agedouinmanoir@laposte.net
Web	chambresgedouin.com

Normandy

La Gautrais

Come for a slice of French farmhouse life. Catherine is quietly friendly, "makes a superb soufflé" and mouthwatering Norman cuisine – she loves it. Naturally hospitable, she and François cook, serve, clear, and always find time for a glass of calvados with their guests. The old granite stable block, built in 1622, was last modernised in the 1970s. Polished floors, spare furnishings, cots in the attic rooms, a couple of kitchenettes and a dining room with a big table make this suitable for families on a budget. The poetically named but perfectly ordinary Two Estuaries motorway provides quick access one kilometre away.

Price	€55. Family room €70 for 3, €80 for 4.
Rooms	4: 2 doubles, 2 family rooms for 3–4.
Meals	Dinner with wine, €20.
Closed	Christmas.
Directions	From A84 exit 32 at St James then D12, following signs for Super U store for Antrain, 1km. On right.

François & Catherine Tiffaine
La Gautrais,
50240 St James,
Manche
Tel   +33 (0)2 33 48 31 86
Email   ctiffaine@hotmail.fr
Web   www.tiffaine.com

Entry 213   Map 3

Normandy

Les Blotteries

Monsieur, formerly a fire officer, is proud of his restoration of the old farm (the B&B is his project; Madame works in town). He is an attentive, positive host, full of smiles and jokes, and has done a good job. Old granite glints as you pass into the softly-curtained entrance; an original hay rack hangs above. One bedroom is on the first floor, another is in the former stable, a third in the old bakery: a ground-floor family room whose large windows overlook the courtyard. The cream breakfast room is simple and elegant and the fields around are open to all so no need to worry about the road at the front.

Price	€70–€75.
Rooms	3: 1 double, 2 family rooms.
Meals	Restaurants 1km.
Closed	Rarely.
Directions	From A84 exit 33; right at r'bout & up hill for approx. 300m to next r'bout; left then left again, D998 for St James; house on right after 5km.

Laurence & Jean-Malo Tizon
Les Blotteries,
50220 Juilley, Manche
Tel   +33 (0)2 33 60 84 95
Email   bb@les-blotteries.com
Web   www.les-blotteries.com

Entry 214   Map 3

Normandy

Belle Vallée

Built in 1800, the tall house stands in acres of woods, pastures and landscaped gardens, with outbuildings (the owners' quarters) and cottage. Footpaths meander to a lovely walled orchard, the kitchen garden provides for table d'hôtes, the hens donate the eggs. Inside are corridors alive with books, five delightful bedrooms – vintage beds, polished floors, boudoir chairs, delicious duvets – and an inviting sitting room with a log fire. In the panelled dining room, hospitable Richard and Victoria, both from the catering industry, serve French breakfasts at crisp tables. Domfront on its hill is wonderfully close.

Price	€60–€90.
Rooms	5: 3 doubles, 2 suites.
Meals	Dinner, 4 courses with wine, €20. Restaurants 5-minute drive.
Closed	Rarely.
Directions	Caen ring road exit 11; D562 thro' Thury Harcourt to Condé s/Noireau; D962 to Domfront; D908 for Bagnoles de l'Orne 2km; left D21 for Dompierre. 500m on left.

	Victoria & Richard Hobson-Cossey Belle Vallée, 61700 Domfront, Orne
Tel	+33 (0)2 33 37 05 71
Email	info@belle-vallee.net
Web	www.belle-vallee.net

Entry 215   Map 4

Normandy

Le Mesnil

There are fresh flowers everywhere and your hosts, retired farmers, offer true country hospitality. Peace is the norm, not the exception, in this deeply rural spot, racehorses graze in the pasture and you are unhesitatingly received into a warm and lively extended family. The rooms, in a converted outbuilding, have an appropriately rustic air with beams, old wardrobes and kitchenettes. The ground-floor room has a little private garden; up steepish stairs the bedroom is bigger. Breakfast is in the family dining room, with tiled floors and a large fireplace. Children are welcome to visit the family farm next door.

Price	€46.
Rooms	2 doubles & kitchenettes.
Meals	Restaurant 5km.
Closed	Rarely.
Directions	From Argentan N158 for Caen; after Moulin sur Orne sign, left; house 800m on left; signed (3.5km from Argentan).

	Janine & Rémy Laignel Le Mesnil, 61200 Occagnes, Orne
Tel	+33 (0)2 33 67 11 12

Entry 216   Map 4

Normandy

Le Prieuré St Michel

An atmospheric time warp for the night on the St Michel pilgrim route: traditional décor in the timbered 14th-century monks' storeroom with tapestry wall covering and antiques, or the old dairy, or a converted stable; a huge 15th-century cider press for breakfast in the company of the Ulrichs' interesting choice of art; a chapel for yet more art, a tithe barn in magnificent condition for fabulous receptions, perfectly stupendous gardens, a sort of medieval revival. Your hosts are totally devoted to their fabulous domain and its listed buildings and happy to share it with guests who appreciate its historical value.

Price	€105-€135.
Rooms	4: 2 doubles, 2 suites for 3.
Meals	Restaurant 4km.
Closed	Rarely.
Directions	From Lisieux D579 for Livarot & Vimoutiers; D916 for Argentan; right 3km after Vimoutiers D703 for Crouttes. Le Prieuré 500m after village.

Jean-Pierre & Viviane Ulrich
Le Prieuré St Michel,
61120 Crouttes,
Orne

Tel	+33 (0)2 33 39 15 15
Email	leprieuresaintmichel@wanadoo.fr
Web	www.prieure-saint-michel.com

Entry 217 Map 4

Normandy

L'Orangerie

The driveway bordered by amusing topiaries leads to a charming hamlet (church, presbytery, mairie, house) where this former orangery is the only trace of the old estate. Very delightful Madame Gran, an American citizen from Geneva, has a talent for enjoying things: painting, bridge, languages, music, people. Breakfast in the large, sunny, familial kitchen, relax on the terrace, make yourself at home. Cosy cottagey bedrooms have small mansard windows, rugs on parquet floors, gracious beds. The wonderful grounds summon you out to Norman woods, walks, horses (yours too, if you wish) – and peace. *Children six and over welcome.*

Price	€60-€80.
Rooms	4: 2 doubles; 1 double, 1 triple, sharing bath.
Meals	Restaurants 12km.
Closed	Christmas & New Year.
Directions	From Vimoutiers for Orbec; D248 for Pontchardon; follow signs for Avernes. House immed. on left after church.

STOP PRESS
No longer doing B&B

Entry 218 Map 4

Normandy

Le Marnis

Barbara's delight in her "corner of paradise" is contagious. In utter peace among the cattle-dotted Norman pastures, here is one brave, outspoken woman, her horse, cats and big waggy Alsatian in a low-lying farmhouse, beautifully rebuilt "from a pile of stones", where old and new mix easily and flowers rampage. The lovely sloping garden is all her own work too – she's getting on but has apparently endless energy. The pastel guest rooms, one upstairs with orchard views, the other down with doors to the garden, are pleasantly floral. The village provides everything, and Sées is nearby. *Babies & children over ten welcome.*

Normandy

Château de la Grande Noë

Much to love here: trompe-l'œil marble and Wedgwood mouldings inherited from an Adam-inspired ancestor who escaped the French Revolution; chamber music in the log-fired drawing room; breakfast in a room wrapped in oak panelling inlaid with precious woods; elegant, alcoved bedrooms full of antiques, books, ancestral portraits, soft comforts; a bathroom through a secret door, a loo in a tower. And the delightful Longcamps are a wonderful couple, she vivaciously cultured and musical, he a retired camembert-maker who enjoys his estate. The French-formal garden overlooks paddocks and agricultural plains; walks start a mile away.

Price	€65-€70.
Rooms	2: 1 double, 1 twin.
Meals	Restaurants in Sées, 15km.
Closed	Rarely.
Directions	From Courtomer, past Mairie, right after last building for Tellières. Left at wayside cross for Le Marnis. 2nd lane on right.

Price	€100-€130.
Rooms	3: 2 doubles, 1 twin.
Meals	Restaurants 5km.
Closed	December-March, except by arrangement.
Directions	From Verneuil sur Avre, N12 SW 24km to Carrefour Ste Anne. Left D918 for Longny au Perche for 4.5km; left D289 for Moulicent. House 800m on right.

	Barbara Goff
	Le Marnis,
	Tellières le Plessis,
	61390 Courtomer, Orne
Tel	+33 (0)2 33 27 47 55
Email	barbara.goff@wanadoo.fr

	Jacques & Pascale de Longcamp
	Château de la Grande Noë,
	61290 Moulicent,
	Orne
Tel	+33 (0)2 33 73 63 30
Mobile	+33 (0)6 87 65 88 47
Email	contact@chateaudelagrandenoe.com
Web	www.chateaudelagrandenoe.com

Normandy

Le Tertre

Pilgrims have trudged by towards Mont St Michel since the 1500s and the search for inner peace continues: yoga and meditation groups come but never overlap with B&B. Anne talks brilliantly about her exotic travels, is active in the village and pours her creative energy into her house, with the help of an excellent restorer. Each elegantly simple room has a clear personality, good beds and sitting space, antiques, soft colours and privacy. One has a six-seater jacuzzi, another a fine set of ivory-backed brushes, the third an impressive bureau. Stunning views, super breakfast in the big kitchen, served with love.

Price	€98-€145.
Rooms	2: 1 double, 1 twin.
Meals	Restaurants 6km.
Closed	January.
Directions	From Alençon D311 to Mamers; on ring-road left D113 for Contilly & Montgaudry 5km. Follow signs.

Anne Morgan
Le Tertre,
61360 Montgaudry,
Orne
Tel   +33 (0)2 33 25 59 98
Email   annemorgan@nordnet.fr
Web   www.french-country-retreat.com

Entry 221   Map 4

Normandy

La Simondrière - La Corbinière

Your English hosts take great care of you in the Percheron farmhouse they have rescued and restored – and enjoy sharing their enthusiasm for this beautiful, unsung, horse-breeding region. Feel free to potter on their land or to venture further afield, then come back to a friendly cup of tea and a truly delicious supper in the dining room. Bedrooms are beamy, cosy and uncomplicated, with good mattresses and warm duvets; in the big square sitting room are books, maps and voluminous easy chairs. A super country place in a forested region, and Rex and Helen are wonderful company. Readers are full of praise.

Price	€70. €85 for 3.
Rooms	2 : 1 triple, 1 family room for 2-4.
Meals	Dinner with wine, €25.
Closed	December.
Directions	From Mortagne au Perche D931 for Mamers for 8km; right on D650 for Coulimer at small x-roads. House 800m on left, last of small hamlet of houses.

Helen Barr
La Simondrière - La Corbinière,
61360 Coulimer,
Orne
Tel   +33 (0)2 33 25 55 08
Email   helenbarr@wanadoo.fr

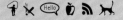

Entry 222   Map 4

Brittany

Photo: www.istockphoto.com

Brittany

Épineu

Fear not, the farm mess is forgotten once you reach the cottage and the long rural views beyond. Yvette, generous, sociable, sprightly and very charming, will lead you into her big, wood-floored and -ceilinged country dining room – warmed in winter by the old stone fireplace. It is uncluttered and soberly French. Bedrooms are a good size, the most characterful one in the main house. The country garden is tended with love and pride and produces vegetables for dinner. Breakfasts are legendary and you will be spoiled outrageously; Madame may join you if you are just two. Deep in the countryside – a joy.

Price	€55. €75 for 3. Extra bed €20.
Rooms	3: 1 triple. Annexe: 1 double, 1 twin sharing bath.
Meals	Dinner €22. Restaurant 3km.
Closed	Rarely.
Directions	From Rennes N137 S exit Poligné D47 for Bourg des Comptes 4km; left & thro' L'Aubriais to next hamlet, Épineu; right into & across farmyard, down lane 20m, cottage on right.

Yvette Guillopé
Épineu,
35890 Bourg des Comptes,
Ille-et-Vilaine
Tel   +33 (0)2 99 52 16 84
Mobile +33 (0)6 25 60 23 22

Brittany

Château du Quengo

Two fascinating generations of an ancient Breton family welcome you open-armed to their inimitable house where history, atmosphere and silence rule: private chapel, bio-garden and rare trees outside, carved chestnut staircase, Italian mosaic floor, 1800s wallpaper, about 30 rooms inside. Anne runs willow classes and plies you with homemade delights; Alfred builds organs and loves animals, gardens, music: the slow life. The bedrooms have antique radiators and are properly old-fashioned, our favourite the family room. No plastic anything, few mod cons – just humorous hosts and a beautiful place. *Sawday self-catering also.*

Ethical Collection: Environment & Food.
See page 410 for details.

Price	€50–€75.
Rooms	5: 1 family room for 3; 2 doubles, 2 twins, sharing 2 baths.
Meals	Guest kitchen. Restaurants 1.5km.
Closed	Rarely.
Directions	From N12 for St Brieuc exit at Bédée D72 to Irodouër; 1st right before church to Romillé; château entrance 600m on left, signed.

Anne & Alfred du Crest de Lorgerie
Château du Quengo,
35850 Irodouër,
Ille-et-Vilaine
Tel   +33 (0)2 99 39 81 47
Email lequengo@hotmail.com
Web   www.chateauduquengo.com

Brittany

Le Mesnil des Bois

Lapped by lawn in a deep-forest clearing is a circle of buildings, a 16th-century estate. The charming, amusing Villettes live in the atmospheric manoir, the guests are in the stable block and the renovation is superb. Beautiful bedrooms have lime plaster walls, sleek wooden floors, brocante chandeliers, paintings and vintage bed linen. In the salon, hip sofas wear bright colours and light floods in through high arched windows. Find a spot in the 'village green' courtyard where peonies, perennials and climbing roses grow, and wild deer wander onto the lawn. A little slice of heaven. *Min. two nights July/August & holiday weekends.*

Price	€95-€150.
Rooms	5: 1 double, 1 twin, 3 family rooms for 2-3.
Meals	Restaurant 1km.
Closed	Mid-November to February.
Directions	From Rennes N137 N exit Miniac Morvan; right to Tressé for Le Tronchet; at x-roads, right D73 for Lanhélin; forest on right, take forest road. Signed.

Martine Villette
Le Mesnil des Bois,
35540 Le Tronchet,
Ille-et-Vilaine

Tel	+33 (0)2 99 58 97 12
Email	villette@le-mesnil-des-bois.com
Web	www.le-mesnil-des-bois.com

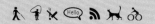

Entry 225   Map 3

Brittany

Le Presbytère

Solid granite, earth energy: inside its walled garden, the vast old priest's house is warm, reassuring and superbly restored: fine old timbers, antiques, panelling, hangings. Some bathrooms are old-fashioned but each bedroom has character... a Breton bed or a canopy, a staircase straight or spiral, antique fabrics, white bedcovers, a garden view; our favourites are those with private entrances. There's a sense of its never ending, there's even a classy mobile home. Madame, a lovely energetic and warmly attentive person, loves cooking. You will leave with new friends in your address book.

Price	€60. €78 for 3.
Rooms	5: 1 double, 2 triples, 1 suite for 3; 1 twin sharing bath.
Meals	Dinner €20. Wine list €8.50-€20.
Closed	Last two weeks in January.
Directions	From Pontorson D219 to Vieux Viel; follow signs for 'Chambres d'Hôtes Vieux Viel'; next to church.

Madeleine Stracquadanio
Le Presbytère,
35610 Vieux-Viel,
Ille-et-Vilaine

Tel	+33 (0)2 99 48 65 29
Email	madeleine.stracquadanio@voila.fr
Web	www.vieux-viel.com

Entry 226   Map 3

Brittany

4 La Hamelinais

The lovely farmhouse goes back to 1718 – Madame has lived here since a child. Expect old beams and exposed stones; few mod cons but bags of charm. Marie-Madeleine makes this place special: up before breakfast to prepare a fire in the huge hearth, making her own breads, cakes and jams, giving her all to garden and orchard. Gentle Jean, retired from the farm, says he "travels through his guests". Rooms are old-fashioned and homely (white bedspreads on comfy beds), your hosts know and love their region intimately and the sea is close. Great value... the best of 'la vieille France'.

Price	€50-€55.
Rooms	2: 1 double, 1 triple.
Meals	Restaurants 4km.
Closed	Rarely.
Directions	From St Malo N137 for Rennes 15km; exit N176 for Mt St Michel 12km. At Dol de Bretagne D80 for St Brolâdre 3km; left D85 for Cherrueix; house sign on right before 3rd bridge.

Jean & Marie-Madeleine Glémot
4 La Hamelinais,
35120 Cherrueix,
Ille-et-Vilaine

| Tel | +33 (0)2 99 48 95 26 |
| Email | lahamelinais@orange.fr |

Entry 227　Map 3

Brittany

Les Mouettes

House and owner are imbued with the calm of a balmy summer's morning, whatever the weather. Isabelle's talent seems to touch the very air that fills her old family house (and smokers are not spurned!). Timeless simplicity reigns; there is nothing superfluous: simple carved pine furniture, an antique wrought-iron cot, dhurries on scrubbed plank floors, palest grey walls to reflect the ocean-borne light, harmonious gingham curtains. Starfish and pebbles keep house and little garden sea-connected, whimsical mobiles add a creative touch. The unspoilt seaside village, popular in season, is worth the trip alone.

Price	€55.
Rooms	5: 4 doubles, 1 twin.
Meals	Restaurants in village.
Closed	Rarely.
Directions	From St Malo N137 for Rennes. 6km after St Malo, right D117 to St Suliac (3km from N137 to village). Road leads to Grande Rue down to port; house at top on right.

Isabelle Rouvrais
Les Mouettes,
17 Grande Rue, 35430 St Suliac,
Ille-et-Vilaine

Tel	+33 (0)2 99 58 30 41
Email	contact@les-mouettes-saint-suliac.com
Web	www.les-mouettes-saint-suliac.com

Entry 228　Map 3

Brittany

Le Clos St Cadreuc

Find peace in this hamlet a pebble's throw from the coast – and driving distance from ten golf courses! There's a welcoming atmosphere in this stone farmhouse, and colour and space in the open-plan dining/sitting room: a friendly place to spend time in. The guest quarters are in the converted stables, very French, very comfortable, with great walk-in showers and hotelly extras; the bright airy mezzanine'd suite 'Viviane' is a triumph. Your warm hosts put Breton dishes on your plate and pour organic wines; between house and stables is a pretty sheltered garden for picnics, potager and DIY barbecues.

Price	€72. Family suites €78.
Rooms	5: 2 doubles, 2 family suites for 4, 1 suite.
Meals	Dinner with wine, €26.
Closed	Rarely.
Directions	From St Malo D168 for St Brieuc. At 1st r'bout after Ploubalay D26 for Plessix Balisson 4km to hamlet; house on right, signed.

Brigitte & Patrick Noël
Le Clos St Cadreuc,
22650 Ploubalay,
Côtes-d'Armor
Tel +33 (0)2 96 27 32 43
Mobile +33 (0)6 82 14 94 66
Email clos-saint-cadreuc@wanadoo.fr
Web www.clos-saint-cadreuc.com

Entry 229   Map 3

Brittany

Malik

The everyday becomes remarkable in these people's hands: we seldom consider modern houses but sensitively designed Malik sailed in. Clad in red cedar, and open-plan, its wood, metal and sliding glass doors are in harmony with the dense trees, and every detail is taken care of. Harmonious covers on good beds, oriental wall hangings on plain walls, private verandas, monogrammed towels and lovely soaps. Breakfast, *un peu brunch*, is carefully attended to, and breads and jams homemade. Lovely people and an exquisitely serene house that seems to hug its garden to its heart. A haven on the edge of a small town.

Price	€79. €122 for 4.
Rooms	2: 1 suite for 2, 1 suite for 2-4.
Meals	Restaurants within walking distance.
Closed	January.
Directions	From Dinan N176 W for St Brieuc approx. 12km; right to Plélan le Petit. Follow signs to Centre & Mairie; at Mairie right for St Maudez, 3rd right, 1st right.

Martine & Hubert Viannay
Malik,
Chemin de l'Étoupe,
22980 Plélan le Petit, Côtes-d'Armor
Tel +33 (0)2 96 27 62 71
Email malikbretagne@free.fr
Web www.malik-bretagne.com

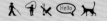

Entry 230   Map 3

Brittany

Le Manoir de la Villeneuve

Wrapped in rolling lawns, wooded parkland and sweeping drive, this manor house seems untouched by the 21st century. Light, airy pools of calm – high ceilings, tall windows, polished floorboards – are furnished with a contemporary elegance while plain walls, beams and tomette floors have been allowed to glow. Bedrooms are comfortable spaces of gentle colours and well-chosen antiques, some with beams and sloping ceilings; the stunning suite with its own salon has a vast bathroom. Breakfast handsomely, then explore Dinan, St Brieuc, the coast... or relax in the garden. A gracious home run by well-organised hosts.

Price	€70–€140.
Rooms	5: 3 doubles, 1 twin/double, 1 suite for 3.
Meals	Restaurant 2km.
Closed	Rarely.
Directions	RN12 Rennes-St Brieuc; exit D768 for Plancoët & Dinard to Lamballe; 1st r'bout to Pleneuf Val Andre; 2nd r'bout to St Aaron; 300m left, follow signs.

Nathalie Peres
Le Manoir de la Villeneuve,
22400 Lamballe,
Côtes-d'Armor
Tel +33 (0)2 96 50 86 32
Email manoirdelavilleneuve@wanadoo.fr
Web www.chambresaumanoir.com

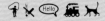

Entry 231   Map 3

Brittany

Château de Bonabry

An extraordinary old château, built in 1373 by the Viscount's ancestor, with vastly wonderful bedrooms, a lively, loveable couple of aristocratic hosts bent on riding, hunting and entertaining you, fields all around and the sea at the end of the drive. Breakfast till ten on crêpes, croissants and quince jam. Madame is using her energy and taste in renovating some of the rooms; in the suite, original painted panelling, silk curtains and a stag's head on a lustrous wall. Windows tall, portraits ancestral, chapel 18th century, roses glorious – and bathrooms with hand-embroidered towels. Incomparable. *Sawday self-catering also.*

Price	€80–€140.
Rooms	2: 1 suite; 1 double with separate bath.
Meals	Bistro in Hillion.
Closed	November-Easter.
Directions	From St Brieuc N12 for Lamballe exit Yffigniac Hillion; left D80 to Hillion; D34 for Morieux, 200m to roadside cross on left by château gates.

Vicomtesse du Fou de Kerdaniel
Château de Bonabry,
22120 Hillion,
Côtes-d'Armor
Tel +33 (0)2 96 32 21 06
Email bonabry@wanadoo.fr
Web www.bonabry.fr

Entry 232   Map 3

Brittany

14 rue des Capucins

Big, solid and well-loved, this place wraps you in comfortable, old-world charm. The Pontbriands and their friendly dog are on hand to suggest restaurants, ferry you to the station…, yet leave you free to enjoy their home. Downstairs is warm with oak doors and panelling, family antiques, oriental rugs, deep sofas and old leather chairs. The two bedrooms and one bathroom are light and prettily old-fashioned with floral wallpapers and a mêlée of furnishings. St Brieuc is on the doorstep, beaches are 15 minutes away, St Malo and Dinan an hour. And there's a lovely walled garden for lazy breakfasts. La vraie France.

Price	€65-€80.
Rooms	2: 1 twin/double, 1 suite for 2-5, sharing bath.
Meals	Guest kitchenette. Restaurant 5-minute walk.
Closed	November-February.
Directions	N12 Rennes-Brest to St Brieuc. House in centre of town; check directions before you go.

Serge & Bénédicte de Pontbriand
14 rue des Capucins,
22000 St Brieuc,
Côtes-d'Armor
Tel   +33 (0)2 96 62 08 21
Email   benedictedepontbriand@hotmail.fr

Brittany

Toul Bleïz

There may be standing stones, badgers and wild boar on the moors but civilisation is a five-minute drive – and you breakfast in a courtyard serenaded by birds. An art teacher in her other life, Julie takes people out painting while Jez concocts delicious vegetarian dishes for your supper. Inside this simple Breton cottage are exposed stone walls, renovated wood, comfy white sofas, a quiet good taste. Light floods in through French windows to your charming ground-floor bedroom with its patchwork quilt and lace pillows, the village is lovely and the Abbey de Bon Repos is nearby. It's bucolic.

Price	€55.
Rooms	1 double.
Meals	Dinner (vegetarian) with wine, €22. Picnic available.
Closed	Rarely.
Directions	From St Brieuc D790 to Corlay; left D44 to Laniscat; D76 for Gouarec; leaivng village 2nd left, over bridge, right for 'Kergoten'; at hilltop left 200m, house on left; check directions before you go.

Julie & Jez Rooke
Toul Bleïz,
22570 Laniscat,
Côtes-d'Armor
Tel   +33 (0)2 96 36 98 34
Mobile   +33 (0)6 88 57 75 31
Email   jezrooke@hotmail.com
Web   www.phoneinsick.co.uk

Brittany

Les Korrigann'ès

The scent of tea lights and Japanese teas washes over you as you enter from the village street. The views, too, are enticing, to courtyard, garden, sundeck, bridge and stream. Frédérique, warm and humorous, has painted her fine old house in the soft lime finishes that she teaches. She is passionate about things natural so 'less is more', nothing is synthetic and wooden floors are white: an airy, harmonious beauty reigns. At dinner, served in the lovely slate-slabbed salon, vegetarians are spoiled, as are lovers of seafood. All is organically sourced and that includes the wine. Cobbled Pontrieux is charming.

Price	€79–€99.
Rooms	5: 4 doubles, 1 family room.
Meals	Dinner €35. Restaurant within walking distance.
Closed	8 January to mid-March.
Directions	N12 to Guingamp; D787 to Pontrieux; entering villlage, antiques shop on left & free parking area; house 50m, same side.

Frédérique Gaby Forner
Les Korrigann'ès,
10 rue des Fontaines,
22260 Pontrieux, Côtes-d'Armor

Tel	+33 (0)2 96 95 12 46
Mobile	+33 (0)6 08 01 17 82
Email	korrigannesgaby@wanadoo.fr
Web	monsite.wanadoo.fr/korrigannes

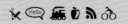

Entry 235 Map 2

Brittany

Manoir de Coat Gueno

The 15th-century, country-cocooned manor house is only a short drive from the fishing ports, headlands and long sandy beaches. Wrapped in a rich fluffy towel, gaze out of your lavishly, florally furnished bedroom onto the lawns below. You may hear the crackling of the log fire in the vast stone hearth downstairs, lit by your affable and perfectionist host, the splash and laughter of guests in the pool, or the crack of billiard balls echoing upwards to the tower. The games room and one gorgeous suite are inseparate buildings in the grounds. Your attentive host is the perfect French gentleman. *Children over eight welcome.*

Price	€100–€110. Suites €135–€165.
Rooms	3: 1 double, 1 suite for 3, 1 suite for 4.
Meals	Dinner €25. Wine €20.
Closed	September–April.
Directions	From Paimpol for Lézardrieux; after bridge left to Pleudaniel; right for Pouldouran; thro' Prat Collet & Passe Porte to sign for Croas Guezou; left; 1st track right 800m. Not easy to find!

Christian de Rouffignac
Manoir de Coat Gueno,
Coat Gueno, 22740 Pleudaniel,
Côtes-d'Armor

Tel	+33 (0)2 96 20 10 98
Email	coatguen@aol.com
Web	mapage.noos.fr/coatgueno

Entry 236 Map 2

Brittany

À la Corniche

Enter and you will see why we chose this modernised house: the ever-changing light of the great bay shimmers in through vast swathes of glass. Each guest room has its own veranda where you can sit and gaze at sea, islands and coastline. Or take ten minutes and walk to Perros for restaurants and beaches. Marie-Clo has enlivened the interior with her patchwork and embroidery, installed a fine new wood-burner in the living space and tea trays in the rooms. It is calm, light, bright; she is attentive, warm and generous, and breakfast is seriously good. Ideal for couples on a gentle seaside holiday.

Price	€80-€85.
Rooms	2 suites.
Meals	Restaurants 400m.
Closed	Rarely.
Directions	From Lannion D788 N to Perros Guirec; follow signs to Port; coastal road round bay for approx. 1km; left at sign. (Will fax map or collect you from railway station.)

Marie-Clotilde Biarnès
À la Corniche,
41 rue de la Petite Corniche,
22700 Perros Guirec, Côtes-d'Armor
Tel   +33 (0)2 96 23 28 08
Mobile   +33 (0)6 81 23 15 49
Email   marieclo.biarnes@wanadoo.fr
Web   perso.wanadoo.fr/corniche

Entry 237   Map 2

Brittany

Manoir de Kerguéréon

Such gracious hosts with a wonderful sense of humour: you feel you are at a house party; such age and history in the gloriously asymmetrical château: tower, turrets, vast fireplaces, low doors, ancestral portraits, fine furniture; such a lovely garden, Madame's own work. Up the spiral stone staircase are bedrooms with space, taste, arched doors, a lovely window seat to do your tapestry in, good bathrooms; and the great Breton breakfast can be brought up if you wish. Aperitifs among the roses, breakfast before the crackling fire; their son breeds racehorses on the estate and now their daughter runs the B&B. Sheer delight.

Price	€100.
Rooms	3: 1 double, 2 twins.
Meals	Restaurants 7km.
Closed	Rarely.
Directions	N12 exit Beg Chra & Plouaret (between Guingamp & Morlaix); Plouaret D11 for Lannion 5.5km; left for Ploumilliau D30; over railway, left to Kerguéréon after 3km, 100m left to end.

M & Mme de Bellefon
Manoir de Kerguéréon,
Ploubezre, 22300 Lannion,
Côtes-d'Armor
Tel   +33 (0)2 96 38 80 59
Mobile   +33 (0)6 03 45 68 55
Email   arnaud.de-bellefon@orange.fr

Entry 238   Map 2

Brittany

L'Ancien Presbytère

Inside an enclosed courtyard, a charming village presbytery. The comfy rooms, shabby chic in places, are stuffed with personal touches. The biggest is the lightest, and has an amazing deep old bath under a faded gilt mirror; the intimate attic rooms have tiny shower rooms and charming toile de Jouy ceilings. Walled gardens and a wildflower orchard for picnics complete the peaceful mood... Madame, easy and approachable, loves gardening and knows the area "like her pocket". She has itineraries for your deeper discovery, so stay awhile. Old-fashioned, authentic and very French.

Brittany

Domaine d'Ar Run

A house to seduce you. From the views of Rosambo château to the candles at breakfast, this is a home of warmth and charm. Polished floors, oriental rugs and antiques reflect its 200-year history, bedrooms are large and inviting. Cushions, drapes, gleaming furniture, chocolates, candelabra, flowers – it's all lovely. Enjoy fabulous breakfasts, doorstep walks or explore the coast (15 mins). Historic Lannion and Morlaix are a short drive; the pretty garden, its Turkish 'hammam' and wooden loungers are to share. Feel thoroughly spoiled by super hosts. *Free access to Turkish bath, spa with jacuzzi & fitness centre.*

Price	€65-€75.
Rooms	3 twins/doubles.
Meals	Dinner with wine, €25.
Closed	November-February.
Directions	From Guingamp N12 for Morlaix, exit Louargat. From Louargat church D33 to Tregrom 7km. At junc. (house with blue shutters on right), go left of church. Entrance thro' blue door in wall.

Price	€95-€115.
Rooms	2 doubles.
Meals	Restaurant 9km.
Closed	January.
Directions	From St. Brieuc on N12, 1st exit after Belle Île en Terre and Total Garage onto D11 dir. Plouaret; follow Lanvellec Château Rosambo; past castle entrance, 2nd left.

Nicole de Morchoven
L'Ancien Presbytère,
22420 Tregrom,
Côtes-d'Armor

Tel   +33 (0)2 96 47 94 15
Email   nicoledemorchoven@orange.fr
Web   tregrom.monsite.orange.fr

Jean-Marie Brun & Jean-François Hurpre
Domaine d'Ar Run,
22310 Plufur, Côtes-d'Armor

Tel   +33 (0)2 96 35 14 05
Mobile   +33 (0)6 72 20 00 33
Email   jeanmariebrun@wanadoo.fr
Web   chambresdarmor.com

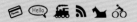

Brittany

La Grange de Coatélan

Yolande is a smiling young grandmother of three, Charlick the most sociable workaholic you could find. They are artistic (he paints) and fun. They have beautifully renovated their old Breton weaver's house and converted other ruins into rooms for guests. Their small auberge is mostly doing table d'hôtes now – a single menu of traditional dishes – and the food is brilliant. Bedrooms under the eaves (some steep stairs) have clever layouts, colour schemes and fabrics and an imaginative use of wood. Joyful rustic elegance deep in the countryside, with animals and swings for children's delight. *Min. two nights in summer.*

Price	€60-€70.
Rooms	5: 2 doubles, 3 quadruples.
Meals	Dinner €22. Wine €17-€57.
Closed	Christmas-New Year.
Directions	From Morlaix D9 south to Plougonven; at 2nd r'bout D109 to Coetélan. House on right, signed.

Charlick & Yolande de Ternay
La Grange de Coatélan,
29640 Plougonven,
Finistère
Tel   +33 (0)2 98 72 60 16
Email   la-grange-de-coatelan@wanadoo.fr
Web   www.lagrangedecoatelan.com

Entry 241 Map 2

Brittany

Manoir de Coat Amour

A dramatic, steep, shrubby drive brings you to a grand old house guarded by stone elephants and a spectacular gem of a chapel: strength and spirit. Set in a paradisical park, the Taylors' house overlooks Morlaix yet the traffic hum is minimal, the seclusion total. Chandeliers and antiques, polished floors, Jouy prints and strong colours add to the house-party atmosphere, refined yet comfortable. Jenny and Stafford (she taught textiles) have enjoyed doing their beautiful house in their own style and chat delightedly about it all. Super bedrooms, some connecting, a high colourful guest sitting room, simple luxury. *Sawday self-catering also.*

Price	€90-€120.
Rooms	5: 2 doubles, 2 triples; 1 family suite.
Meals	Dinner with wine, €35-€54. Restaurant 2km.
Closed	Rarely.
Directions	From Morlaix Route de Paris for St Brieuc; at mini-r'bout left up hill; immed. before mini viaduct sharp left into drive; pale blue gates.

Stafford & Jenny Taylor
Manoir de Coat Amour,
Route de Paris, 29600 Morlaix,
Finistère
Tel   +33 (0)2 98 88 57 02
Email   stafford.taylor@wanadoo.fr
Web   www.gites-morlaix.com

Entry 242 Map 2

Brittany

Domaine de Moulin Mer

Bordeaux shutters against pink-washed walls, graceful steps rising to the front door, attendant palm trees... Stéphane has restored this *maison de maître* to its full glory. The luxurious rooms are a masterly combination of period elegance and modern minimalism (some small showers), the gardens a riot of shady trees and irises, roses and tumbled ruins. Across the road you can glimpse the waters of the estuary and a fine old mill. Stéphane, who used to work in Dublin, is an amusing, genial host. In low season, he will cook you (according to availability and his whim) an inventive dinner using fresh local produce.

Price	€75–€130.
Rooms	4: 2 doubles, 2 suites.
Meals	Dinner with wine & champagne, €40.
Closed	Rarely.
Directions	From Logonna-Daoulas town centre, follow signs to Moulin Mer on D333; Domaine on right of steep downhill bend; pass Domaine, cont. 50m to beach.

Stéphane Pécot
Domaine de Moulin Mer,
34 route de Moulin Mer,
29460 Logonna Daoulas, Finistère

Tel	+33 (0)2 98 07 24 45
Email	info@domaine-moulin-mer.com
Web	www.domaine-moulin-mer.com

Entry 243   Map 2

Brittany

La Ferme de Kerscuntec

In the bucolic heart of the country, yet close to white sand beaches, the 17th-century cider farm has become a delicious B&B. Modern, fresh and calming are the peaceful bedrooms, prolific is the garden, creative and humorous is your hostess. Little confections are left out at all times by Anne for guests to enjoy, zinc pots are stuffed with flowers, bathrooms are for lingering in, and sparkling windows frame the fields. Wake to muffins and hedgerow jams, visit the fishing boats in Sainte Marine harbour and the grand shops of Quimper, set off for the islands. Crêperies and seafood restaurants abound. *Minimum two nights.*

Price	€85–€120.
Rooms	3 doubles.
Meals	Restaurant 2km.
Closed	Rarely.
Directions	From Quimper D34 to Benodet; D44 to Combrit over Pont de Cornouaille; 2nd left to 'Plage de Kermor'. Ferme de Kerscuntec signed on right.

Anne & Bruno Porhiel
La Ferme de Kerscuntec,
Route de Kermor,
29120 Combrit, Finistère

Tel	+33 (0)2 98 51 90 90
Mobile	+33 (0)6 86 99 78 28
Email	vacancesenbretagne@hotmail.fr
Web	www.lafermedekerscuntec.fr

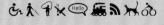

Entry 244   Map 2

Brittany

Manoir de Kerledan

Everyone loves Kerledan, its gargoyles, its sophisticated theatrical décor, its owners' enthusiasm. Peter and Penny have made it stunningly original. Sisal and unstained oak, limed walls, the odd splash of antique mirror or gilded bergère with fake leopard skin create a mood of luxury and calm; slate-floored bathrooms are delicious, candlelit, cut-glass dinners are legendary. Sit by the great dining room fire, stroll in the lovely gardens (baroque courtyard, palisade hornbeam allée, potager), lounge in antique linen in a perfect bedroom and let yourself be pampered by your hosts: arrive as strangers, leave as friends.

Ethical Collection: Food.
See page 410 for details.

Price	€90–€135.
Rooms	3: 1 double, 1 twin/double, 1 family room.
Meals	Dinner, 2-3 courses, €22–€27. Wine from €5.
Closed	Rarely.
Directions	Left out of Carhaix train station; 1st r'bout left, under bridge; 2nd r'bout right; 3rd r'bout right; down hill past 'Gamme Vert' on right; 1st left; 300m; on right.

	Peter & Penny Dinwiddie
	Manoir de Kerledan,
	Route de Kerledan,
	29270 Carhaix-Plouguer, Finistère
Tel	+33 (0)2 98 99 44 63
Email	kerledan@gmail.com
Web	www.kerledan.com

Entry 245   Map 2

Brittany

Lezerhy

A heavenly spot, cradled in a quiet hamlet 200 yards from the river in deepest Brittany. Delightful people: Martine cares for the disabled; Philippe pots and teaches aikido; both have lots of time for guests and daughter Melissa occasionally helps out. In an outbuilding, you have your own living room and kitchen and two big, functionally furnished attic rooms decorated in subtle pastels and fitted with good showers. Birds sing, the two cats are among the best ever, there may be a different kind of cake for breakfast every day, St Nicolas des Eaux has restaurants and kayaks on the river. Cheap, cheerful, bucolic.

Price	€45.
Rooms	2: 1 twin/double, 1 twin.
Meals	Guest kitchen. Restaurants 3km.
Closed	November-Easter, except by arrangement.
Directions	From Pontivy D768 south 12km; exit St Nicolas des Eaux; right immed. after bridge; follow signs for Chambres d'Hôtes & Poterie 3km.

	Martine Maignan & Philippe Boivin
	Lezerhy,
	56310 Bieuzy les Eaux,
	Morbihan
Tel	+33 (0)2 97 27 74 59
Email	boivinp@wanadoo.fr
Web	pagesperso-orange.fr/poterie-de-lezerhy

Entry 246   Map 2

Brittany

Talvern

Separated from the road by a grassy courtyard, this honest old farmhouse once belonged to the château. The dividing stone wall encloses a south-facing terrace, a young fruit-treed garden, space for the Gillots' children – and yours – to play, and a potager. Ask gentle Patrick about his vegetables and his face lights up: he was a chef in Paris (do dine in). Christine teaches English and is the talent behind the very fine, quietly original bedroom décor. There are walks in the woods next door, good cycling, resident peacocks, birdlife all around, the sea just 30 minutes away. *Ask about cookery courses October-March.*

Ethical Collection: Food.
See page 410 for details.

Brittany

Kerimel

The standing stones of Carnac are minutes away, beaches, coastal pathways and golf course close by. Kerimel is a handsome group of granite farm buildings in a perfect setting among the fields. Bedrooms are simple beauties: plain walls, some panelling, patchwork bedcovers and pale curtains, old stones and beams. The dining room is cottage perfection: dried flowers hanging from beams over a wooden table, a spring fire in the vast stone fireplace, breakfasts from Grand-mère that promise a new treat each day. A gentle, generous young family with excellent English... "We talked of flowers", wrote one guest.

Price	€63. €115 for 4.
Rooms	5: 2 doubles, 1 twin/double, 2 suites.
Meals	Dinner with wine, €22.
Closed	Rarely.
Directions	N165 Auray for Lorient; 1st exit to Landévant; after Renault garage, 1st right D24 for Baud 50m; 1st right; continue Rue du Château 1.2km. House on left.

Price	€75-€80.
Rooms	5: 2 twins/doubles, 3 triples.
Meals	Restaurants 3km.
Closed	Rarely.
Directions	From N165 exit for Quiberon & Carnac; on D768, 4km; right to Ploemel; D105 W for Erdeven; sign on right, 1.5km.

Patrick Gillot
Talvern,
56690 Landévant,
Morbihan

Tel	+33 (0)2 97 56 99 80
Mobile	+33 (0)6 16 18 08 75
Email	talvern@chambre-morbihan.com
Web	www.chambre-morbihan.com

Nicolas Malherbe
Kerimel,
56400 Ploemel,
Morbihan

Tel	+33 (0)2 97 56 83 53
Mobile	+33 (0)6 83 40 68 56
Email	chaumieres.kerimel@wanadoo.fr
Web	kerimel.free.fr

Brittany

Kernivilit

Right on the quayside, with the oyster boats under your windows, a very simple but friendly address. French windows open to tiny balconies and bedrooms touch the view; catch the lovely limpid light as you drink coffee on the balcony, listening to the chug-chug of the boats, smelling the sea. Madame worked in England, Germany and the US before coming here to help François farm oysters; he'll take you out in the boats if you ask. Hospitable and generous, alert and chatty, she hangs interesting art in her rooms, lights a fire on cool days and serves a good breakfast (great breads, fine jams) on a terrace shaded by pines.

Price	€70. Apartment €80.
Rooms	3: 1 double, 1 studio & kitchenette, 1 apartment for 3 & kitchenette.
Meals	Restaurant 500m.
Closed	Rarely.
Directions	From Auray D28 & D781 to Crach & Trinité sur Mer; right at r'bout before bridge for La Trinité; house 400m along on left, sign 'François Gouzer'.

	Christine & François Gouzer
	Kernivilit,
	Route de Quéhan, St Philibert,
	56470 La Trinité sur Mer, Morbihan
Tel	+33 (0)2 97 55 17 78
Mobile	+33 (0)6 78 35 09 34
Email	info@residence-mer.com
Web	www.residence-mer.com

Entry 249   Map 2

Brittany

Château de Castellan

Fields and forests and not a house in sight. And, at the end of a lane, this quietly grand château, built in 1732 and a one-time hideout for counter revolutionaries. Ring the bell and Madame will come to greet you. Antique church pews, a wide winding stair, pastoral views are the pleasing first impressions. The owners have the right wing, Grandmère has the left and guests are in the middle, on two floors. Bedrooms are faded but spotless, the best being the double on the first floor with its painted panelling. Delightful Madame cooks, irons, cleans, cooks (very well) and directs you to the prettiest of ancient villages.

Price	€75-€90. Family room €142.
Rooms	3: 1 double, 1 twin, 1 family room for 4, all with separate wcs.
Meals	Dinner €21. Wine €18-€25.
Closed	November-March.
Directions	From Redon D873 to La Gacilly; D777 to St Martin; D149; 1.5km for St Congard. Signs to Castellan.

	Patrick & Marie Cossé
	Château de Castellan,
	56200 St Martin sur Oust,
	Morbihan
Tel	+33 (0)2 99 91 51 69
Email	auberge@club.fr
Web	www.castellan.fr.st

Entry 250   Map 3

Western Loire

Photo: www.istockphoto.com

Château de Coët Caret

Come for a taste of life with the French country aristocracy — it's getting hard to find. Madame greets you on arrival and is on hand during the day, and breakfast is properly formal (at 9am sharp, please!). Your hosts are cultured people, proud of their château tucked into the woods and its 100 hectares of parkland. Bedrooms are faded but comfortable; *Saumon* is carpeted under the eaves and comes with binoculars for the birds. Your hosts are involved with the World Wildlife Foundation and you are in the Brière Regional Park where water and land are inextricably mingled. Wildlife abounds.

Price	€100–€115.
Rooms	4: 3 doubles, 1 twin.
Meals	Restaurants 2km.
Closed	Rarely.
Directions	From N165 exit 15 D774 for La Baule to Herbignac, 10km; fork left D47 for St Lyphard for 4km; house on right.

	Cécile de La Monneraye
	Château de Coët Caret,
	44410 Herbignac,
	Loire-Atlantique
Tel	+33 (0)2 40 91 41 20
Email	infos@coetcaret.com
Web	coetcaret.com

Entry 251   Map 3

Le Manoir des Quatre Saisons

Jean-Philippe, his mother and sister (who speaks English) are attentive hosts, providing both swimming robes and drinks by the pool. Communal breakfasts are flexible, complete with eggs and bacon as well as local choices, and immaculate bedrooms (some in two-storey stone cottages in the grounds) colourfully coordinated; delightful Jean-Philippe has an eye for detail. Expect stripes, patterns, French flourishes and distant sea views. Beach, river and town are walkable but children will enjoy mucking around in the big dog-friendly garden full of secret corners. *Min. two nights July/August & bank holiday weekends.*

Price	€75–€80. Suites €89–€94. Extra person €20.
Rooms	5: 3 doubles. Outbuildings: 2 suites for 2–4 with kitchenettes.
Meals	Restaurants 1.5km.
Closed	Rarely.
Directions	From Guérande to La Turballe; right at entrance to La Turballe to Piriac; on for 1.7km, house on right; check directions before you go.

	Jean-Philippe Meyran
	Le Manoir des Quatre Saisons,
	744 bd de Lauvergnac,
	44420 La Turballe, Loire-Atlantique
Tel	+33 (0)2 40 11 76 16
Mobile	+33 (0)6 87 33 43 86
Email	jean-philippe.meyran@club-internet.fr
Web	www.manoir-des-quatre-saisons.com

Entry 252   Map 3

Western Loire

La Mercerais

These are the sweetest people who really do treat their guests as friends, even if their 'romantic' décor (rosy wallpapers, embroidered sheets) is not to everyone's taste. Madame, bright and sparkling, is proud to show you her decorated books, music scrolls and hats with dried flowers; Monsieur is a retired farmer, quiet, friendly, attached to this place. The house is warm (log fire in winter) and country-furnished; two bedrooms (mind your head on the way up) have family armoires. Picnic in the immaculate award-winning garden with summer kitchen. Breakfast is served in pretty little baskets at the long table.

Price	€50. €65 for 3. Extra bed €15.
Rooms	3: 2 triples; 1 family room for 3 with separate wc.
Meals	Summer kitchen. Restaurant 3km.
Closed	Rarely.
Directions	From Rennes N137 for Nantes 63km; exit Nozay N171 for Blain 8km. At bottom of hill, left at roadside cross; signed.

Yvonne & Marcel Pineau
La Mercerais,
44130 Blain,
Loire-Atlantique

Tel	+33 (0)2 40 79 04 30
Mobile	+33 (0)6 87 90 66 81

Entry 253   Map 3

Western Loire

Logis de Richebonne

Monsieur's parents bought this old *logis Vendéen* when he was six. Years later, researching the history of the house, he found his family had owned it in 1670! In the hall, Madame's family tree goes back to the 14th century. Both are warm, welcoming and not at all grand and the old house is full of personal touches: Madame painted the breakfast china and embroidered the beautiful tablecloths. Vast bedrooms have peaceful views and quantities of fresh and dried flowers. The suite is ideal for a family, the huge grounds hold two pretty ponds (unfenced) and a barbecue: you may picnic here.

Price	€70.
Rooms	3: 2 doubles, 1 suite for 5.
Meals	Picnic possible. Restaurant in village, 1.5km.
Closed	Rarely.
Directions	From Nantes through Legé centre for Challans & Machecoul; on leaving village, left by restaurant Le Paradis; Logis 150m on left.

Mme de Ternay
Logis de Richebonne,
7 impasse Richebonne,
44650 Legé, Loire-Atlantique

Tel	+33 (0)2 40 04 90 41
Email	adeternay@wanadoo.fr

Entry 254   Map 8

Western Loire

Château de la Sébinière

Young, warm, humorous, Anne has exquisite taste, a perfectionist's eye and twin daughters of 13. The house of her dreams, this 18th-century château in its pretty park is a light, sunny and harmonious home. Walls are white or red-ochre, ceilings beamed, bathrooms a blend of old and new. There's an extravagant attention to detail – a pewter jug of old roses by a gilt mirror, a fine wicker chair on an ancient tiled floor. You have your own entrance and the run of the sitting room, log-fired in winter. There may be real hot chocolate at breakfast and, if you wish, a glass of wine on arrival. Nearby Clisson is full of charm.

Price	€95–€120.
Rooms	3 doubles.
Meals	Dinner with wine, €30.
Closed	Rarely.
Directions	From Nantes N249 for Poitiers; 2nd exit N149 for Le Pallet; through village; right just past wine museum; signed.

Anne Cannaferina
Château de la Sébinière,
44330 Le Pallet,
Loire-Atlantique
Tel   +33 (0)2 40 80 49 25
Mobile +33 (0)6 17 35 45 33
Email info@chateausebiniere.com
Web   www.chateausebiniere.com

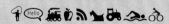

Entry 255   Map 3

Western Loire

Le Verger

The Broux have revived this fine cluster of granite buildings for their family and the guests they welcome so well. At the end of a private lane, one small ancient house of low heavy beams and big stones makes up your quarters: two divans in the sitting area, bedroom upstairs, hand-painted furniture, loads of personality. Across the yard, in the big square family house where noble stone, timber and terracotta also reign, Annick prepares delicious meals for the long bright table. Outside, flowers and vegetables mix in profusion, a white horse grazes in the field. Lovely people, charming place.

Price	€49. €70 for 4.
Rooms	1 suite for 2-4.
Meals	Dinner with wine, €18.
Closed	End October-Easter.
Directions	From Nantes N249 for Poitiers, exit D763 to Clisson. From Clisson N149 for Poitiers. At La Colonne, right D753 to Tiffauges; cont. to Montaigu, 1km; 3rd road on right.

Annick & Marc Broux
Le Verger,
85530 La Bruffière,
Vendée
Tel   +33 (0)2 51 43 62 02
Email broux.annick@wanadoo.fr
Web   pagesperso-orange.fr/le-verger

Entry 256   Map 8

Western Loire

La Maison de Landerie

Annie used to have her own restaurant in Devon so whether you are outside on her little stone terrace overlooking open fields and forest or inside at her long antique table, it will be a Cordon Bleu breakfast. Multi-talented Annie could open an antique shop as well; her lovingly collected artefacts decorate this sweet little farmhouse like a dream from the past. The vintage linens are sumptuous, the towels are thirsty, the mattresses are from heaven. You can walk to town, pick a trail in the forest or rent a canoe and follow the lazy river Lay. Annie's dinners are renowned, even the Mayor comes to dine.

Price	€60-€65.
Rooms	2 doubles.
Meals	Dinner with wine, €28.
Closed	Christmas.
Directions	From La Rochelle N11 then D137 for Chantonnay, thro' Ste Hermine, 3km; 300m after sign for St Juire, left small road to Landerie 800m; 1st house on left.

Annie Jory
La Maison de Landerie,
La Réorthe, 85210 Ste Hermine,
Vendée
Tel +33 (0)2 51 27 80 70
Email richard.jory@wanadoo.fr
Web www.lalanderie.com

Entry 257 Map 8

Western Loire

La Frelonnière

An elegant country house in a peaceful, pastoral setting – who would not love it? The 18th-century farmhouse, complete with musket holes and open rafters, is informal, spacious and delightful. Your English/Scottish hosts are fun, friendly and intimately acquainted with France – they brought their children up here. Now they generously open their living space to guests, their serene pool, their exquisite Monet-style garden. Quietly stylish bedrooms (coir carpets, white walls, fresh flowers, silk flourishes) are divided by a sofa'd library on the landing; dinners may be romantic or convivial. A gem. *Unfenced pool.*

Price	€75.
Rooms	2 doubles.
Meals	Dinner with wine, €30.
Closed	Rarely.
Directions	A83 Nantes-Bordeaux exit Chantonnay; thro' town, D31 to La Caillère, thro' St Philbert & La Jaudonnière; house at end of 2nd lane on right between La Jaudonnière & St Hilaire du Bois.

Julie & Richard Deslandes
La Frelonnière,
85410 La Caillère - St Hilaire du Bois,
Vendée
Tel +33 (0)2 51 51 56 49
Email julie@lafrelonniere.fr
Web www.bandbvendee.com

Entry 258 Map 8

Western Loire

Le Logis de la Clef de Bois

The town, a *ville d'art et d'histoire*, is one of the loveliest in the Vendée. The house stands in lushness at one end of it. Madame has an easy elegance and her home overflows with taste and glamorous touches, from the fabulous Zuber mural in the dining room to the immaculate fauteuils of the salon. Big paintings, a collection of muslin caps from Poitou, bedrooms that celebrate writers... all point to cultural leanings. Rabelais speaks of the Renaissance, Michel Ragon is flamboyant in red and white checks, Rabelais is joyful in trompe l'œil. Come down to a royally elegant breakfast and, perhaps, Madame's own cannelés.

Price	€115–€135.
Rooms	4: 2 doubles, 2 family suites for 2-4.
Meals	Barbecue & picnic possible. Restaurant 100m.
Closed	Occasionally.
Directions	From Nantes A83 for Niort & Bordeaux; exit 8 D938 into Fontenay le Comte; house in town centre.

	Danielle Portebois
	Le Logis de la Clef de Bois,
	5 rue du Département,
	85200 Fontenay le Comte, Vendée
Tel	+33 (0)2 51 69 03 49
Mobile	+33 (0)6 15 41 04 31
Email	clef_de_bois@hotmail.com
Web	www.clef-de-bois.com

Entry 259 Map 8

Western Loire

Le Rosier Sauvage

The pretty village is known for its exquisite abbey and some of that monastic serenity pervades these rooms. We love the family room under the rafters: massive oak door, cool tiled floor, a touch of toile, a simple mix of furniture. Through the family kitchen, breakfast is at a long polished table in the old stable: linger over cake and compote; the old laundry, its huge stone tub intact, is now a sitting room. Guests can picnic in the many-flowered walled garden, overlooked by the abbey and a glorious cedar tree. Energetic Christine is as charming as her house, which is also home to her husband and twin girls.

Price	€47–€50.
Rooms	4: 1 double, 1 twin, 2 family suites (one with separate wc).
Meals	Restaurants within walking distance.
Closed	October-April.
Directions	From Niort N148 for Fontenay le Comte 20km (or A83 exit 9); after Oulmes right to Nieul sur l'Autise to Abbey; house just beyond on left.

	Christine Chastain-Poupin
	Le Rosier Sauvage,
	1 rue de l'Abbaye,
	85240 Nieul sur l'Autise, Vendée
Tel	+33 (0)2 51 52 49 39
Email	lerosiersauvage@yahoo.fr
Web	lerosiersauvage.c.la

Entry 260 Map 8

Western Loire

Demeure l'Impériale

A rare survivor of Cholet's imperial past, when the town flourished on making handkerchiefs, this elegant townhouse was the orangery of a long-gone château. Nothing imperial about Édith, though: she's a natural at making guests feel at home. The bedrooms are bright and beautiful with fine period furniture and modern bathrooms; one sits under the eaves, another overlooks the rose-filled, tree-shaded garden. There are two pretty salons, a glass-roofed dining room in the sunken courtyard, and it's all so spotless you could eat off the parquet. Magnificent breakfasts, excellent dinners; French style and hospitality at its best.

Western Loire

Le Mésangeau

The house is long-faced, and refined; the grounds (superb) come with a fishing pond and 'aperitif gazebo'. The Migons have expertly renovated this unusual house with its barn-enclosed courtyard, two towers and covered terrace. Big, north-facing bedrooms are elegant and comfortable behind their shutters, and keep the housekeepers busy. Expect leather sofas and a suit of armour, colourful beams above antique furniture, two billiard tables, and bikes, ping pong and drums in the barn. At dinner, French cuisine from Madame, and much entertainment from Monsieur, who collects veteran cars and plays bass guitar.

Price	€69-€76. Suite €140.
Rooms	3: 2 doubles, 1 suite for 4.
Meals	Dinner €23. Wine €10-€15.
Closed	Rarely.
Directions	Rue Nationale is a one-way street through Cholet centre. No. 28 200m down on right, near St Pierre church.

Price	€90-€110.
Rooms	5: 3 doubles, 1 suite for 4, 1 suite for 5.
Meals	Dinner with wine, €35.
Closed	Rarely.
Directions	Exit A11 at Ancenis for D763; at Liré, right D751. Left at Drain for St Laurent des Autels D154. House 3.5km after church, on left.

	Édith & Jean-René Duchesne
	Demeure l'Impériale,
	28 rue Nationale, 49300 Cholet,
	Maine-et-Loire
Tel	+33 (0)2 41 58 84 84
Email	demeure.imperiale@wanadoo.fr
Web	demeure-imperiale.com

	Brigitte & Gérard Migon
	Le Mésangeau,
	49530 Drain,
	Maine-et-Loire
Tel	+33 (0)2 40 98 21 57
Email	le.mesangeau@orange.fr
Web	www.loire-mesangeau.com

Loire-Charmilles

A house and garden full of surprises and a dazzling mix of styles. Chunky beams and old floors are set against slabs of slate, Japanese art and some very modern furniture. Up wooden stairs, through a low doorway (mind your head), bedrooms have huge beds, dimmer switches, antique desks with perspex chairs and ultra-chic bathrooms, one with a repro bath. The enclosed garden teems with roses, mimosa and orchids; breakfast and dinner are on the veranda on warm days or in the huge-windowed orangery; bubbly Nadia cooks on a fireplace grill; she and Jean-Pierre, son Jules and the lovely lab, make this a warm family house.

Price	€59.
Rooms	2: 1 double, 1 twin.
Meals	Dinner with wine, €23. Guest kitchenette.
Closed	Rarely.
Directions	From St Florent le Vieil D751 for Montjean; entering Le Mesnil, signed Loire-Charmilles; house on right.

Nadia Leinberger
Loire-Charmilles,
9 rue de l'École, 49410 Le Mesnil en Vallée, Maine-et-Loire
Tel +33 (0)2 41 78 94 74
Mobile +33 (0)6 77 10 69 66
Email nadia@loire-charmilles.com
Web www.loire-charmilles.com

Entry 263 Map 3

La Rousselière

A hymn to peace and gentle living. The impeccably lovely garden is Monsieur's pride and joy; château-like reception rooms open one into another – glass doors to glass doors, billiards to dining to sitting – like an indoor arcade; family portraits follow you wherever you go; Mass is still said in the private chapel on 16 August. But it's never over-grand. Bedrooms are highly individual with their antiques and hand-painted armoires (courtesy of an artistic sister), many bathrooms are new and Madame is the most delightful smiling hostess and a fine cook; your lovely hosts join you for an aperitif before dinner.

Ethical Collection: Food.
See page 410 for details.

Price	€60-€95.
Rooms	5: 2 doubles, 1 twin, 1 family room, 1 family suite for 5.
Meals	Dinner with wine, €30.
Closed	Rarely.
Directions	From Angers D723 for Nantes; exit St Georges sur Loire; left at 1st r'bout for Chalonnes; left at 2nd r'bout for Chalonnes. Immed. before bridge left to La Possonnière; 1.5km; left; signed.

François & Jacqueline de Béru
La Rousselière,
49170 La Possonnière,
Maine-et-Loire
Tel +33 (0)2 41 39 13 21
Mobile +33 (0)6 60 67 60 69
Email larousseliere@unimedia.fr
Web www.anjou-et-loire.com/rousseliere

Entry 264 Map 3

Le Manoir de la Noue

On the edge of little Dénee, beyond the avenues of a residential estate, discover this: a walled garden resplendent with the colours of the seasons and a 16th-century manor. In 2002 your hosts discovered the world of wine after pursuing other careers; each of their vintages has earned them praise. Now the former barn has become a stylish chambres d'hôtes: bedrooms above, breakfast area below. All is comfortable and characterful: oak beams and bold colour-washed walls, big beds and generous bathrooms. After feasting on Catherine's jams and 'gelées', seek out the lovely village-island of Béhuard.

Prieuré de l'Épinay

Such happy, interested, interesting people, and meals the greatest fun – local farm chicken and asparagus, raspberries and lettuces from their own organic potager. Facing the big grassed garden, the ancient priory has changed so little that the monks would feel at home here today, though the swimming pool, large and lovely, might be a surprise. Your hosts gladly share their home and its history; lofty ceilings, 15th-century beams, a fascinating *cave*, a rare fireplace. The two-storey rooms in the barn are simple and big, summer breakfasts are served in the chapel. What value! *Ask about wine tours.*

Price	€70-80.
Rooms	4 doubles.
Meals	Guest kitchen. Restaurant 5km.
Closed	Rarely.
Directions	From Angers A87 for Cholet & La Rochelle exit 23; right at 2nd r'bout in Denée; just after village sign, right 3 times.

Price	€80.
Rooms	3: 1 suite for 2, 2 suites for 4-5.
Meals	Dinner with wine, €30. Picnic available.
Closed	October-April.
Directions	From Angers D723 for Nantes 18km; through St Georges; cont. 1.5km; left after garage. Pass château; house on left. Park outside, walk thro' gate.

Catherine & Olivier de Cenival
Le Manoir de la Noue,
49190 Denée,
Maine-et-Loire
Tel   +33 (0)2 41 78 79 80
Email   odecenival@wanadoo.fr
Web   www.domainedeschesnaies.com

Bernard & Geneviève Gaultier
Prieuré de l'Épinay,
49170 St Georges sur Loire,
Maine-et-Loire
Tel   +33 (0)2 41 39 14 44
Email   bernard.gaultier3@wanadoo.fr

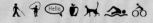

Western Loire

Logis de la Roche Corbin

Smack in the middle of old Angers, a secret, special place. Behind a high wall: a cobbled path, a climbing rose, a bunch of lettuces to keep the tortoise happy. Off this delightful courtyard garden is your room, aglow with 18th-century charm; off a French-grey hallway, an exquisite zen-like bathroom. Breakfast is up the magnificent rough-hewn oak stair, in a Japanese-touched room with a rooftop view. Behind this hugely sympathetic restoration of a 16th-century house are a fine, talented couple, Michael, an American painter with a studio across the road, and Pascale from Paris, warm, relaxed and enthusiastic about B&B.

Price	€85. Whole house available July/August.
Rooms	1 double.
Meals	Occasional dinner with wine, €15–€30.
Closed	Rarely.
Directions	A11 to Angers; exit for hospital; opp. hospital (urgences) Rue de l'Hommeau. House at end of street on corner of Rue de la Harpe. Parking available.

	Michael & Pascale Rogosin
	Logis de la Roche Corbin,
	3 rue de la Harpe, 49100 Angers,
	Maine-et-Loire
Tel	+33 (0)2 41 86 93 70
Email	logisdelaroche@wanadoo.fr
Web	www.logisdelaroche.com

Entry 267   Map 4

Western Loire

La Pinsonnière

'Pinson' means finch – but most of the happy chirping comes from satisfied guests after one of Olivier's superb meals accompanied by natural wines: their 15th-century troglodyte caves are ageing some fine nectars. Tired of city life, your hosts now reign over a mini hamlet. The old barn is a communal feasting space with noble timbers, original fireplace, stone walls, and a super long table for guaranteed conviviality. Pascale's bedrooms are sprinkled about, each with its own entrance; expect exposed stone, wooden floors, antique finds and handsome slate bathrooms with Italian showers. Unpretentious and fun.

Ethical Collection: Food.
See page 410 for details.

Price	€65–€84. Extra bed (adult) €25. Child bed €19.
Rooms	4: 2 doubles, 1 family room for 3–5, 1 family room for 2–4. Yurt available.
Meals	Dinner €32–€37.
Closed	2 weeks in February.
Directions	From Poitiers for Saumur to Montreuil Bellay; D77 for Puy Notre Dame; left at stop; left Sanziers, 1km. Park in lot next to entrance.

	Pascale & Olivier Petitout Schvirtz
	La Pinsonnière,
	Rue des Clos, Sanziers,
	49260 Vaudelnay, Maine-et-Loire
Tel	+33 (0)2 41 59 12 95
Mobile	+33 (0)6 61 70 63 42
Email	pascale@la-pinsonniere.fr
Web	www.la-pinsonniere.fr

Entry 268   Map 4

Western Loire

La Closerie

Nothing pretentious about this quiet village house – or its owners, genuine country folk. Carmen, retired English teacher, has a great sense of humour; Hervé looks after vegetables and hens and is the creator of delicious traditional French dinners. Bedrooms, in the old farmhouse or off the shady courtyard, two with their own entrances, are simply decorated with small shower rooms. One has a magnificent stone fireplace; another, old beams, stone walls and pretty yellow fabrics; the two-room family suite is deeply old-fashioned. Trees almost engulf the house and the sunny conservatory dining room looks over a bosky garden.

Price	€55-€60.
Rooms	4: 1 double, 2 family suites for 4 (1 with sofabed), 1 family cottage for 5.
Meals	Dinner with wine, €28. Restaurant 4km.
Closed	Rarely.
Directions	From A85 exit 2 Longué; N147 for Saumur; at Super U r'bout D53 to St Philbert. House on right in centre of village.

	Carmen & Hervé Taté
	La Closerie,
	29 rue d'Anjou, 49160 St Philbert du Peuple, Maine-et-Loire
Tel	+33 (0)2 41 52 62 69
Email	herve.tate@wanadoo.fr
Web	www.bandb-lacloserie.com

Entry 269   Map 4

Western Loire

Domaine de l'Oie Rouge

Recline in bed and watch the Loire flow by. The 19th-century townhouse sits in a large peaceful garden; Christiane runs an art gallery in a smaller building. One bedroom has an astonishingly ornate 1930s brown-tiled bathroom with the tub bang in the middle, another opens to the garden and its trees; all the rooms are lavishly French and art-hung. Monsieur is chef, Madame hosts dinner, especially fun when a number of guests are staying. Both your hosts will be happy to help you decide what to see and make the most of your stay. The lovely garden is definitely worth exploring if you are green-fingered.

Price	€73-€90.
Rooms	5 doubles.
Meals	Dinner with wine, €25.
Closed	Rarely.
Directions	From Saumur D952 for Angers for 15km. Domaine on right at village entrance.

	Christiane Batel
	Domaine de l'Oie Rouge,
	8 rue Nationale, 49350 Les Rosiers sur Loire, Maine-et-Loire
Tel	+33 (0)2 41 53 65 65
Email	c.batel@wanadoo.fr
Web	domaine-oie-rouge.com

Entry 270   Map 4

Western Loire

Château de Salvert

This highly sculpted neo-gothic folly is home to a couple of unselfconscious aristocrats and lots of cheerful children. The baronial hall is properly dark and spooky, the dining room and salon elegant and plush with gilt chairs and ancestors on the walls. In the vast suite, a sitting area and a library in an alcove. One double has the shower in one turret, the loo in another (off the corridor). All are well decorated with fine French pieces and modern fabrics. The park is huge, wild boar roam, spring boarlets scamper, and Madame plays the piano and holds concerts. *Arrivals after 4pm. Sawday self-catering also.*

Price	€49-€90. Suites €99-€160.
Rooms	5: 1 double, 1 suite for 2. Le Brosse: 2 doubles, 1 suite.
Meals	Dinner €44. Wine €22-€35.
Closed	Rarely.
Directions	From A85 exit Saumur on D767 for Le Lude. After 1km, left on D129 to Neuillé. Signed.

	Monica Le Pelletier de Glatigny
	Château de Salvert,
	Salvert, 49680 Neuillé,
	Maine-et-Loire
Tel	+33 (0)2 41 52 55 89
Mobile	+33 (0)6 15 12 03 11
Email	info@salvert.com
Web	www.chateau-de-salvert.fr

Entry 271   Map 4

Western Loire

Le Gué de la Fresnaie

On a small road, but with little traffic, this 19th-century farmhouse has whitewashed walls, ancient beams, tiled floors and a lovely park-like garden behind. Bedrooms are in the main building with their own entrance; sprinkled with antiques and interesting farmyard relics, they are airy and white, while bathrooms are unexpectedly modern. Calm Madame is a gifted cook who grows her own vegetables – you'll eat well. Take a book to the large comfortable sitting room and admire more antiques, wander the fruit garden, watch the river, borrow a bike or a canoe. Wonderfully serene.

Price	€65.
Rooms	2 doubles (with sofabeds).
Meals	Dinner with wine, €27.
Closed	Rarely.
Directions	From D347 exit Beaufort en Vallée; D59 to Gée; 3rd right; 5th house on left.

	M & Mme Fernandez
	Le Gué de la Fresnaie,
	Les Planches, Chemin du Petit Jusson,
	49250 Beaufort en Vallée, Maine-et-Loi
Mobile	+33 (0)6 61 11 42 60
Email	rjcg-fernandez@club-internet.fr
Web	rjcg-fernandez.club.fr

Entry 272   Map 4

Western Loire

Les Bouchets

Beams, beams and more beams. The house was a ruin when the Bignons found it but they managed to save all the old timbers and stones, then added lovely antiques, open fires and fresh flowers. The result is a seductively warm cheerful house with bedrooms cosy and soft, two upstairs, one with an entrance off the garden. Passionate about food, they used to run a restaurant where Michel was chef; the signs are everywhere: coppers in the kitchen/ entrance hall, memorabilia in the family sitting room. Géraldine, bright, friendly and organised, loves needlework… and serving beautiful food and the wines of Anjou.

Price	€60–€70.
Rooms	3: 1 double, 1 twin/double, 1 family room.
Meals	Dinner with wine, €26.
Closed	Rarely.
Directions	From Baugé D60 for Beaufort en Vallée; at Chartrené, right at x-roads; 2nd left. Signed.

Michel & Géraldine Bignon
Les Bouchets,
49150 Le Vieil Baugé,
Maine-et-Loire
Tel +33 (0)2 41 82 34 48
Mobile +33 (0)6 71 60 66 05
Email bignonm@wanadoo.fr
Web www.lesbouchets.com

Entry 273 Map 4

Western Loire

La Besnardière

"Divine," says a happy guest. Lovely Joyce brims with knowledge about all things horticultural, cooks beautiful vegetarian food, welcomes art, yoga and meditation workshops in her meditation room and shares her fresh, tranquil, comfortable home with generosity. Beams spring everywhere in the 500-year-old farmhouse, roof and velux windows are new, and the big, warm, book-filled bedrooms are tucked under the rafters, one with steps to a courtyard below. Be charmed by log fires, a soft-pink sofa'd sitting room, a garden full of wildflowers, a donkey, goats, ducks, hens and views. *Massage & reflexology. Sawday self-catering also.*

Ethical Collection: Food.
See page 410 for details.

Price	€60.
Rooms	2: 1 double, 1 triple, sharing bathroom.
Meals	Dinner (vegetarian or vegan) with wine, €20.
Closed	Rarely.
Directions	A11 to Durtal; D138 to Fougeré; D217 for Baugé; 1.5km, house on left.

Joyce Rimell
La Besnardière,
Route de Baugé, 49150 Fougeré,
Maine-et-Loire
Tel +33 (0)2 41 90 15 20
Email rimell.joyce@wanadoo.fr
Web www.holiday-loire.com

Entry 274 Map 4

Western Loire

Château de Montriou

The park will explode your senses — and once the visitors have gone home, what a treat to have it all to yourselves: the lake, the famous sequoia, the waves of crocuses in spring, the tunnel of squashes, ravishing at summer's last flush. The 15th-century château has been lived in and tended by the same family for 300 years and Monsieur and Madame know exactly how to make you feel at home. A spiral stone staircase leads to properly formal bedrooms whose bold colours were design flavour of the period; wooden floors, thick rugs and antiques are only slightly younger. And the venerable library is now a guest sitting room. Unique.

Price	€85–€100. Suite €165.
Rooms	4: 2 doubles, 1 double & kitchen, 1 suite for 4 & kitchen.
Meals	Restaurant 6km.
Closed	Rarely.
Directions	From Angers A11 exit 16 to Cantenay Epinard & Feneu; D768 for Champigné 4.5km; at La Croix de Beauvais, left D74 for Sceaux d'Anjou 300m.

	Régis & Nicole de Loture Château de Montriou, 49460 Feneu, Maine-et-Loire
Tel	+33 (0)2 41 93 30 11
Email	chateau-de-montriou@wanadoo.fr
Web	www.chateau-de-montriou.com

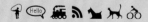

Entry 275   Map 4

Western Loire

Manoir du Bois de Grez

An old peace lingers over the unique fan-shaped yard, the old well, the little chapel: the Manoir oozes history. Your doctor host, an amateur painter, and his gracious, charming wife, much-travelled antique-hunters with imagination and flair, set the tone with a bright red petrol pump and a penny-farthing in the hall. Generous bedrooms (including a superb family room) hung with well-chosen oriental pieces and paintings come in good strong colours that reflect the garden light. You share the big sitting room with your lovely hosts, lots of plants and a suit of armour. The grand gardens are dotted with ornamental trees.

Price	€80–€90.
Rooms	4: 2 doubles, 1 twin, 1 family room.
Meals	Picnic on request. Guest kitchen. Restaurant 1.5km.
Closed	Rarely.
Directions	From Angers D775 for Laval; at Grieul right D291 to Grez Neuville; leave village on Sceaux d'Anjou road 900m; right Allée du Bois de Grez.

	Marie Laure & Jean Gaël Cesbron Manoir du Bois de Grez, Route de Sceaux d'Anjou, 49220 Grez Neuville, Maine-et-Loire
Tel	+33 (0)2 41 18 00 09
Mobile	+33 (0)6 22 38 14 56
Email	cesbron.boisgrez@wanadoo.fr
Web	www.boisdegrez.com

Entry 276   Map 4

La Croix d'Étain

Frisky red squirrels decorate the stone balustrade, the wide river flows past the lush garden: it feels like deep country yet this handsome manor has urban elegance in its very stones. Panelling, mouldings, subtly muted floor tiles bring grace, traditional French florals add softness. It looks fairly formal but sprightly Madame adores having guests and pampers them, in their own quarters, with luxury. Monsieur is a hoot, makes jam, loves fishing! Expect plush, lacy, flowery, carpeted bedrooms, three with river views, all with sunny bathrooms. The yacht-side setting is stunning – it could be the Riviera.

Price	€65–€100.
Rooms	2: 1 double, 1 twin.
Meals	Dinner with wine, €30. Crêperie 50m.
Closed	Rarely.
Directions	From Angers N162 for Le Lion d'Angers; 20km to Grieul; right D291 to Grez Neuville. At church, Rue de l'Écluse towards river on left.

Jacqueline & Auguste Bahuaud
La Croix d'Étain,
2 rue de l'Écluse,
49220 Grez Neuville, Maine-et-Loire

Tel +33 (0)2 41 95 68 49
Email croix.etain@loire-anjou-accommodation.com
Web www.loire-anjou-accomodation.com

Entry 277   Map 3

Le Frêne

Unbroken views of the countryside, and not a whisper of the 21st century. The austere topiaried spinning-tops flanking the drive belie the warm, sunny rooms ahead – this house breathes books, music and art. Richard, who once had a book shop in Angers, is charming and funny; Florence runs art courses from home. Built on the ramparts of the old fortified village, the house has a 'hanging' garden whose beds are themed by colour. Bedrooms are colourful-cosy; the big attic suite, ideal for families, holds a Russian billiard table – and Florence's charming watercolours. Delicious food, delicious garden.

Price	€60. Suite €95.
Rooms	4: 1 double, 2 twins, 1 suite for 4.
Meals	Dinner €19. Wine from €7.
Closed	Rarely.
Directions	From Angers N162 to Le Lion d'Angers; D863 to Segré; right D923 then left D863 to l'Hôtellerie de Flée; D180 to Châtelais; entering village 1st left for Bouillé Ménard.

Richard & Florence Sence
Le Frêne,
22 rue St Sauveur,
49520 Châtelais, Maine-et-Loire

Tel +33 (0)2 41 61 16 45
Mobile +33 (0)6 89 41 62 55
Email lefrene@free.fr
Web lefrene.free.fr

Entry 278   Map 3

Western Loire

La Marronnière

This pretty white-shuttered house overlooking the river has been in the family for ever. The vicomte and vicomtesse give you a gracious, smiling welcome and large, serene bedrooms most lovingly revived. Choose a bed tucked into a poppy-papered alcove, or butterflies fluttering pinkly on the walls; all rooms have river views. Madame loves cooking and breakfast is a moveable feast: dining room in winter, terrace in summer. The warmly authentic sitting room provides a winter fire in a stone hearth, Italian ochres, silk drapes, family portraits and – on warm nights – doors open to the Loire.

Price	€94–€114.
Rooms	3: 1 double, 2 twins/doubles.
Meals	Dinner €30. Wine from €20.
Closed	Rarely.
Directions	From Angers A11 for Paris; exit 14b Tiercé; at Tiercé for Cheffes, at r'bout Soulaire & Bourg; left 100m after village; house 300m on right by River Sarthe.

Jean & Marie-Hélène de la Selle
La Marronnière,
49125 Cheffes,
Maine-et-Loire
Tel +33 (0)2 41 34 08 50
Email j.delaselle@wanadoo.fr
Web www.lamarronniere.fr

Entry 279 Map 4

Western Loire

La Maison du Roi René

The famous old auberge has become a charming B&B. Scrunch up the drive serenaded by soft roses to a lovely welcome from Madame. Part medieval, part 18th century, like the village around it, it has corners, crannies and a stunning central stone fireplace. The Valicourts are the happy new owners of these magnificent oak doors and rosy tomette floors; bedrooms are beamed and very pleasing – one opens to the garden, three to the tower. There's a pretty paved terrace for breakfast with viennoiseries and a room of auberge proportions for dinner; the family join you for true table d'hôtes – and speak four languages!

Price	€65–€85.
Rooms	4: 2 doubles, 1 twin (with sofabed), 1 suite for 2.
Meals	Supper tray available, €15. Restaurant 100m.
Closed	Rarely.
Directions	From Paris A11 for Nantes; exit 10 for Sablé sur Sarthe; in Sablé D399 for d'Angers; D27 for 10km.

Dominique de Valicourt
La Maison du Roi René,
4 Grande Rue, 53290 St Denis d'Anjou
Mayenne
Tel +33 (0)2 43 70 52 30
Mobile +33 (0)6 89 37 87 12
Email roi-rene@orange.fr
Web www.roi-rene.fr

Entry 280 Map 4

Le Logis du Ray

All who stay at the Logis du Ray are sure to be wonderfully looked after – and we don't mean only the guests. Jacques and Martine run a carriage-driving school, own four horses, three carthorses, two Shetland ponies and one Irish cob stallion, and house them in spotless pens and paddocks. Bedrooms are equally immaculate, their lovely old waxed terracotta floors setting off fine antiques and smart colourful fabrics to perfection; the décor is refined-traditional French. The house is handsome, the owners attentive, the village historic and the area both rural and charming. Readers love the breakfasts.

Château de Craon

Such a close and welcoming family, whose kindness extends to include you. It's a magnificent place, with innumerable expressions of history, taste and personality, and gracious Loïk and Hélène, young grandparents, treat you like friends. A sitting room with sofas and a view of the park, an Italianate hall with sweeping stone stair, classic French bedrooms in lavender, blue, cream… an original washstand, a canopied bed, a velvet armchair. Everywhere a feast for the eyes; paintings, watercolours, antiques. Outside, 40 acres of river, meadows, lake, ice house, tennis court, pool, and a potager worth leaving home for.

Price	€72.
Rooms	2 family rooms for 3.
Meals	Restaurant in village.
Closed	Rarely.
Directions	A11 exit 10, D306 to Sablé sur Sarthe; thro' town, D309 to St Denis d'Anjou; 1st left entrance to village, follow signs École d'Attelage; right to house.

Price	€100-€160. Single €70. Suite €260.
Rooms	6: 3 doubles, 1 twin, 1 single, 1 suite for 2-4.
Meals	Restaurants in village, within walking distance.
Closed	November-March.
Directions	From Laval D771; clear signs as you enter town. 30km south of Laval.

Martine & Jacques Lefebvre
Le Logis du Ray,
53290 St Denis d'Anjou,
Mayenne
Tel   +33 (0)2 43 70 64 10
Email ecoleattelageduray@orange.fr
Web   www.ecoleattelageduray.com

Loïk & Hélène de Guébriant
Château de Craon,
53400 Craon,
Mayenne
Tel   +33 (0)2 43 06 11 02
Email chateaudecraon@wanadoo.fr
Web   www.craoncastle.com

Western Loire

Le Rocher

Being the Richecours' only guests means a free run of Madame's delightful conversation (travel, history, houses, gardens, people), her lovingly designed garden (an abundance of old roses), and the delicious house that they have restored with such care and imagination. Your room is in the 17th-century part above the old kitchen, so attractive in its wealth of fitted cupboards and slabs of slate. Character fills the big guest room: original tiles, iron bed, great old timbers. The meadow sweeps down to the river where the family pedalo awaits to take you to the restaurant on the opposite bank. Elegance and great warmth – perfection!

Price	€90–€120. Extra person €30.
Rooms	1 family room for 2-3.
Meals	Restaurants within 7km.
Closed	Rarely.
Directions	From Château Gontier N162 for Laval 4km; left for St Germain de l'Hommel; immed. right; on to village; left, signed 'no through road', 500m 2nd house called Rocher.

Mme de Richecour
Le Rocher,
St Germain de l'Hommel,
53200 Fromentières, Mayenne
Tel   +33 (0)2 43 07 06 64
Email   eva2richecour@free.fr
Web   manoirdurocher.fr

Entry 283   Map 3

Western Loire

Villeprouvé

Of vast age and character – and an ancient, leaning stair – this farmhouse is home to a humorous and talented couple who juggle cattle, children and guests. Delicious dinners end with a flaming presentation of 'grog maison' to guarantee deep sleep. In the big, soft rooms, every bed is canopied except the single box-bed which is carved and curtained to a tee. There are nooks, crannies and crooked lines, terracotta floors, half-timbered walls, antiques, books on art, tourism, history – and pretty new bathrooms. Ducks paddle in the pond, cows graze, the wind ruffles the trees, apples become cider – bucolic peace.

Price	€50.
Rooms	4: 2 doubles, 1 triple, 1 family room.
Meals	Dinner €16. Wine €10.
Closed	Rarely.
Directions	From Laval N162 for Château Gontier 14km; right through Villiers Charlemagne to Ruille Froid Fonds; in village near church left C4 for Bignon 1km; signed.

Christophe & Christine Davenel
Villeprouvé,
53170 Ruille Froid Fonds,
Mayenne
Tel   +33 (0)2 43 07 71 62
Email   christ.davenel@orange.fr
Web   pagesperso-orange.fr/villeprouve

Entry 284   Map 4

Western Loire

Château de la Villatte

From the village, a drive rises to the top of the butte where a 19th-century château sits in splendour. Isabelle arrived some years ago and her loving restoration knows no bounds – the fine outbuildings are next – yet still she finds time to enjoy her guests. Dimensions are generous throughout and bedrooms are vast, their parquet floors strewn with rugs. Tall windows overlook the steeply sloping park and the valley below, there are marble fireplaces, paintings in gilt frames, an original claw-foot bath. Breakfast on the balcony or in the grand salon, borrow bikes, or explore the lovely tree'd grounds.

Price	€75-€93. Suite €168.
Rooms	2: 1 double, 1 twin/double (rooms can interconnect to form suite).
Meals	Cold dinner €18. Wine €14-€39. Summer kitchen.
Closed	Rarely.
Directions	From Laval D171 for St Nazaire 8km; left for Montigné le Brillant; thro' village for l'Huisserie; on for 600m; house on right, signed.

	Isabelle Charrier
	Château de la Villatte,
	53970 Montigné le Brillant,
	Mayenne
Tel	+33 (0)2 43 68 23 76
Email	info@lavillatte.com
Web	www.lavillatte.com

Western Loire

La Rouaudière

Prize-winning cows in the fields, an adorable family in the house, and a wagging farm dog. Thérèse, her farming son and husband (retired) are exceptionally engaging, relaxed people and their conversation is the heart and soul of this place. Dinners are divine, breakfasts in front of the crackling fire are estimable – delicious fresh everything and lashings of coffee. You'll find roses, pergolas, a rare magnolia and birdsong in the garden (Madame is a nature lover and keen plantswoman) and bedrooms that are straightforward, spotless and simple: plain walls, a few antiquey bits and bobs, pretty window boxes. Lovely.

Price	€50-€58.
Rooms	3: 1 double, 1 twin, 1 triple.
Meals	Dinner with wine, €22.
Closed	Rarely.
Directions	From Fougères N12 east for Laval 15km; farm sign on right.

	Maurice & Thérèse Trihan
	La Rouaudière,
	Mégaudais, 53500 Ernée, Mayenne
Tel	+33 (0)2 43 05 13 57
Mobile	+33 (0)6 89 50 10 11
Email	therese-trihan@wanadoo.fr
Web	www.chambresdhotesauxportes delabretagne.com

Western Loire

Le Cruchet

The garden is a wonderful tree-laden haven, the 'gentilhommière', handsome and perfectly restored, dates from 1640, and the pepperpot tower with its spiral stone stair houses a big atmospheric suite for three. In the fine dining room downstairs, an excellent breakfast is served to the chiming of the church clock; otherwise the village is as peaceful as can be. The charming, unintrusive Nays, fluent English speakers, enjoy sharing their family home with guests. The rooms are elegant with antiques, the bathrooms are spotless, the modern suite is in the stable, and readers love "the character of the place". Stay at least a night.

Price	€45–€50.
Rooms	2: 1 suite for 2, 1 family suite for 3.
Meals	Guest kitchenette. Restaurants 3km.
Closed	Rarely.
Directions	From Laval N157 for Le Mans; at Soulgé sur Ouette D20 left to Evron; D7 for Mayenne; signed in Mézangers.

Léopold & Marie-Thérèse Nay
Le Cruchet,
53600 Mézangers,
Mayenne

Tel +33 (0)2 43 90 65 55
Email reservation@lecruchet.com
Web www.lecruchet.com

Entry 287 Map 4

Western Loire

La Garencière

Lovely old stone buildings tumbled with flowers, a few livestock, a pool in a barn with a view: it's a delightful, deep-rural address. These charming young parents – she the fine cook, he the smiling waiter – love their new enterprise and make a spirited team. The two-storey 'boulangerie' – pretty bedsteads, huge old bread oven – is the most characterful of the guest rooms, the vistas are long, the dinners are generous and very, very good. Breakfasts are feasts. Spill outside for pétanque as children explore Wendy house, trampoline, swings and huge space. Great B&B. *Small, well-behaved pets only.*

Price	€60. Extra person €15.
Rooms	5: 1 double, 2 family rooms for 4, 1 family room for 6, 1 family suite for 4.
Meals	Dinner with wine or cider, €25. Restaurant 5km.
Closed	Rarely.
Directions	A28 exit 19 for Alençon; left at r'bout D55 for Champfleur, left at 2nd r'bout. Thro' Champfleur, for Bourg le Roi 800m; 1st house on left.

Carine & Frédéric Brindjonc
La Garencière,
72610 Champfleur,
Sarthe

Tel +33 (0)2 33 31 75 84
Mobile +33 (0)6 89 38 06 33
Email lagarenciere@orange.fr
Web www.garenciere.fr

Entry 288 Map 4

Western Loire

Château de Monhoudou

Hunting trophies, timeless tranquillity, candlelit dinners and delicious desserts. Madame is the nicest, easiest of aristocrats, determined to keep the family home alive in a dignified manner – 19 generations on. A jewel set in remote rolling parkland, sheep and horses grazing under mature trees, swans on the pond, peacock, deer, boar... inside, antiques on parquet floors, hats and helmets in the hall, charming bathrooms from the 70s and loos in turrets. Also: an elegant dining room with portraits and silver, a sitting room with log fire, a piano to play, a small library – and do ask to see the chapel upstairs.

Price	€110-€180.
Rooms	6: 4 doubles, 1 twin, 1 suite for 3.
Meals	Dinner with wine, €44.
Closed	Rarely.
Directions	From Alençon N138 S for Le Mans, approx. 14km; at La Hutte left D310 for 10km; right D19 through Courgains; left D132 to Monhoudou; signed.

Michel & Marie-Christine
de Monhoudou
Château de Monhoudou,
72260 Monhoudou, Sarthe
Tel   +33 (0)2 43 97 40 05
Mobile   +33 (0)6 83 35 39 12
Email   info@monhoudou.com
Web   www.monhoudou.com

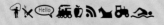

Western Loire

La Maison du Pont Romain

Cross Monfort's exquisite stone bridge to this pretty house on the banks of the river. Enter the grounds and forget the world in heavenly peace among very old trees. Gentle Madame saved it all from ruin and gives you two comfortable rooms upstairs, privately off the courtyard, both with fine armoires. The suite is in the old stables: salon below, bright bedrooms above. There are delicious jams at the big table for breakfast and a family salon for guests. Visit Montfort's castle and the lovely, unsung villages and vineyards of the Sarthe. For children? Forest animals at Pescheray and an aquapark in the village.

Price	€56-€66.
Rooms	3: 2 doubles, 1 suite for 3-4.
Meals	Dinner with wine, €22.
Closed	Rarely.
Directions	From Le Mans, D323 (formerly N23) for Chartres. At La Belle Inutile, left for Montfort le Gesnois. Over bridge, house immed. on left.

Chantal Paris
La Maison du Pont Romain,
26 rue de l'Église,
72450 Montfort le Gesnois, Sarthe
Tel   +33 (0)2 43 76 13 46
Email   chantal-paris@wanadoo.fr
Web   www.le-pont-romain.fr

Western Loire

Éporcé

You may think yourself as lucky to stay in this relaxedly grand place as the owner and his young family to have inherited it, so fine and genuine inside and out. Pure 17th century with a magnificent avenue of trees, moat, lofty beamed ceilings, three salons for guests, it brims with atmosphere and antiques, books, pictures, engravings and butterfly collections yet never overwhelms and is thoroughly lived-in. First-floor rooms are proper château stuff, and if you choose the 'gourmet' dinner, your host will set out the family silver and Wedgwood. Endearing and delightful. *Chapel & coach house available for weddings.*

Price	€90–€150.
Rooms	3: 2 doubles, 1 twin/double.
Meals	Dinner with wine, €40.
Closed	Rarely.
Directions	From A11 exit 8; N157 for Laval; D28 for La Quinte; left by church for Coulans; 1km, wayside cross, fork right; entrance on left.

	Rémy de Scitivaux
	Éporcé,
	72550 La Quinte,
	Sarthe
Tel	+33 (0)2 43 27 70 22
Email	eporce@wanadoo.fr

Entry 291 Map 4

Western Loire

Château de l'Enclos

The Guillous welcome you to their grand château in its elegant setting as long-lost friends. Sociable and fun, they are proud of their parkland with its fine trees, llamas and donkeys, magical Finnish treehouse in a monumental sequoia and new gypsy caravan, decked, fenced, lantern'd and decorated in cosiest Romany style. Back in the château, a staircase sweeps you up to handsome bedrooms of parquet and rich carpets, writing desks and tall windows; two have balconies. The charming salon opens to a stage-set-perfect garden, and you dine with your hosts in liveliest table d'hôtes style. There's masses to do in little Brûlon.

Price	€110. Treehouse €160. Gypsy caravan €140.
Rooms	5: 2 doubles, 1 twin, 1 treehouse for 2, 1 gypsy caravan for 2.
Meals	Dinner with wine, €45.
Closed	Rarely.
Directions	From A81 Le Mans-Laval; exit 1 to Brûlon. Château on right at end of town. Signed.

	Annie-Claude & Jean-Claude Guillou
	Château de l'Enclos,
	2 avenue de la Libération,
	72350 Brûlon, Sarthe
Tel	+33 (0)2 43 92 17 85
Email	jean-claude.guillou5@wanadoo.fr
Web	www.chateau-enclos.com

Entry 292 Map 4

Western Loire

Le Perceau

A happy house, part farm, part *maison bourgeoise*, where the smell of baking may greet you and the results be on the table by the morning: fabulous. Your easy, amusing hosts have three charming sons and Mr Alfred the donkey – and space indoors for little ones to run their socks off when they tire of the wild garden. Then it's up the spiral staircase to a serene cassis-and-orange bedroom; or the lavender room where a huge stone fireplace has pride of place. On a residential extremity of the village, find grass, space, freedom and lovely meadow views – and direct access to the towpath by the beautiful river Sarthe.

Price	€50.
Rooms	2: 1 double, 1 family room for 4.
Meals	Restaurants 800m.
Closed	Rarely.
Directions	From Le Mans D323 for Angers/ La Flèche; at Fontaine St Martin right D8 Malicorne sur Sarthe; D23 for Le Mans; house on corner of first lane on left.

Catherine & Jean-Paul Beuvier
Le Perceau,
72270 Malicorne,
Sarthe
Tel +33 (0)2 43 45 74 40
Email leperceau@orange.fr
Web pagesperso-orange.fr/
leperceau.malicorne

Entry 293   Map 4

Western Loire

Château de Montaupin

Outside, a virginia creeper has the façade in its clutches – to pretty effect! Find a rosebush tunnel, some big shrubs and lots of green plastic furniture. There's a laid-back feel here that families will appreciate, and sweet, friendly, easy-going Marie to care for you all. An impressive suspended spiral staircase leads to the upper floors; some rooms look onto a 400-year-old cedar, all have interesting furniture and are gradually being updated. The best suite is up a steep staircase, its roof timbers exposed. Breakfasts are robust and table d'hôtes is classic French – be sure you try the family wines. *French courses.*

Price	€70–€75. Extra person €20.
Rooms	5: 1 double, 2 triples, 2 suites for 5.
Meals	Dinner with wine, €22.50.
Closed	Occasionally.
Directions	From Le Mans D323 for La Flèche to Cérans Foulletourte; D31 to Oizé; left on D32; sign to right.

Marie David
Château de Montaupin,
Montaupin, 72330 Oizé,
Sarthe
Tel +33 (0)2 43 87 81 70
Mobile +33 (0)6 83 56 60 40
Email chateaudemontaupin@wanadoo.fr

Entry 294   Map 4

Western Loire

Le Moulin Calme

Weeping willow-fringed millponds dreamy with lilies and irises, a duck house, a charming hump-backed bridge, create a magic waterworld that wraps you in calm. Add quietly spoken Joëlle's excellent cooking (guests return for favourite dishes) using organic produce from the garden and served by ebullient Jean-Luc in the conservatory or by the pond, and you may feel no need to explore the surrounding Loire. There's fishing, a heated pool, swings and a pedalo; young children may need watching. Three exterior staircases lead to rooms in the former millhouse – homely, traditional, with views over water or wooded hills.

Price	€60.
Rooms	5: 2 doubles, 1 twin, 2 family rooms for 3.
Meals	Dinner €20. Wine €8–€25. Auberge in village.
Closed	Christmas–New Year.
Directions	From Le Mans D338 for Tours to Ecommoy then Luceau. Signed in village.

	Joëlle Combries
	Le Moulin Calme,
	Gascheau, 72500 Luceau, Sarthe
Tel	+33 (0)2 43 46 39 75
Email	moulincalme@wanadoo.fr
Web	www.lemoulincalme.com

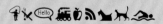

Entry 295   Map 4

Western Loire

Le Moulin du Prieuré

The brilliantly converted watermill is this couple's labour of love, down to the smooth cogwheels that turn in the great kitchen. Marie-Claire, who used to live in London, is so relaxed and unflappably efficient, such good company, such fun, it's hard to believe she has four teenage children. The sitting room bursts with books and videos; simple, attractive rooms have good beds, old tiled floors, stone walls; the garden is heaven for little ones. The atmosphere embraces you, the country sounds of stream and daytime Angelus prayer bells soothe, the area brims with interest. People love it. *Massage & spa. Unfenced water.*

Price	€66. Family room €90.
Rooms	5: 4 doubles, 1 family room.
Meals	Restaurant nearby.
Closed	Rarely.
Directions	From Tours D338 for Le Mans 45km to Dissay sous Courcillon; left at lights; mill just past church.

	Marie-Claire Bretonneau
	Le Moulin du Prieuré,
	3 rue de la Gare,
	72500 Dissay sous Courcillon, Sarthe
Tel	+33 (0)2 43 44 59 79
Email	moulinduprieure@wanadoo.fr
Web	www.moulinduprieure.fr

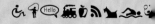

Entry 296   Map 4

Le Prieuré

Bushels of history cling to the beams and vaulted ceilings of the moated priory, snug beneath its old church. Built in the 12th, extended in the 16th, it had monks until the 20th century. Christophe loves telling the history, Marie-France does the decorating, brilliantly in keeping with the elegant old house: oriental rugs on old tiled floors, pale-painted beams over stone fireplaces, fine old paintings on plain walls, good beds under soft-coloured covers. They are attentive hosts, happy to share their vaulted dining room and pretty, peaceful garden, and the road is not an inconvenience. *Ask about local wine tours.*

La Châtaigneraie

Outside is a fairy tale: mellow old stone, white shutters, green ivy, a large leafy garden, a clematis-covered well, a little wood and glimpses of the 12th-century castle round the corner (this house used to be the castle's servants' quarters). Green-eyed Michèle, modern, intelligent and interested in people, shares the hosting with Michel. The suite is made up of three pastel-hued interconnecting bedrooms that look onto garden or endless fields. Stay a while and connect with the soft hills, woods, streams and châteaux. Guests can be as independent as they like (separate entrance) and can take one, two or three rooms.

Price	€90–€130.
Rooms	3: 2 doubles, 1 twin.
Meals	Auberge opposite; restaurants nearby.
Closed	November–February, except by arrangement.
Directions	From Le Mans A28 for Tours; exit 26 Château du Loir; D338 to Dissay sous Courcillon; left at lights, house on left.

Price	€60–€100.
Rooms	1 suite of 3 rooms (1 double, 2 singles).
Meals	Dinner with wine, €15. Child €12. Restaurant 2km.
Closed	November–March.
Directions	From Le Mans, RD138 for Tours. After Dissay sous Courcillon, left onto small road on bend & follow signs.

Christophe & Marie-France Calla
Le Prieuré,
1 rue de la Gare,
72500 Dissay sous Courcillon, Sarthe

Tel	+33 (0)2 43 44 09 09
Mobile	+33 (0)6 15 77 84 48
Email	ccalla@club-internet.fr
Web	www.chateauprieure.com

Michèle Letanneux & Michel Guyon
La Châtaigneraie,
72500 Dissay sous Courcillon,
Sarthe

Tel	+33 (0)2 43 79 36 71
Mobile	+33 (0)6 16 44 45 97
Email	michele.marie.celeste@wanadoo.fr

Western Loire

Le Moulin de la Diversière

In a loop of a small river, a honey-coloured mill surrounded by trees, silence and willow-fringed paths leading to two cottages – yours for self-catering or B&B - that Anne and Jean-Marc have lovingly converted in tune with the setting and their green ideals. Outside: a big sloping garden, a play area for your children (and theirs), shady arbours, an above-ground pool. Inside: old tomettes and limewashed walls, cane chairs and fresh flowers, pretty kitchens and showers with pebble floors. Breakfast is brought to your door; table d'hotes is at your hosts' friendly table, by a roaring fire in winter. Special indeed.

Price	€60–€70.
Rooms	2 cottages: 1 for for 2-4, 1 for 2-5.
Meals	Dinner with wine, €23.
Closed	Rarely.
Directions	From Le Lude D306 for La Flèche 1.5km; left D305 to Savigné sous le Lude. Entering village, right for La Flèche; over small bridge, immed. right 600m; driveway on right.

Anne & Jean-Marc Le Foulgocq
Le Moulin de la Diversière,
72800 Savigné sous le Lude,
Sarthe

Tel	+33 (0)2 43 48 09 16
Mobile	+33 (0)6 77 44 79 95
Email	contact@moulin-de-la-diversiere.com
Web	www.moulin-de-la-diversiere.com

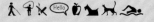

Entry 299   Map 4

Photo: Lesley Chalmers

Loire Valley

Photo: www.istockphoto.com

Loire Valley

Le Moulin de Lonceux

A placid river sets ancient mill stones grinding and flour flows; ducks dip, swans preen, geese saunter; gardens are beset by roses, herbs, bantams, goats, a hammock. The mill has been ingeniously restored by this hard-working family (she a geologist, he an engineer) into a home and – alongside, separate – a B&B managed with verve. Sleep in stables complete with manger; a flint-walled cider press; a two-room loft suite; a smart Miller's Room with fireplace. Breakfast in the dayroom (sofa, games, candles, log fire) on fresh pastries from home-milled flour (of course). Chartres is close, Paris an easy train ride. A gem.

Price	€105-€155.
Rooms	4: 3 doubles, 1 suite for 2-4.
Meals	Catered meals & cold tray on arrival, on request. Restaurant 3km.
Closed	Rarely.
Directions	A11 exit Ablis, N10 for Chartres; left at Essars r'bout for Auneau 3km; right for Levainville to Garnet; D122 for Oinville. House 300m on left.

	Isabelle Heitz
	Le Moulin de Lonceux,
	Hameau de Lonceux,
	28700 Oinville sous Auneau, Eure-et-Loir
Mobile	+33 (0)6 70 00 60 45
Email	heitzi@orange.fr
Web	www.moulin-de-lonceux.com

Entry 300   Map 5

Loire Valley

Maison JLN

Come to enjoy this gentle, charming family and the serene vibes of their old Chartrain house. Up two steep twisting spirals to the attic, through the family's little prayer room (a shell for each pilgrim who's stayed here), the sweet, peaceful bedroom feels like a chapel itself with its honey floorboards and small windows (no wardrobe). Lots of books; reminders of pilgrimage, just beneath the great cathedral; Madame knowledgeably friendly, Monsieur, who speaks nine languages, quietly amusing, both interested in your travels, both happy to sit and talk when you get back. An unusual and special place, in a timeless town.

Price	€50.
Rooms	1 twin with separate shower & wc on floor below.
Meals	Restaurants nearby.
Closed	Rarely.
Directions	In Chartres follow signs for IBIS Centre; park by Hotel IBIS Centre (Place Drouaise); walk 20m along Rue de la Porte Drouaise to Rue Muret (100m car to house).

	Jean-Loup & Nathalie Cuisiniez
	Maison JLN,
	80 rue Muret, 28000 Chartres,
	Eure-et-Loir
Tel	+33 (0)2 37 21 98 36
Mobile	+33 (0)6 79 48 46 63
Email	jln.cuisiniez@orange.fr
Web	monsite.orange.fr/maisonjln

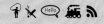

Entry 301   Map 4

Loire Valley

Chambres d'Hôtes Les Champarts

This was Dagmar's country cottage until she left Paris to settle here. She left her native Germany and adopted France many moons ago. Come for compact, cosy, immaculate B&B set in a pretty village. Breakfast is a feast: hot croissants, home-made jams, smoked salmon, farm butter. The cottage garden is cherished and, if you time it right, every old wall will be covered with roses. Up the steep stairs, one bedroom is wood-panelled, the other more typical with sloping rafters; fabrics are flowered and varnished floors symmetrically rugged. Traditional, authentic, friendly, and great fun.

Price	€50-€60.
Rooms	2: 1 double, 1 suite. Extra beds available.
Meals	Restaurants 3km.
Closed	Rarely.
Directions	From Verneuil sur Avre D939 for Chartres; in Maillebois left D20 to Blévy; in Blévy left for Laons-Dreux 200m; left D133 for Laons; house 1st on right after 50m.

Dagmar Parmentier
Chambres d'Hôtes Les Champarts,
2 route des Champarts,
28170 Blévy, Eure-et-Loir
Tel   +33 (0)2 37 48 01 21
Email   leschamparts@bab-blevy.com
Web   www.bab-blevy.com

Loire Valley

Les Charmettes

This robust 18th-century townhouse by the canal has inherited an expansive atmosphere from its wine-merchant builders; they were loading wine onto barges on the canal until the 1930s. That was the past. Nowadays, you dine with your elderly, refined hosts in a chandelier'd dining room, sleep in highly individual old-style rooms (space for 12, three bathrooms, one in a bedroom), breakfast off ravishing Gien china with fruit from the pretty garden, chat with your effusive hostess, who's been doing B&B since 1984, and her good-natured husband over a glass of local wine. She keenly arranges visits to winegrowers.

Price	€80. €150 for 4. €160 for 5.
Rooms	2: 1 suite for 4; 1 family apartment for 8 (3 bedrooms, 2 bathrooms, one in a bedroom).
Meals	Dinner with wine, €30.
Closed	Rarely.
Directions	From Orléans N60 E for Montargis & Nevers; exit to Fay aux Loges; through Fay, cross canal, left D709; house 1st on left arriving in Donnery.

Nicole & Jacques Sicot
Les Charmettes,
40 avenue Ponson du Terail,
45450 Donnery, Loiret
Tel   +33 (0)2 38 59 22 50
Email   n.sicot@wanadoo.fr

Loire Valley

Domaine de la Thiau

A vast estate by the Loire, a 19th-century house for the family, a 17th-century one for guests, exotic pheasants and peacocks strutting around the splendid grounds. Your hosts – he is a busy vet, she elegantly looks after house, gîtes and you – make it feel welcoming despite the apparent grandeur. Peaceful bedrooms are carefully decorated with carved bedsteads and papered walls – extremely, Frenchly traditional. There's a smart Victorian-style conservatory for breakfast, furnished with a large oval table and blue velvet chairs. A good address for summer. *Minimum two nights weekends, bank holidays & high season.*

Price	€58–€68.
Rooms	3: 2 doubles, 1 suite for 3 & kitchen.
Meals	Gastronomic dinner available for 2+ night stays. Restaurants 4km.
Closed	Rarely.
Directions	From A6 onto A77 for Nevers, exit Briare; D952 for Gien. Between Briare & Gien: sign Granit Design shop.

Bénédicte François
Domaine de la Thiau,
45250 Briare,
Loiret

Tel	+33 (0)2 38 38 20 92
Email	info@lathiau.fr
Web	www.lathiau.fr

Entry 304   Map 5

Loire Valley

Les Vieux Guays

Looking for seclusion? This house sits in 200 acres of woods, its grassy shrubby garden, larder for legions of fearless rabbits, rambling down to the duck-loved lake. Sandrine and Alvaro, a tennis professional, returned from Chile to the family home, now alive with two youngsters. They are a poised and friendly couple easily mixing old and modern, bright and dark. You breakfast at their long dining table before the bucolic lake view, relax in green leather in your own log-fired sitting room. In another wing, bedrooms are high quality too: antiques, excellent new bedding, plain walls and floral fabrics. Very special.

Price	€80.
Rooms	5: 2 doubles, 2 twins, 1 family suite for 4.
Meals	Dinner with wine, €30.
Closed	Rarely.
Directions	A6 from Paris; A77 exit Gien; D940 Argent sur Sauldre; D948 to Cerdon; D65 for Clémont; immed. right after level crossing; 1.5km left onto track; straight on.

Sandrine & Alvaro Martinez
Les Vieux Guays,
45620 Cerdon du Loiret,
Loiret

Tel	+33 (0)2 38 36 03 76
Mobile	+33 (0)6 80 16 53 76
Email	lvg45@orange.fr
Web	www.lesvieuxguays.com

Entry 305   Map 5

Loire Valley

La Brissauderie

Utter peace… this 1970s farmhouse is cradled in tumbling woodland and wrapped in birdsong. Goats softly bleat on the farm below. Madame is chatty and genuine, she still helps out with the animals and can arrange goat visits for children. The suite upstairs is perfect for families. It has stencilled furniture, some good family pieces, tongue-and-groove pine cladding throughout. Walls, ceilings and doors are alive with fun murals: sunflowers shine, bees bumble and butterflies flutter by. Your tasty breakfast comes with honey from a friend's bees and, of course, goat's cheese. Remarkable value.

Price	€45. €55 for 3. €75 for 4-5.
Rooms	1 suite for 4-5.
Meals	Restaurants nearby.
Closed	Mid-December to mid-January.
Directions	From Sancerre D923 for Jars & Vailly sur Sauldre; 2km before Jars right on track into wood; house at end of track, signed.

Madeleine Jay
La Brissauderie,
18260 Jars,
Cher
Tel   +33 (0)2 48 58 74 94
Email   madeleine.jay@wanadoo.fr
Web   www.labrissauderie.com

Entry 306   Map 5

Loire Valley

Moulin Guillard

Just outside the village of Subligny, not far from Sancerre, is this enchanting blue-shuttered mill; where flour was once produced is a stylish and delightful B&B. Dorothée, a fascinating and cultured woman who once ran a bookshop in Paris, divides her time between an exquisite garden of rare plants and her guests. She offers you a smallish, softly serene double upstairs, and a two-bedroom suite across the way, its private sitting room with piano downstairs. In summer you breakfast between the two, in a barn overlooking the stream and Dorothée's several breeds of free-roaming hen. Dinners are superb.

Ethical Collection: Environment.
See page 410 for details.

Price	€85.
Rooms	2: 1 double, 1 suite for 4 with sitting room.
Meals	Dinner €25. Wine from €18.
Closed	Rarely.
Directions	From Briare N7 S 8km; right to Chatillon s/Loire. D49 thro' Pierrefitte ès Bois & Sury ès Bois; follow signs to Subligny; thro' village for Cosne; last lane on right before roadside crucifix.

Dorothée Malinge
Moulin Guillard,
18260 Subligny,
Cher
Tel   +33 (0)2 48 73 70 49
Mobile   +33 (0)6 61 71 15 30
Email   malinge.annig@orange.fr

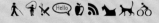

Entry 307   Map 5

Loire Valley

La Verrerie

Deep countryside, fine people, fantastic bedrooms. In a pretty outbuilding, the double, with a green iron bedhead, old tiled floor and Provençal quilt, looks onto the garden from the ground floor; the suite's twin has the same tiles underfoot, beams overhead and high wooden beds with an inviting mix of white covers and red quilts. The Count and Countess, who manage forests, farm and hunt, enjoy doing B&B-they are charming and thoroughly hospitable. If you would like to dine in, you will join them for dinner in the main house. Members of the family run a vineyard in Provence, so try their wine.

Price	€75-€110. Suite €99, €122 for 3, €145 for 4.
Rooms	3: 2 doubles, 1 family suite for 2-4.
Meals	Dinner with wine, €20-€30. Guest kitchen. Restaurants 10km.
Closed	Rarely.
Directions	From Bourges D940 to Chapelle d'Angillon; D12 to Ivoy le Pré. At church left D39 dir. Oizon; Château de la Verrerie 2.5km, gate on right.

Étienne & Marie de Saporta
La Verrerie,
18380 Ivoy le Pré,
Cher

Tel	+33 (0)2 48 58 90 86
Email	m.desaporta@wanadoo.fr
Web	www.laverreriedivoy.com

Entry 308   Map 5

Loire Valley

La Grande Mouline

Ten years ago, your hosts came to raise their family in this rustic haven where the natural garden flows into woods and fields, deer roam and birdlife astounds. Jean is a kindly grandfather, proud of his efforts in converting his outbuildings for B&B. Bedrooms reflect his far-flung travels: Indian rugs, Moroccan brasses, a collection of fossils in an old chemist's cabinet, lots of old farmhouse stuff – nothing too sophisticated. Breakfast is in the main house where family life bustles. Return after contemplating Bourges to meditate in this sweet corner of God's garden or share the above-ground pool.

Price	€47. €62 for 3. €77 for 4.
Rooms	4: 2 triples, 1 quadruple, 1 family room.
Meals	Restaurant 2.5km.
Closed	Rarely.
Directions	From Bourges D944 for Orléans. In Bourgneuf left at little r'bout; immed. right & follow signs 1.5km.

Jean Malot & Chantal Charlon
La Grande Mouline,
Bourgneuf, 18110 St Éloy de Gy,
Cher

Tel	+33 (0)2 48 25 40 44
Email	jean-m4@wanadoo.fr
Web	pagesperso-orange.fr/lagrandemouline

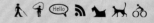

Entry 309   Map 10

Loire Valley

Domaine de l'Ermitage

In historic Berry-Bouy, in the heartland of France, this articulate husband-and-wife team run their beef and cereals farm and Menetou-Salon vineyards (tastings arranged), make their own jam and still have time for their guests. Vivacious and casually elegant, Laurence runs an intelligent, welcoming house. The big, simple yet stylishly attractive bedrooms of her superior 18th-century farmhouse are of pleasing proportions, one up a steep and twisting stair in the brick-and-timber tower, others with views over the graceful park. Guests may use the swimming pool, set discreetly out of sight, between 6 and 7pm.

Price	€71–€74. Triple €102. Quadruple €130.
Rooms	5: 2 doubles, 1 twin, 1 triple, 1 quadruple.
Meals	Restaurants in village.
Closed	Rarely.
Directions	From Vierzon N76 for Bourges through Mehun sur Yèvre; D60 right to Berry Bouy & on for approx. 3km; farm on right.

Laurence & Géraud de La Farge
Domaine de l'Ermitage,
18500 Berry-Bouy,
Cher

Tel   +33 (0)2 48 26 87 46
Email   domaine-ermitage@wanadoo.fr
Web   www.hotes-ermitage.com

Entry 310   Map 10

Loire Valley

Les Bonnets Rouges

Cross the secret garden courtyard to this venerable 15th-century house, once a coaching inn (Stendhal slept here). Beyond the breakfast room where ancient timbers, wraparound oak panels and stone alcoves dance in all their mixed-up glory for the fresh fruit and Turkish rugs, the knight in shining armour beckons you up. Bedrooms, not four-star but wonderfully quaint, have antique beds (one a four-poster), new mattresses, marble fireplaces and a claw-footed bath; the pretty attic double is festooned with beams. Your charming host lives just across the courtyard. Sleep among angels beneath that unsurpassed cathedral.

Price	€58–€80. Extra person €20.
Rooms	4: 2 doubles, 2 suites for 3–4.
Meals	Restaurants within walking distance.
Closed	Rarely.
Directions	In Bourges centre behind cathedral, Rue Bourbonnoux, 2nd on right. Park in yard if space available, otherwise phone; house 300m from cathedral.

Olivier Llopis
Les Bonnets Rouges,
3 rue de la Thaumassière,
18000 Bourges, Cher

Tel   +33 (0)2 48 65 79 92
Email   bonnets-rouges@bourges.net
Web   bonnets-rouges.bourges.net

Entry 311   Map 10

Domaine de la Trolière

The beautifully proportioned house in its big shady garden has been in the family for over 200 years. The sitting room is a cool blue-grey symphony, the dining room smart yellow-grey with a rare, remarkable maroon and grey marble table: breakfast is in here, dinner, sometimes *en famille*, always delicious, is in the big beamed kitchen. Each stylishly comfortable room has individual character and Madame has a fine eye for detail. She is charming, dynamic, casually elegant and has many cats. Visitors have poured praise: "quite the most beautiful house we've ever stayed in", "the evening meals were superb".

Price	€49-€70.
Rooms	4: 3 doubles; 1 double with separate wc.
Meals	Dinner with wine, €23-€25.
Closed	Rarely.
Directions	From A71 exit 8; at r'bout D925 W for Lignières & Châteauroux. Sign 500m on right.

	Marie-Claude Dussert
	Domaine de la Trolière,
	18200 Orval,
	Cher
Tel	+33 (0)2 48 96 47 45
Mobile	+33 (0)6 72 21 59 76
Email	marie-claude.dussert@orange.fr

Entry 312   Map 10

La Croix Verte

Vincent and Élisabeth's serene home lies plumb in the heart of George Sand country. Linger under lime trees in a secret courtyard garden while relishing a plentiful breakfast; enjoy a dinner of home-grown produce; get cosy in the family sitting room before an open fire. A staging post in the 12th century, La Croix Verte stands in the heart of the village but you won't hear a peep as you slumber under a hand-stitched bed-cover; the two charming loft bedrooms in natural tones share sofas, books and games. Come for heaps of character, unspoilt countryside, and artist hosts (potter and painter) who are an absolute delight.

Price	€55.
Rooms	3: 2 doubles, 1 twin.
Meals	Dinner €22. Restaurant 1.5km.
Closed	Rarely.
Directions	From Châteauroux D943 for La Châtre. Left after Corlay D69 to St Chartier. House in village on right, just after château.

	Élisabeth Portier
	La Croix Verte,
	Le Bourg, 12 rue des Maîtres Sonneurs,
	36400 St Chartier, Indre
Tel	+33 (0)2 54 31 02 71
Email	contact@veportier.com
Web	www.veportier.com

Entry 313   Map 10

Loire Valley

Château de la Villette

More pretty 19th-century hunting lodge than grand château, la Villette sits in 40 idyllic acres of parkland, close to a huge spring-fed lake: borrow the row boat and potter. Capable, hospitable, generous Karin – dynamic gardener, fine cook – loves and cares for each inch of the place. A winding staircase leads to a beauty of a bedroom done in Biedermeier style, with a sloping ceiling and serene views; the second room too is seductive. Feather duvets will cosset you, elegant breakfasts and dinners at the convent table will delight you, and nothing is too much trouble for Karin. *New natural swimming pool.*

Price	€80–€90.
Rooms	2: 1 double; 1 double with separate bath.
Meals	Dinner with wine, €25.
Closed	Rarely.
Directions	From Châteauroux D943 to La Châtre, after Ardentes left D14 for St Août 6km; left at La Villette sign 400m.

Karin Verburgh
Château de la Villette,
St Août, 36120 Ardentes,
Indre
Tel   +33 (0)2 54 36 28 46

Entry 314   Map 10

Loire Valley

La Chasse

This delightful and hard-working English couple came to farm in France with their two boys and invite you to drive down a long bumpy track through pretty woods where wild deer roam to their farmhouse. Expect wellie boots by the door and Jack Russells on arrival, a dining room in the sitting room, some old beams still and a stone fireplace, and restful bedrooms that are big, pale-floored and 1970s comfortable. Alison gives you cereals and muesli for breakfast, Robin may tell you tales of keeping cattle, shearing French sheep or where to gaze on rare orchids. Argenton, 'Venice of the Indre', is a must.

Price	€58. Family room €72.
Rooms	3: 1 double; 1 double, 1 family room for 4, sharing bath & separate wc.
Meals	Dinner with wine, €28.
Closed	January-March.
Directions	From Châteauroux A20 exit 16 to Tendu; 1st left in village. Pass Mairie, fork left at church for Chavin & Pommiers for 1.5km; left up track for 2km.

Robin & Alison Mitchell
La Chasse,
36200 Tendu,
Indre
Tel   +33 (0)2 54 24 07 76
Email   mitchell.robin@wanadoo.fr

Entry 315   Map 9

Loire Valley

Le Canard au Parapluie Rouge

This pretty 17th-century house has been welcoming travellers for most of its history: it was once the Auberge de la Gare; the station has gone but a TGV occasionally shoots past, disturbing the sleepy calm. Kathy and Martin are great fun – she's from Ohio, he's from Wiltshire – and will make you feel instantly at home. Each of the sunny little bedrooms has a charm and flavour of its own and the low-beamed sitting room opens onto a big, enclosed garden. Meals are served in the elegant dining room or out under the trees. Kathy loves cooking and Martin grows the vegetables. It's all absurdly good value.

Price	€55–€85.
Rooms	4 doubles.
Meals	Dinner with wine, €22.
Closed	Rarely.
Directions	A20 exit 19 for Celon; 1st right as you enter village; signed.

Martin & Kathy Missen
Le Canard au Parapluie Rouge,
3 rue des Rollets,
36200 Celon, Indre

Tel	+33 (0)2 54 25 30 08
Email	info@lecanardbandb.com
Web	lecanardbandb.com

Entry 316   Map 9

Loire Valley

La Gaucherie

A peaceful young family, a gentle welcome, and a beautifully restored, L-shaped farmhouse hidden away in the conifer forests of the Sologne, with plenty of grassed space around it and a pretty orchard. Aurélia, who ran a restaurant and studied art in New York, loves light and simplicity: colours are beige and ecru, furniture wooden and roughly planed. The stable conversion has a rustic sitting room with wood-burning stove and red sofas; floors are terracotta or seagrass, bathrooms are pebbled or mosaic'd. Rejoice in ponies and hens for the children, home-produced eggs and lamb, a lake with boat and a fenced, heated pool.

Price	€65–€145.
Rooms	5: 2 doubles, 1 twin/double, 2 suites for 4.
Meals	Dinner with wine, €25.
Closed	Mid-January to mid-February.
Directions	From Langon, right at bakery & past church for Romorantin; at top of hill fork for Bois aux Frères, cont. for 7km; right at T-junc. 500m; right, 1st right.

Aurélia Curnin
La Gaucherie,
Route de Méry, Dep 76,
41320 Langon, Loir-et-Cher

Tel	+33 (0)2 54 96 42 23
Mobile	+33 (0)6 88 80 45 93
Email	lagaucherie@wanadoo.fr
Web	www.lagaucherie.com

Entry 317   Map 5

Loire Valley

Le Bouchot

Come not for luxury but for deep country authenticity – and to make friends with a generous, charming, free-thinking family who gave up Paris for this lush corner of France. They have restored, renovated and eco-converted a run-down farm, insulated it with hemp, wattle and daub, then added wood-burning stoves, organic breakfasts… and cats, dogs, horses, hens, donkeys, sheep. Bedrooms in outbuildings round the courtyard are wood-clad with sloping celings, rudimentary furnishings, mix and match bed linen, the odd rug. Dinner is in the kitchen diner – or the barns when there are campers. A place for new horizons.

Ethical Collection: Environment.
See page 410 for details.

Price	€65-€75.
Rooms	3: 1 family room for 3, 1 family room for 4, 1 suite for 2-7.
Meals	Dinner with wine, €25. Restaurant 2km.
Closed	Rarely.
Directions	From Orléans A71 for Vierzon, exit 3 to Lamotte Beuvron; D23 & D55 to Pierrefitte sur Sauldre; right in church square onto D126 for Chaon; 1km to house.

	Anne & Jean-Philippe Beau-Douëzy
	Le Bouchot,
	Route de Chaon, 41300 Pierrefitte sur Sauldre, Loir-et-Cher
Tel	+33 (0)2 54 88 03 33
Mobile	+33 (0)6 71 57 61 26
Email	contact@lebouchot.net
Web	www.lebouchot.net

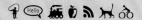

Entry 318   Map 5

Loire Valley

Les Bordes

With a sweeping farmyard, a pond and absolutely charming hosts, this is, as one reader puts it, "a gem of a B&B". Élisabeth and Guy are a smiling couple who give you their time without invading your space and are delighted to show you round their immaculate farm, orchard and vegetable garden should you be interested; they also do genuine table d'hôtes. Spotless bedrooms have floral walls and firm mattresses, furniture is modest, bathrooms are deeply raftered, and the farmhouse breathes through its timbers. You can gaze for miles across fields filled with lark song and cereals; it is serenely peaceful here.

Price	€43-€46. €86-€92 for 4.
Rooms	2: 1 double, 1 suite for 4.
Meals	Dinner with wine, €20.
Closed	Rarely.
Directions	From Vendôme D957 for Blois 6km. Right to Crucheray & Chambres d'Hôtes. 4km from turning; signed.

	Élisabeth & Guy Tondereau
	Les Bordes,
	41100 Crucheray,
	Loir-et-Cher
Tel	+33 (0)2 54 77 05 43
Email	ge.tondereau@wanadoo.fr

Entry 319   Map 4

Loire Valley

Carrefour de l'Ormeau

A woody minimalism from Alain, music lover, painter, craftsman, keen cyclist and font of local knowledge, and Isabelle, who loves to cook. In big bedrooms of monastic simplicity, nothing distracts from the natural warmth of old tiles and Alain's smooth, contemporary, local-wood furniture: all is light, space, harmony. The magnificent room under the rafters is used for exhibitions of Alain's creativity. Isabelle's lush village garden centres on its potager and there's a little path through the 'wild' wood beyond: this big house is a meeting of market-place and wilderness where people grow. *Shiatsu massage. Organic cookery courses.*

Ethical Collection: Environment & Food. See page 410 for details.

Price	€53. Triple €70. Suite €87–€104.
Rooms	4: 1 double, 2 triples, 1 suite for 4–5.
Meals	Dinner with wine, €25.
Closed	Rarely.
Directions	From Le Mans N157 for Orléans 52km; left D921 to Mondoubleau; Carrefour de l'Ormeau is central village junction; house on corner opp. Ford garage.

	Alain Gaubert & Isabelle Peyron-Gaubert Carrefour de l'Ormeau, 41170 Mondoubleau, Loir-et-Cher
Tel	+33 (0)2 54 80 93 76
Email	isabelle@carrefour-de-lormeau.com
Web	www.carrefour-de-lormeau.com

Entry 320   Map 4

Loire Valley

L'île ô reflets

Just below the troglodyte village of Trôo is a mill in a deliciously green setting. With its river banks, wash houses, barns and wisteria-clad cottages, it has the air of an old-fashioned hamlet. Martial adores it and has big plans. He's converting an old turbine for electricity and has restored the main house to perfection: each fresh, comfortable, French-feminine bedroom is inspired by a La Fontaine fable, bathrooms are spotless. Outside are terraces and topiary, an orchard and a meadow mown by donkeys. Best of all, the place has its own island, reached by a bridge.

Ethical Collection: Environment, Food & Community. See page 410 for details.

Price	€60–€80.
Rooms	4: 1 double, 1 family room for 3, 2 suites for 3. Cots available.
Meals	Dinner with wine, €25.
Closed	Rarely.
Directions	From Vendôme D917 for Château du Loir & La Flèche 25km thro' Montoire sur le Loir to Trôo; thro' village for Sougé; left to Moulin de la Plaine at exit of Trôo.

	Martial Chevallier L'île ô reflets, Moulin de la Plaine, 41800 Trôo, Loir-et-Cher
Tel	+33 (0)2 54 72 57 84
Email	martial.chevallier@wanadoo.fr
Web	www.moulindelaplaine.com

Entry 321   Map 4

Loire Valley

La Villa Médicis

Why the Italian name, the Italianate look? Queen Marie de Médicis used to take the waters here in the 17th century: the fine garden still has a hot spring and the Loire flows regally past behind the huge old trees. Muriel, a flower-loving perfectionist (artificial blooms as well as fresh), has let loose her decorative flair on the interior. It is unmistakably yet adventurously French in its splash of colours, lush fabrics and fine details. Fine antiques and brass beds grace some rooms, while the suite is a great 1930s surprise with a super-smart bathroom. You are wonderfully well looked after in this elegant and stylish house.

Price	€69.50. €79 for 3.
Rooms	4: 2 twins, 1 triple, 1 suite.
Meals	Dinner with wine, €32.
Closed	In winter, except by arrangement.
Directions	Macé is 5km north of Blois along D2152 for Orléans. In village follow signs.

Muriel Cabin-Saint-Marcel
La Villa Médicis,
Macé, 41000 St Denis sur Loire,
Loir-et-Cher
Tel   +33 (0)2 54 74 46 38
Email   medicis.bienvenue@wanadoo.fr
Web   lavillamedicis.com

Entry 322   Map 4

Loire Valley

16 place St Louis

In the cobbled streets of Blois, smack bang in front of the cathedral, is this elegant townhouse. Inside, an antique staircase twists up three floors filled with treasures: an old gramophone, a grandfather clock, bright Malian paintings. The best room at the top has a Turner–inspired view over rooftops to the river Loire. Marie, anglophile, a passionate historian and a perfect hostess, makes fresh, copious, high-quality breakfasts; eat in a courtyard bursting with flowers in summer. Then head for the countryside – or hop in a hot air balloon and spy the châteaux from above. A dreamy place. *Minimum two nights July/August.*

Price	€80-€140.
Rooms	3: 1 double, 1 twin, 1 suite.
Meals	Restaurants in town.
Closed	Rarely.
Directions	From Tours A10 for Blois/Paris exit 17; N252 then N152, right Bd Eugène Riffault; 1st left. House on cathedral square opp. car park.

Marie Escoffre
16 place St Louis,
41000 Blois,
Loir-et-Cher
Tel   +33 (0)2 54 74 13 61
Mobile   +33 (0)6 14 54 36 68
Email   16placesaintlouis@free.fr
Web   www.16placesaintlouis.fr

Entry 323   Map 4

Loire Valley

Le Clos Pasquier

Plumb in château country, Blois forest and the Loire on the doorstep, here is what the gracious Nicots left busy jobs for: a beautiful house with chunky beams and stone floors in a sweet, peaceful setting. Delicious furniture and a huge fireplace fit the garden suite; smaller Salamandre and Porc-épic – royal emblems – are minimalist and classy. In the salon are winter fires and tempting jars of sweets; at breakfast you feast on Claire's own brioches, croissants and jams, and smoothies in summer. Explore the Loire on a borrowed bike, delve into historic Blois. Stunning. *Amma massage available. Min.two nights July/August.*

Price	€110. Suites €130.
Rooms	4: 2 twins, 2 suites.
Meals	Restaurants in Blois, 6km.
Closed	Rarely.
Directions	From A10 exit 17 to Blois; N152 along Loire for Tours 4km; right to Auberge de Jeunesse; right at church; Rue de l'Hôtel Pasquier to woods. Left at r'bout.

Laurent & Claire Nicot
Le Clos Pasquier,
10-12 impasse de l'Orée du Bois,
41000 Blois, Loir-et-Cher

Tel	+33 (0)2 54 58 84 08
Mobile	+33 (0)6 07 35 20 14
Email	leclospasquier@orange.fr
Web	www.leclospasquier.fr

Entry 324   Map 4

Loire Valley

Château de Nanteuil

Rushing water is a constant here: the river speeds below your window into lush meadows. It's a landscape unaltered by time, just like this grand old wisteria-hung house – once Grand-mère's. Rooms have a faded, film-set quality: frescoes and trunks in the hall, stags' heads and chandeliers in the dining room, floral wallpapers and marble fireplaces in the bedrooms. These are light-filled and unstylishly old-fashioned, but there's charm in 'Roi' and 'Rose'. Bathrooms, in contrast, are modern. Most of all, you'll love Frédéric's fabulous organic cooking – tuck into asparagus in season and baked fillet of perch. Best in summer.

Ethical Collection: Food.
See page 410 for details.

Price	€70-€85.
Rooms	5: 2 doubles, 2 family rooms for 3, 1 family suite for 4.
Meals	Dinner with wine, €28.
Closed	Rarely.
Directions	A10 for Tours, exit 16 Mer for Chambord; D33 right to Huisseau sur Cosson; cont. 4km; right to château. Entrance on right thro' high stone-pillared gateway.

Frédéric Théry
Château de Nanteuil,
41350 Huisseau sur Cosson,
Loir-et-Cher

Tel	+33 (0)2 54 42 61 98
Mobile	+33 (0)6 88 83 79 84
Email	chateau.nanteuil@free.fr
Web	www.chateau-nanteuil.com

Entry 325   Map 4

Loire Valley

Les Chambres Vertes

Flowers fill the quadrangle formed by the house (16th- and 19th-century) and an old wall; a fountain adds coolness. Your rooms are in the former stables opposite Sophie's house, each with a slate porch; her's has this slate running its full length, giving shelter from sun and rain. Outside the quadrangle is a covered patio for drinks and delicious organic meals, overlooking countryside... all this just a stone's throw from the village. The rooms, on the ground floor, are uncluttered, exquisitely simple, with attractive no-frills bathrooms. The mood is natural, artistic, delightful. Parisienne Sophie lives the dream.

Ethical Collection: Environment & Food. See page 410 for details.

Price	€61-€67.
Rooms	3: 2 doubles, 1 twin.
Meals	Dinner with wine, €24.
Closed	Occasionally.
Directions	A10 from Paris, exit Blois for Châteauroux D956, 15km; left just after village sign Cormeray 800m; left. 1st house on left.

Sophie Gélinier
Les Chambres Vertes,
Le Clos de la Chartrie,
41120 Cormeray, Loir-et-Cher
Tel   +33 (0)2 54 20 24 95
Email   sophie@chambresvertes.net
Web   www.chambresvertes.net

Entry 326   Map 4

Loire Valley

Le Cormier

Wake in the morning and sigh with pleasure at the beauty of the garden: box hedges and cottage flowers, sweet herbs, poplars and an iris-fringed pond. Then think about breakfasting on garden fruits and homemade banana bread... Californian Michael and Dutch Marie-Louise rescued this long, low farmhouse and barn from ruin; it's hard to imagine more endearing hosts. The suites are exceedingly pretty, with creamy stone walls, overhead beams, dainty fabrics and ethnic rugs; each has its very own salon with kettle, fridge, books, magazines, logs for the fire. One has its own little kitchen. Perfect peace, and not another house in sight. *Unfenced water.*

Price	€90-€100.
Rooms	2 suites, one with kitchen.
Meals	Restaurant nearby.
Closed	November-April.
Directions	From Blois cross Loire; D751 to Chailles; D764 to Sambin centre; right to Chaumont 1.5km; left at sign for Le Cormier; 3km to house.

Michael & Marie-Louise Harvey
Le Cormier,
41120 Sambin,
Loir-et-Cher
Tel   +33 (0)2 54 33 29 47
Email   michael@lecormier.com
Web   www.lecormier.com

Entry 327   Map 4

Loire Valley

Prieuré de la Chaise

Sheer delight for the senses: stunning ancient buildings outside, Madame's decorations within. The 13th-century chapel, still used on the village feast day, and the 'new' manor house (1500s) are awash with history, 16th-century antiques, tapestries and loveliness – huge sitting and dining rooms, and a winding staircase to the room in the tower. One room has a large stone fireplace, a magnificent rug, and limewashed beams. The setting is superb, mature trees shade the beautiful gardens, there are horses in the paddock and you are surrounded by vines; ask your friendly, dynamic hostess to arrange tastings.

Price	€70–€90. Suites €130 for 2, extra person €20.
Rooms	5: 2 doubles, 2 suites for 3, 1 suite for 5.
Meals	Restaurants nearby.
Closed	Rarely.
Directions	St Georges is between Chenonceau & Montrichard on N76. In town centre, up hill to La Chaise; on up Rue du Prieuré. No. 8 has heavy wooden gates.

Danièle Therizols
Prieuré de la Chaise,
8 rue du Prieuré, 41400 St Georges
sur Cher, Loir-et-Cher

Tel	+33 (0)2 54 32 59 77
Email	prieuredelachaise@yahoo.fr
Web	www.prieuredelachaise.com

Entry 328   Map 4

Loire Valley

Le Moulin du Port

An irresistible walk starts at your doorstep: Thierry will tell you how to follow the wide, beautiful river Cher all the way to Chenonceau. The tall 19th-century mill, in its own wooded grounds, is also handy for other Loire châteaux. The bedrooms (to which there's a lift) are shamelessly pretty, the bathrooms new and luxurious, and there's a pleasant ground-floor sitting area overlooking the old mill wheel. The friendly Moreaus, busy with gîtes, young family and B&B, serve a fabulous breakfast, in the yellow-walled veranda/dining room, based on local produce and, perhaps, Isabelle's apple and strawberry juice.

Ethical Collection: Food.
See page 410 for details.

Price	€100–€120.
Rooms	5: 4 doubles, 1 twin.
Meals	Restaurant 800m.
Closed	Rarely.
Directions	From Tours D976 for Vierzon to St Georges sur Cher; left at r'bout & 2nd left into lane; entrance on right, high iron gates.

Isabelle Moreau
Le Moulin du Port,
26 rue du Gué de l'Arche,
41400 St Georges sur Cher, Loir-et-Cher

Tel	+33 (0)2 54 32 01 37
Email	info.alsam@lemoulinduport.com
Web	www.lemoulinduport.com

Entry 329   Map 4

Le Moutier

The artist's touch and Jean-Lou's paintings vibrate throughout this house of tradition and originality where you will feel instantly at home. Note one of the bedrooms is accessed via the owner's studio, heaving with paintings and brushes! Of the four, we like best the top-floor one in the house, cosy and bright with white walls, dark green woodwork and a yellow spread over a sturdy brass bed. There's an understated elegance in the sitting and dining rooms, a charming garden, throngs of fruit trees and some loitering hens. Above all, great table d'hôtes: good food and wine generously low. *Ask about painting & French courses.*

Price	€65.
Rooms	4: 2 doubles. Studio: 2 doubles.
Meals	Dinner with wine, €30.
Closed	Rarely.
Directions	From Blois D956 to Contres; D675 to St Aignan; over bridge; D17 right to Mareuil sur Cher. House on left in hamlet La Maison des Marchands (just before cat breeder sign) before main village.

Martine & Jean-Lou Coursaget
Le Moutier,
13 rue de la République,
41110 Mareuil sur Cher, Loir-et-Cher

Tel	+33 (0)2 54 75 20 48
Email	lemoutier.coursaget@wanadoo.fr
Web	www.chambresdhotesdumoutier.com

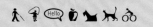

Entry 330   Map 4

Le Moulin de Montrésor

Do you dream of living in a watermill? Your hosts have converted theirs, near the magnificent château of Montrésor, in stylish and simple good taste: a wooden staircase leading to a coconut-matted landing, family portraits, super colours, pretty rooms with lots of light and original features... and quiet flows the water over the wheel beneath the glass panel in the dining room. Madame is cultured and well-travelled, her family has had the château for 200 years but no-one stands on ceremony and there's a sense of timeless peace here. The plain garden has a fenced, child-friendly pool.

Price	€70–€80. Under 4s free.
Rooms	4: 1 double, 1 twin, 2 triples.
Meals	Dinner €25. Restaurants within 5km.
Closed	Rarely.
Directions	From Loches D760 to Montrésor; left for Chemillé; mill on left; signed.

Sophie & Alain Willems de Ladersous
Le Moulin de Montrésor,
37460 Montrésor,
Indre-et-Loire

Tel	+33 (0)2 47 92 68 20
Email	alain.willems@wanadoo.fr
Web	www.moulindemontresor.fr

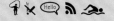

Entry 331   Map 9

Loire Valley

La Tinellière

A pretty hamlet farmhouse, a gentle old goose wandering the garden, a glass of homemade *épine*. Éliane, a welcoming, enthusiastic hostess, loves talking to people about their interests and hers and is constantly improving her rooms, a ground-floor, mezzanine'd quadruple (with ladder and gate), now exotic with Vietnamese hangings, and another larger room in the converted stable. Parts of the house are 17th-century with massive beams and well-mixed new and old furniture, wild and dried flowers, colours and fabrics. The living room is darkish, beamed and cosy, the guests' kitchenette brand new.

Price	€52–€55.
Rooms	2 quadruples.
Meals	Guest kitchenette. Auberge 3km.
Closed	Rarely.
Directions	From A10 exit 24.1 for Sorigny. Passing Sorigny, right D910 for 9.5km; left D101 through St Catherine de Fierbois for Bossé; right 3km to La Tinellière. Signed.

	Éliane Pelluard
	La Tinellière,
	37800 Ste Catherine de Fierbois,
	Indre-et-Loire
Tel	+33 (0)2 47 65 61 80
Mobile	+33 (0)6 59 05 75 49
Email	elianepelluard@neuf.fr

Loire Valley

Le Moulin de St Jean

The restored mill in its delicious island setting is all ups and downs, nooks and crannies, big rooms and small, character and variety. Your delightful hosts fled city jobs for a quieter life, he bringing his love of Loire wines (just ask), she her passion for quilts and her cooking skills. Assorted wallpapers, patterns, frills and furniture – and a welcome bottle of wine – make for a warm, homely feel. Plus new mattresses and good bathrooms, two sitting rooms, numerous DVDs and books, a shady garden, a heated pool – and all the fascinations of the Loire Valley. *Not suitable for young children: unfenced water.*

Price	€75–€85.
Rooms	4: 2 doubles, 1 twin, 1 suite.
Meals	Dinner €15–€25. Wine from €10.
Closed	Rarely.
Directions	From Tours A85 exit Esvres; D943 to Loches 25km; cont. D943 thro' Perusson; D492 to St Jean; 300m to small bridge over river Indre. Entrance from bridge on left.

	Barbara & John Maxwell
	Le Moulin de St Jean,
	St Jean - St Germain,
	37600 Loches, Indre-et-Loire
Tel	+33 (0)2 47 94 70 12
Email	lemoulinstjean@club-internet.fr
Web	www.lemoulinstjean.com

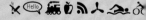

Loire Valley

La Demeure St-Ours

Climb the twisting rustic staircase of this slender 16th-century house, breathe in the history of Loches' ancient cobbles. Your entertaining host loves this old quarter, plumb in the town centre. Enter, by day, through an art gallery to rooms cosily stacked on top of each other like a vertical jigsaw puzzle. Gauzy curtains and bed-covers come in red, yellow and orange 'à l'orientale'; a table and chair for reading or writing, books on the Touraine to browse. Downstairs, the old-beamed, tiled dining room doubles as a sitting room. Flexible breakfast includes local goat's cheese and eggs. The markets of Loches are memorable.

Loire Valley

Les Bournais

Philippe and Florence are outstanding hosts in a jewel of a place. The old farm, lovingly restored, is set round a pretty courtyard. Flo has a studio at one end, where she paints and the bedrooms are in the rustic stables, upstairs and down. Each is delightful with heaps of space, stripy fabrics and brocante finds, armchairs, bolsters, books and fresh flowers. Walls are stone, floors tiled and spotless. Showers are walk-in and colourful. Excellent traditional dinners with innovative touches are served round a rustic table and breakfasts are moveable feasts. Cats, horses and hens add to the country charm.

Price	€50–€75.	Price	€68.
Rooms	3: 1 double, 1 twin, 1 triple.	Rooms	4 doubles, each with extra bed.
Meals	Restaurant 20m.	Meals	Dinner with wine, €20.
Closed	Rarely.		Barbecue available.
Directions	From Loches centre for Château/ Cité Médiévale; free parking Porte Royale, 50m from Rue des Fossés St Ours, next to Rue du Château.	Closed	Rarely.
		Directions	Leave A10 at Ste Maure de Touraine; D760 to L'île Bouchard; cross river; D757 for Richelieu. Les Bournais signed left just before entering Brizay.

Claude Reben
La Demeure St-Ours,
11 rue du Château,
37600 Loches, Indre-et-Loire
Mobile +33 (0)6 33 74 54 82
Email   saintours@orange.fr
Web   www.saintours.eu

Philippe & Florence Martinez
Les Bournais,
37220 Theneuil,
Indre-et-Loire
Tel   +33 (0)2 47 95 29 61
Email   les.bournais@orange.fr
Web   www.lesbournais.net

Entry 334   Map 9

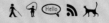

Entry 335   Map 9

Loire Valley

Domaine de Beauséjour

Dug into the hillside with the forest behind and a panorama of vines in front, this wine-grower's manor successfully pretends it was built in the 1800s. Venerable oak beams and stone cut by troglodyte masons create a mood of stylish rusticity. Charming bedrooms have carved bedheads, big puffy eiderdowns, old prints, vases of fresh and artificial flowers; bathrooms are elegant and the sweetest rooms are in the tower by the pool. Make sure you buy some (discounted) wine to take home. When not away at a wine fair, Parisienne Marie-Claude looks after you with panache. *Minimum two nights. Sawday self-catering also.*

Price	€70–€90. €120 for 4.
Rooms	3: 2 doubles, 1 suite for 3-4.
Meals	Restaurants 5km.
Closed	Rarely.
Directions	From Chinon D21 to Cravant les Côteaux. On towards Panzoult; house on left after 2km.

Marie-Claude Chauveau
Domaine de Beauséjour,
37220 Panzoult,
Indre-et-Loire
Tel   +33 (0)2 47 58 64 64
Email   dom.beausejour@wanadoo.fr
Web   www.domainedebeausejour.com

Loire Valley

La Baumoderie

Anne designed interiors in Paris, Jean-François managed hotels, now they do B&B from their imaginatively restored farmhouse on the top of a hill. Lively, charming people, they serve excellent French dinners in a modern chandelier'd conservatory and give guests two rustic-elegant rooms: one cool and spacious on the ground floor (with just French windows) and a suite at the top of an outside stone staircase; wake to splendid views. You can walk from the house, canoe on the Vienne, taste the wines of Chinon. The garden blends into the landscape, the small village is up the road, and peace reigns supreme.

Price	€90–€125.
Rooms	2: 1 double, 1 suite.
Meals	Lunch or dinner €30, with wine. Restaurant 4km.
Closed	Rarely.
Directions	From Tours D751 for Chinon; at Azay le Rideau D757 for L'Île Bouchard; at r'bout 3km before L'Ile Bouchard, right to Panzoult, 1st right. Signed.

Anne Tardits
La Baumoderie,
17 rue d'Étilly, 37220 Panzoult,
Indre-et-Loire
Mobile   +33 (0)6 08 78 00 73
Email   anne@labaumoderie.fr
Web   www.labaumoderie.fr

Loire Valley

Les Camélias de Pallus

Follow the pathway through Patricia's pretty garden to her long low farmhouse and you'll find yourself in a cool, stone-flagged hall guarded by a rocking horse. Beyond is the cosy guest sitting room where meals are served; the food is excellent and much of the fruit and vegetables come fresh from the garden. Open stairs lead to the attic suite: two airy, very charming rooms divided by a sitting area, with a good-sized bathroom. (They're under the rafters but have fans for warm nights.) The house is in a gently sloping valley, with fine walks through the vineyards to the river and the forest.

Price	€82–€115.
Rooms	2: 1 suite for 4. Outbuilding: 1 double & kitchenette.
Meals	Dinner €30. Wine €10–€18.
Closed	Rarely.
Directions	From A10 exit Ste Maure de Touraine for L'Île Bouchard; D21 to Panzoult & cont. for Cravant. House on left 2.8km after Panzoult.

Patricia & Christian Périn-Nguyen
Les Camélias de Pallus,
37500 Cravant les Côteaux,
Indre-et-Loire

Tel	+33 (0)2 47 93 08 94
Mobile	+33 (0)6 60 23 26 29
Email	camelias.pallus@wanadoo.fr
Web	www.lescamelias.fr

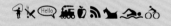

Entry 338   Map 9

Loire Valley

Le Clos de Ligré

This former wine-grower's house sings in a subtle harmony of traditional charm and contemporary chic under Martine's thoroughly modern touch. Sponged walls, creamy beams and eye-catching fabrics breathe new life into rooms with old tiled floors and stone fireplaces – and there are two newer big beamy doubles in the attic. Windows are flung open to let in the light and the stresses of city living are forgotten in cheerful, easy conversations with your hostess, who joins guests for candlelit dinners. Bookcases, billiard table and baby grand, buffet breakfasts at the long table, a pool for the energetic – delightful.

Price	€100–€110.
Rooms	5: 4 doubles, 1 family suite.
Meals	Dinner with wine, €35.
Closed	Rarely.
Directions	From Chinon D749 for Richelieu; 1km after r'bout D115 right for 'Ligré par le vignoble' 5km; left to Le Rouilly; left at Dozon warehouse; house 800m on left.

Martine Descamps
Le Clos de Ligré,
Le Rouilly, 37500 Ligré,
Indre-et-Loire

Tel	+33 (0)2 47 93 95 59
Email	mdescamps@club-internet.fr
Web	www.le-clos-de-ligre.com

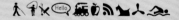

Entry 339   Map 9

Loire Valley

Le Châtaignier

A pretty old stone farmhouse on the edge of a hamlet, beautifully restored by Odile – and Jean-Joseph who loves his garden. With open lawns, swings, boules, fruit trees and a vast chestnut tree that gives the house its name, it's a joy to spend time in; and now there's a summer kitchen. The décor is cool and charming, the bedrooms, each with a private entrance, are inviting. Artistic Odile who speaks good English, presents you with a homemade lavender bag on leaving, a typically delightful touch. Sunny, country-elegant sitting and dining rooms open to the garden, and the fields stretch for miles. Special!

Price	€68. €110 for 4.
Rooms	2: 1 suite for 2 & sofabed, 1 suite for 4 (2 twin rooms separated by outside stair).
Meals	Summer kitchen. Restaurant 3km.
Closed	Rarely.
Directions	From Tours D751 to Chinon; cont. onto D759 for Loudun 6.5km. At Beuxes left to La Roberderie. Left at x-roads in hamlet, 4th house on left.

	Odile & Jean-Joseph Crescenzo
	Le Châtaignier,
	16 rue du Carroi, La Roberderie,
	37500 Marcay, Indre-et-Loire
Tel	+33 (0)2 47 93 97 09
Mobile	+33 (0)6 71 42 22 15
Email	info@lechataignier.com
Web	lechataignier.free.fr

Entry 340   Map 9

Loire Valley

84 quai Jeanne d'Arc

An elegant, screened townhouse by the stately river Vienne, lived in by a delightful, devoted couple – she exuberant and chic, he literary and musical. Deep chairs round the brass coffee table call for bright, convivial conversation; the dining alcove brings gasps of delight; the bedrooms have huge, beautiful personalities, each detail lovingly chosen. A sleigh bed here, a Chinese carpet there, a pretty mirror over a basin with a border painted in trompe l'œil, beautifully laundered linen. In the centre of medieval Chinon with the nicest possible hosts and 'gourmand' breakfasts. *Minimum two nights.*

Price	€95.
Rooms	1 twin/double.
Meals	Restaurants within walking distance.
Closed	October-March.
Directions	Entering Chinon on D751 from Tours, along river past bridge & Rabelais statue; house just after post office.

	Jany & Jean Grosset
	84 quai Jeanne d'Arc,
	37500 Chinon,
	Indre-et-Loire
Tel	+33 (0)2 47 98 42 78
Email	lamaisondesbellesvues@orange.fr
Web	www.lamaisondesbellesvues.com

Entry 341   Map 4

Loire Valley

Cheviré

Wonderful hosts, wonderful surroundings. You stay in the well-converted stable block of a traditional farmhouse on the edge of a peaceful village – all a-shimmer in the Loire's inimitable light. Welcome to the protected wetlands between the Loire and the Vienne. Pretty, uncluttered bedrooms, each a good size, display a happy mix of old and new; there's space to sit and cook, and new bathrooms gleam. The meadows are full of birds and fritillaries, and the treasures of Chinon await, as do the wines of Bourgueil and Saumur. "Very clean, very friendly, very good breakfasts," say our readers. Superb value, too.

Price	€43–€50.
Rooms	3: 1 double, 2 triples with extra bed.
Meals	Guest kitchenette. Restaurant 1km.
Closed	Mid-November to mid-March.
Directions	From Chinon D749 for Bourgueil 6km; left to Savigny en Véron; in village follow 'Camping'; house 1km after campsite on right.

Marie-Françoise & Michel Chauvelin
Cheviré,
11 rue Basse, 37420 Savigny en Véron,
Indre-et-Loire
Tel +33 (0)2 47 58 42 49
Email chauvelin.michel@wanadoo.fr
Web www.ch-hotes-chevire.fr

Entry 342   Map 4

Loire Valley

La Chancellerie

Unwind in this elegant 18th-century house, set apart from the village by rather grand walled gardens. An energetic perfectionist, Élisabeth loves to entertain and gives you delicious meals on fine china in the rustic kitchen or the sophisticated salon. Guests are treated to sofas, a bar and games in the large 'cave', and stylish bedrooms in two wings. Expect sweeping tiled and carpeted floors, exposed beams, big beds, polished antiques, and a tiny oratory in the Azur suite: the peace of the convent here. Outside are lawn, swings, fenced pool and a semi-wild 'English' garden. Delightful. *Minimum two nights July/August.*

Price	€119–€144.
Rooms	3: 1 double, 2 family suites for 4.
Meals	Dinner with wine, €40.
Closed	Rarely.
Directions	From Chinon D16 to Huismes. After 400m, left on entering village; house on corner, 100m.

Élisabeth & Christian Maury
La Chancellerie,
37420 Huismes,
Indre-et-Loire
Tel +33 (0)2 47 95 46 76
Email christian.maury1@oange.fr
Web www.lachancellerie.com

Entry 343   Map 4

Loire Valley

Le Moulin de Touvois

Delightful, good-natured, hospitable Myriam and Jean-Claude have renovated the old miller's house in a blend of styles; now stonework, beams and terracotta mix with good modern furniture. The Moroccan tiled dining table looks great beside the big old stone fireplace; simple, smallish, comfortable bedrooms have tiled or parquet floors and crisp bedding. Best of all is the garden, with its planked bridge, orchard, swings and pool, and shady terrace by the bucolic stream. Three hens contentedly roam, horses dot the paddock, the food is delicious and Jean-Claude arranges visits to wine growers. Wonderful value.

Price	€60–€65.
Rooms	5: 2 doubles, 2 twins/doubles, 1 triple.
Meals	Dinner with wine, €25.
Closed	Mid-November to mid-February.
Directions	From A85 exit Saumur; D10 & D35 to Bourgueil; at r'bout on Bourgueil ring road (north), D749 for Gizeux 4km; right in Touvois after bridge on bend; 200m on left.

Myriam & Jean-Claude Marchand
Le Moulin de Touvois,
3 rue du Moulin de Touvois,
37140 Bourgueil, Indre-et-Loire
Tel   +33 (0)2 47 97 87 70
Email info@moulindetouvois.com
Web   www.moulindetouvois.com

Entry 344   Map 4

Loire Valley

Domaine de la Blanche Treille

Chic Madame has sparkling eyes and a warm energy; Monsieur is charming and loves gardening; the house (in a wine village) is the last word in luxury. So meticulously furnished are the rooms that, as you sip coffee from the silver pot, you may wish yourself in twinset and pearls… No matter; your Parisian hosts love swapping travellers' tales and inspiration from the elegant orient informs the décor – pictures, prints, wicker elephants for tables. Bedrooms ooze comfort: a toile de Jouy quilt, a Directoire bed, linen embroidered by Madame. The garden has been tamed and the vineyards stretch to the hills.

Price	€100.
Rooms	3 doubles.
Meals	Restaurants 4km.
Closed	Rarely.
Directions	A85 exit 5 Bourgueil; D749 to Bourgueil; entering town, bear right past abbey to D635 for Restigné; in Fougerolles, house on left, after Auger winery.

Aimée Rabillon
Domaine de la Blanche Treille,
56 route de Bourgueil,
37140 Fougerolles, Indre-et-Loire
Tel   +33 (0)2 47 97 93 30
Email rabillon.c@free.fr

Entry 345   Map 4

Loire Valley

20 rue Pilate

In the lovely Loire valley where the intimate and the romantic reign, you have the little house in the garden all to yourselves: a kitchen and a bathroom downstairs, two bedrooms upstairs and a private piece of flower-filled garden for breakfasts. Or you can join your delightful hosts at the long check-clothed table in the cheerful kitchen where baskets hang from beams. Cultured, dynamic and a superb maker of jams, Ghislaine is involved in visiting artists and writers to this peaceful Touraine town. Be charmed by the genuine welcome, unpretentious comfort, wisteria in the natural garden and bird song all around.

Price	€60. €100 for 4.
Rooms	Cottage for 4.
Meals	Dinner with wine, €25.
Closed	November-March.
Directions	A28 from Le Mans exit Neuillé Pont Pierre. D766 to Beaumont la Ronce; after 1km, onto D2 to Neuvy le Roi. The house has a blue front door, opp. turning to Louestault.

Ghislaine & Gérard de Couesnongle
20 rue Pilate,
37370 Neuvy le Roi,
Indre-et-Loire
Tel +33 (0)2 47 24 41 48
Email ggh.coues@gmail.com

Loire Valley

La Louisière

Simplicity, character and a marvellous welcome make La Louisière special. Madame delights in her role as hostess; Monsieur, who once rode the horse-drawn combine, tends his many roses, and his paintings of bucolic bliss line the walls. A caring and unpretentious couple, both are active in their community. The traditional bedrooms have well-chosen colour schemes and sparkling bathrooms; touches of fun, too. Surrounded by chestnut trees, the farmhouse backs onto the gardens of the château and is wonderfully quiet. Tennis, bikes, tractors, horses to ride and an old-fashioned playground – it's bliss for children.

Price	€55-€60.
Rooms	3: 1 twin, 1 triple, 1 suite for 5.
Meals	Auberge 800m.
Closed	Rarely.
Directions	From Tours D29 to Beaumont la Ronce; signed in village.

Michel & Andrée Campion
La Louisière,
37360 Beaumont la Ronce,
Indre-et-Loire
Tel +33 (0)2 47 24 42 24
Mobile +33 (0)6 78 36 64 69
Email andree.campion@orange.fr

Loire Valley

Le Chat Courant

Traditional materials – soft Touraine stone, lime render, wood and slate – and old furniture, pale colours and lots of light make this house a stylish haven by the Cher where the birdsong drowns out the trains. Éric, a warm, humorous and talented host (ask to see his photographs of the Loire) has local lore to tell, wines for you to taste and a fascinating walled garden for you to admire. The lovely suite is in the summer house. Everywhere you'll find cool colours, natural textures, bits of antiquery (one bedhead is an adapted Breton 'lit clos'), oodles of taste and flowers inside and out. Outdoors: bikes, ping-pong and pool.

Price	€70-€75. Suite €100.
Rooms	2: 1 double. Summer house: 1 family suite for 2-5.
Meals	Restaurant 5 minutes by car.
Closed	Rarely.
Directions	From Tours D7 to Savonnières; right across bridge; left for 3.5km; on right.

Éric Gaudouin
Le Chat Courant,
37510 Villandry,
Indre-et-Loire
Tel   +33 (0)2 47 50 06 94
Mobile   +33 (0)6 37 83 21 78
Email   info@le-chat-courant.com
Web   www.le-chat-courant.com

Entry 348   Map 4

Loire Valley

Château du Vau

At the end of a long bumpy drive is a house of great character run with good humour: delightful philosopher Bruno has turned his family château into a stylish refuge for travellers. Generations of sliding young have polished the banisters on the stairs leading to the large, light bedrooms, freshly decorated with seagrass and family memorabilia round splendid brass bedsteads. Dinners showcase estate produce and, on summer evenings, garden buffets can take you to a favourite corner of the vast grounds; deer bound in the meadow, sheep graze in the orchard. There's a fine pool, and a golf course bang opposite.

Price	€130.
Rooms	5: 3 doubles, 1 family room, 1 triple.
Meals	Dinner with wine, €42. Summer buffets in garden, €26.
Closed	Rarely.
Directions	From Tours for A85 Saumur; 1st exit for Ballan Miré; signs for Ferme Château du Vau & golf course at motorway exit. Entrance opp. golf course.

Bruno Clément
Château du Vau,
37510 Ballan Miré,
Indre-et-Loire
Tel   +33 (0)2 47 67 84 04
Email   info@chateau-du-vau.com
Web   www.chateau-du-vau.com

Entry 349   Map 4

Loire Valley

Les Mazeraies

Beautifully sculpted from the same ancient cedar trees that stalked the splendid grounds 100 years ago, this thoroughly contemporary mansion on the old château foundations in the Garden of France is a real delight. Humour, intelligence and love of fine things inhabit this welcoming family and their guest wing is unostentatiously luxurious in rich fabrics, oriental and modern furniture, good pictures and lovely, scented, cedar-lined bathrooms. Ground-floor rooms have a private terrace each, upstairs ones have direct access to the roof garden. Marie-Laurence is utterly charming.

Price	€100.
Rooms	4: 1 double, 2 twins/doubles, 1 suite for 3-4.
Meals	Restaurants nearby.
Closed	Rarely.
Directions	From Tours D7 for Savonnières; 3km before village left after Les Cèdres restaurant; 800m on left.

Marie-Laurence Jallet
Les Mazeraies,
Route des Mazeraies,
37510 Savonnières, Indre-et-Loire

Tel	+33 (0)2 47 67 85 35
Email	les.jallet@wanadoo.fr
Web	www.lesmazeraies.com

Loire Valley

La Cornillière

Just 15 minutes from the centre of Tours yet you're deep in the countryside where deer, and even the occasional wild boar, invite themselves into the garden from the surrounding woods. The Espinassous live in an 18th-century farmhouse and have turned their longère into a delightfully rustic guest suite with all creature comforts. Croissants and fresh bread will be delivered to you each morning and the rambling gardens are yours to explore, including the formal walled garden, Monsieur's special pride and joy. These are friendly, cultured people who know the area well and will advise on places to visit. *Sawday self-catering also.*

Price	€90–€150.
Rooms	1 suite for 2-4.
Meals	Picnic in garden on request. Restaurants nearby.
Closed	Rarely.
Directions	From Tours D938 for Le Mans, right to Mettray. In village follow one-way system round church, right for St Antoine du Rocher; 2nd right, signed.

Catherine Espinassou
La Cornillière,
Mettray, 37390 Tours,
Indre-et-Loire

Tel	+33 (0)2 47 51 12 69
Mobile	+33 (0)6 03 13 66 12
Email	kakimail@orange.fr
Web	www.gites-lacornilliere-touraine.com

Loire Valley

Les Hautes Gâtinières

High on a cliff above the Loire, house and garden gaze over village, valley and vines. Les Hautes Gâtinières may be modern imitating old, but we chose it for Jacqueline's five-star hospitality. All is immaculate and meticulous within: glossy wooden floors, smart wallpapers, French repro furniture. There's a big living area with a tiled floor warmed by rugs, and views over the large sloping garden, perfect for children (and Api, the fluffy white dog) to romp in. Giant breakfasts, a lovely welcome and a delightful restaurant just down the hill – great value for the Loire. Châteaux, gardens, vineyards beckon.

Price	€58. Suite €93.
Rooms	3: 2 doubles, 1 suite for 4.
Meals	Restaurants in village, 500m.
Closed	Rarely.
Directions	From Tours A10 for Paris; cross Loire; exit 20 to Vouvray. In Rochecorbon left at lights & right up steep narrow lane; signed.

	Jacqueline Gay
	Les Hautes Gâtinières,
	7 chemin de Bois Soleil,
	37210 Rochecorbon, Indre-et-Loire
Tel	+33 (0)2 47 52 88 08
Email	gatinieres@wanadoo.fr
Web	www.gatinieres.eu.ki

Entry 352   Map 4

Loire Valley

La Falotière

A cave suite! Hewn long ago into the rock beside a bell-topped presbytery, deliciously cool and light, it's a spacious retreat. Step from private courtyard to sitting room with big fireplace and old bread oven, smart wicker chairs, red lamps, tiled floors. Burrow through to a cushioned, red-carpeted bedroom sculpted into whitewashed rock; soak in a theatrical free-standing bath. Locals and walkers, your delightful hosts serve home-laid eggs at breakfast, enjoy sharing their lovely shady garden and this intriguing town, wedged in a gully ten minutes from Tours amid the Loire's vineyards and châteaux. Private, unique, fantastic.

Price	€120. Child bed, €15.
Rooms	1 suite for 2.
Meals	Restaurant 150m.
Closed	Rarely.
Directions	From Tours D952 (right bank of Loire) for Vouvray approx 3km; left Rue du Dr Lebled after Tourist Office; up hill, last house on left before Mairie.

	Dominique & Jean-Pierre Danderieux
	La Falotière,
	51 rue du Docteur Lebled,
	37210 Rochecorbon, Indre-et-Loire
Mobile	+33 (0)6 50 65 41 49
Email	contact@falotiere.com
Web	www.falotiere.com

Entry 353   Map 4

Loire Valley

Château de Nazelles

Even the pool is special: a 'Roman' bath hewn out of the hillside with a fountain and two columns, set on one of several garden levels that rise to the crowning glory of vines where grapes are grown by natural methods. The young owners brim with enthusiasm for their elegant, history-laden château, built in 1518 to gaze across the Loire at Amboise. Every detail has been treated with taste and discretion. Rooms, two in the main house, two smaller in the adorable old pavillon, are light and fresh with lovely wooden floors, the suite carved from the rock itself – and there's a big living room with books, internet and games.

Price	€110-€150.
Rooms	4: 3 doubles, 1 suite for 4.
Meals	Summer kitchen. Restaurants in Amboise.
Closed	Rarely.
Directions	From A10 exit 18 for Amboise 12km; right D1 to Pocé sur Cisse & Nazelles Négron; in village centre, narrow Rue Tue la Soif between Mairie & La Poste.

	Véronique & Olivier Fructus
	Château de Nazelles,
	16 rue Tue la Soif,
	37530 Nazelles, Indre-et-Loire
Tel	+33 (0)2 47 30 53 79
Email	info@chateau-nazelles.com
Web	www.chateau-nazelles.com

Entry 354   Map 4

Loire Valley

Le Clos du Golf

Fourteen hectares of heron, wild boar, deer *and* a nine-hole golf course: a vast expanse of green. Mark, a gallicised Englishman, and Katia, an anglicised Frenchwoman, travellers both, are in love with their beautiful home; and are brilliant at B&B. The old farmhouse, a Loire 'longère', has been masterfully restored and is filled with a pleasing mix of English and French. Expect immaculate bedrooms beneath old beams, good antiques and delicious dinners of local seasonal things at one big sociable table. Swimming, tennis and the splendours of the Loire lie just down the road. A wonderful, hospitable place.

Price	€70-€85. Extra bed €18.
Rooms	3 doubles.
Meals	Dinner with wine, €35.
Closed	December-January.
Directions	From A10 exit 18 on D31 for Amboise to Autrèche; left D55 to Route de Dame Marie les Bois; right D74; 2nd house on left after woods.

	Mark & Katia Foster
	Le Clos du Golf, Le Plessis,
	Route de Dame-Marie-les-Bois,
	37530 Cangey-Amboise, Indre-et-Loire
Tel	+33 (0)2 47 56 07 07
Email	closdugolf@wanadoo.fr
Web	www.bonadresse.com/val-de-loire/cangey-amboise.htm

Entry 355   Map 4

Loire Valley

Manoir de la Maison Blanche

Your 17th-century manor sits in blissful seclusion yet you can walk into the centre of old Amboise. Annick is the perfect host, loves people, loves life, and gives you three fabulous, generous, lofty bedrooms in a converted outbuilding. One is tiled and beamed with a small patio overlooking the garden, another, under the eaves, reached via an outdoor spiral stair, is charming. The garden is surprisingly huge, bursting with roses and irises that may make their way to your room. Look out for the 16th-century pigeon loft – a historical rarity. Delicious breakfasts, super rooms, and châteaux all around. One of the best.

Price	€90.
Rooms	3: 2 triples, 1 family suite.
Meals	Guest kitchenette. Restaurants within walking distance.
Closed	Rarely.
Directions	From Place du Château in Amboise for Clos Lucé; round park; straight on at 1st stop sign, right at 2nd stop sign, 1st left; signed.

	Annick Delécheneau
	Manoir de la Maison Blanche,
	18 rue de l'Épinetterie,
	37400 Amboise, Indre-et-Loire
Tel	+33 (0)2 47 23 16 14
Mobile	+33 (0)6 88 89 33 66
Email	annick.delecheneau@wanadoo.fr
Web	www.lamaisonblanche-fr.com

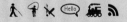

Entry 356   Map 4

Loire Valley

Belleroche

Faint sounds sometimes drift upwards from the embankment far below but Belleroche remains serene. Only a 15-minute walk from the centre of Amboise, this fine house stands poised and aloof in a three-hectare garden high above the Loire. Florence searched high and low for the perfect place for her B&B; having found it, she and her vet husband have devoted energy and imagination to its restoration. The exquisite bedrooms and the guest sitting room, once the old library, overlook the river. So, too, does a little 18th-century pavilion under the lime trees where Florence may serve breakfast on sunny mornings. Heaven.

Price	€100–€120.
Rooms	2: 1 suite for 4; 1 double with separate bath.
Meals	Restaurants nearby.
Closed	Mid-October to mid-April.
Directions	From Tours, D751 along river to Amboise centre; pass bridge & château, take lower road Quai Charles Guinot becoming Quai des Violettes; right Rue du Clos de Belleroche. House 1st on left, blue gates.

	Florence Janvier
	Belleroche,
	1 rue du Clos de Belleroche,
	37400 Amboise, Indre-et-Loire
Tel	+33 (0)2 47 30 47 03
Mobile	+33 (0)6 73 89 60 16
Email	belleroche.amboise@orange.fr
Web	www.belleroche.net

Entry 357   Map 4

Loire Valley

Le Pavillon de Vallet

When she moved to this little valley, charming, gracious Astrid had no B&B plans at all – "it happened" and she loves it, taking huge care over the rooms (new beds in all) and breakfast (delicious). She and her pilot husband are escapees from Paris. The *tuffeau* stone is light and bright, the lawns run down to the Cher and wisteria covers the breakfast *gloriette*. Guests have a lofty, tiled living room full of lightness and well-being. The bread-oven bedroom is sweet with its flowery wallpaper, painted beams and private courtyard; in another, an enormous four-poster looms beneath a canopy of joists. Special.

Price	€70-€90.
Rooms	3: 1 double, 2 triples.
Meals	Restaurants 4km.
Closed	Rarely.
Directions	From Tours D976 for Bléré; pass sign for Athée sur Cher, cont. to Granlay; immed. left to Vallet; down lane; left at bottom of hill; last house on right.

Astrid Lange
Le Pavillon de Vallet,
4 rue de l'Aqueduc,
37270 Athée sur Cher, Indre-et-Loire
Tel +33 (0)2 47 50 67 83
Mobile +33 (0)6 87 00 51 27
Email pavillon.vallet@orange.fr
Web www.pavillon-de-vallet.com

Entry 358 Map 4

Loire Valley

Le Belvédère

Madame, ex air hostess and English teacher, treats you to superb breakfasts, and is a mine of information on the region. From plain street to stately courtyard magnolia to extraordinary marble-walled spiral staircase with dome atop – this is a *monument historique*, a miniature Bagatelle Palace with a circular salon, in the centre of sleepy Bléré. The light, airy, elegant rooms, small and perfectly proportioned, are soft pink and grey; lean out and pluck a grape from the vine-clad pergola, prettily illuminated at night. Monsieur was a pilot and still flies vintage aircraft; ask about flights over the Loire châteaux.

Price	€90. Suite €140.
Rooms	3: 2 doubles, 1 suite for 4.
Meals	Restaurants in Bléré.
Closed	Occasionally.
Directions	A85 exit 11; D31 to Bléré; in Bléré follow signs for Centre Culturel (house is in same street). OR collection from private airfield 5km.

Dominique Guillemot
Le Belvédère,
24 rue des Déportés,
37150 Bléré, Indre-et-Loire
Tel +33 (0)2 47 30 30 25
Email jr.guillemot@wanadoo.fr
Web lebelvedere-bednbreakfast.com

Entry 359 Map 4

Loire Valley

Moulin de la Follaine

Great wooden doors open to courtyard and garden beyond: Follaine is a deeply serene place. Ornamental geese adorn the lake, the tended garden has places to linger, colourful bedrooms have antique furniture, fabulous mattresses and lake views; one opens to the garden. Upstairs is a lovely light sitting room – and a guest fridge for picnics in the garden. Amazingly, the old milling machinery in the breakfast area still works – ask and Monsieur will turn it on for you; there are relics from the old hunting days, too. Your hosts, once in the hotel trade, know the area intimately and are utterly charming. *Sawday self-catering also.*

Price	€70-€80.
Rooms	4: 2 doubles, 2 suites.
Meals	Bar-restaurant 800m; choice in Loches.
Closed	December-February.
Directions	From Tours D943 for Loches; left D58 to Reignac; D17 to Azay sur Indre; left opp. restaurant; at fork, left (over 2 bridges); mill below fortified farm on right.

	Danie Lignelet
	Moulin de la Follaine,
	2 chemin du Moulin,
	37310 Azay sur Indre, Indre-et-Loire
Tel	+33 (0)2 47 92 57 91
Email	moulindelafollaine@wanadoo.fr
Web	www.moulindefollaine.com

Entry 360   Map 4

Loire Valley

Les Moulins de Vontes

"Magical," say readers. Three old mills side by side on a glorious sweep of the Indre, boats for messing about in, wooden bridges to cross from one secluded bank to another, a fine view of the river from the terrace. No dinners so gather a picnic en route and your entertaining hosts will happily provide cutlery, rugs and anything else you need. The airy, elegant, uncluttered rooms are in historic style and have stunning river views (the rushing water becomes a gentle murmur at night). Bathrooms sparkle. Billiards in the sitting room, home honey for breakfast, swimming and fishing in the river, eco-aware owners. Heaven.

Price	€130-€140.
Rooms	3: 1 twin; 2 doubles, each with separate wc.
Meals	Restaurants 2.5km.
Closed	October-March.
Directions	From Tours D943 for Loches; at 3rd r'bout right to Esvres centre; left on D17; 200m after village exit sign, turn right; continue to end of road.

	Odile & Jean-Jacques Degail
	Les Moulins de Vontes,
	37320 Esvres sur Indre,
	Indre-et-Loire
Tel	+33 (0)2 47 26 45 72
Email	info@moulinsdevontes.com
Web	www.moulinsdevontes.com

Entry 361   Map 4

Loire Valley

La Lubinerie

Built by Elizabeth's grandfather, its typical brick-and-tile face still looking good, this neat townhouse is a spirited mixture of nostalgic and modern. Strong colours and delicate muslin, elegant mirrors and her own patchwork, and a fascinating collection of paintings, prints, old cartoons and… teapots. Elizabeth lived for years in England, collected all these things and calls her delicious rooms Earl Grey, Orange Pekoe, Darjeeling. Your hosts love sharing their stories and knowledge with guests. Two lovely dogs, a friendly little town, a sweet cottagey garden – and, we are told, the best croissants ever.

Price	€80–€140.
Rooms	3: 2 doubles, 1 suite for 4.
Meals	Restaurants 3km.
Closed	Rarely.
Directions	From Tours D143 for Loches; exit r'bout for Esvres; left at stop to centre ville; after church for St Branchs; at mini-r'bout, 1st left then 1st right. House opp. École Maternelle.

	Elizabeth Aubert-Girard
	La Lubinerie,
	3 rue des Écoles,
	37320 Esvres sur Indre, Indre-et-Loire
Tel	+33 (0)2 47 26 40 87
Mobile	+33 (0)6 82 89 00 95
Email	lalubinerie@orange.fr
Web	www.lalubinerie.com

Entry 362   Map 4

Photo: Lesley Chalmers

Poitou – Charentes

Photo: www.istockphoto.com

Poitou - Charentes

L'Aumônerie

This old hospital priory beside the original moat (now a boulevard bringing new neighbours, garden centre included) has eight drama-packed centuries to tell. The L'Haridons have put back several original features and alongside picture windows the old stone spiral leads up to the suite (big warm sitting room, low oak door to fresh beamed bedroom with extra bed). The small ground-floor double is utterly charming; outside is a playhouse for children. Madame is well-travelled, loves old buildings and gardens and is a most interesting and considerate hostess who also has a passion for patchwork.

Price	€42–€55. Suites €55–€130.
Rooms	3: 1 double, 1 suite for 2-3, 1 family suite for 2-6.
Meals	Restaurants within walking distance.
Closed	Rarely.
Directions	From Fontevraud, take Loudun centre; cross traffic lights; at r'bout (Hôtel de la Roue d'Or on right) take 1st exit for Thouars. Entrance 200m on right opp. Cultural Centre.

Christiane L'Haridon
L'Aumônerie,
3 bd Maréchal Leclerc,
86200 Loudun, Vienne
Tel   +33 (0)5 49 22 63 86
Mobile   +33 (0)6 83 58 26 18
Email   chris.lharidon@wanadoo.fr
Web   www.l-aumonerie.biz

Entry 363   Map 9

Poitou - Charentes

Domaine de Bourgville

Time slows down here. In the converted stable block of a 17th-century 'gentil-hommière' the style is gentle, provincial France, in tune with the rolling countryside of forests, hamlets and hills. The first-floor bedrooms wrap you in a soft embrace of old French bedsteads and shiny seagrass, flowers, rush-seated chairs and views to garden or terrace; all is intimacy and calm. Breakfast in the airy sitting room with its comfortable, well-chosen furnishings; John is a superb cook so stay for dinner. Explore Loire châteaux, medieval Chinon, walk the trails, then return to the rambling garden. Supremely restful.

Price	€50–€60.
Rooms	4 doubles.
Meals	Dinner with wine, €23. Restaurants in village.
Closed	Rarely.
Directions	From Richelieu for Châtellerault; after approx. 2km, right D24 to Mont sur Guesnes; signed in village.

John & Glyn Ward
Domaine de Bourgville,
Allée de Bourgville,
86420 Mont sur Guesnes, Vienne
Tel   +33 (0)5 49 98 74 79
Mobile   +33 (0)6 61 71 92 97
Email   b-b.bourgville@wanadoo.fr
Web   www.vie-vienne.com

Entry 364   Map 9

Poitou - Charentes

Château de la Motte

Nothing austere about this imposing, lovingly restored 15th-century castle. A wide spiral stone staircase leads to grandly high yet simply decorated rooms where family furniture, vast stone fireplaces and rich canopies, finely stitched by talented Marie-Andrée, preserve the medieval flavour; bathrooms are state of the art. The lofty, light-filled sitting room is engagingly cluttered, the elegant dining room witnesses excellent, organic, home cooking and enlightened conversation with your dynamically green, cultured and charming hosts. Everyone is welcome here, families included. *Sawday self-catering also. Shared pool.*

Ethical Collection: Environment & Food.
See page 410 for details.

Price	€80-€130. Extra bed €25.
Rooms	4: 1 twin, 1 triple, 2 suites.
Meals	Dinner with wine, €30. Child under 12, €20.
Closed	Mid-November to mid-March.
Directions	A10 exit 26 Châtellerault Nord; at r'bout after toll for Usseau 5km; D749 for Richelieu; D75 to Usseau.

	Jean-Marie & Marie-Andrée Bardin
	Château de la Motte,
	2 La Motte,
	86230 Usseau, Vienne
Tel	+33 (0)5 49 85 88 25
Mobile	+33 (0)6 19 03 35 35
Email	chateau.delamotte@wanadoo.fr
Web	www.chateau-de-la-motte.net

Entry 365   Map 9

Poitou - Charentes

Manoir de la Boulinière

Laughter echoes in this 15th-century country manor where descendants of Scottish royalty once lived. Share with Alain, Marie-Pierre and son Henri the great gothic windows, the stone-flagged floors, the huge fireplaces, a living room replete with period pieces and their art collection. Alain is generous with the Loire valley's secrets, Marie-Pierre offers cookery mornings; table d'hôtes dinners burst with fresh herbs. The walled garden, too, is delightful, with giant cedar, plums, cherries, vines, a pretty gazebo. Two-room suites, up spiral stairs, revel in canopied beds, gorgeous bathrooms and a heady sense of history.

Price	€130.
Rooms	2 family suites for 4.
Meals	Dinner €25. Child under 12, €15.
Closed	Rarely.
Directions	A10 exit 26; D749 for Richelieu; D79 to Usseau; D9 for Leigné sur Usseau; 3km after Château de la Motte, right by bus shelter; 400m on left.

	Marie-Pierre Guillon-Hardyau
	Manoir de la Boulinière,
	7 Manoir de la Boulinière,
	86230 Usseau, Vienne
Tel	+33 (0)5 49 85 07 49
Mobile	+33 (0)6 87 03 58 84
Email	manoir.bouliniere@hotmail.fr
Web	www.manoirdelabouliniere.fr

Entry 366   Map 9

Poitou - Charentes

La Grenouillère

In an unexpectedly lovely cluster of old buildings on a residential road, a wonderful B&B. Impossible not to be charmed by these warm, easy, good-hearted people who offer you extremely good food, flowing wine, meals on a shady terrace in summer and, always, flowers on the table. The bedroom in the converted woodshed has beams, a blue-and yellow- tiled floor and a view over the garden – rambling and delightful with a long pond and weeping willows. More rooms await in the house across the courtyard where Madame's charming mother lives (and makes delicious jam). There's even a yurt... and a rowing boat to mess about in.

Price	€50–€57. Yurt €95 for 2.
Rooms	6: 3 doubles, 2 triples, 1 yurt for 4.
Meals	Dinner, 4 courses with wine, €27.
Closed	Rarely.
Directions	From Tours D910 S for Châtellerault 55km. In Dangé St Romain, right at 3rd traffic lights, cross river, keep left on middle of little square. House 200m along on left; signed.

Annie & Noël Braguier
La Grenouillère,
17 rue de la Grenouillère,
86220 Dangé St Romain, Vienne
Tel   +33 (0)5 49 86 48 68
Email   lagrenouillere86@aliceadsl.fr

Entry 367   Map 9

Poitou - Charentes

Château de La Plante

You'll be charmed by this graceful stone château, looking proudly over the countryside to the wooded Vienne valley. 'La Plante' refers to the vines that were harvested for wine by Madame's ancestors. Period elegance drifts through rooms where the family grew up, leaving canopied beds, parquet floors and the odd empty picture frame in bedrooms lovingly named after great-grandmothers. Serenity reigns supreme; breakfast is in the old music room, a fittingly classic cream-blue affair. Join your hosts for an aperitif on the balustraded terrace or under the spreading lime tree. If houses could sing, this one surely would.

Price	€75–€130.
Rooms	4: 3 doubles; 1 family suite with bath & separate wc.
Meals	Restaurants 10-minute drive.
Closed	Rarely.
Directions	A10 exit 26; at r'bout D1 for Châtellerault. Right D749 still signed Châtellerault; left D43 for Thuré 1.5km. Entrance to château on right.

Patrick & Françoise Dandurand
Château de La Plante,
86540 Thuré,
Vienne
Tel   +33 (0)5 49 93 86 28
Email   patrick.dandurand@orange.fr
Web   www.chateaudelaplante.fr

Entry 368   Map 9

Poitou - Charentes

Château de Labarom

A great couple in their genuine family château of fading grandeur; mainly 17th century, it has a properly aged face. From the dramatic hall up the superbly bannistered staircase, you reach the salon gallery that runs majestically through the house. Here you may sit, read, dream of benevolent ghosts. Bedrooms burst with personality and wonderful old beds. Madame's hand-painted tiles adorn a shower, her laughter accompanies your breakfast (organic garden fruits and four sorts of jam); Monsieur tends his trees, aided by Polka the dog – he's a fount of local wisdom. A warm, wonderful, authentic place.

Price	€75-€79.
Rooms	2: 1 double, 1 twin/double, sharing bathroom.
Meals	Auberge nearby; choice 3km.
Closed	Rarely.
Directions	From A10 Futuroscope exit D62 to Quatre Vents r'bout; D757 to Vendeuvre; at r'bout left D15 through Cheneché. Labarom 800m on right after leaving Cheneché.

Éric & Henriette Le Gallais
Château de Labarom,
Route de Thurageau,
86380 Cheneché, Vienne
Tel   +33 (0)5 49 51 24 22
Mobile   +33 (0)6 83 57 68 14
Email   chateau.de.labarom@wanadoo.fr
Web   www.labarom.com

Entry 369   Map 9

Poitou - Charentes

La Roseraie

Country B&B with one foot in the town: Neuville is a mere stroll. Warm and generous, Heather and Michael live in an elegant townhouse in four enclosed acres with orchard, vegetable garden and two rows of vines. The sitting area is cosy, the pool is fabulous, the bedrooms are immaculate, restful and calm: seagrass floors, white tub chairs, a carved bedhead, a balcony here, a patio off the garden there. Put the world to rights over Heather's delicious dinner served at the big table, or under the pergola in summer: gîte and B&B guests combine. Doves coo, Jack Russells frolic, Poitiers is the shortest drive. *Sawday self-catering also.*

Price	€68-€88. Suites €110-€140.
Rooms	5: 3 doubles, 2 family suites for 4-5.
Meals	Dinner with wine, €28.
Closed	Rarely.
Directions	A10 exit 28 (Futuroscope); D62 to Neuville; entering town, D347 for Mirebeau; left at r'bout for centre ville. House on right on one-way system, just before water tower.

Michael & Heather Lavender
La Roseraie,
78 rue Armand Caillard,
86170 Neuville de Poitou, Vienne
Tel   +33 (0)5 49 54 16 72
Email   heather@laroseraiefrance.fr
Web   www.laroseraiefrance.fr

Entry 370   Map 9

Poitou - Charentes

La Pocterie

A "passionate gardener" is how Martine describes herself, with a soft spot for old-fashioned roses: they ramble through the wisteria on the walls and gather in beautifully tended beds. The 'L' of the house shelters a very decent pool (alarmed) while furniture is arranged in a welcoming spot for picnics. Martine works but will see you for breakfast (in the delightful dining room or under the pretty arbour) or in the evening: she's the one with the big smile. A fresh, polished and peaceful retreat with Futuroscope minutes away. Bikes and tennis nearby, and a huge range of day trips to choose from: excellent for families.

Price	€65. Triple €75.
Rooms	2: 1 double, 1 triple.
Meals	Restaurants 3km.
Closed	Rarely.
Directions	From Châtellerault D749 for Chauvigny & Limoges approx. 13km; Vouneuil on right; cont. for 3km, then left for 750m; down track to end.

Michel & Martine Poussard
La Pocterie,
86210 Vouneuil sur Vienne,
Vienne

Tel	+33 (0)5 49 85 11 96
Mobile	+33 (0)6 76 95 49 46
Email	martinelapocterie@orange.fr
Web	lapocterie.chambres.free.fr

Entry 371 Map 9

Poitou - Charentes

Les Hauts de Chabonne

A pleasant 'stop off' for guests looking to discover this lovely undiscovered part of the Vienne. The Penots have converted a fine big barn into guest quarters, where two impressively sized bedrooms await. Older than the main house, the building has been renovated well, then decorated in muted colour schemes with ethnic rugs and good furniture. Ask if you may sit on the cobbled terrace if the evening is warm and gaze across the wide landscape as the wind plays in the poplars. There's a nature reserve on the doorstep – dragonflies a speciality – and a famously beautiful golf course at Saint Cyr.

Price	€65. €80 for 3.
Rooms	2: 1 double, 1 triple.
Meals	Dinner with wine, €25.
Closed	Rarely.
Directions	From Châtellerault D749 to Vouneuil sur Vienne; left in church square & follow Chambres d'Hôtes signs. Last house on right in hamlet of Chabonne.

Florence & Antoine Penot
Les Hauts de Chabonne,
Chabonne,
86210 Vouneuil sur Vienne, Vienne

Tel	+33 (0)5 49 85 28 25
Email	penot.antoine@wanadoo.fr
Web	www.chabonne.com

Entry 372 Map 9

Logis du Château du Bois Doucet

Naturally, graciously, aristocratically French, owners and house are full of stories and eccentricity. Beautiful treasures abound: a jumble of ten French chairs, bits of ancient furniture, pictures, heirlooms, lamps in a stone-flagged salon, a properly elegant dining room, old dolls and family hunting buttons. There are statues inside and out and bedrooms with personality; the two-storey suite in the main house is fit for a cardinal. Monsieur's interests are history and his family, Madame's are art and life, and the garden is listed, a symphony in green. Feel part of family life in this delightful people- and dog-orientated house.

Château de Masseuil

In the big flagstoned kitchen of the crag-perched, pepper-potted château, friends and family chat over the jam-making. Hunting trophies, family portraits and sepia photographs adorn the sunny breakfast room and parade up the stairs; comfortable, fresh bedrooms have old family pieces, a shower each, new beds; charming, courteous and unstuffily aristocratic hosts are hugely knowledgeable about local Romanesque art and tell stories of monks and brigands. Sixteenth-century castles didn't have en suite loos: there are chamber pots in case you can't face the stairs! Seemingly remote yet Poitiers is down the road. Wonderful value.

Price	€80–€90. Suites €150.
Rooms	3: 1 family suite with wc on ground floor. Wing: 1 double, 1 family suite for 4-6.
Meals	Dinner with wine, €30.
Closed	Rarely.
Directions	From A10 exit Poitiers Nord, N10 for Limoges 7km; right to Bignoux; follow signs to Bois Dousset.

Price	€75.
Rooms	2: 1 double, 1 twin/double, sharing wc.
Meals	Restaurants 3km.
Closed	Rarely.
Directions	A10 exit Poitiers Nord N149 for Nantes 12km; at bottom of hill left for Masseuil.

	Vicomte & Vicomtesse de Villoutreys de Brignac
	Logis du Château du Bois Doucet, 86800 Lavoux, Vienne
Tel	+33 (0)5 49 44 20 26
Mobile	+33 (0)6 75 42 79 78
Email	mariediane1012@yahoo.fr

	Alain & Claude Gail
	Château de Masseuil, 17 rue du Château, 86190 Quinçay, Vienne
Tel	+33 (0)5 49 60 42 15

Entry 373   Map 9

Entry 374   Map 9

Poitou - Charentes

Poitou - Charentes

La Théophilière

Jean-Louis, a genial twinkly man, keeps vegetables and chickens and is involved in numerous local events; Geneviève is a perfectionist. Their traditional Poitevin farmhouse, rendered a sunny ochre, has a modern conservatory along its width and rooms opening off either side. You come to it from the back, up a long tree-lined drive; it's a surprise to discover it's in the middle of the village. Bedrooms are fresh and immaculate with great colours, furniture is suitably old: the canopy over the double bed was made for Madame's great-grandmother's wedding. Don't miss their delicious pine aperitif before dinner. *Heated pool.*

Le Logis de Bellevue

You're within strolling distance of one of the prettiest towns in the Marais Poitevin. The green-shuttered lodge has been transformed by this happy, hospitable British couple into a colourful home with the guest suite on the first floor: white walled, wooden floored, clean-limbed and spotless. The garden is immaculate too, with lawns and colourful borders, croquet, table tennis and (shared with gîtes) super pool. Garden fruits make an appearance at breakfast in homemade juices and jams; clever Marylyn even makes brioche. Dinner might include goat's cheese from the area and lamb from the farmer next door. A treat.

Price	€53-€66. Family room €79-€95.
Rooms	2: 1 family room; 1 twin with separate wc.
Meals	Dinner with wine, €20.
Closed	Rarely.
Directions	From A10 exit Poitiers Sud N10 for Angoulême to Vivonne; 2nd exit D4 to Champagne St H. & Sommières du C.; right D1 for Civray 8km; left to Champniers; signed.

Price	€85. €160 for 4.
Rooms	1 family suite for 2-4.
Meals	Dinner with wine, €30. Child €15. Restaurants 400m.
Closed	Rarely.
Directions	A83 exit 9 for Benet; D148 to Benet; right into Benet; D1 to Coulon; house on right 100m after Coulon sign.

	Geneviève & Jean-Louis Fazilleau
	La Théophilière,
	86400 Champniers,
	Vienne
Tel	+33 (0)5 49 87 19 04
Email	jeanlouis.fazilleau@free.fr
Web	chambres-hotes-poitou-charente.ifrance.com

	Marylyn & Anthony Kusmirek
	Le Logis de Bellevue,
	55 Route de Benet,
	79510 Coulon, Deux Sèvres
Tel	+33 (0)5 49 76 75 45
Email	kusmirek@orange.fr
Web	www.lelogisdebellevue.com

Château de Tennessus

It's all real: moat, drawbridge, dreams. Two steep stone spirals to "the biggest bedroom in France": granite windowsills, giant hearth, canopied bed, shower snug; on the lower floors of the keep, the medieval family room: vast timbers, good mattresses, arrow slits for windows. Furniture is sober, candles are lit, fires always laid, and you breakfast – beautifully – at a massive table on 14th-century flagstones. The whole place is gloriously authentic, the charming gardens glow from loving care (medieval potager, modern pool), the views reach far, and Pippa is a bundle of energy and generosity. *Children over six welcome.*

Price	€120–€145.
Rooms	2: 1 double & kitchenette, 1 family suite for 4.
Meals	Gourmet picnic basket with wine, €29.50. Restaurants 500m.
Closed	Christmas.
Directions	From A10 exit 29 on N147; N149 W to Parthenay; round Parthenay northbound; on N149 for Bressuire; 7km north of Parthenay right at sign for château (D127).

Nicholas & Philippa Freeland
Château de Tennessus,
79350 Amailloux,
Deux Sèvres

Tel	+33 (0)5 49 95 50 60
Email	tennessus@orange.fr
Web	www.tennessus.com

Le Beach House

Ever dream about your own cabin on an island with glorious sunsets and views to the horizon? This one has a private dune to boot – and a first-row balcony seat from which to contemplate the waves or the sparkling Milky Way. Breakfasts are superb, aperitifs come from the honesty bar, and everything is shipshape in the little blue and white cabin ten steps from the house: quietly stylish wicker furniture and luxurious linen. Antoinette is huge fun, Philippe knows his oysters, there's a pool here, a colourful port nearby, and plashy waves to lull you to sleep at night. *Min. two nights in high season (three at weekends).*

Price	€110–€150.
Rooms	2: 1 double. Cabin: 1 double.
Meals	Occasional dinner with wine, €30. Restaurant 1km.
Closed	November–March.
Directions	Directions on booking.

Antoinette & Philippe Girard
Le Beach House, Plage de la
Faucheprère, La Cotinière, 17310 St Pierre
d'Oléron, Charente-Maritime

Tel	+33 (0)5 46 47 19 70
Mobile	+33 (0)6 86 82 38 39
Email	contact@lebeachhouse.com
Web	www.lebeachhouse.com

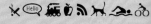

Poitou - Charentes

La Grande Barbotière

Between the fruit trees a hammock sways, breakfast is served next to a sparkling pool and sculpted chickens peck. Tucked behind gates in the heart of a bustling village is a *maison de maître* of elegance and charm. Your hosts (she half Belgian, he from Yorkshire) have a wicked sense of humour and have created a luxurious and eclectic décor – gazelle antlers, pebbled showers, delicious French linen – for suites with private terraces. Table tennis, croquet, toys for children, bikes to borrow, jasmine, lavender and, everywhere, that spirit-lifting light that you find on this cherished stretch of coastline. *Min. two nights.*

Price	€90-€125. €100-€135 for 3.
Rooms	2 suites for 3.
Meals	Restaurants 4km.
Closed	Rarely.
Directions	A10 to Niort; N11 to La Rochelle ring road; N137 south; exit Châtelaillon & St Vivien; D113 1km to St Vivien.

Christopher & Jacqui McLean May
La Grande Barbotière,
10 rue du Marais Doux,
17220 St Vivien, Charente-Maritime
Tel   +33 (0)5 46 43 76 14
Mobile   +33 (0)6 43 12 11 04
Email   info@mcleanmay.com
Web   www.lagrandebarbotiere.com

Entry 379   Map 8

Poitou - Charentes

A l'Ombre du Figuier

A rural idyll, wrapped in birdsong. The old farmhouse, lovingly restored and decorated, is simple and pristine; its carpeted rooms under eaves that are polished to perfection overlook a pretty garden where you may picnic. Your hosts are an interesting couple of anglophiles. Thoughtful, stylish Madame serves generous breakfasts of homemade jams, organic breads, cheeses and cereals under the fig tree in summer. Monsieur teaches engineering in beautiful La Rochelle; follow his suggestions and discover its lesser-known treasures. Luscious lawns are bordered by well-stocked beds. Great value.

Price	€59-€75.
Rooms	2: 1 family suite for 2-6. Annexe: 1 family room for 2-4.
Meals	Occasional dinner with wine, €23. Guest kitchen. Auberge 3km.
Closed	Rarely.
Directions	From La Rochelle N11 E for 11km exit Longèves; D112, signed to village. In village, past church; right at 'bar-pizzas', 1st left, signed. 700m on left.

M-Christine & J-François Prou
A l'Ombre du Figuier,
43 rue du Marais,
17230 Longèves, Charente-Maritime
Tel   +33 (0)5 46 37 11 15
Email   mcprou@wanadoo.fr
Web   www.alombredufiguier.com

Entry 380   Map 8

Poitou - Charentes

Le Clos de la Garenne

Charming owners and animals everywhere, from boxer dog to donkey to hens! Brigitte and Patrick gave up telecommunications for their dream of the country and the result is this heart-warming, small-village B&B. Avid collectors, they have decorated their roomy 16th-century house with eclectic flair, and old and new rub shoulders merrily; discover doll's house furniture and French cartoon characters, old armoires and antique treasures. Harmony breathes from walls and woodwork, your hosts are endlessly thoughtful, food is exotic organic (and delicious), and families are truly welcome. *Minimum three nights July/August.*

Ethical Collection: Food.
See page 410 for details.

Price	€71. Suite €172. Cottage €131.
Rooms	4: 2 doubles, 1 suite for 6, 1 family cottage (in same street) for 5.
Meals	Dinner with wine, €27.
Closed	Rarely.
Directions	From Surgères Gendarmerie & fire station D115 for Marans & Puyravault; 4km, left on D205. In Puyravault, right. Signed.

	Brigitte & Patrick François
	Le Clos de la Garenne,
	9 rue de la Garenne,
	17700 Puyravault, Charente-Maritime
Tel	+33 (0)5 46 35 47 71
Email	info@closdelagarenne.com
Web	www.closdelagarenne.com

Entry 381   Map 8

Poitou - Charentes

Les Grands Vents

In a lovely sleepy village in the heart of wine and cognac country, roadside but peaceful, the former pineau farmhouse has simple limewashed walls and a traditional French décor. You have your own entrance so you can be as private as you like, but Valérie and Nicolas are super generous hosts and happy for you to have the run of the place, making this wonderfully relaxing for families. Bedrooms, with views onto a well-pruned garden, are large, fresh and catch the morning or evening sun. There's a lush pool and a new covered terrace for simple summer breakfasts. Good value.

Price	€58. Extra person €16–€20.
Rooms	2: 1 triple, 1 suite for 4.
Meals	Restaurants in Surgères, 8km.
Closed	Rarely.
Directions	From A10 exit 33 E601 to Mauzé sur le Mignon; D911 to Surgères; D939 4km, right to Chervettes; behind iron gates.

	Valérie & Nicolas Godebout
	Les Grands Vents,
	17380 Chervettes,
	Charente-Maritime
Tel	+33 (0)5 46 35 92 21
Mobile	+33 (0)6 07 96 68 73
Email	godebout@club-internet.fr
Web	www.les-grands-vents.com

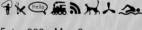

Entry 382   Map 8

Poitou - Charentes

Little Meadows

An English rose and a country doctor have transformed a Charentaise farmhouse with talent and love: wine-red shutters against exposed stone, a pergola heaving with scented roses, potted plants happy in their lustrous jars on the terrace. Through the cathedral ceiling'd salon, new oak stairs lead to a salon/landing (make yourself a cuppa) beamed bedrooms; one baldaquin'd in sun-yellow, the other canopied in valentine-red with views on leafy fig and lemon trees. Cédric is a busy GP, Alison is charming, cultured and cooks divinely. You may be lucky and spot the owls and European buzzards in the barn. *French courses.*

Price	€65.
Rooms	3: 1 double, 1 triple, 1 suite for 2-4.
Meals	Lunch €20. Dinner with wine, €26-€35.
Closed	Rarely.
Directions	From Niort for St Jean d'Angely 25km; left at Tout Y Faut for Aulnay. 2nd left, last house on right. Red signs.

Cédric & Alison Bergoend-Gaffyne
Little Meadows,
Rue des Petits Prés, 17330 La Croix
Comtesse, Charente-Maritime

Tel	+33 (0)5 46 32 24 32
Mobile	+33 (0)6 09 80 41 54
Email	alisonbergoendgaffyne@anglofrench.info
Web	www.anglofrench.info

Entry 383   Map 9

Poitou - Charentes

Les Hortensias

Behind its modest, wisteria-covered mask, this 17th-century former wine-grower's house hides a charming interior – and a magnificent garden that flows through orchard to topiary, a delight in every season. Soft duck-egg colours and rich trimmings make this a warm and safe haven, light airy bedrooms are immaculate (one with its original stone sink, another with a pretty French pink décor), the bathrooms are luxurious, the walls burst with art and the welcome is gracious, warm and friendly. Superb value, scrumptious dinners and blackcurrants from the potager – Madame's sorbets are the best.

Ethical Collection: Environment & Food. See page 410 for details.

Price	€59-€66. Extra person €17.
Rooms	3: 2 doubles, 1 triple.
Meals	Dinner with wine, €24. Summer kitchen. Restaurant in village.
Closed	Rarely.
Directions	From A10 exit 34 on D739 to Tonnay Boutonne; left D114 to Archingeay; left for Les Nouillers; house just after turning, with hydrangea at door.

Marie-Thérèse Jacques
Les Hortensias,
16 rue des Sablières,
17380 Archingeay, Charente-Maritime

Tel	+33 (0)5 46 97 85 70
Email	jpmt.jacques@wanadoo.fr
Web	www.chambres-hotes-hortensias.com

Entry 384   Map 8

Poitou - Charentes

Le Manoir Souhait

Built by a cognac merchant in 1888 (outbuildings contain the presses), the mellow manoir has pretty porcelain in elegant cabinets, sprigs of lavender on fat pillows, white-painted beams, a majestic antique bed, a sparkling chandelier: Liz's attention to detail is irresistible. That includes lavish dinners on which guests heap praise, and breakfasts of fresh fruits, charcuterie, viennoiseries and griddled muffins. Further treats await outside in the form of badminton, table tennis, swings and a terraced heated pool. A luxurious B&B run by friendly super-organised English hosts, Liz and Will. *Sawday self-catering also.*

Poitou - Charentes

Le Logis de Bresdon

Immerse yourself in a secluded 19th-century manor house in "the sunniest region of France." Kathy is a marvellous cook and serves locally sourced dinners in her chic dining room – and in the meditation garden under the stars. The gardens are well-kept, the views are stunning and you'll sleep blissfully in smart, light bedrooms with the smoothest linen and lovely antiques. Treat yourself to a massage, soak in the hot tub, sip something cool by the shrub-surrounded pool, retreat with a book to the drawing room. Cognac and Saintes are a half-hour drive, La Rochelle is an hour. *Sawday self-catering also.*

Price	From €85.
Rooms	3: 1 double, 2 suites for 2-4.
Meals	Dinner, 4 courses, €29.
Closed	Rarely.
Directions	From A10 exit 34; D939 to Matha bypass 20km; left D739 for Aigre 6km; left to Gourvillette. Manor signed in village.

Price	€70–€85. Gîte €600–€1,200 per week.
Rooms	3 + 1: 2 doubles, 1 family room. Gîte for 4.
Meals	Dinner with wine, €30. Restaurants 5km.
Closed	Rarely.
Directions	From Matha D739 to Bresdon; right D222 for Anville; pass cemetery on left, Mairie on right, left fork after 100m; over x-roads, round to right, blue gates on right.

Will & Liz Weeks
Le Manoir Souhait,
7 rue du Château d'Eau,
17490 Gourvillette, Charente-Maritime
Tel   +33 (0)5 46 26 18 41
Mobile   +33 (0)6 08 48 27 34
Email   weeks@manoirsouhait.com
Web   www.manoirsouhait.com

Kathy Fortescue
Le Logis de Bresdon,
4 impasse des Tilleuls, Vinerville Bas,
17490 Bresdon, Charente-Maritime
Tel   +33 (0)5 46 25 09 44
Mobile   +33 (0)6 13 82 18 39
Email   kathy.fortescue@orange.fr
Web   www.logis-de-bresdon.com

Entry 385   Map 9

Entry 386   Map 9

Poitou - Charentes

La Rotonde

Stupendously confident, with priceless river views, this city mansion seems to ride the whole rich story of lovely old Saintes. Soft blue river light hovers into high bourgeois rooms to stroke the warm panelling, marble fireplaces, perfect parquet (the studios are less fine). Double glazing, yes, but ask for a room at the back, away from river and busy road. The Rougers love renovating, and Marie-Laure, calm and talented, has her own sensitive way with classic French furnishings: feminine yet not frilly, rich yet gentle. Superb (antique) linen and bathrooms, too, breakfasts with views and always that elegance.

Price	€100.
Rooms	7: 4 doubles, 1 twin, 2 studios (with kitchenettes) for 2.
Meals	Restaurants in town centre.
Closed	Rarely.
Directions	A10 exit Saintes; at lights before bridge over river, right Quai de la République; keep river on left to Place Blair. On right-hand side, on corner of Rue Monconseil.

	Marie-Laure Rouger La Rotonde, 2 rue Monconseil, 17100 Saintes, Charente-Maritime
Tel	+33 (0)5 46 74 74 44
Mobile	+33 (0)6 87 51 70 92
Email	laure@laboutiquedelarotonde.com
Web	www.laboutiquedelarotonde.com

Entry 387   Map 8

Poitou - Charentes

Le Chiron

The big old well-lived-in house is all chandeliers, ceiling roses and heavy dark furniture. The Toile de Jouy triple has a rustic elegance, La Rose is… pink. Bathrooms are more functional than luxurious but with so much natural beauty to hand who wants to stay in anyway? Madame's regional cooking is a treat, served in a conservatory big enough for many. Genuinely welcoming, your farmer hosts stay and chat (in French, mostly!) when they can. They'll also show you the fascinating old cognac still. Big, off the beaten track and great for families (they run a campsite next door). *Mobile homes available at farm campsite.*

Price	€50. Suite €80.
Rooms	6: 2 doubles, 1 twin, 2 triples, 1 family suite for 4.
Meals	Dinner with wine, €18.
Closed	Rarely.
Directions	From A10 Pons exit, D700 for Barbezieux Archiac. After Echebrune D148 (1st left) for Lonzac-Celles; right D151 & follow signs.

	Micheline & Jacky Chainier Le Chiron, 16130 Salles d'Angles, Charente
Tel	+33 (0)5 45 83 72 79
Email	mchainier@voila.fr

Entry 388   Map 9

Poitou - Charentes

Le Chatelard

This is a gem of a place to stay, both grand and intimate. Béatrice inherited the exquisitely French neo-gothic château and she lovingly protects it from the worst of modernisation (though the hurricane took its toll and trees have had to be replanted). Sleep between old linen sheets, sit in handsome old chairs and be charmed by a bedroom in a tower. The sitting room has that unusual quirk, a window over the fireplace, the dining room a panelled ceiling studded with plates. Béatrice, a teacher, and Christopher, a lecturer in philosophy, are interesting, cultured hosts who enjoy eating with their guests.

Le Bourg

Stone cottages, nodding hollyhocks, ducks in the lane: Mareuil epitomises rural France, and the house sits in its heart. Arrive to a sweeping drive, an immaculate pool, a grand façade and Ron and Vanessa, who have travelled the world. After a final posting in Paris they have landed in sunny Charente, and are happy. Bedrooms are bright, airy and comfortable, with farmhousey bathrooms; dinners, in the ample dining room or the cosy snug, are gastronomic, cosmopolitan, entertaining and preceded by pineau de Charente. You are surrounded by sunflowers and vines and Cognac is close. Friendly, interesting, great fun.

Price	€50-€60.
Rooms	4: 1 double; 1 double, 1 twin, 1 family suite, each with separate wc.
Meals	Dinner with wine, €20. Restaurant 1km.
Closed	Rarely.
Directions	From A10 exit 36 to Pons, Archiac & Barbezieux; N10 exit Barbezieux; D731 for Chalais 12km. At Passirac, 1st right thro' village; château on left.

Price	€75-€85.
Rooms	3: 2 doubles, 1 twin.
Meals	Dinner with wine, €30.
Closed	Rarely.
Directions	D939 from Rouillac for Matha. At Sonneville left to Mareuil. In village take Jarnac road up hill; house on left with green gates.

	Béatrice de Castelbajac & Christopher Macann
	Le Chatelard,
	Passirac, 16480 Brossac, Charente
Tel	+33 (0)5 45 98 71 03
Email	c.macann@wanadoo.fr
Web	www.lechatelard.tk

	Vanessa Bennett-Dixon
	Le Bourg,
	16170 Mareuil,
	Charente
Tel	+33 (0)5 45 66 29 75
Email	lebourg-charente@wanadoo.fr
Web	www.lebourg-charente.com

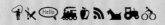

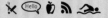

Poitou - Charentes

La Fontaine des Arts

Along the narrow street in the charming, bustling town, through the heavy oak gates, under the ancient arch, is a cottage by the Charente with a little boat for trips up the river. Beautifully coiffed Marie-France combines the glamour of the city with the warmth of a country hostess: guests love her. Breakfast in the conservatory alongside Gérard's easel and piano, or in the courtyard by the pretty fountain pool. Décor is quintessential French: shiny gold taps, striped and flowered walls, a white dressing table. There's a shared guest kitchenette – and a surprising open-gallery bathroom in the double. Great for summer.

Price	€66-€73.
Rooms	3: 1 double, 1 twin, 1 triple.
Meals	Guest kitchenette. Restaurant within walking distance.
Closed	Rarely.
Directions	RN10 between Angoulême & Poitiers, exit Mansle; towards centre ville; between tourist office & L'Hotel Beau Rivage, straight on to No. 13.

Marie-France Pagano
La Fontaine des Arts,
13 rue du Temple,
16230 Mansle, Charente
Tel +33 (0)5 45 69 13 56
Email mfpagano@wanadoo.fr
Web www.la-fontaine-des-arts.com

Entry 391   Map 9

Poitou - Charentes

La Cochère

Cool off by the lush pool, listen to the clacking and cheering of summer Sundays' boules. Kathy, John and Bob the St Bernard are the proud protectors of this dreamlike place where the long table groans with fresh compôtes, croissants and coffee at breakfast and the tranquil garden, John's delight, is sprinkled with lanterns at dusk. In the old coach house, antique iron beds wear floral quilts and crisp linen, and pretty stone peeps through timeworn render. Who wouldn't fall for this heart-warming blend of sophistication and rusticity in a sleepy farming village? Don't miss the fascinating Jardins Européens project.

Price	€60. Triple €70.
Rooms	4: 2 doubles, 1 twin. Studio: 1 triple (May-Sept only).
Meals	Restaurant 6km.
Closed	Christmas.
Directions	A10 to Poitiers; exit N10 S; 10km after Ruffec leave N10 for Salles de Villefagnan D27; in village by Salle des Fêtes, right for Villefagnan; house 200m on right.

John & Kathy Anderson
La Cochère,
Le Bourg, 16700 Salles de Villefagnan, Charente
Tel +33 (0)5 45 30 34 60
Email la.cochere@wanadoo.fr
Web www.lacochere.com

Entry 392   Map 9

Poitou - Charentes

Lesterie

This English farming family lives in a roadside country house with many original delights as well as their working farm and mobile sawmill. Balconies look out onto the dog-run wooded garden and crops, while a sweeping staircase leads to basic bedrooms and rugged bathrooms on the first floor (their teenage children now occupy the attic floor). Stephen and Polly are busy but generally find time to sit round the table with guests. For evenings there's a little guest sitting room in soft pinks and greens. Bring your line and tackle – there's fishing in the lake opposite. Children love the swing-ball and trampoline.

Price	€45–€55.
Rooms	2: 1 double, 1 twin.
Meals	Dinner with wine, €18.
Closed	November-March.
Directions	From Confolens, D948 for Limoges for 4km; sign on road.

Stephen & Polly Hoare
Lesterie,
St Maurice des Lions,
16500 Confolens, Charente
Tel +33 (0)5 45 84 18 33
Email polly.hoare@gmail.com
Web www.lesterie.com

Entry 393 Map 9

Poitou - Charentes

Le Pit

What a remote, interesting and gentle place – heaven for walkers, and for children. Pets doze by the fire, llamas munch on the hillside. Simple, floral bedrooms are in a converted outbuilding, the larger one overlooking the lake. Dinner is unusual (venison pâté perhaps), delicious (produce from the precious vegetable garden) and preceded by a glass of homemade pineau. Alex left London for French farming with a difference and runs a thriving farm shop; Hélène loves pergolas: there are many little corners of rustic charm and colour from which to enjoy the fascinating surroundings. Fun and hugely welcoming.

Price	€53. Triple €75. Quadruple €95.
Rooms	2: 1 triple, 1 quadruple.
Meals	Dinner with wine, €27.
Closed	Rarely.
Directions	From Poitiers D741 S for Confolens 50km. 10km after Pressac, left on D168 for St Germain de Confolens; sign after 2km.

Alex & Hélène Everitt
Le Pit,
Lessac, 16500 Confolens,
Charente
Tel +33 (0)5 45 84 27 65
Mobile +33 (0)6 82 30 74 98
Email everitt16@aol.com
Web www.lepit.fr

Entry 394 Map 9

Aquitaine

Photo: www.istockphoto.com

Aquitaine

Château Bavolier

The classic pale-stone building lies low among unfussy lawns and trees. Inside, the space, light and simplicity of décor are striking. Your charming talented hostess uses a restrained palette to give a floaty, dreamy quality: beige and white paint, pale-straw sisal, impressive decorations (she is restoring some hand-painted panelling). The first bedroom is beautiful in white, gilt and black Louis XVI. The second is enormous, breathtaking, with myriad windows, play of dark and light across the huge brass bed and monochrome oils of Paris. And in each a magnificent chandelier. Amazing.

Price	€110-€160.
Rooms	2 doubles.
Meals	Restaurant nearby.
Closed	October-March.
Directions	From St André de Cubzac D137 to St Christoly de Blaye. Right to St Savin after 50m, left after 2-3 mins; château on right.

Ann Roberts
Château Bavolier,
33920 St Christoly de Blaye,
Gironde
Tel   +33 (0)5 57 42 59 74
Email   info@chateau-bavolier.com
Web   www.chateau-bavolier.com

Entry 395   Map 8

Aquitaine

Château de la Grave

Come for three sweeping bedrooms, two balconies with vineyard views, a stone entrance hall – and a wrought-iron terrace for a glass of the Bassereaus' own dry white semillon (their red is superb, too). They are a hard-working and confident young couple in an 18th-century château with too much good taste to make it sumptuous – thank heavens. It is relaxed and easy – even busy – with three pleasant teenagers, six friendly cats and deer in the woods. Breakfast is on the terrace, wine-tasting in the magnificent *salle de dégustation*. The small pool is for evening dippers rather than sun-worshippers. Good value.

Price	€75-€100. Family room €130.
Rooms	3: 1 double, 1 triple, 1 family room for 4.
Meals	Restaurants in Bourg, 2km.
Closed	November-March; 2 weeks in August.
Directions	From A10 exit 40a or 40b thro' St André de Cubzac; D669 thro' Bourg for Blaye; quickly right D251 for Berson for 1km; sign on right, up lane.

Philippe & Valérie Bassereau
Château de la Grave,
33710 Bourg sur Gironde,
Gironde
Tel   +33 (0)5 57 68 41 49
Email   reservation@chateaudelagrave.com
Web   www.chateaudelagrave.com

Entry 396   Map 8

Aquitaine

Le Castel de Camillac

Perched above vineyards and the lazy Dordogne, a perfect mini-château. Madame has restored its 18th-century spirit with passion, giving rooms delicious drama: panelled walls, vast tapestries, Turkish rugs, elegant antiques. Bedrooms, gleaming with polished wood and lush fabrics, feel like intimate family rooms while head-ducking beams and odd-shaped but sparkling bathrooms add to the charm. Breakfast in the voluptuous dining room or on the terrace, swim in the discreet circular pool, play tennis on the floodlit court, enjoy a round of billiards by the wood-burner. A rich experience, 30 minutes from Bordeaux.

Price	€80–€95.
Rooms	3 doubles.
Meals	Restaurant 2km.
Closed	Occasionally.
Directions	A10 exit St André de Cubzac for Bourg sur Gironde; thro' Bourg, cont. 1.5km, left to Pain de Sucre. Entering Pain de Sucre small street on right after approx. 10m. Keep right round wall.

Élisabeth Frape
Le Castel de Camillac,
1 Camillac, 33710 Bourg,
Gironde
Mobile +33 (0)6 74 31 15 85
Email   elizabeth.frape@orange.fr
Web   lecasteldecamillac.com

Entry 397   Map 8

Aquitaine

83 rue de Patay

Martine may have just one room but she's used to making guests feel welcome: she owns a restaurant in the middle of the old town. Le Loup has been serving local specialities since 1932: you will probably want to pay a visit. This old stone townhouse is a welcome retreat after days visiting the city (ten minutes by tram) or those renowned vineyards. Martine has given it a light modern touch which works well. Your cosy-wosy little bedroom is approached up a curved stone staircase and you have the floor to yourselves. It overlooks a small courtyard garden and has a desk and other pieces stencilled by a friend.

Price	€70.
Rooms	1 twin/double.
Meals	Martine's restaurant near Cathedral.
Closed	Rarely.
Directions	From Bordeaux south take Les Boulevards to Barrière de Pessac; 1st right, right again onto Rue de Patay.

Martine Peiffer
83 rue de Patay,
33000 Bordeaux,
Gironde
Tel   +33 (0)5 56 99 41 74
Mobile +33 (0)6 19 81 22 81
Email   mpeifferma95@numericable.fr

Entry 398   Map 8

Aquitaine

Ecolodge des Chartrons

A many-splendoured delight: city-centre and eco-friendly, with lovely materials and the warmth of simplicity. Your relaxed and friendly hosts have put their earth-saving principles to work, stripping the wonderful wide floorboards, insulating with cork and wool, fitting solar water heating and sun pipes to hyper-modern shower rooms, organic linen and blankets to beds and providing all-organic breakfasts. At the bottom of this quiet road flows the Garonne where cafés, shops and galleries teem in converted warehouses (English wine merchants traded here 300 years ago) and a mirror fountain baffles the mind.

Ethical Collection: Environment, Food & Community. See page 410 for details.

Price	€98–€134.
Rooms	5: 2 doubles, 2 twins/doubles, 1 triple.
Meals	Restaurant 100m.
Closed	Rarely.
Directions	On foot from cathedral: west on Cours d'Alsace & de Lorraine to river; left along quay 1.5km to Quai des Chartrons; Rue Raze on left; check directions before you go.

Véronique Daudin
Ecolodge des Chartrons,
23 rue Raze, 33000 Bordeaux,
Gironde

Tel	+33 (0)5 56 81 49 13
Mobile	+33 (0)6 99 29 33 00
Email	veronique@ecolodgedeschartrons.com
Web	www.ecolodgedeschartrons.com

Entry 399   Map 8

Aquitaine

Château Lestange

Come for vendanges! We are filled with admiration for Anne-Marie, who keeps this proud old place and its vineyards afloat. Built in 1645, it was 'modernised' after the Revolution, but the faded Louis XV paintwork and imperfect tiles simply add to its charm. Beautiful wooden floors, panelled walls and old furniture create a well lived-in feel, and the very private family suites, furnished with mirrors and portraits Anne-Marie is still unearthing from the attic, are capacious. Bathrooms are incongruously modern. Breakfast in a vast room beneath a grand mirror; stroll to dinner in the restaurant down the road. *Minimum two nights.*

Price	€130–€190. €160–€220 for 3.
Rooms	2 family suites for 3.
Meals	Restaurant in village.
Closed	Rarely.
Directions	From Bordeaux ring-road exit 22; after 6km left at roundabout to Quinsac; halfway up hill, on left (porch).

Anne-Marie Charmet
Château Lestange,
33360 Quinsac,
Gironde

Mobile	+33 (0)6 73 00 86 19
Email	charmet@chateau-lestange.com
Web	www.chateau-lestange.com

Entry 400   Map 8

Aquitaine

Château Monlot

If you appreciate good wine you will enjoy this coolly restrained, very beautiful manor among the vines, just a mile from St Émilion... with luck you'll be invited to taste the tempting goods in the cellars. It has been in the family for nine generations, though the owners leave their delightful nephew and relaxed manager to look after you. Charming bedrooms, with plain sandstone or painted walls and sober antiques, offer space, comfort and tranquillity; the shrubby garden has an arch of trees that gives dappled shade as you walk towards the distant statue.

Price	€80–€98.
Rooms	5: 4 doubles, 1 twin.
Meals	Guest kitchen. Restaurants 2km.
Closed	Rarely.
Directions	From A10 exit St André de Cubzac through Libourne for Bergerac; 3km after Bigaroux left D234e for St Laurent; before railway right for St Hippolyte; house on left.

Bernard & Béatrice Rivals
Château Monlot,
St Hippolyte, 33330 Saint Émilion,
Gironde

Tel	+33 (0)5 57 74 49 47
Email	mussetrivals@chateaumonlot.com
Web	www.chateaumonlot.com

Entry 401   Map 9

Aquitaine

Domaine de Barrouil

As befits its calling, this old winegrower's house stands in a sea of vines whose liquid fruits you will taste. Inside the colourful and immaculate house, greens, reds and creams set off gilt-framed mirrors, fine bathrooms, and bedcovers made by Madame. Your hosts believe in big thick towels too. They have lived in French Guiana so Madame's superb French dinners, served in the beautifully tiled dining room, may bring echoes of more exotic lands. She is charming and chatty, a former English teacher; he, a former journalist, knows masses about wine. Ask about watercolour painting classes.

Price	€55–€90.
Rooms	3: 2 doubles, 1 family suite for 2-4.
Meals	Dinner with wine, €28.
Closed	Rarely.
Directions	A10 exit St André de Cubzac to Libourne Bergerac. At Castillon D17 south 8km; at D126 x-roads left; 1st house on left.

Annie & Michel Ehrsam
Domaine de Barrouil,
Bossugan, 33350 Castillon La Bataille,
Gironde

Tel	+33 (0)5 57 40 59 12
Email	info@barrouil.com
Web	www.barrouil.com

Entry 402   Map 9

Aquitaine

Château de Carbonneau

Big château bedrooms bedecked in soft linens with splashes of splendid detail, a fine old bed in the Peony room, huge bathrooms done with rich tiles – here is a self-assured family house where quality is fresh, history stalks and there's plenty of space for three young de Ferrières and a dozen guests. Visit Wilfred's winery and taste the talent handed down by his forebears. Jacquie, a relaxed dynamic New Zealander, provides tasty alternatives to the ubiquitous duck cuisine and a relaxed approach to dining; a dab hand at interiors, she has also cultivated a luminescent, airy guest sitting room close to the orangerie.

Price	€90-€130.
Rooms	5: 2 doubles, 3 twins/doubles.
Meals	Dinner €27. Wine €8-€20.
Closed	December-February.
Directions	D936 to Castillon la Bataille-Bergerac; from Réaux, right to Gensac, Pessac; at r'bout D18 to Ste Foy la Grande; 2km on right.

Jacquie Franc de Ferrière
Château de Carbonneau,
33890 Pessac sur Dordogne,
Gironde

Tel	+33 (0)5 57 47 46 46
Mobile	+33 (0)6 83 30 14 35
Email	carbonneau@orange.fr
Web	www.chateau-carbonneau.com

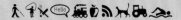

Entry 403 Map 9

Aquitaine

La Cigogne

Croaking frogs, prune-drying paraphernalia and a wacky springwater pool – this is rural, unstuffy, great fun. In its leafy garden, La Cigogne (the name of the nearby stream) is a typical farmhouse inherited by Véronique and modernised by this charmingly natural couple to give simple and wonderfully individual guest rooms, each with its own vine- and rose-shaded terrace. There's a cosy sitting room for winter evenings; the huge barn, its old mangers still intact, makes a comfortable retreat – with billiards – for damp summer days. Yves, a talented golfer, is happy to give you a free lesson and cycle paths pass the door.

Price	€75.
Rooms	2 doubles.
Meals	Dinner with wine, €20.
Closed	November-March.
Directions	From La Réole D670 for Sauveterre 1km; right D668 to Monségur; right D16 for Ste Gemme 2.5km; after 3 bends left for Château les Arqueys; house 500m.

Yves & Véronique Denis
La Cigogne,
5 le Grand Janot,
33580 Ste Gemme, Gironde

Tel	+33 (0)5 56 71 19 70
Mobile	+33 (0)6 75 93 66 32
Email	lacigogne.33@orange.fr
Web	www.chambres-lacigogne.fr

Entry 404 Map 9

Aquitaine

Chambres d'hôtes Janoutic

Charming Jean-Pierre finds the finest organic produce for his table. From croissants to charcuterie, 'poulets fermier' to orchard jams (apricot, blackcurrant, redcurrant, fig), it sounds delicious. This is a well-restored old farmhouse in the hamlet of Janoutic, two miles from the motorway, a great little stopover between Bordeaux and Toulouse. We like the two bright, carpeted bedrooms upstairs best, their rustic rafters hung with tobacco leaves in memory of old farming days; all have big walk-in showers. There's more: leather sofas and a great log fire; a wild garden with an aviary and a pool for newts and birds.

Ethical Collection: Environment & Food.
See page 410 for details.

Price	€65. Extra bed €22.
Rooms	3: 2 doubles, 1 family room for 3.
Meals	Dinner €22. Child under 12, €17.
Closed	Rarely.
Directions	A62 (Bordeaux/Toulouse) exit 4 La Réole; left D9 for Aillas; after water tower on left, left D124 for Sigalens; after 1300m take gravel path on left.

Jean-Pierre Doebele
Chambres d'hôtes Janoutic,
2 Le Tach, 33124 Aillas,
Gironde

Tel	+33 (0)5 56 65 32 58
Mobile	+33 (0)6 81 97 02 92
Email	jpdoebel@club-internet.fr
Web	www.chambresdhotesjanoutic.com

Entry 405   Map 9

Aquitaine

Maison d'Agès

In an intriguing mixture of typical brickwork and colonial verandas, this noble manor stands among fabulous old hardwoods and acres of pines. Nature rejoices, cranes fly overhead, thoroughbreds grace the paddock (they breed horses), hens range free and Madame deploys boundless energy to ply you with exquisite food from the potager, myriad teas, lovely antique-filled, sweet-coloured bedrooms (with her own framed embroidery): she adores entertaining. Monsieur smiles, while teenage Jonathan is all discretion. A huge open fire, baby grand piano and panelled sitting room tell it perfectly.

Ethical Collection: Food.
See page 410 for details.

Price	€65-€85.
Rooms	3: 1 double, 1 twin, 1 suite for 2.
Meals	Dinner with wine, €25.
Closed	Rarely.
Directions	N10 Bordeaux & Bayonne exit Morcenx; D38 for Mont de Marsan; in Ygos right to Ousse Suzan; in Ousse pass 'Kaleo'; signed Chambres d'Hôtes; up lane; Domaine 1.5km on left.

Élisabeth Haye
Maison d'Agès,
40110 Ousse Suzan,
Landes

Mobile	+33 (0)6 86 87 56 08
Email	maisondages@hotmail.fr
Web	www.hotes-landes.fr

Entry 406   Map 13

Aquitaine

Domaine de Sengresse

In the undiscovered Landes, two hours from Spain, a remote and ravishing 17th-century domaine. A solid stone house, a cathedral-like barn, an elegant pool, red squirrels in many luscious acres and a 'petite maison' whose bread oven served the area's farms: such are the riches in store. A Godin stove and six-oven Aga feed today's guests in gourmet style (from a wonderful array of homemade produce), the rooms are bathed in light and everything sparkles, from the luxurious bedrooms with their calming colours to the library brimful of books. More country hotel than B&B, run by the loveliest people. *Sawday self-catering also.*

Price	€95–€130.
Rooms	4 + 1: 3 doubles, 1 twin. House for 2–6.
Meals	Dinner with wine, from €28.
Closed	Rarely.
Directions	12km from N124 Dax & Mont de Marsan; exit Tartas for Mugron D924, 4km, right Mugron D332; right at junc. D3 to Mugron. 2nd right Gouts D18; entrance on right after Cap Blanc Kiwi sign.

Michèle & Rob McLusky &
Sasha Ibbotson
Domaine de Sengresse, Route de Gouts,
40250 Souprosse, Landes
Tel +33 (0)5 58 97 78 34
Email sengresse@hotmail.fr
Web www.sengresse.com

Entry 407 Map 13

Aquitaine

Château de Bezincam

An atmosphere of dream-like tranquillity wafts over this grand and appealing old French country house, with its elegant doors and polished oak floors. Just outside the park gates is the beautiful river Adour, abundant in bird and wildlife – every ten years or so it comes and kisses the terrace steps. Two of the gilt-mirrored bedrooms overlook the water and a great spread of meadows where animals graze. There is a vast choice for 'flexitime' breakfast on the terrace or in the rustic-chic dining room. Madame, an energetic and interesting hostess, was a publisher in Paris for many years.

Price	€70–€80.
Rooms	3: 2 doubles, 1 triple.
Meals	Restaurants 2km.
Closed	Rarely.
Directions	From A63 exit 8 to St Geours de Maremne; D17 S 5km to Saubusse; right just before bridge; château 600m on right.

Claude Dourlet
Château de Bezincam,
600 quai de Bezincam,
Saubusse les Bains, 40180 Dax, Landes
Tel +33 (0)5 58 57 70 27
Email dourlet.bezincam@orange.fr
Web www.bezincam.fr

Entry 408 Map 13

Aquitaine

Maison Capcazal de Pachioü

Fall asleep by a crackling fire, wake to the clucking of the hens. You'll love this house, with its original panelling (1610) and its contents accumulated by the family for 14 generations: portraits from the 17th century onwards, spectacular bedrooms with canopied antique beds, strong colours, luscious armoires, embroidered linen. One luminous bathroom has a marble-topped washstand, the living room is handsome with twin grandfather clocks and huge stone fireplace, and François has stepped into his mother's shoes seamlessly, nurturing goats, donkeys, pets and guests; brilliant dinners, too. Exceptional.

Ethical Collection: Food.
See page 410 for details.

Price	€50-€90.
Rooms	4 doubles.
Meals	Dinner with wine, €20.
Closed	Rarely.
Directions	From Dax D947 for Pau & Orthez; from r'bout at edge of Dax cont. 10km; at r'bout on D947 ignore sign for Mimbaste; next right C16; follow discreet yellow signs for 1km.

François Dufourcet-Alberca
Maison Capcazal de Pachioü,
606 route de Pachioü,
40350 Mimbaste, Landes

Tel   +33 (0)5 58 55 30 54
Email   francois.alberca@wanadoo.fr
Web   www.capcazaldepachiou.com

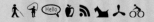

Entry 409   Map 13

Aquitaine

Domaine de Peyron

The family estate – a pretty cluster of beautifully maintained buildings – has been feted in design magazines; you can tell that Maylis adored creating her interiors. Three bedrooms lie peacefully in the barn, alongside a glowing salon. One is wood-panelled, like a swish ski lodge; one, with ceiling fan and draped four-poster, has its heart in Africa; all are luxurious. The Cottards' five children frolic in the pool in high summer – you may prefer out of season – and the views are far-reaching. Maylis loves people and is a great cook: dinners are intimate or convivial, breakfasts are feasts.

Price	€80-€90.
Rooms	3 doubles.
Meals	Lunch €24. Dinner €29. Wine €16-€45. Guest kitchenette.
Closed	Rarely.
Directions	From Hagetmau D2 to St Cricq Chalosse; through village; on outskirts fork left, signed.

Maylis & Louis Cottard
Domaine de Peyron,
240 chemin de Bordes,
40700 St Cricq Chalosse, Landes

Tel   +33 (0)5 58 79 85 64
Mobile +33 (0)6 32 31 90 47
Email   lcottard@wanadoo.fr
Web   www.domainedepeyron.com

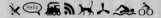

Entry 410   Map 13

Aquitaine

Domaine de la Carrère

Wow! Country-house grandeur in modest, pretty Arthez. Fritz and Mike moved to France from Wales and spent three years perfecting this 17th-century mansion. Oak panelling, parquet floors and ancient beams are the backdrop to gleaming antiques, original paintings and rich rugs. Bedrooms are classically elegant with high ceilings, carved bedheads, flamboyant drapes; bathrooms are high luxe. Quiet corners display plump sofas while the garden is lush with terraces, lawns and dreamy pool. Historic Pau is 20 minutes away and glorious Biarritz 40; return to Fritz's fabulous dinner amid candles and cut glass!

Price	€95–€125.
Rooms	5: 4 doubles, 1 twin.
Meals	Dinner with wine, €35.
Closed	Rarely.
Directions	A64 exit 9; N117 for Orthez 7km; D31 right to Arthez. In village centre left to La Place; house 500m to west, signed.

	Fritz Kisby & Mike Ridout
	Domaine de la Carrère,
	54 rue la Carrère, 64370 Arthez
	de Béarn, Pyrénées-Atlantiques
Tel	+33 (0)5 24 37 61 24
Mobile	+33 (0)6 32 96 34 62
Email	info@domaine-de-la-carrere.fr
Web	www.domaine-de-la-carrere.fr

Entry 411   Map 13

Aquitaine

La Closerie du Guilhat

Through the iron gates, up the tree-lined drive to an astonishing kingdom of plants of all shapes and sizes: a hidden garden of exotica. Weave your way through rhododendrons and magnolias, bananas and bamboos to secret benches for quiet reading and the Pyrenees as a backdrop – sheer delight for all ages. To the sturdy Béarn house with solid old furniture and traditional décor Marie-Christine has added her own decorative touches; bedrooms are spotless. Table tennis is shared with gîte guests, dinners are delicious. The otherworldliness is restorative yet the spa town of Salies is a bike-ride away.

Price	€59–€65. €75 for 3.
Rooms	3: 1 double, 1 twin, 1 suite for 3.
Meals	Dinner €22.
Closed	Rarely.
Directions	From A64 exit 7; right for Salies '5 tonnes'; next right to Le Guilhat 1.8km; house on left beside nurseries at junction with Chemin des Bois.

	Marie-Christine Potiron
	La Closerie du Guilhat,
	64270 Salies de Béarn,
	Pyrénées-Atlantiques
Tel	+33 (0)5 59 38 08 80
Email	guilhat@club-internet.fr
Web	www.holidayshomes.com/guilhat

Entry 412   Map 13

Aquitaine

Villa Le Goëland

It is lush, lavish, inviting. Dominating the ocean, yards from the beaches of glamorous Biarritz, the only privately owned villa of its kind to have resisted commercial redevelopment has opened its arms to guests. Turrets were added in 1903; Paul's family took possession in 1934; now he and his wife, young, charming, professional, are its inspired guardians and restorers. Be ravished by oak floors, magnificent stairs, tall windows and balconies that go on for ever. Two bedrooms have terraces, beds are king-size, bathrooms are vintage or modern, breakfasts flourish sunshine and pastries. And the surfing is amazing.

Price	€150-€270.
Rooms	4: 3 doubles, 1 suite for 3.
Meals	Restaurant 20m.
Closed	November-February.
Directions	From Place Clémençeau in Biarritz centre follow signs for place Ste Eugénie by Rue Mazagran; after pharmacy 1st right Rue des Goélands. House between antique shop & bar, narrow street.

Paul & Elisabeth Daraignez
Villa Le Goëland,
12 plateau de l'Atalaye,
64200 Biarritz, Pyrénées-Atlantiques
Tel   +33 (0)5 59 24 25 76
Mobile +33 (0)6 87 66 22 19
Email   info@villagoeland.com
Web   www.villagoeland.com

Aquitaine

Bidachuna

The electronic gate clicks behind you and 29 hectares of forested peacefulness is yours – with wildlife. Open wide your beautiful curtains next morning and you may see deer feeding; lift your eyes to feast on long vistas to the Pyrenean foothills; trot downstairs to the earthly feast that is Basque breakfast; fall asleep to the hoot of the owl. Shyly attentive Isabelle manages all this impeccably and keeps a refined house where everything gleams; floors are chestnut, bathrooms are marble, family antiques are perfect. Pop off to lovely St Jean de Luz for lunch, return to this manicured haven and blissful cosseting.

Price	€120.
Rooms	3: 2 doubles, 1 twin.
Meals	Restaurant 6km.
Closed	Mid-November to mid-March.
Directions	From Biarritz railway station to Bassussary & Arcangues; D3 for St Pée; 8km after Arcangues house on left; signed.

Isabelle Ormazabal
Bidachuna,
Route Oihan Bidea D3, 64310 St Pée sur Nivelle, Pyrénées-Atlantiques
Tel   +33 (0)5 59 54 56 22
Email   isabelle@bidachuna.com
Web   www.bidachuna.com

Aquitaine

Les Volets Bleus

High in these ancient hills stands this beautiful new farmhouse built with old Basque materials. Chic, clever Marie has made a perfect creation. Through the magnificent double-arch door is a flagged entrance hall, then a terrace with rattan chairs and weathered pine tables. Up stone staircases are bedrooms in restful colours with wood or tiled floors, gilt mirrors, embroidered sheets, ancestral paintings; exquisite bathrooms have iron towel rails and aromatic oils. Marie is also an accomplished gardener so retreat to her garden for a read or a swim – or lounge in the sitting room on deep comfy sofas. It's heaven.

Price	€108-€170. Suite €138-€186.
Rooms	4: 2 doubles, 1 twin, 1 suite.
Meals	Restaurants 1.5km.
Closed	Rarely.
Directions	From Biarritz D3 for Arcangues; left at r'bout to St Pée sur Nivelle; end of village, sign to Arcangues, 3rd right; house 1st on left up slope.

Marie de Lapasse
Les Volets Bleus,
Chemin Etchegaraya, 64200 Arcangues,
Pyrénées-Atlantiques

Mobile	+33 (0)6 07 69 03 85
Email	maisonlesvoletsbleus@wanadoo.fr
Web	www.lesvoletsbleus.fr

Entry 415   Map 13

Aquitaine

Domaine de Silencenia

The house cornerstone, the magnificent magnolia, the towering pines were all planted on one day in 1881. A pool and lake (with fountain, boat, trout and koi carp) are set in spacious parkland, and a billiard room, sauna and fitness area (for a small charge) are on tap. This sensitive restoration includes a Blue Marlin room, canopied pine beds, modern fittings, a desk made from wine cases and respect for the original chestnut panelling. Philippe, discreetly helped by his mother with dinner, knows about wine too: his cellar is brilliant. And there's great walking in the surrounding hills.

Price	€90.
Rooms	5: 3 doubles, 2 triples.
Meals	Dinner with wine, €30-€35.
Closed	Rarely.
Directions	A63 exit 5 onto D932 through Ustaritz & Cambo les Bains; left into Louhossoa; straight over x-roads. House 800m on left.

Philippe Mallor
Domaine de Silencenia,
64250 Louhossoa,
Pyrénées-Atlantiques

Tel	+33 (0)5 59 93 35 60
Mobile	+33 (0)6 72 63 81 66
Email	domaine.de.silencenia@orange.fr
Web	www.domaine-silencenia.com

Entry 416   Map 13

Aquitaine

Maison Marchand

A lovely face among all the lovely faces of this listed village, the 16th-century Basque farmhouse, resuscitated by its delightful French/Irish owners, is run with well-organised informality. Dinners round the great table are lively; local dishes are excellent. Light, well-decorated bedrooms, each with their own terrace, have beams, exposed wafer bricks, thoughtful extras. Summer breakfast is in the beautiful walled garden on the covered terrace – beyond: deckchairs and a hammock. Extrovert Gilbert shares his knowledge of culture and rugby, and will teach you *la pelote basque*! *Ask about massage treatments.*

Price	€65–€85.
Rooms	3: 2 doubles; 1 double & extra bed for 2 children.
Meals	Dinner with wine, €25.
Closed	Mid-November to mid-March.
Directions	From A64 exit 4 for Urt & Bidache; right D936; right D123 at mini-island to La Bastide Clairence. House in main street, opp. bakery.

Valerie & Gilbert Foix
Maison Marchand,
Rue Notre Dame, 64240 La Bastide
Clairence, Pyrénées-Atlantiques

Tel	+33 (0)5 59 29 18 27
Email	maison.marchand@wanadoo.fr
Web	pagesperso-orange.fr/maison.marchand

Aquitaine

La Maison de la Fontaine

The venerable stone house stands proudly in tiny ancient Araux. Jon and Kate – well-travelled, well-read – imprint their relaxed personalities on the place. Glimpse Latin America, Asia, the Orient; find interesting books in fine big rooms. The sitting room's antiques glow in firelight while the salon, with its 1904 Blüthner grand piano, resounds with recitals. Unwind in the large pool, lavender garden, orchard or Béarn's forests and châteaux. Return to dinner in the fire-warmed kitchen; the veg garden provides the herbs, children collect the eggs, the neighbour makes the pâté, your hosts supply all the rest.

Price	€90. Extra bed €25.
Rooms	4: 2 doubles, 1 twin, 1 family room for 3.
Meals	Dinner with wine, from €25. Picnic lunch €10–€15.
Closed	Christmas.
Directions	From A64 exit 8, D9 to Mourenx; D111 to Navarrenx; D936 for Bayonne 5km; thro' Viellenave; left into Araux, signs to Maison de la Fontaine.

Jonathan & Katherine Siviter
La Maison de la Fontaine,
1 rue de la Fontaine, 64190 Araux,
Pyrénées-Atlantiques

Tel	+ 33 (0)5 59 66 20 10
Mobile	+ 33 (0)6 81 70 49 36
Email	info@maisondelafontaine.com
Web	www.maisondelafontaine.com

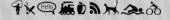

Aquitaine

Domaine Lespoune

Renovated with panache in unsung Pays Basque, this 18th-century manor calms and charms. Easy-going and interesting, Nicole and Yves poured their hearts into its restoration: panelling, tiled and wooden floors, original doors, and added modern touches: colourwashed walls, contemporary art, walk-in showers. The ground-floor bedroom has a striking black-and-white tiled floor and a private terrace; the rooms upstairs are palely soft (one with veranda). Breakfast under the spreading magnolia, spend the day fishing, return to Nicole's beautiful food – and a Navarrenx cigar in the garden. *Free sauna & spa with two-night stay.*

Price	€70-€90.
Rooms	3: 2 doubles, 1 twin.
Meals	Dinner with wine, €25-€35.
Closed	Mid-November to mid-March.
Directions	From Oloron Ste Marie D936 for Bayonne 20km; left to Castetnau Camblong centre; house on right after church; signed.

Yves & Nicole Everaert
Domaine Lespoune,
20 route de Camblong, 64190 Castetnau
Camblong, Pyrénées-Atlantiques
Tel   +33 (0)5 59 66 24 14
Email   contact@lespoune.fr
Web   www.lespoune.fr

Entry 419   Map 13

Aquitaine

Maison L'Aubèle

The Desbonnets transformed their grand 18th-century village house after finding it and this sleepy village in the Pyrenean foothills: both house and owners are quiet, elegant, sophisticated and full of interest. He collects precious old books, she binds them, and the furniture is a feast for the eyes. As you breakfast off fine china ask what you need to know about the region, and do delve into their tempting library. The light, airy bedrooms have more interesting furniture on lovely wooden floors. La Rose is very chic, La Verte is a dream, large and luminous with views of the mountains and a 'waltz-in' bathroom.

Price	€70.
Rooms	2 doubles.
Meals	Restaurants 4km.
Closed	Rarely.
Directions	From Navarrenx D2 for Monein to Jasses; right D27 for Oloron Ste Marie; in Lay Lamidou left, 1st right, 2nd house on right.

Marie-France Desbonnet
Maison L'Aubèle,
4 rue de la Hauti, 64190 Lay Lamidou,
Pyrénées-Atlantiques
Tel   +33 (0)5 59 66 00 44
Mobile +33 (0)6 86 22 02 76
Email   desbonnet.bmf@infonie.fr
Web   chambrehote.ifrance.com

Entry 420   Map 13

Aquitaine

Clos Mirabel

Fifteen minutes from city lights yet bucolic and surrounded by vineyards. French-Canadian André is a retired diplomat, Ann worked in travel, Emily goes to the village school. They fell in love with Clos Mirabel five years ago, now they delightedly welcome guests. The 18th-century manor is flanked by a winery and gatehouse; inside, rooms are light, airy and restful, their gracious proportions enhanced by Ann's elegant eye. A spiral staircase links the Gustavian apartment's three levels, there's a pool terrace with breathtaking Pyrenean views and breakfast honey comes from André's bees. A delight.

Price	€95–€140. Extra person €35.
Rooms	3: 2 doubles, 1 apartment for 4 (with kitchen).
Meals	Restaurants 3km.
Closed	Rarely.
Directions	From Pau N134 for Saragosse to Jurançon; cont. for Gan; right at traffic lights for Chapelle de Rousse. At top of hill right Av des Frères Bartélémy.

	Ann Kenny & André Péloquin
	Clos Mirabel,
	276 avenue des Frères Barthélémy,
	64110 Jurançon, Pyrénées-Atlantiques
Tel	+33 (0)5 59 06 32 83
Email	info@closmirabel.com
Web	www.closmirabel.com

Entry 421   Map 13

Aquitaine

Maison Rancèsamy

Painters love this haven and respond to Isabelle's own gentle talent. From terrace and pool you can see for ever into the Pyrenees – sunlit snowy in winter, all the greens in summer. Beside the 1700s farmhouse, the barn conversion shelters artistic, uncluttered, stone-walled bedrooms and incredible views. The superb dining room – Isabelle's trompe-l'œil floor, huge carved table – reflects the origins (Polish, French, South African) of this happy, relaxed family. On balmy summer evenings, the food (book ahead) is deliciously garden-aromatic: Simon is a powerful, eco-aware gardener. Wonderful. *Min. two nights July/August.*

Price	€75–€90. Family room €108–€125.
Rooms	5: 2 doubles, 1 twin, 2 family rooms.
Meals	Dinner with wine, €32.
Closed	Rarely.
Directions	From Pau N134 S for Saragosse to Gan; right at lights after chemist, D24 for Lasseube 9km; left D324. Follow Chambres d'Hôtes signs; cross 2 small bridges; house on left up steep hill.

	Simon & Isabelle Browne
	Maison Rancèsamy,
	Quartier Rey, 64290 Lasseube,
	Pyrénées-Atlantiques
Tel	+33 (0)5 59 04 26 37
Email	missbrowne@wanadoo.fr
Web	www.missbrowne.com

Entry 422   Map 13

Aquitaine

Beth Soureilh

Marie-Noëlle is charming and so is her house: perched on the edge of the forest, it is light, bright, eco-warm and filled with colour. Cheerful pinks and greens romp through the sitting/dining room; step out onto the terrace and find a pretty garden with the greenest views. Upstairs are very generous bedrooms with wooden floors, big beds, bright colours and gleaming white-tiled shower rooms, one with a view. Breakfast and supper are organic and delicious – much is home-grown – and there are excellent local wines. If you hear 'La Marseillaise' a-humming, you haven't over indulged: it's just Coco the parrot.

Price	€59–€68.
Rooms	2: 1 double, 1 twin.
Meals	Dinner with wine, €22.
Closed	Rarely.
Directions	From Pau D938 for Lourdes 15km; D936 left to Bénéjacq; cont. D936 for 2km; up hill; after 2 bends house on left, signed.

Marie-Noëlle Pée
Beth Soureilh, 3 côte du Bois de Bénéjacq, 64800 Coarraze, Pyrénées-Atlantiques
Tel   +33 (0)5 59 53 70 75
Mobile +33 (0)6 07 66 90 11
Email   info@chambres-hotes-pyrenees.net
Web   www.bed-breakfast-france-pyrenees.com

Entry 423   Map 14

Aquitaine

Château de Rodié

Paul and Pippa did the triumphant restoration themselves, with two small children and a passionate commitment to the integrity of this ancient building: brash modernities are hidden and the telephone lurks behind a model ship. Expect two stone staircases, patches of fresco, fine old country furniture, a vast hall with a giant fireplace and table, an atmospheric room in the tower, a lovely pool – and dogs, geese, ducks, sheep: this is a working farm. The family is super welcoming, veggie-friendly, and Pippa, who favours organic produce, cooks gorgeous dinners that last for hours. *Sawday self-catering also.*

Ethical Collection: Environment & Food. See page 410 for details.

Price	€78–€110.
Rooms	5: 4 doubles, 1 suite.
Meals	Dinner with wine, €20.
Closed	Rarely.
Directions	From Fumel D102 to Tournon; D656 for Agen 300m; left to Courbiac, past church, right at cross for Montaigu 1km; house on left.

Paul & Pippa Hecquet
Château de Rodié,
47370 Courbiac de Tournon,
Lot-et-Garonne
Tel   +33 (0)5 53 40 89 24
Email mail@chateauderodie.com
Web   www.chateauderodie.com

Entry 424   Map 14

Aquitaine

Château de Grenier

One minute you're bowling along a fairly busy road, the next you've pulled up at the doors of an 18th- and 19th-century *belle demeure*. Painted wood and dried flowers set the tone of this large, light, comfortable home. Discreet, charming Madame ushers you up to beautifully proportioned bedrooms with tall windows; ask for one facing the garden. Expect pristine white bathrooms, a sun-streamed double, a generous twin with pink walls, a two-room suite off the garden – more basic but ideal for families. Dinners are serenely elegant affairs, your hosts share the cooking. *Ask about furniture painting & sculpture courses.*

Price	€90. Family suite €140.
Rooms	5: 3 doubles, 1 twin, 1 family suite.
Meals	Dinner with wine, €30. Restaurants nearby.
Closed	Rarely.
Directions	A62 exit 6; D8 N for Agen approx. 4km; château on right just before river Garonne. Signed.

	Chantal Breton le Grelle
	Château de Grenier,
	47160 St Léger,
	Lot-et-Garonne
Tel	+33 (0)5 53 79 59 06
Email	info@chateaudegrenier.com
Web	www.chateaudegrenier.com

Entry 425   Map 14

Aquitaine

Chez Kelly

The orangery, with Warhol's Marilyn prints and red sofas, sets the boutique-château tone. But expect a relaxed touch: Siamese cats and golden retriever play; hosts Brendan and Keld – a Kiwi and a Dane – help you unwind. Easy in this setting, the château laps serenely at the banks of the canal. Boats, bikes, tennis court and pool await your discovery, a wildflower garden is in the making and orchids beautify chic, themed rooms: Iona, Alhambra… the suite is African in mood, with zebra stripes on its bed and polished floor. Dinner, elegant and convivial, starts with champagne on the terrace. *Minimum two nights in July/August.*

Price	€95–€145.
Rooms	5: 4 doubles, 1 suite.
Meals	Dinner with wine, €25. Snacks by the pool. Picnics available.
Closed	Rarely.
Directions	From Marmande D993 for Casteljaloux 1km; right D116 7km; left D3, almost immed. right D116; follow canal 2km; house signed on sharp bend.

	Keld & Brendan Kelly
	Chez Kelly,
	Château Sauvin, 47180 Meilhan sur Garonne, Lot-et-Garonne
Tel	+33 (0)5 53 20 13 07
Email	chezkelly@orange.fr
Web	www.chezkelly.eu

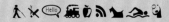

Entry 426   Map 9

Aquitaine

Manoir de Levignac

Walk through the entrance hall into the handsome country kitchen and thence into the peaceful grounds, with nature reserve and views. Or stay and dine, beautifully, in a room with a big fireplace, pottery pieces and carved cupboard doors. In the sitting room, terracotta tiles, kilim rugs, and grand piano give a comfortably artistic air. Adriana is Swiss-Italian, Jocelyn South African; they are thoughtful and kind and do everything well. You get a lush bedroom with rural views, a sitting room and an immaculate bathroom. Outside, a small pine wood, a daisy-sprinkled lawn and a pool surrounded by palms.

Price	€70–€80.
Rooms	2 suites for 4.
Meals	Dinner with wine, €25.
Closed	Rarely.
Directions	From A10 exit St André de Cubzac to Ste Foy La Grande; D708 to Duras; 4km after Duras left C1 to St Pierre.

	Jocelyn & Adriana Cloete
	Manoir de Levignac,
	St Pierre sur Dropt,
	47120 Duras, Lot-et-Garonne
Tel	+33 (0)5 53 83 68 11
Email	cloete@wanadoo.fr
Web	manoir.de.levignac.free.fr

Entry 427   Map 9

Aquitaine

Château Lavanau

The Uharts aren't just playing at being farmers – as the wine crates beside their pink-washed farmhouse prove. After spending 15 years in Paris, they now produce 100,000 bottles of Côtes de Duras a year; Paul – half French – is happy to guide you round the vineyard. There's an art studio, too: Juliana trained at St Martin's and runs courses. The bedrooms are simple and very charming, with old country furniture and splashes of colour. A half wall separates each room from its narrow stylish bathroom. There's also a small kitchen where you can prepare snacks. And a garden just leaving its infancy.

Price	€70–€80.
Rooms	5: 3 doubles, 2 twins.
Meals	Guest kitchen. Restaurant 1km.
Closed	Rarely.
Directions	From Bordeaux D936 to Ste Foy la Grande; right D708 for Duras 9km; at Margueron, fork left for La Sauvetat/Miramont 1.5km; left for Monestier; château signed.

	Juliana & Paul Uhart
	Château Lavanau,
	Les Faux, 47120 Loubès Bernac,
	Lot-et-Garonne
Tel	+33 (0)5 53 94 86 45
Mobile	+33 (0)6 74 97 57 04
Email	juliana.uhart@googlemail.com
Web	www.chateaulavanau.com

Entry 428   Map 9

Aquitaine

Manoir de Roquegautier

In a beautiful park with rolling views, this gracious house is wondrously French. Drapes, swags and interlinings all by Brigitte, and memorable rooms in the tower with their own entrance and spiral stone stair. There are claw-footed baths and huge old basins and taps, and each top-floor suite has one round tower room. Bliss for families: swings, games room and discreet pool, gazebos around the garden and mature trees to shade your picnic lunches. Delicious food fresh from the family farm are shared with your hosts, but note: the French language may dominate at dinner. *Upholstery courses out of season. Golf 4km.*

Price	€80. Suites €120-€133.
Rooms	4: 2 doubles, 2 family suites: 1 for 3, 1 for 4.
Meals	Dinner with wine, €26. Child €12.
Closed	November-Easter.
Directions	From Villeneuve sur Lot N21 north for Cancon 15.5km. Manoir signed on left 3.5km before Cancon.

Brigitte & Christian Vrech
Manoir de Roquegautier,
Beaugas, 47290 Cancon,
Lot-et-Garonne
Tel +33 (0)5 53 01 60 75
Email roquegautier@free.fr
Web www.roquegautier.fr

Entry 429   Map 9

Aquitaine

Domaine du Moulin de Labique

Soay sheep on the drive, ducks on the pond, goats in the greenhouse and food *à la grand-mère*. Shutters are painted with *bleu de pastel* from the Gers and the 13th-century interiors have lost none of their charm. In house and outbuildings there are chunky beams, seagrass on ancient tiles, vintage iron bedsteads, antique mirrors, and wallpapers flower-sprigged in raspberry, jade and green. Outside are old French roses and young alleys of trees, a bamboo-fringed stream, a restaurant in the stables, an exquisite pool. Wonderful hosts, the Bruxellois owners loved this place for years; now they are its best ambassadors.

Price	€110-€135. Suite €170.
Rooms	6: 2 doubles, 2 twins, 1 suite for 4, 1 apartment.
Meals	Dinner €27. Wine €16-€30.
Closed	Rarely.
Directions	From N21 at Cancon D124 for Monflanquin 5.5km; left D153 through St Vivien; on right 1km after St Vivien.

Patrick & Christine Hendricx
Domaine du Moulin de Labique,
St Vivien, 47210 Villeréal,
Lot-et-Garonne
Tel +33 (0)5 53 01 63 90
Email moulin-de-labique@wanadoo.fr
Web www.moulin-de-labique.fr

Entry 430   Map 9

Aquitaine

Le Prieuré du Château de Biron

Beneath the imposing fortress, the church gazes over the little village, hiding this very old priory. Cross the tiny cobbled courtyard to an ornate knocker on a nail-studded door. You're greeted in a stone floored hall and ushered up an elegant stair. Fireplaces take pride of place in huge first-floor rooms, along with exposed stone walls, the glow of antiques, fine linens and shades of powder blue and pale gold: Elisabeth has exquisite taste. Timbers fly across the palely gracious rooms under the roof; heavenly views reach across the fields. Harmonious, rich, thoroughly welcoming and not to be missed. *Over 12s welcome.*

Price	€120–€160. Apartment €950–€1,130 per week.
Rooms	5 + 1: 3 suites, 2 family suites for 3. Apartment for 3.
Meals	Breakfast €8 (apartment only). Dinner €28. Restaurant 50m.
Closed	Mid-November to February.
Directions	From St Cyprien D703 for Bergerac; left D710 to Belvès; D53 to Monpazier; D2 for Villeréal 5km, left D53 to Biron. Parking below château.

Elisabeth Vedier
Le Prieuré du Château de Biron,
Le Bourg, 24540 Biron,
Dordogne
Tel +33 (0)5 53 61 93 03
Mobile +33 (0)6 84 31 38 38
Email leprieurebiron@gmail.com
Web www.leprieurebiron.com

Entry 431   Map 9

Aquitaine

Domaine des Faures

Near the lovely bastide village of Monpazier, yet secluded, is this immaculately restored 17th-century house of quiet stone. Log fires and heated 300-year-old flagstones keep you toasty in winter, fans cool you in summer, wooden floors and smooth white walls create a mood of delicious calm. Classic French breakfast of baguettes and organic jams is served at a circular glass table with black dining chairs: classy. Swim in the saltwater pool, cycle through woods to Château Biron. New to farming, the Standens have a herd of organic Aubrac-Salers cattle grazing their rolling acres. Super place, super people.

Ethical Collection: Environment & Food. See page 410 for details.

Price	€95–€115. Whole house €1,500–€2,750 per week.
Rooms	4: 3 doubles, 1 family room for 3.
Meals	Dinner with wine, €28. Restaurant 2km.
Closed	Rarely.
Directions	From Bergerac, follow signs for Issigeac, Villeréal & Monpazier. Right at wooden cross just before Monpazier on country road; Les Faures signed.

Ray & Jacinta Standen
Domaine des Faures,
24540 Gaugeac,
Dordogne
Tel +33 (0)5 53 27 98 08
Email raystanden@domainedesfaures.com
Web www.domainedesfaures.com

Entry 432   Map 9

Aquitaine

Château Gauthié

Outside a perfect bastide village, here is château B&B run with warmth and energy. Stéphane cooks brilliantly and loves wine; Florence charms her guests brightly. Restful, light-filled, traditional bedrooms have white bathrooms. An infinity pool overlooks the lake below, above it perches the treehouse steeped in rusticity, its balcony gazing over meadows and cows, its mother tree thrusting two branches through the floor. Solar-lit paths lead you down through the trees at night, a breakfast basket is winched up in the morning. Later… play badminton, fish in the lake, spin off on a bike. *Minimum two nights.*

Price	€85–€160.
Rooms	5: 3 doubles, 1 twin. Treehouse: 1 double.
Meals	Dinner €40. Wine €15–€90.
Closed	Mid-November to March.
Directions	From Bergerac N21 10km; left D14 to Issigeac; right D21 for Castillones 2km; just after Eyrenville/Monmarvès x-roads, left for château.

Florence & Stéphane Desmette
Château Gauthié,
24560 Issigeac Monmarvès,
Dordogne
Tel +33 (0)5 53 27 30 33
Web www.chateaugauthie.com

Entry 433   Map 9

Aquitaine

Le Logis Plantagenet

A medieval house, part of an earlier château, on a tree-lined square in old Bergerac, a minute's walk from the lovely limpid river – a peaceful, centre ville address. Your well-travelled and welcoming hosts give you light-filled bedrooms painted in soft colours with pretty rugs on polished floors, excellent beds, full-length baths and fabulous linen. Breakfasts are served in the courtyard garden in summer and in the big modern kitchen in winter, at one merry table. After a day visiting châteaux and gardens and tasting fine wines, return to two delightful country-house sitting rooms. *Ask about house-party cookery courses.*

Price	€85–€95.
Rooms	3: 1 double, 2 twins.
Meals	Dinner with wine, €28. Restaurants nearby.
Closed	Rarely.
Directions	In old quarter of Bergerac; owner's house with yellow shutters faces old port; Le Logis Plantagenet is directly behind. Ring bell of 6 Quai Salvette.

Bruce & Rosetta Cantlie
Le Logis Plantagenet,
5 rue du Grand Moulin,
24100 Bergerac, Dordogne
Tel +33 (0)5 53 57 15 99
Email bruce.cantlie@wanadoo.fr
Web www.lelogisplantagenet.com

Entry 434   Map 9

Aquitaine

La Ferme de la Rivière

The large farmhouse auberge sits alone and surrounded by its fields in a hamlet of a dozen houses. The Archer family honour tradition; he is a poultry breeder, she is an industrious (decidedly non-vegetarian) cook and the recipes for handcrafting pâtés and foie gras are their heirlooms. Readers talk of fabulous meals and delicious aperitifs...The honey stones of the building are impeccably pointed and cleaned, bedrooms have functionality rather than character, shower rooms are large and pristine and there's an open-fired sitting room just for guests. Good for families (a climbing frame in the garden). Utterly French.

Price	€56.
Rooms	2: 1 double, 1 triple.
Meals	Dinner with wine, €21.
Closed	November-February.
Directions	From airport D660 for Sarlat; in Mouleydier over bridge on D21; after bridge 1st left D37; follow signs 2nd on right; cont. to house. Don't go into St Agne.

Marie-Thérèse & Jean-Michel Archer
La Ferme de la Rivière,
24520 St Agne,
Dordogne
Tel   +33 (0)5 53 23 22 26
Email   archer.marietherese@wanadoo.fr
Web   www.lafermedelariviere.com

Entry 435   Map 9

Aquitaine

Pauliac

The exuberant hillside garden, full of blossom and bamboo, has gorgeous views of sunflowers and an overflowing stone plunge pool. John and Jane's talents are a restful atmosphere, great dinners, and interiors that are a brilliant marriage of cottage simplicity and sparks from African throws and contemporary paintings. Beautiful bedrooms have a separate entrance. Delightful, energetic Jane offers superb, imaginative food in the sun-splashed veranda with its all-season views, or the bright, rustic dining room with roaring log fire — and early suppers for children. Lovely people in a tranquil view-drenched spot. *Cookery & painting courses.*

Ethical Collection: Food.
See page 410 for details.

Price	€70-€75.
Rooms	4: 2 doubles, 1 twin, 1 suite for 4.
Meals	Dinner €25. Wine €10.
Closed	Rarely.
Directions	From Angoulême D393 for Périgueux 29km; right D12 for Ribérac to Verteillac. Left at Boulangerie on D1 for Celles; after 5km right D99 for Celles. After 400m, sign to left.

Jane & John Edwards
Pauliac,
Celles, 24600 Ribérac,
Dordogne
Tel   +33 (0)5 47 23 40 17
Email   info@pauliac.fr
Web   www.pauliac.fr

Entry 436   Map 9

Aquitaine

Les Hirondelles

Carine, half-Greek, energetic, charming and fun, makes you feel welcome in the sunny kitchen of her restored farmhouse on the top of a hill. She enjoys cooking French and international dishes, sometimes organises barbecues round the big pool and makes amazing walnut jam. Simple, dim-lit, inexpensive bedrooms are in a converted barn set back from the house, each with a terrace delineated by concrete planters. The pool is far enough away not to disturb your siesta. Spend two or three nights and get to know this beautiful village and the whole area; Carine knows the best places to go. *Minimum two nights July/August.*

Price	€50-€54.
Rooms	4: 2 doubles, 2 twins.
Meals	Dinner with wine, €19.
Closed	November-April.
Directions	From Le Bugue go to Ste Alvère; at main x-roads there, D30 for Pezuls. House 3rd right, 500m after sign Le Maine at top of hill.

Carine Someritis
Les Hirondelles,
Le Maine, 24510 Ste Alvère,
Dordogne
Tel   +33 (0)5 53 22 75 40
Email   leshirondelles.carine@orange.fr

Entry 437   Map 9

Aquitaine

Le Moulin Neuf

Watch the ducks waddle by on their way to the lake. Robert or Stuart's greeting is the first line of an ode to hospitality written in warm stone and breathtaking gardens, set to the tune of the mill stream. Immaculate rooms in the guest barn are comfortingly filled with good beds and fresh flowers, bathrooms are sheer luxury, and views sweep over the lawns. Wake up to delicious breads, croissants, patisseries, homemade jams, succulent fruits and tiny cheeses served on white tablecloths on the vine-shaded terrace. All is lovingly tended, in perfect peace. *Ask about pets. Over tens welcome. Min. three nights in winter.*

Price	€85-€89.
Rooms	5: 2 doubles, 1 twin/double, 1 family room for 3, 1 suite.
Meals	Restaurant in Paunat, 1km.
Closed	Rarely.
Directions	From Le Bugue D703 & D31 through Limeuil. Past viewpoint to x-roads; D2 for Ste Alvère; after 100m fork left; house 2km on left at small x-roads.

Robert Chappell & Stuart Shippey
Le Moulin Neuf,
Paunat, 24510 Ste Alvère,
Dordogne
Tel   +33 (0)5 53 63 30 18
Email   moulin-neuf@usa.net
Web   www.the-moulin-neuf.com

Entry 438   Map 9

Aquitaine

Le Domaine de la Millasserie

Near lovely lively Trémolat, and the Dordogne with its watery charms, is this classy and immaculate B&B. American Byrne and Alain from Bordeaux have swapped literature and antiques for hospitality – and do they do it well. Alongside their honey-hued 18th-century manor overlooking the woods, a fine new building in traditional style houses four generous rooms. French windows open to private terraces, huge beds are dressed in toile de Jouy, gorgeous antiques glow: armoires, paintings and mirrors. Lazy breakfasts, by the pool if you prefer, flourish fruits, viennoiseries and homemade preserves. *Minimum two nights.*

Price	€95.
Rooms	4 doubles.
Meals	Restaurants 5km.
Closed	Rarely.
Directions	From Bergerac D660 to Lalinde; D703 thro' Sauveboeuf; cont. D703 7km; at x-roads, right for Millasserie (signs), property immed. on left.

	Byrne Fone & Alain Pioton
	Le Domaine de la Millasserie,
	24150 Mauzac & Grand Castang,
	Dordogne
Tel	+33 (0)5 53 57 78 01
Email	byrnefone@wanadoo.fr
Web	www.bandbfrancedordogne.com

Entry 439   Map 9

Aquitaine

Manoir de la Brunie

An elegant village manor in a glorious setting. The owners live in Paris but the friendly manager will introduce you to a fine living room full of warm bright colours overlooking a sweeping lawn – play the piano, browse the books – and excellent bedrooms. The tower suite and small double have a modern feel, the three other rooms, huge and high-ceilinged, are more traditional; all have subtle colours, new wooden floors, sitting areas and good lighting. Breakfasts are sumptuous, bathrooms delightful… there's a heated pool shared with gîte guests, a beach nearby on the Dordogne, and riding next door.

Price	€65-€99. Extra bed €17.
Rooms	5: 3 doubles, 1 twin/double, 1 suite.
Meals	Breakfast €8-€12. Dinner with wine, €27.
Closed	December-January.
Directions	From Sarlat D57 to Beynac; D703 to St Cyprien; cont. 7km, right to Coux & Bigaroque; thro' village, left after Mairie approx. 1km; house on right, just past wayside cross.

	Joyce Villemur
	Manoir de la Brunie,
	La Brunie, 24220 Le Coux
	et Bigaroque, Dordogne
Tel	+33 (0)5 53 31 95 62
Email	manoirdelabrunie@wanadoo.fr
Web	www.manoirdelabrunie.com

Entry 440   Map 9

Aquitaine

La Guérinière

Once a charterhouse, this good-looking Périgord house, peacefully atop a hill facing Domme in private parkland, is a tribute to the rich sober taste of the area. Inside reflects outside: the same dark timbers against pale stone and the owners have redecorated the bedrooms most charmingly, gradually replacing the modern furniture with country antiques; the feel is warmly authentic. Moreover, they used to run a restaurant: we hear great reports of the food. There's a big table for house guests and you may find more gourmets in the beamed dining room (outsiders are occasionally allowed in). A gem. *Sawday self-catering also.*

Price	€70-€95.
Rooms	5: 1 double, 2 twins, 1 triple, 1 quadruple.
Meals	Dinner €25. Wine €20.
Closed	November-March.
Directions	From Sarlat D46 to Cénac St Julien. At end of village on for Fumel. House 3rd turning on right.

Brigitte & Christophe Demassougne
La Guérinière,
Baccas, 24250 Cénac & St Julien,
Dordogne
Tel   +33 (0)5 53 29 91 97
Email contact@la-gueriniere-dordogne.com
Web   www.la-gueriniere-dordogne.com

Aquitaine

Château de Mombette

Built in the 1600s-1700s by the same family, Mombette has the simple, harmonious elegance that natural style brings to an organically-grown house; from its hilltop perch, it gazes across to the splendid medieval fortifications of Domme. Madame is welcoming and easy and has travelled a lot, especially to North Africa, where her father was a general. The character of her house is made of fine, generous spaces and good regional antiques, an attractive library and very lovely gardens. Bedrooms are comfortably homely and you are within reach of all the delights of the Dordogne. Real France – with a super pool.

Price	€100.
Rooms	3: 1 double, 1 twin, 1 triple.
Meals	Restaurants within walking distance.
Closed	Mid-November to March.
Directions	From Sarlat D46 to Cénac & St Julien; D50 right for St Cybranet for 300m; left at sign.

Michèle Jahan
Château de Mombette,
24250 Cénac & St Julien,
Dordogne
Tel   +33 (0)5 53 28 30 14
Mobile +33 (0)6 81 15 17 16
Email   michele.jahan@orange.fr

Aquitaine

Château de Puymartin

Neither dream nor museum, Puymartin is a chance to act the aristocrat for a spell, and survey the day visitors from your own wing. The fireplace in the tapestried baronial dining room would take a small tree, painted beams draw the eye, the carved stone staircase asks to be stroked, the furniture is authentic 17th-century Perigordian, history oozes from every corner. Bedrooms are vastly in keeping – twin four-posters, a faded ceiling painting, a loo in a turret, thick draperies. The elderly, ever-elegant Comtesse is friendly and very French; her son helps in the château and speaks good English; both are delightful.

Price	€120.
Rooms	2: 1 twin, 1 family suite.
Meals	Restaurant 5km.
Closed	November-March.
Directions	From Sarlat D47 for Les Eyzies 8km. Château signed regularly.

Comtesse de Montbron
Château de Puymartin,
24200 Sarlat la Canéda,
Dordogne
Tel   +33 (0)5 53 59 29 97
Email   chateaupuymartin@gmail.com
Web   www.chateau-de-puymartin.com

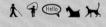

Entry 443   Map 9

Aquitaine

Les Charmes de Carlucet

An 18th-century house with a poignant history: Jewish families were sheltered here during the 2nd World War. Now the welcoming Edgars – he French, she English – live here with their children. In a vast walled garden on the edge of the village, the house has been completely renovated. Living and dining rooms are cool compositions of natural stone, white walls, pale fabrics. Pitch-ceilinged, L-shaped bedrooms under the eaves have gleaming floors, spotless bath or shower rooms, fans for summer. Should you tire of the heated pool (Éric says this hardly ever happens), you can stroll to the clipped hedges of Eyrignac. *Sawday self-catering also.*

Price	€99-€119. Extra bed €20.
Rooms	2 doubles, each with extra bed.
Meals	Restaurant 500m.
Closed	Rarely.
Directions	From Sarlat D60 for St Crépin & Carlucet; for Salignac passing stadium on right. After 500m right for Carlucet 1.5km; fork left 300m; right & right again.

Éric & Helen Edgar
Les Charmes de Carlucet,
24590 St Crépin & Carlucet,
Dordogne
Tel   +33 (0)5 53 31 22 60
Email   lescharmes@carlucet.com
Web   www.carlucet.com

Entry 444   Map 9

Aquitaine

Le Moulin de Leymonie du Maupas

The Kieffers did the utterly successful restoration of their remote Dordogne mill themselves, their gardening past speaks softly in the herb-scented patio and the little brook trembles off past grazing horses to the valley. Inside, levels juggle with space, steep stairs rise to small rooms of huge character with stone and wood walls, rich rugs and selected antiques; loos are tiny. Your sitting room is seductive with its logs on the fire and timbers overhead. Add a relaxed, bubbly welcome, organic dinners served with crisp linen and candles, homemade bread and jams for breakfast, and you have great value.

Ethical Collection: Food.
See page 410 for details.

Price	€70.
Rooms	2: 1 double, 1 twin. Children's room available.
Meals	Dinner €20. Wine €9.
Closed	Rarely.
Directions	In Mussidan, at church, for Villamblard 4km; left D39E; cont. 4km; in valley on right; check directions before you go.

Jacques & Ginette Kieffer
Le Moulin de Leymonie du Maupas,
24400 Issac,
Dordogne
Tel   +33 (0)5 53 81 24 02
Mobile   +33 (0)6 88 10 81 74
Email   jacques.kieffer2@wanadoo.fr
Web   perso.wanadoo.fr/lemoulindeleymonie

Entry 445   Map 9

Aquitaine

Briançon

The 14th-century walnut mill is a house full of riches and light, and the English garden, blessed with a burbling brook, is resplendent with rare plants. Inside, sofas wear colourful throws, boho-stylish bedrooms burst with personality and shower rooms have retro touches. Dinners, served at the big old country table, sound enticing: wines from Michael's cellar, produce from Katie's potager, herbs and garlic scattered with studied abandon, and plenty for vegetarians. Katie and Michael, from London, have created a sophisticated yet laid-back home and it's a treat to stay. *Workshops in knitting, writing, yoga, flamenco.*

Price	€90–€110.
Rooms	3 doubles.
Meals	Dinner €25. Restaurant 2km.
Closed	December–March.
Directions	From Angoulême D708 to Verteillac; right at church D1 for St Martial de Viveyrol; 2km, house on left.

Katie Armitage
Briançon,
24320 Verteillac,
Dordogne
Tel   +33 (0)5 53 91 38 40
Email   katie@elliottarmitage.com
Web   www.elliottarmitage.com

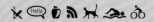

Entry 446   Map 9

Aquitaine

La Maison des Beaux Arts & The Aurora

The name is well chosen. Delia is a British artist and her striking canvases (from pop art jugs to oversized flowers) set off the house's well-preserved features. Once home to the mayor, the grand 19th-century house faces the main street and backs onto countryside. The only new addition, a glass conservatory, exploits the wonderful valley views. Sumptuous bedrooms are painted in a sizzling array of colours – sunflower yellow, duck-egg blue, Tiffany green – and filled with flowers. Should Delia's enthusiasm and talent inspire, she presents art packages too. *Min. two nights. Self-catering in The Aurora.*

Price	€75–€90 for 2. Apt €450–€600 per week.
Rooms	5 + 1: 3 doubles, 2 family rooms for 3. Apartment for 2.
Meals	Restaurants nearby.
Closed	Rarely.
Directions	From Limoges N21 exit Chalus; right at D6; D85 to Nontron; left over bridge to centre; house opp. post office, next to tourist information.

Delia Cavers
La Maison des Beaux Arts & The Aurora,
7 avenue du Général Leclerc,
24300 Nontron, Dordogne

Tel	+33 (0)5 53 56 39 77
Mobile	+33 (0)6 71 09 64 72
Email	delia@deliacavers.co.uk
Web	www.la-maison-des-beaux-arts.com

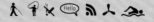

Photo: Lesley Chalmers

Limousin

Photo: www.istockphoto.com

Limousin

La Roche

It's homely yet exciting with Michel's artistry everywhere: sculptures take you magically through the garden; in the old stables, a carved door frame opens to a big living room, an iron balustrade leads up to generous, painting-hung bedrooms and simple showers. An interesting, likeable couple of ex-Parisians, proud of doing things their way, Michel has a fascinating studio and a clutch of collector cars, Josette loves cooking for vegetarians – and the opulent curtains and tented ceiling are her work. The beautiful forested valley alone is worth the visit: stay and walk in peace for miles.

Price	€63.
Rooms	2 doubles.
Meals	Dinner with wine, €20.
Closed	Rarely.
Directions	From A20 exit 35 D979 to Eymoutiers; D30 for Chamberet. House in village of La Roche, 7km beyond Eymoutiers.

Michel & Josette Jaubert
La Roche,
87120 Eymoutiers,
Haute-Vienne
Tel   +33 (0)5 55 69 61 88
Web   clos.arts.free.fr

Limousin

Magnac

In an ancient manor of enormous personality, your live-wire hostess, once a Parisian designer, now paints porcelain, organises cultural events and struggles to renovate the family house and its wild park with deep respect for its originality. Utterly endearing in its battered aristocracy, it is one room deep: light pours in from both sides onto heavy floorboards, 18th-century panelling and a delightful tower cocktail room. The traditional-style bedroom in the main house is vast, the snugger suite in the half-timbered orangery is ideal if you'd rather be independent. *1km from motorway exit. Children over 12 welcome.*

Price	€90.
Rooms	2: 1 twin/double, 1 suite for 3.
Meals	Light suppers available.
Closed	November to mid-May.
Directions	From A20 exit 41 for Magnac Bourg centre, over r'bout (Auberge de l'Étang), continue 100m, left thro' open gates into yard.

Catherine & Bertrand de la Bastide
Magnac,
87380 Magnac Bourg,
Haute-Vienne
Mobile +33 (0)6 03 08 79 19
Email   cathdelabastide@gmail.com

La Chapelle

Wonderful walking country; the emphasis here is outside, fields and woodlands are your garden. Deeply committed to the welfare of the land and all ecosystems, your hosts left city life to run a bio-dynamic goat farm and be as self-sufficient as possible. Modernised inside, the old farmhouse has four quietly strong, pine-clad bedrooms that wear good colours and share a kitchen/living room. Have supper with this genuine, unpretentious couple if you can: they are excellent company, their food is all home-grown and nourishing, their cheeses remarkable. Children love helping to milk the goats and collect eggs.

Ethical Collection: Environment, Food & Community. See page 410 for details.

Moulin de Marsaguet

The nicest people, they have done just enough to this proud old building so it looks as it did 200 years ago when it forged cannon balls. The farm is relaxed and natural, the bedrooms quaint, they have ducks and animals (including Lusitanian horses), three teenagers and a super potager, and make pâtés and 'confits' by the great mill pond, hanging the hams over the magnificent hearth in their big stone sitting room with its old-fashioned sofa. Relish the drive up past tree-framed lake (boating possible) and stone outbuildings and the prospect of breakfasting on home-grown ingredients. *Ask about pets when booking.*

Price	€46–€48.
Rooms	4: 3 doubles, 1 triple.
Meals	Supper €10. Wine from €7. Guest kitchen.
Closed	Rarely.
Directions	From A20 exit 41 to Magnac Bourg; D215 (between Total service station & Brasserie des Sports) SW. Follow signs 4km to La Chapelle & Chambres d'Hôtes.

Price	€53.
Rooms	3 doubles.
Meals	Restaurant 3km.
Closed	November to mid-April.
Directions	From A20 exit 39 to Pierre Buffière; cross river, D15 & D19 for St Yrieix 15km. At Croix d'Hervy, left D57 for Coussac Bonneval; mill on left after lake (7km).

Patrick & Mayder Lespagnol
La Chapelle,
87380 Château Chervix,
Haute-Vienne
Tel   +33 (0)5 55 00 86 67
Email   plespagnol@laposte.net
Web   gite.lachapelle.free.fr

Valérie & Renaud Gizardin
Moulin de Marsaguet,
87500 Coussac Bonneval,
Haute-Vienne
Tel   +33 (0)5 55 75 28 29
Email   gizardin.renaud@akeonet.com
Web   www.moulindemarsaguet.com

Limousin

Les Drouilles Bleues

High on a granite hill, with views to set your imagination on fire, the low stone house and its greenly rocky garden creak with age and history. As does the whole region. Paul and Maïthé, a most intelligent and attentive couple, take their hosting to heart, revelling in the wide variety of people who gather for an evening or two at their convivial and tasty dinner table. In converted outbuildings, handsome bedrooms large (the suite) and smaller are done with care, soft colours and gentle character. All have working fireplaces, sleeping quarters on mezzanines, good shower rooms. Deeply, discreetly, welcoming.

Price	€63. Suite €84.
Rooms	3: 2 doubles, 1 suite for 4.
Meals	Dinner with wine, €22.
Closed	Rarely.
Directions	From A20 exit 39 N or 40 S onto D15 thro' Nexon & St Hilaire les Places; approx. 1.5km beyond St Hilaire, 3rd turning on right to top of lane: La Drouille.

Maïthé & Paul de Bettignies
Les Drouilles Bleues,
La Drouille, 87800 St Hilaire les Places,
Haute-Vienne

Tel	+33 (0)5 55 58 21 26
Email	drouillesbleues@free.fr
Web	drouillesbleues.free.fr

Entry 452   Map 9

Limousin

Château Ribagnac

Patrick and Colette are intelligent, thoughtful and enthusiastic, and their splendid château, built in 1647, is a treat. With a growing family in London, this was their dream – superbly achieved. In fine big rooms, the conversion is authentic and elegantly comfortable: rugs on oak floors, old and newish furniture, superb new bathrooms (one loo in its turret). Ask for a lighter room with views over park and lake. Fruit and veg grow in their organic garden, the local meat is succulent, there is a deep commitment. Conversation flows with the wine. *Swimming lake with beach 1.5km. Golf nearby.*

Ethical Collection: Food.
See page 410 for details.

Price	€90–€160.
Rooms	5 suites for 2-5.
Meals	Dinner with wine, €45.
Closed	Rarely.
Directions	From A20 exit 27 to Ambazac; ahead to r'bout, right for St Léonard; under bridge 500m; right D56 to St Martin Terressus 3km. Château on right.

Patrick & Colette Bergot
Château Ribagnac,
87400 St Martin Terressus,
Haute-Vienne

Tel	+33 (0)5 55 39 77 91
Email	reservations@chateauribagnac.com
Web	www.chateauribagnac.com

Entry 453   Map 9

Limousin

Château du Fraisse

After 800 years of family and estate symbiosis, Le Fraisse is a living history book, mainly a rustic-grand Renaissance gem by the great Serlio – pale limestone, discreetly elegant portico, Henry II staircase and an astonishing fireplace in the vast drawing room. Your cultured hosts, two generations now, will greet you with warmth, happily tell you about house and history and show you to your room: fine furniture, paintings and prints, traditional furnishings; one bathroom has a fragment of a 16th-century fresco. If you return late at night you must climb the steep old spiral stair to your room as the main door is locked. *Golf 5km.*

Price	€72.50-€82.50. Suites €95-€170.
Rooms	4: 1 double, 1 twin, 1 suite for 3, 1 suite for 4.
Meals	Auberge 3km.
Closed	Mid-December to mid-January.
Directions	From A20 exit 23 to Bellac; N147 for Poitiers 7km; D951 to Mézières sur Issoire; left for Nouic 2.5km; château on right.

Marquis & Marquise des Monstiers
Mérinville
Château du Fraisse,
Le Fraisse, 87330 Nouic, Haute-Vienne

Tel	+33 (0)5 55 68 32 68
Email	infos@chateau-du-fraisse.com
Web	www.chateau-du-fraisse.com

Entry 454   Map 9

Limousin

La Flambée

You will find simple French value and a sweet, hard-working young couple in this organic smallholding. They genuinely like sharing their country fare, created from home-grown vegetables and home-reared lamb, duck, pigeon and rabbit (delicious pâtés). Myriam cares for their children, potager and guests and is redoing the rooms with fun and colour; Pierre, a builder by trade, looks after the animals and myriad house improvements. The 18th-century roadside farmhouse has characterful old wood – a great oak staircase, beams, timber framing – family clutter, fireplaces, peaceful bedrooms and a garden full of toys.

Price	€45.
Rooms	4: 1 double, 1 triple, 2 family rooms.
Meals	Dinner with wine, €15.
Closed	Rarely.
Directions	In Bellac follow signs to Limoges; just before leaving Bellac D3 right for Blond 4km to Thoveyrat. House sign on left.

Pierre & Myriam Morice
La Flambée,
Thoveyrat, 87300 Blond,
Haute-Vienne

Tel	+33 (0)5 55 68 86 86
Email	chambrehote@freesurf.fr
Web	www.laflambee.info

Entry 455   Map 9

Limousin

Château de Sannat

The serene 18th-century château stands proud for all to see on the site of an ancient fort – oh, the panorama! Bedrooms are mostly vast, traditionally furnished, regally wallpapered, modern bathroomed; the whole places oozes authenticity and easy family living and breakfast is superb. The atmosphere in the spectacular west-facing dining room, with its pale blue and yellow panelling, high-backed tapestried chairs and antique table may be informal, but the surroundings impose civilised dressing for dinner. Madame is an exceptionally warm and interesting lady; make the most of her lovely company. *Golf nearby.*

Price	€100–€190. Extra bed €40.
Rooms	5: 2 doubles, 2 twins, 1 suite.
Meals	Restaurant 5km.
Closed	Rarely.
Directions	From Poitiers N147 towards Limoges, through Bellac; left D96 for St Junien les Combes. 1st left in village for Rançon approx. 1km.

	Aucaigne de Sainte Croix
	Château de Sannat,
	87300 St Junien les Combes,
	Haute-Vienne
Tel	+33 (0)5 55 68 13 52
Mobile	+33 (0)6 82 57 98 19
Email	chateausannat@wanadoo.fr
Web	www.chateausannat.com

Entry 456   Map 9

Limousin

Maison Numéro Neuf

Lisa and Duncan from England have embraced life in southern La Souterraine. She is the least ruffled, most contented of chefs; he serves wines with finesse; both love house, children, guests, and their secret garden with hens. Now, at last, the renovation of the former residence of the Marquis de Valady is complete. So much to enjoy: the fine proportions, the sweeping balustrade, the antique mirrors, the crystal-drop chandeliers, the pale walls, the glowing parquet… and superb breakfasts and dinners. If Lisa pops a hot water bottle into your bed it will be encased in white linen: the hospitality here is exceptional.

Price	€60–€105.
Rooms	3: 2 doubles; 1 twin, sharing shower.
Meals	Dinner €20–€40. Wine €15.
Closed	Rarely.
Directions	A20 exit 23 for Guéret. Follow signs to La Souterraine & centre ville; signed.

	Duncan & Lisa Rowney
	Maison Numéro Neuf,
	Rue Serpente,
	23300 La Souterraine, Creuse
Tel	+33 (0)5 55 63 43 35
Email	reservations@maisonnumeroneuf.com
Web	maisonnumeroneuf.com

Entry 457   Map 9

Limousin

Château de Memanat

Roger and Pauline are passionate about their château. It is fabulously comfortable yet keeps strict faith with its past. Bedrooms are light and beautifully furnished, one with its own sitting room; bathrooms are superb. The food's great, too: Pauline adores cooking and uses local and organic suppliers. Opt for the simple menu and she and Roger will dine with you; go for gourmet and they'll join you for dessert. The grounds are vast: 1km of trout river, a walled garden with play area and solar-heated pool, and parkland planted with specimen trees by guests of the first owner, the scientist Dr Louis Queyrat. Marvellous.

Price	€95-€110.
Rooms	2 suites.
Meals	Dinner €34. Wine €15.
Closed	Christmas & New Year.
Directions	70km from Limoges for Aubusson N141/D941; after St Hilaire le Château, right for Chavanat D10; 2nd right to Memanat D45, white gates on right on entering village.

Roger & Pauline Ketteringham
Château de Memanat,
Memanat, 23250 Chavanat,
Creuse

Tel	+33 (0)5 55 67 74 45
Email	enquiries@memanat.com
Web	www.memanat.com

Limousin

L'Abbaye du Palais

Everything here is generous, light-hearted: each bathroom has rolltop tub and walk-in shower; high, square bedrooms have delectable old furniture and embroidered linen; there are two pianos, one in the downstairs loo, some stupendous trees and much heartfelt friendship. Martijn and Saskia left powerful jobs to bring their children to a life of nature and creativity by the ruined Cistercian abbey. With endless charm, they'll share its wonders with you. Martijn's sociable dinners, early suppers for children in the apple orchard, a sprig of rosemary on your pillow for sweet dreams. *Ask about cookery courses. Sawday self-catering also.*

Price	€75-€100.
Rooms	5: 2 doubles, 1 twin, 2 suites for 4.
Meals	Dinner with wine, from €35. Picnics available.
Closed	January/February.
Directions	From Limoges D941 east through Bourganeuf for Pontarion; just after Bourganeuf, left D940A. Abbaye with blue gates 5km on right.

Martijn & Saskia Zandvliet-Breteler
L'Abbaye du Palais,
23400 Bourganeuf,
Creuse

Tel	+33 (0)5 55 64 02 64
Email	info@abbayedupalais.com
Web	www.abbayedupalais.com

Manoir XV Domaine de Peyrafort

Come to be spoiled by homemade bread and cakes, picnics if you want them and delicious, locally-sourced dinners; Frances and Ian look after you with quiet ease in their 15th-century manor house. Find mullioned windows, a huge open fire in the sitting room, big beams, stripped floors and a long wooden table for shared meals; it may be smart but it's also relaxed. Bedrooms vary in size and all are well turned out with super beds, navy and gold fabrics and small modern bathrooms. Acres of garden to explore, walking and cycling routes galore, and the glories of little-known Corrèze to unearth. *Min. two nights July/August.*

La Souvigne

Jacquie, half-French, and Ian, half-Hungarian, are passionate Francophiles who know the local people, history, flora and building regs intimately. In fact, they're passionate about many things. Jacquie makes myriad jams, Ian serves superb food with a flourish and wines from his cellar… aperitifs and dinner, even breakfasts in the separate guest house, are not for shrinking violets! Their clever renovation of the little house on the village square has produced an intimate kitchen/diner, a biggish, old-style downstairs bedroom and two cosily updated rooms under the rafters with some nice furniture. The place is a gem. *Ask about wine appreciation stays.*

Ethical Collection: Food.
See page 410 for details.

Price	€65–€90.
Rooms	4: 1 double, 1 single, 1 family room for 3-4, 1 suite for 2.
Meals	Dinner with wine, €27.
Closed	Rarely.
Directions	From north D1120 (ex-N120) into Tulle; on for 1.2km, left & follow signs to Les Fontaines, Peyrafort & Manoir XV.

Price	€41–€44.
Rooms	3: 2 doubles, 1 twin.
Meals	Dinner with wine, €20.
Closed	Rarely.
Directions	From Tulle D1120 for Argentat & Aurillac. At Forgès, left up towards church, park below.

Frances & Ian Black
Manoir XV Domaine de Peyrafort,
Chemin de Peyrafort,
19000 Tulle, Corrèze
Tel +33 (0)5 55 29 93 58
Mobile +33 (0)6 16 71 12 72
Email info@peyrafort.com
Web www.peyrafort.com

Ian & Jacquie Hoare
La Souvigne,
1 impasse La Fontaine,
19380 Forgès, Corrèze
Tel +33 (0)5 55 28 63 99
Email info@souvigne.com
Web www.souvigne.com

Limousin

La Farge

The stone hamlets take you back to another age along the rugged valleys. The delightful Archibalds have adopted the country and nationality, the stones and the peace, updating them with their English sense of fine finish: an ancient cart carefully restored before being flooded with flowers, new windows fitted with the latest fly screens, first-class beds and showers. Fresh pastel bedrooms have honey-boarded floors and a teddy each; modern pine mixes with antique oak; the kitchen's solid farmhouse table, wood-burner and super food are at the heart of this house. Heaven. *Minimum two nights. Sawday self-catering also.*

Ethical Collection: Food.
See page 410 for details.

Price	€65.
Rooms	3: 2 doubles; 1 twin with separate bath.
Meals	Dinner with wine, €32.50.
Closed	Rarely.
Directions	From Argentat D12 W 10km; D83E1 right for Le Vialard & Moustoulat 3km; right for La Farge; right again; 2nd house on right in village with black gates.

Keith & Helen Archibald
La Farge,
19400 Monceaux sur Dordogne,
Corrèze
Tel   +33 (0)5 55 28 54 52
Email   info@chezarchi.com
Web   www.chezarchi.com

Entry 462   Map 10

Limousin

Jeanne Maison d'Hôtes

Where tree-clad hills surge up from valleys and sprinklings of fortified towns cling gloriously to hilltops is this turreted, redstone village. Hidden from tourist bustle behind high walls is a green shady garden, roses in abundance, a 15th-century tower and three floors of living space. Big bedrooms have sisal and sofas, heavy old armoires, the odd redstone wall and one, a stone terrace; white bathrooms sparkle. She did PR in Paris, he was a restaurateur, both are fine, interesting hosts and speak good English. You eat well; mushrooms are gathered in season and Brigitte is proud of her breakfast gâteaux.

Price	€95.
Rooms	5: 3 doubles, 2 twins/doubles.
Meals	Dinner with wine, €35.
Closed	Rarely.
Directions	From Brive A20 exit 52; D38 to Collonges la Rouge; right at 2nd parking sign, follow signs down lane, park in field on right.

Brigitte & Pascal Monteil
Jeanne Maison d'Hôtes,
BP 28 Le Bourg,
19500 Collonges la Rouge, Corrèze
Tel   +33 (0)5 55 25 42 31
Email   info@jeannemaisondhotes.com
Web   www.jeannemaisondhotes.com

Entry 463   Map 9

Auvergne

Photo: www.istockphoto.com

Auvergne

Auvergne

Château du Ludaix

Pure château with a touch of humour, Ludaix is glamorous, dramatic and utterly welcoming. David and Stephanie have boundless energy, love people (they run a training company) and lavish care on house and guests. David is exploring the archives ("Ludaix is a living history book"), rebuilding the ancient waterworks and shady walks in the wood. Stephanie's talent cossets the rich warm rooms with English and French antiques ancient and modern, myriad hats, clocks and costumes, the odd tented ceiling. Gorgeous rooms, imaginative bathrooms, delicious food, great conversation – and lots more… *Extra rooms for groups or seminars.*

Manoir Le Plaix

Thick, thick walls, great old stones and timbers: the immense age of this gloriously isolated farmhouse (once a fortified manor) is evident but it has been beautifully restored. Big, warm, cosy, subtly-lit rooms, lovingly decorated with family antiques and memorabilia, are reached by a treat of a spiral staircase. A hundred head of cattle graze safely in the surrounding fields – you can walk, fish, and hunt mushrooms in season. Easy and good-natured, Madame Raucaz opens her heart, her intelligence and her breakfast table to all – and you can picnic in the garden. Relax and feel at home. Wonderful value for money.

Price	€120. Whole house available.
Rooms	2 suites.
Meals	Dinner, 4 courses with wine, €40.
Closed	January/February.
Directions	A71 exit 11 for Montmarault; left at r'bout, left D4/D13 to Lapeyrouse/Montaigut; right T-junc. D2144; left D502; 2nd house on left.

Price	€55.
Rooms	3: 1 double, 2 triples.
Meals	Picnics available. Restaurants 4km.
Closed	Rarely.
Directions	From Nevers N7 S 22km; right D978a to Le Veudre; D13 then D234 to Pouzy Mésangy. Chambres d'Hôtes signs.

David Morton & Stephanie Holland
Château du Ludaix,
Rue du Ludaix,
03420 Marcillat en Combraille, Allier
Tel   +33 (0)4 70 51 62 32
Mobile   +44 (0)7739 431918
Email   stephanie@rapport-online.com
Web   www.chateauduludaix.com

Claire Raucaz
Manoir Le Plaix,
Pouzy Mésangy,
03320 Lurcy Levis, Allier
Tel   +33 (0)4 70 66 24 06
Email   leplaix@yahoo.fr
Web   manoirleplaix.blogspot.com

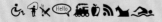

Auvergne

Cognet

Billowing hilly pastures wrap the hamlet in sensuality. Built in 1886 as a rich man's summer place, here is a generous, sophisticated house informed by Madame's broad cultural interests, her father's paintings and her fine Provençal furniture that looks perfect beside the beautiful original panelling and wide fireplace. Up steep shiny stairs, the guest space is a sweep of pine floor and ceiling; light floods over sitting area, big pine bed, old chest; a proud tree shades the splendid shower room. Deep rest, super breakfast and conversation, Romanesque jewels to visit, beauty sessions in Vichy – a must.

Price	€60.
Rooms	1 twin/double.
Meals	Light supper first night €15. Wine €10. Restarants 5km.
Closed	November-February.
Directions	A75 exit Gannat to Vichy; over Allier; immed. right Bd JFK, left for Cusset; over r'way; 5 lights, D906 right for Ferrières; right D995 9km; left D121 1.2km; right to Cognet 800m; iron gates.

	Bénita Mourges
	Cognet,
	03300 La Chapelle,
	Allier
Tel	+33 (0)4 70 41 88 28
Mobile	+33 (0)6 98 47 54 48
Email	maison.cognet@free.fr
Web	maison.cognet.free.fr

Entry 466   Map 10

Auvergne

La Rambaude

A generous and handsomely decorated family house: the volcanoes gave their lava for dining room and staircase floor slabs; the hall is resplendent with hand-blocked wallpaper by Zuber. Ancestors gave their names to bedrooms, where their faded photographs and intricate samplers fill the walls; others left some fine old ornaments and pieces of furniture and built the stupendous brick barns that shelter the garden. Élisabeth is dynamic, intelligent and full of wry humour, once a trace of shyness has worn off, and serves her deliciously wholesome breakfast in the garden, studded with wild violets in spring.

Price	€70-€78.
Rooms	3 doubles.
Meals	Restaurants 7km.
Closed	November-March, except by arrangement.
Directions	From A71 exit Riom; N144 for Combronde & Montluçon; 2.5km after Davayat, right D122 to Chaptes.

	Élisabeth Beaujeard
	La Rambaude, 8 route de la Limagne
	Chaptes, 63460 Beauregard Vendon,
	Puy-de-Dôme
Tel	+33 (0)4 73 63 35 62
Email	elisabeth.beaujeard@orange.fr
Web	www.la-rambaude.com

Entry 467   Map 10

Auvergne

Château de Vaulx

Is it real or a fairy tale? Creak along the parquet, pray in the chapel, swan around the salon, sleep in one tower, bath in another. It's been in the family for 800 years, well-lived-in rooms have evocative names and romantic furnishings – worthy of the troubadours who sang here. Breakfast on home-hived honey, brioche, yogurt, eggs, cheese, get to know your delightfully entertaining hosts, visit the donkey, walk into the sweeping view. Feeling homesick? Have a drink in Guy's crazy 'pub' with its huge collection of beer mats. A dream of a place: the next generation will nurture it just as imaginatively.

Price	€70–€90.
Rooms	2: 1 double, 1 triple.
Meals	Dinner with wine, €15–€30. Auberge 3km.
Closed	Rarely.
Directions	From A89 exit 3 on D7 through Celles sur Durolle to Col du Frissonnet. Château 1st right after Col du Frissonnet.

Guy & Régine Dumas de Vaulx, Philippe & Martine Vast
Château de Vaulx,
63120 Ste Agathe, Puy-de-Dôme

Tel	+33 (0)4 73 51 50 55
Email	philippe.vast@chateaudevaulx.fr
Web	www.chateaudevaulx.fr

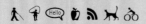

Entry 468   Map 10

Auvergne

Domaine de Gaudon - Le Château

Out in wildest Auvergne, here be surprises: new Venuses and urns outside, 19th-century splendour inside – glossy oak panelling, ceiling roses, original wall coverings. Alain and Monique, endearingly natural and loving their new life, have created a setting of astonishing brass and satin, gilt and quilted glamour for their superb French antiques. Add luxurious bathrooms, dazzling breakfasts, specimen trees, innumerable frogs, bats, birds and insects (some in frames), herons fishing in the pond – and Connemara ponies in the park. Children and adults love it, one and all. *Wildlife conservation area.*

Price	€110. Suite €130. Extra person €25.
Rooms	5: 3 doubles, 1 twin, 1 suite.
Meals	Supper trays available. Restaurant 4km.
Closed	Rarely.
Directions	A75 from Montpellier exit 9; D229 then D996 to St Dier d'Auvergne. At end of village D6 for Domaize 3km. Right for Ceilloux 1km.

Alain & Monique Bozzo
Domaine de Gaudon - Le Château,
63520 Ceilloux,
Puy-de-Dôme

Tel	+33 (0)4 73 70 76 25
Email	domainedegaudon@wanadoo.fr
Web	www.domainedegaudon.fr

Entry 469   Map 10

Auvergne

Les Frênes

Perched above Saint Nectaire, the old farmhouse has stupendous views from its hillside garden of the Romanesque jewel below and woods and mountains soaring beyond. Monique, chatty and knowledgeable, enthuses her guests with descriptions of the Auvergne in perfect English. She doesn't pretend to offer luxury, just the cosy comfort of a real home. You stay in an attached one-bedroom cottage with a shower and kitchen area downstairs. Breakfast is in Monique and Daniel's vaulted dining room, full of exposed beams and stone; eat copiously and enjoy the humour and zest of a couple who were born to hospitality. Great value for money.

Price	€50.
Rooms	Cottage for 2. 2 extra beds for children.
Meals	Restaurants in St Nectaire, 2km.
Closed	Rarely.
Directions	From A75 exit 6 to St Nectaire then to St Nectaire le Haut; at church D150 for 1.5km; left D643 to Sailles, 3rd lane on right in hamlet, signed.

Monique Deforge
Les Frênes,
Sailles, 63710 St Nectaire,
Puy-de-Dôme
Tel   +33 (0)4 73 88 40 08
Email   daniel.deforge@orange.fr
Web   deforge.pagesperso-orange.fr/lesfrenes/

Auvergne

La Closerie de Manou

The rambling old house sits solid among the ancient volcanoes of Auvergne where great rivers rise and water is pure. There's a fine garden for games, a family-sized dining table before the great fireplace and a mixed bag of friendly armchairs guarded by a beautiful Alsatian stove in the salon. The décor is properly, comfortably rustic, bedrooms are lightly floral, no bows or furbelows, just pretty warmth and good shower rooms. Maryvonne, intelligent and chatty, knows and loves the Auvergne in depth and serves a scrumptious breakfast. *Minimum two nights July/August.*

Price	€85-€90. Extra person €30. Whole house available.
Rooms	3: 1 double, 2 family rooms for 3.
Meals	Restaurant in village, 0.3km.
Closed	Mid-October to March.
Directions	From A75 exit 6 on D978 then D996 to Le Mont Dore; pass Mairie & take Avenue des Belges (still D996); 3km to Le Genestoux; house signed.

Françoise & Maryvonne Larcher
La Closerie de Manou,
Le Genestoux, 63240 Le Mont Dore,
Puy-de-Dôme
Tel   +33 (0)4 73 65 26 81
Mobile   +33 (0)6 08 54 50 16
Email   lacloseriedemanou@orange.fr
Web   www.lacloseriedemanou.com

Auvergne

Château de Pasredon

Whichever splendid room is yours – we loved the four-poster *Jouy* with its waltz-in bathroom – you will feel grand: here a superbly inlaid armoire, there an exquisite little dressing room, everywhere shimmering mirrors, fabulous views of uninterrupted parkland, ancient trees, the Puy-de-Dôme: acres of space for those who like to read in a secluded spot to the magical sound of birdsong. The vast, panelled, period-furnished drawing and dining rooms are quite dramatic. A perfectly cultured, relaxed hostess, Madame makes you feel instantly at ease and helps you plan your day over a delicious breakfast. Really very special.

Price	€85–€105.
Rooms	3: 2 doubles, 1 twin.
Meals	Restaurants 2km.
Closed	Mid-October to mid-April.
Directions	From Clermont Ferrand A75 exit 13 to Parentignat; D999 for St Germain l'Herme 6km; sign on right. (8km from A75 exit.)

Henriette Marchand
Château de Pasredon,
63500 St Rémy de Chargnat,
Puy-de-Dôme
Tel +33 (0)4 73 71 00 67
Email chateau.de.pasredon@orange.fr

Entry 472 Map 10

Auvergne

Le Relais de la Diligence

Soon after escaping to this pretty village in rugged country, Peter and Laurette opened their doors so guests could enjoy the simplicity of their aptly named house and the local flora and fauna. Peter's craftsman's skills and their shared passion for restoration come together in this old coaching inn with its carefully restored beams, warm colours and sweet painted furniture. Comfortable beds in sunny bedrooms, cosy sitting room with glorious wood-burner and simple light suppers at a refectory table speak of thoughtful, kind hosts. Next morning, wave to Fleur as she jumps on the school bus, driven by Laurette.

Price	€50. €80 for 4.
Rooms	3: 1 double, 1 family room for 3, 1 family suite for 4.
Meals	Dinner with wine, €18.
Closed	Rarely.
Directions	From La Chaise Dieu D906 for Ambert; at Arlanc D300 left for St Germain L'Herm, 13km to St Bonnet; Le Relais on left in middle of village.

Peter & Laurette Eggleton
Le Relais de la Diligence,
Le Bourg, 63630 St Bonnet le Chastel,
Puy-de-Dôme
Tel +33 (0)4 73 72 57 96
Email leseggleton@aliceadsl.fr
Web www.relais-diligence.com

Entry 473 Map 10

Auvergne

Ma Cachette

Pierre is the gardener, Johan the cook. Both South African and charming, they left the film and television world for this elegant village house in the heart of the Regional Park. A few steps from the romantic garden, lush with roses, ancient fruit trees and flourishing potager, and you'll be walking some of the most stunning trails in Auvergne. Rooms are big with oriental carpets and garden flowers; the stylish living room is for guests. Dinner will be exceptional, the conversation as much as the European-inspired food: Johan's debilitating Parkinson's in no way affects his quick mind or enjoyment of people.

Price	€55-€65.
Rooms	4: 3 doubles, 1 twin.
Meals	Dinner with wine, €28.
Closed	Rarely.
Directions	From A72 exit 2, D906 for Le Puy en Velay 67km. Entering Arlanc follow Chambres d'Hôtes signs; near St Pierre Romanesque church.

Johan Bernard & Pierre Knoesen
Ma Cachette,
10 rue du 11 Novembre,
63220 Arlanc, Puy-de-Dôme
Tel +33 (0)4 73 95 04 88
Email cachette@club-internet.fr
Web www.ma-cachette.com

Auvergne

La Déchetterie

Known to all in this sleepy Auvergnat village, our funky low-carbon retreat stands in stunning contrast to its neighbouring *prieurés* and *manoirs*. Distinctively minimalist and modern, bedrooms are bubble-shaped with porthole windows and individual colour themes. 'Spécial Verre' is tinted in shades of olive (listen to tinkling glass day and night), and there's reading material a-plenty in the urban-designed 'Papier' pod. Breakfast is a selection of organic matter delivered by neighbours doing their bit for the environment. It's a bring-your-own policy for drinks – but there's sure to be a drop or two about. Unique.

Price	Money back in exchange for your empties.
Rooms	3 pods.
Meals	Irregular but varied.
Closed	Rarely. Often full but always possible to cram a few more in.
Directions	From Tri Sélectif village centre follow signs; if lost, just follow the smell or try and spot a dustbin lorry heading the same way.

Sidward Emballage
La Déchetterie,
Rue de la Conservation,
63460 Tri Sélectif, Puy-de-Dôme
Email la_poubelle@recyclage.fr
Web www.stayinarecyclingbin.com

Auvergne

La Jacquerolle

Built on the ramparts of the ancient town, just below the medieval Abbey whose August music festival draws thousands, the big, atmospheric old house has been lined with wood and lovingly filled with flowers in every form – carpets, curtains, wallpaper, quilts. It is a soft French boudoir where mother and daughter, quietly attentive, welcome their guests to sleep in cosy bedrooms, some with wonderful views out to the hills, all with firm beds and good little bathrooms. (Ask for the largest.) French country cuisine is served on bone china with bohemian crystal before a huge stone fireplace.

Price	€60.
Rooms	3: 1 double, 1 twin, 1 family room for 4.
Meals	Dinner with wine, €25.
Closed	Rarely.
Directions	From Brioude D19 to La Chaise Dieu centre ville; facing Abbey, right Place du Monument; bottom rt-hand corner: down Rue Marchédial; right Rue Fontgiraud, park on right.

Carole Chailly
La Jacquerolle,
Rue Marchédial,
43160 La Chaise Dieu, Haute-Loire
Tel   +33 (0)4 71 00 07 52
Email lajacquerolle@hotmail.com
Web   lajacquerolle.com

Entry 476   Map 10

Auvergne

Château de Chazelles

Off the beaten track amid the mountains of the Auvergne, a renovated château, an understated gem. Outside are romantic, child-friendly walled gardens awash with lime trees, pines and weeping birch; inside are large, light, impeccable bedrooms with sublime views. Ornate four-posters, Jouy-print wallpaper, framed 30s fashion ads and fine painted furniture exude stylish comfort, deep roll top baths are delicious after a day's hiking, the lovely sitting room has books, maps and guides to supplement your delightful, well-travelled hosts' tips for trekking, riding and exploring – and Frank's travel pics are stunning.

Price	€75.
Rooms	3: 1 double, 1 suite for 2-4, 1 suite for 4-6.
Meals	Dinner with wine, €20. Picnic lunch available. Restaurant 4km.
Closed	November-March.
Directions	From Craponne D9, follow St André de Chalencon signs, left before garage (sign for Stade), left into village. Green gates 200m on left.

Cathy Wainwright
Château de Chazelles,
43130 St André de Chalencon,
Haute-Loire
Tel   +33 (0)4 71 58 49 17
Email info@chateau-chazelles.com
Web   www.chateau-chazelles.com

Entry 477   Map 11

Auvergne

Château de Durianne

Since moving in seven years ago the Chambons have poured hearts and souls into rescuing the family château. Nothing had been touched for a century; in the attics was 120-year-old wallpaper which they lovingly re-used. Now the place, its portraits and antiques, feels like home. The huge bedroom overlooks a farm where the Chambons plan to keep sheep; the as-yet uncultivated garden is long and grassy, the orchard is home to two donkeys and a pony, and the village is just down the lane. Breakfast is generous (homemade tarte, juice from their apples) and you may be joined by delightful Madame for coffee and a chat.

Ethical Collection: Environment & Food. See page 410 for details.

Price	€60–€70. Whole castle €800 per week (June-August).
Rooms	1 family suite for 2-4.
Meals	Dinner with wine, €25. Restaurant 3km.
Closed	Rarely.
Directions	Le Puy en Velay D103 for Lavoute/Vorey 2km; right D103 to Durianne; in village, take the only right, unmarked; château 50m on left.

Françoise & Jean-Nicolas Chambon du Garay
Château de Durianne,
43700 Le Monteil, Haute-Loire

Tel	+33 (0)4 71 02 90 36
Mobile	+33 (0)6 80 70 59 32
Email	info@chateaudedurianne.com
Web	www.chateaudedurianne.com

Entry 478   Map 11

Auvergne

Château de Lescure

On the southern slope of Europe's largest extinct volcano, where nine valleys radiate, stands an atmospheric 18th-century château guarded by a medieval tower where two rustic vaulted bedrooms soar. The twin has the right furbelowed drapery, and, in the big inglenook kitchen, Sophie, a committed environmentalist, serves home-smoked ham, veg from her organic garden, fruit from her orchard. Michel's passions are heritage conservation and blazing trails across the hills straight from the door. They are bilingual hosts who may invite you to join in bread-making, cooking, visiting their medieval garden… *Min. two nights in summer.*

Ethical Collection: Environment, Food & Community. See page 410 for details.

Price	€85–€90. Extra person €25.
Rooms	3: 1 twin; 1 double with separate shower, 1 double with separate shower room downstairs.
Meals	Dinner with wine, €20–€30. Child €10.
Closed	December–January.
Directions	From Clermont Ferrand A75 to St Flour; up to old town; left D921 10km; right D990 to St Martin. Right for Brezons; château 3km on right.

Michel Couillaud &
Phoebe Sophie Verhulst
Château de Lescure,
15230 St Martin Sous Vigouroux, Canta

Tel	+33 (0)4 71 73 40 91
Email	michel.couillaud@orange.fr
Web	sites.google.com/site/chateaudelescure

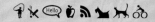

Entry 479   Map 10

Auvergne

La Roussière

Not another house in sight. Just the Cantal hills and a chattering stream. Brigitte and Christian live here with their young son and have done much of the restoration themselves. Christian is a genius at woodwork: his golden staircase and panelling sit happily with mellow stone, old armoires, ancient ceiling hooks… There's an Alpine air to the place. Beds are excellent, meals 'en famille' are a delight: great food, good wine, mineral water from the spring. Be calmed by a serene, rustic elegance. No actual garden but their green rolling hectares, a haven for wildlife, are perfection enough. *Min. two nights July/August.*

Price	€75-€90.
Rooms	3: 1 double, 1 suite for 2-3, 1 suite for 3-4.
Meals	Dinner with wine, €25.
Closed	Rarely.
Directions	From Massiac N122 for Aurillac; in Vic sur Cère left for Pailherols; D54 for 6km up to col de Curebourse; continue to Pailherols; left before bridge; continue straight on 4km.

Christian Grégoir & Brigitte Renard
La Roussière,
15800 St Clément,
Cantal

Tel	+33 (0)4 71 49 67 34
Email	info@laroussiere.fr
Web	www.laroussiere.fr

Entry 480   Map 10

Auvergne

Ferme des Prades

A real creaky old farmhouse – warm, atmospheric, unpretentious. A sweet, down-to-earth couple, Françoise and Philippe welcome company: their sons are away studying, and this is 'la France profonde'! The farm covers 150 hectares; walk for hours through pure air and inspiring landscapes – you need not see another soul. The house, destroyed in the French Revolution, was rebuilt by Napoleon's confessor. Within its solid walls are stripped floors and panelling, big rooms, comfortably worn sofas, fine armoires, muslin curtains – and Françoise's bedside tables fashioned from milk churns. Convivial dinners are great value. A treat.

Ethical Collection: Food.
See page 410 for details.

Price	€67-€82.
Rooms	5: 3 doubles, 2 family rooms.
Meals	Dinner with wine, €22.
Closed	First two weeks in September.
Directions	A75 exit 23 (Massiac); N122 for Murat 25km; right D21 to Allanche; D679 for Marcenat 7km; Les Prades farm on right.

Françoise & Philippe Vauché
Ferme des Prades,
Les Prades, Landeyrat,
15160 Allanche, Cantal

Tel	+33 (0)4 71 20 48 17
Mobile	+33 (0)6 88 30 79 67
Email	les-prades@wanadoo.fr
Web	www.fermedesprades.com

Entry 481   Map 10

Midi – Pyrénées

Photo: www.istockphoto.com

Midi - Pyrénées

La Croix du Bournissard

In 2005, Tina and Robert opted out of running a busy restaurant in the south of France for a life of quiet quality. Robert now revels in cooking succulent home-grown vegetables for just a few appreciative guests; Tina delightedly makes jam and bakes in the old bread oven — it's all organic. They restored the old farmhouse with the same care, keeping the best original features and opening up rooms to fill the house with fresh new light. Bedrooms and garden have the tended natural look: a hammock between two pear trees beside the potager, birdsong for breakfast, stars for dinner, parquet and linen curtains for bedtime.

Price	€120.
Rooms	2 doubles.
Meals	Dinner €33.
Closed	Rarely.
Directions	A20 exit 55 for Souillac 2km; D803 for Martel 7km; left D33 at Baladou for Cuzance. House 5-6km on right.

	Tina Karsenti
	La Croix du Bournissard,
	46600 Le Bournissard, Lot
Tel	+33 (0)5 65 27 12 92
Mobile	+33 (0)6 14 49 18 15
Email	bournissard@orange.fr
Web	lacroixdubournissard.over-blog.com/articles-blog.html

Entry 482   Map 9

Midi - Pyrénées

Moulin de Goth

The 13th-century mill — imaginatively, magically restored by its Australian owners — guards a garden of rare peace and beauty. Lily pads and lawns, willows, water and two sculpted herons — it is ineffably lovely. Humorous and exuberant, Coral cooks like an angel; Bill makes tables and intelligent conversation — join him for snooker in the barn. Big, dramatically raftered rooms have decorative iron beds, soft fabrics, antique chests. The stone-walled dining room, its arrow slits intact, is stunningly barrel-vaulted — but meals are mostly in the enchanting garden. Readers adore this place. *Children over eight welcome.*

Price	€70-85.
Rooms	2: 1 double, 1 triple.
Meals	Dinner with wine, €28.
Closed	Rarely.
Directions	From Martel D23 for Creysse 3km; fork right for Le Goth 1.5km; 1st house on right after stone bridge.

	Coral Heath-Kauffman
	Moulin de Goth,
	46600 Creysse, Lot
Tel	+33 (0)5 65 32 26 04
Mobile	+33 (0)6 98 63 41 80
Email	coral.heath@orange.fr
Web	www.moulindugoth.com

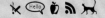

Entry 483   Map 9

Midi - Pyrénées

Château de Termes

The views! Sublime when the mists hang in the valleys and the sun glints on the summits. Your hospitable hosts, he a small-plane instructor who offers flying for guests, she quietly busy with her ten gîtes, have created a marvellous escape for families. More domestic than grand, their 1720s château promises four good rooms (two with bath and loo in the bedroom), a garden, a pool, play areas, short tennis, a big terrace, a small bar. Floors are stripped wood or chunky terracotta, furniture 'distressed', the suite opens to the garden, the whimsical doubles are in the tower. Kids love it. *Airport 20-min. drive. No dinner July/Aug.*

Price	€68–€85.
Rooms	3: 2 doubles, 1 family suite for 3.
Meals	Dinner with wine, €20–€25.
Closed	Rarely.
Directions	From Paris A20 exit 54 to Martel; D803 for Vayrac & St Céré, 4.5km on left.

Pierre & Sophie Nadin
Château de Termes,
St Denis,
46600 Martel, Lot
Tel +33 (0)5 65 32 42 03
Email infos@chateau-de-termes.com
Web www.chateau-de-termes.com

Midi - Pyrénées

Le Moulin de Latreille

The mill is 13th century and Cistercian, the owners are talented and attentive, the setting is magical. Kingfishers and wild orchids, herons, hammocks and happy dogs… and it is just as wonderful inside. Furniture has been renovated and painted, books peep from alcoves, bathrooms are delightful, and you get a little private sitting room with a wood-burner. Down its own bumpy track from the village, with timeless views of cliffs, woods and weir, let the chorus of birdsong and the rush of the millrace wash over you; they even generate their own electricity. Heaven in Quercy. *Minimum two nights. Unfenced water.*

Ethical Collection: Environment.
See page 410 for details.

Price	€85.
Rooms	2 doubles.
Meals	Dinner with wine, €25. Light lunches & picnics available. Restaurant in village.
Closed	Rarely.
Directions	From Payrac D673 to Calès. Opp. Le Petit Relais, left for La Cave, immed. right (for Le Petit Relais parking), round to left, down hill (rough road); only house at bottom.

Giles & Fi Stonor
Le Moulin de Latreille,
Calès,
46350 Payrac, Lot
Tel +33 (0)5 65 41 91 83
Email gilesetfi@wanadoo.fr
Web moulindelatreille.com

Midi - Pyrénées

La Buissonnière

The converted 18th-century barn with its stone outbuilding feels instantly like home. Well-travelled bi-lingual Élisabeth, warm, full of life, loves cookery and ceramics and uses her creative touch everywhere – including the terrace and the lovely sloping garden; she is a fount of historical and cultural lore. The open-plan living room, where old skylights deliver splashes of sky, is full of artistic character with oak floors, old stove and pretty antiques beneath paintings of all periods. The airy ground-floor guest room has its own antique writing table, watercolours and a glazed stable door to the garden. Charming.

Price	€60.
Rooms	2: 1 double. Outbuilding: 1 double & kitchenette.
Meals	Dinner with wine, €18–€20. Restaurant in village.
Closed	Rarely.
Directions	From Gramat D840 (previously N140) for Figeac; left for 'Le Bout du Lieu' after sign for Thémines; house, 100m on right; signed.

Élisabeth de Lapérouse Coleman
La Buissonnière,
Le Bout du Lieu,
46120 Thémines, Lot
Tel   +33 (0)5 65 40 88 58
Mobile +33 (0)6 43 41 69 33
Email   edelaperouse.coleman@wanadoo.fr
Web   leboutdulieu.weebly.com

Entry 486   Map 10

Midi - Pyrénées

Les Jardins de la Contie

Ken and Sabine have rescued a ruined hamlet and created a place of rustic charm. It is delightfully quirky, very comfortable, all knobbly-stone walls, flagged floors, beams, arches and inglenooks. Traditional bedrooms in separate buildings, each with a private outdoor spot, have country antiques, cosy beds, good linen. In the huge breakfast room you feast on hams, cheeses and fruit from their trees: the lush gardens are full of them, fragrant shrubs too, so pick a lounger and settle in. Lovely people, big saltwater pool, great walks from the house, views to die for – yet the shortest drive from civilisation.

Price	€60–€95.
Rooms	2: 1 double, 1 suite for 2 & kitchenette.
Meals	Restaurants 3km.
Closed	November-Easter.
Directions	From Figeac D840 for Decazeville. 1km after Capdenac Port, left to Lunan & Église Romane; right at town hall; follow signs.

Sabine & Ken Lazarus
Les Jardins de la Contie,
La Contie,
46100 Lunan, Lot
Mobile +33 (0)6 11 64 78 57
Email   sablaz@nordnet.fr
Web   www.lacontie.com

Entry 487   Map 10

Mas de Garrigue

Match natural Irish hospitality with the personality of a many-layered French house and you have a marriage made in heaven. Sarah creates fine pâtés from the pigs Steve raises on the veg patch in winter and serves them with onion jam made with onions grown there in summer: they care deeply about their food and its sourcing. The big, unusual house has an elegance all its own: vast rooms, supremely beamed and raftered, are furnished with quiet taste, Irish antiques and the occasional contemporary flourish; beds are the best you've ever slept in, each bathroom a poem. They are a lovely, witty couple, generous to a fault.

Téranga

This happy, secluded house – its front facing the main road, its back surveying a cedar-forested bank – is charged with childhood memories. Agnès, vivacious ex-English teacher, and Francis, wine-lover and retired architect, have filled the rooms with Senegalese touches and take immense pleasure in welcoming guests. Bedrooms have wooden floors and ethnic hangings, the gardens hide a delicious pool and the long vine-strewn veranda is the perfect spot for breakfast gâteaux and jams. Discover restaurants in old Pradines, history in lovely Cahors (a short drive), and the river Lot for watery adventures. *Minimum two nights.*

Price	€85–€100.
Rooms	4: 3 doubles, 1 twin.
Meals	Dinner with wine, €30.
Closed	Rarely.
Directions	From A20 exit 57; right for St Géry, D653 to Vers; D622 for Cajarc. Leaving Larnagol, right over bridge 2km; left at junc.; left over bridge; 1st house on left in hamlet.

Price	€65.
Rooms	2 doubles.
Meals	Restaurants 10-minute walk.
Closed	November-March.
Directions	From Cahors D8 for Pradines/Luzech; after 4th r'bout for Douelle 1km; continue for 1km; small road on left at No 303.

Sarah Lloyd & Steven Allen
Mas de Garrigue,
La Garrigue,
46160 Calvignac, Lot
Tel   +33 (0)5 65 53 93 31
Mobile   +33 (0)6 33 78 66 90
Email   info@masdegarrigue.com
Web   www.masdegarrigue.com

Agnès & Francis Sevrin-Cance
Téranga,
303 route de Douelle,
46090 Pradines, Lot
Tel   +33 (0)5 65 35 20 51
Email   chambres.teranga@orange.fr
Web   www.chambresteranga.com

Entry 488   Map 10

Entry 489   Map 9

laynac

fter all these years, this delightful, heerful couple offer heart-warming B&B. till ready for a drink and a chat (in French), our hosts genuinely love visitors and are appy for you to linger over breakfast all ay on the peaceful terrace (the table may e shared with gîte guests or members of he big Faydi tribe), revelling in the eavenly views and flowering garden. ime-warp floral wallpapers, lino and amily furniture are in keeping with the feel f the place. No dinner but lots of home-rown wine and aperitif, fruit from their rees and 'gâteau de noix' with their own oney – flowing as in paradise. Great value.

La Théronière

This mellow stone 19th-century farmhouse, secure in its delightful grounds, is within walking distance of the pretty market town of Prayssac: you have the best of all worlds. Bedrooms, subtly hued and flower-themed, are lovely, Gardenia on the ground floor, Lavande with a Juliet balcony. After a day's canoeing on the Lot, lapping up the honey'd streets of Sarlat, the region's markets and the cave paintings of Lascaux, it's delicious to return to cool gardens and a pool. Friendly and civilised, Karen and Tony are well-versed in looking after guests and enjoy sharing their home. *Sawday self-catering also.*

rice	€48.
ooms	1 double.
Meals	Auberge 2km.
losed	Rarely.
irections	From Cahors D8 for Pradines 6km; at sign for Flaynac, follow Chambres d'Hôtes sign on right, then right & right again.

Price	€68.
Rooms	5: 4 doubles, 1 single.
Meals	Dinner with wine, €28. Restaurants in Prayssac, 1km.
Closed	Rarely.
Directions	From Cahors D911 for Fumel 25km to Prayssac. At post office right D67 2km; left after garden centre for Dom. du Théron; house on right.

M & Mme Faydi
Flaynac,
46090 Pradines,
Lot
el   +33 (0)5 65 35 33 36

Karen Durant-Pritchard
La Théronière,
Route de Théron,
46220 Prayssac, Lot
Tel   +33 (0)5 65 20 15 47
Email   info@theroniere.com
Web   www.theroniere.com

Entry 490   Map 9

Entry 491   Map 9

Midi - Pyrénées

Mondounet

The golden Lot stone glows and the wonderful view from the breakfast terrace sweeps over two valleys. On a peaceful through road with just the postman going by, the 17th-century farmhouse has been restored to its original character, including outbuildings for gîte guests. Make friends round the fenced-in salt-purified pool, or over dinner, served before the generous fire. Zoé will charm you, see you have a good time, serve breakfast when you like. Peter plays the guitar and sings – his musical evenings are great fun. Off the lovely living room is the bedroom, simple, spacious, delightful – as is the whole place.

Price	€60.
Rooms	1 double.
Meals	Dinner with wine, €22.
Closed	Rarely.
Directions	From Cahors for Toulouse; at r'bout D653 for Agen 16km; at junc. right D656 for 14km; thro' Villesèque, Sauzet, Bovila; after Bovila, 3rd left; signed.

	Peter & Zoé Scott
	Mondounet,
	46800 Fargues,
	Lot
Tel	+33 (0)5 65 36 96 32
Email	scotsprops@aol.com
Web	www.mondounetholidaysandhomes.com

Entry 492   Map 14

Midi - Pyrénées

Lamoulère

Wrapped in 20 acres of soft pastures, th white Quercy farmhouse sparkles in th sun. At night, magical views reach to th village, floodlit on its hill. Sue serves dinne on white china, Paul takes care of the wine both happy to share evenings with guest it's all so lovely you'll long to return. Th bedroom is calm and inviting (in the mai house but with its own entrance), aglov with old stone walls and new plaste creamy colours and a dash of rose-rec terracotta floors beautifully restored… an a dream of a shower. Lauzerte is up th road, the garden is delicious, so is the pool *Min. two nights July / Aug.*

Price	€60-€70.
Rooms	1 double/twin.
Meals	Dinner with wine, €30. Restaurant 3km.
Closed	Rarely.
Directions	From Montauban D927 to Lafrançaise; D2 to Durfort Lacapelette; right D953 to Lauzerte; right D34 for Cazes Mondenard. Signed.

	Sue & Paul Roberts
	Lamoulère,
	82110 Lauzerte,
	Tarn-et-Garonne
Tel	+33 (0)5 63 95 29 31
Mobile	+44 (0)7966 514134
Email	paul.roberts543@orange.fr
Web	www.lamouleregite.com

Entry 493   Map 14

Midi - Pyrénées

Green Chambre d'Hôte

Under pollution-free skies, amid acres of meadow and woodland, a green paradise unfolds. Taking on a hunter's shack, this couple renovated their patch simply and with love and attention. Sid and Laura are a delight, as is their colourful organic garden. Landscape gardeners and experts on wildlife, they are also virtually self-sufficient; home-grown veggie cuisine for supper, solar powered everything and natural pest control. Overlooking lavender garden and vine-covered terrace is a cosy bedroom. Watch birds by day, listen to frogs sing at night, immerse yourself in unspoilt beauty. *Station transfers; baggage transfers for walkers.*

Ethical Collection: Environment, Food & Community. See page 410 for details.

Price	€65-€80. Child bed, €15.
Rooms	1 double (extra single bed).
Meals	Dinner (vegetarian) with wine, €20. Picnic lunch available. Restaurants 10-minute drive.
Closed	Rarely.
Directions	From St Antonin D5 for Caussade; 2nd left for St Cirq & Gouvern 2km; in small hamlet, left for Tourondol 500m, 1st house on right.

Laura & Sid Havard
Green Chambre d'Hôte,
Lausoprens, 82140 St Antonin
Noble Val, Tarn-et-Garonne
Tel +33 (0)5 63 30 53 77
Mobile +33 (0)6 31 99 94 31
Email green.havard@gmail.com
Web www.greenchambredhote.com

Entry 494 Map 14

Midi - Pyrénées

La Résidence

Your charming hosts love being part of village life – and what a village: medieval to the core and with a famous Sunday market. It is a joy to stay in a townhouse in the heart of it all, with an airy hall and a great spiral staircase, rosy floor tiles and old stone walls, and views to a delicious, sculpture-rich garden. Three of the big tranquil bedrooms overlook the garden, another has a divine terrace with rooftop views; sunlight dapples the soft colours and uncluttered spaces, modern paintings and old country pieces. Seriously into food, Sabine and Evert do excellent dinners – do book. *Studio available.*

Price	€80-€98.
Rooms	5: 3 doubles, 2 twins.
Meals	Dinner €27. Wine €15-€25.
Closed	Rarely.
Directions	From Montauban N20, 22km to Caussade; right D926 for 7km; right D5 to St Antonin Noble Val 12km; in centre, behind town hall.

Evert & Sabine Weijers
La Résidence,
37 rue Droite, 82140 St Antonin
Noble Val, Tarn-et-Garonne
Tel +33 (0)5 63 67 37 56
Email info@laresidence-france.com
Web www.laresidence-france.com

Entry 495 Map 15

Midi - Pyrénées

Maison Lavande

Cosy up with delightful Bob and Lorraine in a townhouse that snoozes at the village edge. They love looking after people and have turned their two top floors into a 'home from home' with snug living areas (wood-burner, Chinese carpets, family photos, guest fridge) and bedrooms upstairs tinged with cuddly pinks and blues. You have to nip down to the loos (gowns provided), though the Pink Room has a communicating shower. Lorraine cooks (extremely well) in the cheery kitchen and Bob makes a great paella: eat sociably on the terrace or in the garden by the apple tree and teensy pool. So welcoming. *Minimum two nights.*

Price	€85. Child bed €20.
Rooms	2: 1 double; 1 double with separate shower. Both wc's downstairs.
Meals	Dinner with wine, €12–€21. Picnic €8. Restaurant 2km.
Closed	Rarely.
Directions	From Caussade to St Antonin Noble Val; D115 for Varen 12km; left D33 for Verfeil 1km; in Arnac, house on left just after cemetery.

	Lorraine & Bob Walker
	Maison Lavande,
	Rue de la Bascule,
	Arnac, 82330 Varen, Tarn-et-Garonne
Tel	+33 (0)5 63 27 26 84
Email	boblorrainew@msn.com
Web	www.maison-lavande.com

Midi - Pyrénées

Le Mas des Anges

An exciting venture for a super couple who are squeaky-green too, running their organic vineyard. You find a very pretty house surrounded by lovely shrubs, a pool, and a separate entrance to each bedroom with terrace. Ground-floor rooms have fabulous colours, big good beds, bathrooms with thick towels. The sitting area is airy and modern with stacks of books, magazines and interesting sculpture and art. Sophie gives you a huge breakfast with homemade bread and jams, fresh fruit, cheeses and yogurt. Mountauban is only 7km away and you are near enough to amazing Albi for a day trip.

Price	€70. €90 for 3. €100 for 4.
Rooms	3: 2 doubles, 1 family room for 3-4.
Meals	Restaurants in Montauban, 7km.
Closed	Rarely.
Directions	From Montauban D999 for Albi, 2km; r'bout 3rd exit onto D92. House on left after approx. 1.6km, signed.

	Juan & Sophie Kervyn
	Le Mas des Anges,
	1623 route de Verlhac Tescou,
	82000 Montauban, Tarn-et-Garonne
Tel	+33 (0)5 63 24 27 05
Mobile	+33 (0)6 76 30 86 36
Email	sophiekervyn@hotmail.com
Web	www.lemasdesanges.com

Midi - Pyrénées

Au Château

A beguiling mix of grandeur and informality. The house is filled with light and life, thanks to this young Anglo-French family. Softly contemporary bedrooms, two in a separate building, are airy spaces that mix the best of modern with the loveliest of traditional: pale beams and white plaster walls, bold colours, luxurious silks, elegant antiques. There's a country-style breakfast room and a kitchenette so you can make your own suppers – then eat al fresco on the terrace. Visit historic towns, explore the Canal du Midi, let the kids roam free in the garden, stroll the charming village. *Gourmet, wine & bridge breaks.*

Price	€61-€89.
Rooms	5: 1 double, 1 twin, 1 family suite for 4, 2 suites for 2-3.
Meals	Guest kitchenette. Restaurant 5km.
Closed	Rarely.
Directions	From Valence d'Agen D813 for Moissac; after Malause right to St Nicolas de la Grave; cross river Garonne. Entering St Nicolas de la Grave, 1st r'bout left, château on left.

Kathrin Barker
Au Château, 1 bd des Fossés de Raoul,
82210 St Nicolas de la Grave,
Tarn-et-Garonne
Tel   +33 (0)5 63 95 96 82
Email   kathrin.barker@sfr.fr
Web   www.au-chateau-stn.com

Entry 498   Map 14

Midi - Pyrénées

Tondes

Warm country people, the Sellars left a Sussex farm for a smallholding in deepest France to breed sheep, goats and poultry the natural way: no pesticides, no heavy machines, animals roaming free. Their hard work has earned them great respect locally and their recipe for a simple rewarding life includes receiving guests happily under the beams, by the wood-burning stove, in pretty-coloured, country-furnished rooms with super walk-in showers. While Julie creates homemade marvels from her farmhouse kitchen, you relax on the terrace with a glass of homemade orange liqueur and admire the garden — as wonderful as all the rest.

Ethical Collection: Food.
See page 410 for details.

Price	€50.
Rooms	2: 1 double, 1 family room.
Meals	Dinner with wine, €21.
Closed	Rarely.
Directions	A62 exit 9; D813 to Moissac; D7 for Bourg de Visa. At Fourquet, left at r'bout. After 500m, right at Chambres d'Hôtes 2km. 2nd sign on left, house at top of drive.

Julie & Mark Sellars
Tondes,
82400 Castelsagrat,
Tarn-et-Garonne
Tel   +33 (0)5 63 94 52 13
Email   willowweave@orange.fr

Entry 499   Map 14

Le Petit Feuillant

Magret de canard, beans from the garden, wines from the Côtes de Gascogne, melons from over the hill: table d'hôtes (and lots of French guests) is pure pleasure for David and Vikki. In a hilltop, out-of-the-way village, this well-restored house and barn, with its several terraces and outstanding views, has become a B&B of huge comfort and charm. Find old stone walls and tiled floors, whitewashed beams and weather-worn shutters, soft colours and uncluttered spaces, and homemade croissants for breakfast. Foodies come for the cookery courses, astronomers for the night skies. Great value.

La Lumiane

Such a surprise to step off a side street into a delightful garden with loungers, pool and sweet-smelling shrubs. Chatty Alain and chef Gisèle have restored this gracious house with style: rooms in the main house, up the stunning staircase, breathe tradition and space, old fireplaces, big windows and antiques; those in the garden annexe have a sweetly contemporary feel. All have an uncluttered mix of florals and stripes and simple, spotless bathrooms. Eat well on local, seasonal produce in the formal dining room or on the terrace by candlelight, wake to the sound of the church bells. Much authenticity and charm.

Price	€60.
Rooms	5: 4 doubles; 1 suite for 2 with separate shower.
Meals	Dinner with wine, €22. Auberge in village 50m.
Closed	Rarely.
Directions	From Montauban D928 to Montech & Beaumont de Lomagne. 6km after B-de-L, right D7 through St Clar; D40 to Gramont; up hill to village.

Price	€42-€67.
Rooms	5 doubles.
Meals	Dinner with wine, €24.
Closed	Rarely.
Directions	From Condom D654 to Saint Puy. Grande Rue in centre of village by church.

David & Vikki Chance
Le Petit Feuillant,
Le Bourg, 82120 Gramont,
Tarn-et-Garonne

Tel	+33 (0)5 63 29 11 04
Email	david.chance@neuf.fr
Web	www.gasconcook.co.uk/ accomodation.html

Alain & Gisèle Eman
La Lumiane,
Grande Rue,
32310 St Puy, Gers

Tel	+33 (0)5 62 28 95 95
Mobile	+33 (0)6 78 18 32 24
Email	info@lalumiane.com
Web	www.lalumiane.com

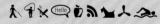

Midi - Pyrénées

Belliette

On a hill near the winding Douze river sits a 300-year-old farmhouse. It is gorgeous inside and out. Arum lilies run along the half-timbered façade, an ancient bread oven and rose-brick chimney stand at its core, beautifying each simple bedroom. The Cormiers' affection for Gascon culture and armagnac shines through. Join them for an evening meal, be serenaded by your engaging host and his guitar. Outside, deer roam and there's a delightful chicken coop full of feathery inhabitants. Catch a wisp of the Pyrenees on a clear day, enjoy vales-lovely walks, historic Eauze, summer markets and summertime jazz in Marciac.

Price	€60-€70. Suite €90.
Rooms	3: 2 rooms, 1 suite.
Meals	Dinner with wine, €22.
Closed	Rarely.
Directions	From A62 exit 7 for Condom; D931 to Eauze (80km); D626 for Cazaubon 8km; follow signs for Belliette.

Marie Cormier
Belliette,
Cutxan,
32150 Cazaubon, Gers
Tel   +33 (0)5 62 08 18 68
Email   marie.cormier@wanadoo.fr
Web   www.belliette.fr

Entry 502   Map 14

Midi - Pyrénées

Lieu Dit Fitan

Complete tranquillity, beautiful gardens, charmed pool, and Dido, who loves people – an inspiration to us all. In 1999 this was just another derelict barn in the undulating Gers countryside; the restoration is a wonder. At the door, the whole superb space opens before the eyes, English antiques gleam and the fine modern kitchen sparkles (available for a small fee). Two luscious bedrooms, one upstairs, one down: raw stones punctuate soft white walls, patchwork cheers, books tempt. Dido loves cooking, has travelled thousands of miles and is highly cultured. A corner of paradise, it even smells heavenly.

Price	€70-€80.
Rooms	2: 1 double, 1 twin.
Meals	Dinner with wine, €35. Use of kitchen €8.
Closed	Rarely.
Directions	From Marciac D134 north; cross D946, continue to Louslitges church on left, 2nd right, Fitan 3/4 up on right. Pale green shutters.

Dido Streatfeild-Moore
Lieu Dit Fitan,
32230 Louslitges,
Gers
Tel   +33 (0)5 62 70 81 88
Email   deedoenfrance@wanadoo.fr
Web   www.chezdeedo.com

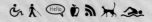

Entry 503   Map 14

Midi - Pyrénées

Domaine de Peyloubère

The sober buildings don't prepare you for the explosion inside: 80 years ago, an Italian painter spread his heart and love of form and colour over ceilings and doors. 'His' suite has vast space, fine antiques, a dream of a bathroom, dazzling paintings. Theresa and Ian fell for the romantically wild house and glorious domaine and left high-pressure London jobs to save the whole place from dereliction – their enthusiasm and sensitive intelligence show in every room. The waterfall, the wild orchids, the wildlife, the hosted dinners – there's no other place like it. Heaven for children – or an anniversary treat. *Sawday self-catering also.*

Ethical Collection: Environment, Food & Community. See page 410 for details.

Price	€80-€110.
Rooms	2 suites.
Meals	Dinner with wine, €30.
Closed	Rarely.
Directions	From Auch N21 south 3km; left D929 for Lannemezan; in Pavie, left after Mairie, cross old bridge, 1st right, signed Auterrive; house 1km on left.

	Theresa & Ian Martin
	Domaine de Peyloubère,
	32550 Pavie,
	Gers
Tel	+33 (0)5 62 05 74 97
Email	martin@peyloubere.com
Web	www.peyloubere.com

Entry 504   Map 14

Midi - Pyrénées

La Garenne

Youthful, outgoing and warm-hearted, Mireille (who loves to practise her English) is an inspired cook and a delight to be with; Olivier too is a warm presence. Together, they fill the cosy house with antique plates, prints, pictures and furniture. The guest room is tiny – no lounging space – and there's no guest sitting room, but on a fine day you could sit out in the garden and listen to the birds. This is a relaxed and unpretentious family home with the essential dogs and cats and a swimming pool shared with the gîte guests. An easy address for families, and babysitting is available.

Price	€60.
Rooms	1 double. Children's room available.
Meals	Dinner with wine, €20. Restaurant 24km.
Closed	Rarely.
Directions	From Auch N21 for Tarbes 2km; left D929 for Lannemezan; in Masseube, left for Simorre 4km; left for Bellegarde; 1st left, before church & castle.

	Mireille & Olivier Courouble
	La Garenne,
	Bellegarde,
	32140 Masseube, Gers
Tel	+33 (0)5 62 66 03 61
Mobile	+33 (0)6 88 71 84 49
Email	ocourouble@wanadoo.fr
Web	www.lebalconvertdespyrenees.com

Entry 505   Map 14

Midi - Pyrénées

À Larroustat

A tranquil space is yours in the large upstairs suite, whether there are two of you or four. The two airy bedrooms are filled with antique pine furniture, soft and homely fabrics and handmade wooden beds; the bathroom is big enough for a party. Chill out in the sitting room with its books, maps and comfy chairs. Breakfast and dinner are taken at one table in the lovely handcrafted kitchen or on the terrace: much is home-grown, the duck is local, all is seasonal, and Posy makes delicious puddings. You don't have to go anywhere once you've arrived; just loll by the pool or find a shady spot and dream.

Price	€75. €120 for 4.
Rooms	1 family suite for 2-4.
Meals	Dinner with wine, €25.
Closed	Mid-December to 1st week in January.
Directions	L'Isle Jourdain D632 for Boulogne sur Gesse; 4km before Boulogne D12 right for Lunax; D228 left to St Blancard. Leave village, château on left; left; D228 right for Manent Montané; house on right.

Posy & Mike Fallowfield
À Larroustat,
32140 Manent Montané,
Gers

Tel	+33 (0)5 62 66 16 88
Mobile	+44 (0)7814 705586
Email	webland@wanadoo.fr
Web	www.coin-du-gers.com

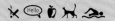

Entry 506   Map 14

Midi - Pyrénées

Martinn-Maubourguet

Martine loves life, children (hers now all grown up), house, guests, gastronomy. Food is served at the big kitchen table with gusto: homemade breads and jams, exotic teas, Sunday brunches, Moroccan dinners (or Spanish, or Italian); gourmet picnics too. She is warm, genuine, generous, proud of her freshly decorated bedrooms with their big bathrooms and polished wooden floors; three feed off a wraparound balcony that overlooks the courtyard below. And then, a garden, small park and serene pool, marvellous surprises at this village-centre farmhouse. Maps, bikes, WiFi, DVDs – Martine gives you it all.

Ethical Collection: Food.
See page 410 for details.

Price	€85-€98. Extra bed €10-€30, baby €5.
Rooms	4: 3 doubles, 1 twin.
Meals	Dinner with wine, €28-€42. Sunday brunch €20. Picnics available.
Closed	Mid-November to February.
Directions	From Pau D943 thro' Morlaas to Lembeye; cont. right to Maubourget; cont. D943 right for Marciac; over 1st r'bout; at fork straight on. Yellow house on right.

Martine Jablonski-Cahours
Martinn-Maubourguet,
88 route de Sauveterre,
65700 Maubourguet, Hautes-Pyrénées

Tel	+33 (0)5 62 96 01 07
Mobile	+33 (0)6 23 55 34 82
Email	info@mart-inn.com
Web	www.mart-inn.com

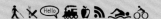

Entry 507   Map 14

Midi - Pyrénées

Maison de l'Évêque

You could weep, this valley is so beautiful; so are the house, its story, garden, owners. A doctor built it (see the caduceus on the great newel post), then it fostered one Bishop Laurence, who 'proved' Bernardette's miracles and set Lourdes up for glory. Arlette, a miracle of industry and human warmth, decorates prettily, cooks simply and brilliantly and still finds plenty of time for guests. Quiet and attentive, Robert will point you in the right direction for hiking and fishing in that gorgeous valley (Pyrenean high-mountain trout are the best, naturally). A very special place.

Price	€55–€62.
Rooms	4: 3 doubles, 1 triple.
Meals	Restaurant 1.5km.
Closed	November–March.
Directions	From Lourdes N21 S for 2km; left at bridge; immediately left again D26 to Juncalas; house in village centre on right.

Arlette & Robert Assouère
Maison de l'Évêque,
Impasse Monseigneur Laurence,
65100 Juncalas, Lourdes, Hautes-Pyrénées
Tel   +33 (0)5 62 42 02 04
Mobile   +33 (0)6 80 22 42 08
Email   robert.assouere@wanadoo.fr
Web   www.maisondeleveque.com

Midi - Pyrénées

Eth Berye Petit

Beauty, harmony, tranquillity... all who stay, long to return. The grand old village *maison de maître*, in Henri's family for centuries, opens to soft green rolling meadows and the majestic Pyrenees – the finest view in all France! Ione, graceful, smiling mother of two, ushers you up the venerable stair to wonderful warm bedrooms in pastel hues – one with a balcony – and luscious beds wrapped in antique linen. The living room, where a fire roars and a fine dinner is served on winter weekends, is a delight to come home to after a day's skiing or hiking. For summer? A dreamy garden. Exceptional.

Price	€58–€64.
Rooms	3: 1 double, 1 twin, 1 suite for 3.
Meals	Dinner with wine, €20. Auberge 100m.
Closed	Rarely.
Directions	From Lourdes for Argelès Gazost; 10km; left at r'bout for Beaucens, follow Eth Berye Petit signs.

Henri & Ione Vielle
Eth Berye Petit,
15 route de Vielle,
65400 Beaucens, Hautes-Pyrénées
Tel   +33 (0)5 62 97 90 02
Email   contact@beryepetit.com
Web   www.beryepetit.com

Midi - Pyrénées

La Ferme du Buret

In an enchanting Heidi-esque valley in the Haute (but gently rolling) Pyrenees is a long low stone cattle stable tucked into the hills, with a barn attached. Each superb structure houses two guest bedrooms. From the loftiest beam to the chunkiest floor, interiors are lined with thick wide planks of cedar, chestnut, acacia and oak; rustic-chic fabrics and sleek white bathroom fittings add to the spare, but never spartan, charm. Cathy is a champion skier and can ski-guide you, Pierre is an inspired chef of regional dinners served at the big table. Sports and thermal spas abound, the scenery makes the heart sing.

Price	€80-€100.
Rooms	4: 2 twins/doubles, 2 family rooms for 3.
Meals	Dinner with wine, €25.
Closed	Mid-November to January (open Christmas to New Year).
Directions	From Tarbes A64 exit Tournay; N117 dir. Toulouse; in Ozon D14 right to Bourg de B; enter on D84 up to D26, 6km dir. Bulan; at Asque sign, keep to upper D26, 2km; left; 700m.

Pierre & Cathy Faye
La Ferme du Buret,
65130 Asque,
Hautes-Pyrénées
Tel   +33 (0)5 62 39 19 26
Mobile   +33 (0)6 86 77 33 71
Email   info@lafermeduburet.com
Web   www.lafermeduburet.com

Entry 510   Map 14

Midi - Pyrénées

Domaine de Jean-Pierre

Madame is gracefully down to earth and her house and garden an oasis of calm where you may share her delight in playing the piano or golf (3km) and possibly make a lifelong friend. Built in Napoleon's time, her house has an elegant hall, big airy bedrooms and great bathrooms, while fine furniture and linen sheets reflect her pride in her ancestral home – a combination of uncluttered space and character. The huge quadruple has space to waltz in and the smallest bathroom; the colours chosen are peaceful and harmonious; and breakfast comes with an array of honeys and civilised conversation. Great value.

Price	€58. Triple €73.
Rooms	3: 2 doubles, 1 triple.
Meals	Restaurants 3km.
Closed	Rarely.
Directions	From Toulouse A64 exit 17 for Montréjeau/Tarbes/Pinas 11km; at church D158 for Villeneuve. House 1km on right.

Marie-Sabine Colombier
Domaine de Jean-Pierre,
20 route de Villeneuve,
65300 Pinas, Hautes-Pyrénées
Tel   +33 (0)5 62 98 15 08
Email   marie@domainedejeanpierre.com
Web   www.domainedejeanpierre.com

Entry 511   Map 14

Midi - Pyrénées

La Souleillane

Fabienne and Jean-Luc have done an amazing restoration, and guest rooms at 'Sunnyside' are appropriately big and bright: the cheery yellow family room in the house, the restful doubles in the barn. Having young boys of their own, they make children very welcome and give them the run of the walled garden. Your hosts work so you may be left alone in the morning; come evening, Fabienne enjoys cooking and chatting round the table while Jean-Luc, Pyrenean born and bred, is an interesting source of mountain-eering escapades. No sitting room but a large covered terrace for summer. And there's cross-country skiing nearby. Lovely.

Ethical Collection: Food.
See page 410 for details.

Price	€58-€78.
Rooms	3: 1 family room for 4. Barn: 2 doubles.
Meals	Dinner with wine, €19.
Closed	Rarely.
Directions	From Toulouse A64 exit 17; D938 west 7km; signed. 8km from Lannemezan station.

Fabienne & Jean-Luc Garcia
La Souleillane, 4 rue de
l'Ancienne Poste, 65150 St Laurent
de Neste, Hautes-Pyrénées
Tel +33 (0)5 62 39 76 01
Email info@souleillane.com
Web www.souleillane.com

Entry 512 Map 14

Midi - Pyrénées

La Genade

Up in her beloved mountains with the wild streams splashing and an unbroken view of 13th-century Lordat, Meredith loves sharing her heaven. A passionate climber and skier, she has rebuilt her ruined auberge: old stones and new wood, craggy beams, precious furniture and a cheery fire make it rustic, warm and elegant. Under truly American care, rooms have beautiful bed linens, oriental rugs and books. The welcome is genuine, the dinners are animated – and delicious. Walkers and cyclists should stay a week, and there's a repair room specially for bikes. *Over sevens welcome. Minimum two nights (one for cyclists).*

Ethical Collection: Environment & Food.
See page 410 for details.

Price	€50-€65.
Rooms	3: 2 doubles, 1 twin.
Meals	Dinner with wine, €20-€23.
Closed	Rarely.
Directions	From Toulouse A61 then A66-N20/E9 for Andorra. 4-lane road ends Tarascon; cont. E9/N20 to Luzenac; left D2 then D55 for Château de Lordat. After Lordat left, Axiat 1km, 1st on left, facing church.

Meredith Dickinson
La Genade,
La route des Corniches,
09250 Axiat, Ariège
Tel +33 (0)5 61 05 51 54
Email meredith.dickinson@orange.fr
Web www.chambre-dhote-pyrenees-lagenade.com

Entry 513 Map 14

Impasse du Temple

Breakfast among the remains of a Protestant chapel, sleep in a townhouse, one of a terrace constructed in 1758; John and Lee-anne are its second owners. Delightful, humorous Australians, they are restoring their elegant mansion and loving it. Graciously high ceilings, a sweeping spiral staircase, lovely great windows in an oasis of ancient, stream-kissed oaks… arrive as strangers, depart as friends. The food is fantastic and the guest rooms are generous, in pastels and with just enough antiques; one even has the vast original claw-footed bath. Readers sing their praises. *Sawday self-catering also.*

Le Castelou

The history and the architecture of their beautifully restored ducal house fascinate this warm, friendly couple; ask about the stained glass, the neo-gothic tiles, the rococo-esque plasterwork. Amanda is an artist, Andy is a film maker, together they host exhibitions and concerts, and attention to detail is their hallmark. The walled garden is delightful and the bedrooms are elegant, all sweeping wooden floors and masses of light; one has its own lookout tower. Breakfasts are generous, the house is atmospheric and Leran has a bustling Friday night market.

Price	€80-€90. Suite €116-€130.
Rooms	5: 2 doubles, 2 triples, 1 suite for 4.
Meals	Dinner €25. Wine €9-€20.
Closed	Rarely.
Directions	From Toulouse A61 for Montpellier; exit 22 on D4/D119 to Mirepoix; left D625 for Lavelanet 11km; at Aigues Vives left for Léran D28.

Price	€80-€90.
Rooms	4: 2 doubles, 2 family suites for 2-4.
Meals	Occasional dinner (vegetarian). Restaurant 200m.
Closed	Rarely.
Directions	From Mirepoix, D625 for Lavelanet, left to Léran; left after church. 1st house on left after school.

John & Lee-anne Furness
Impasse du Temple,
09600 Léran,
Ariège
Tel   +33 (0)5 61 01 50 02
Mobile   +33 (0)6 88 19 49 22
Email   john.furness@wanadoo.fr
Web   www.chezfurness.com

Andrew & Amanda Attenburrow
Le Castelou,
8 cours St Jacques,
09600 Léran, Ariège
Tel   +33 (0)5 61 65 44 36
Email   attenburrow@wanadoo.fr
Web   www.lecastelou.com

La Ferme de Boyer

Your hosts, fun, humorous and with interesting pasts, have filled the big rambling farmhouse with polished mahogany and family memorabilia and the garden with shrubs and lawns. He was once a helicopter engineer and loves classic cars, she is a Cordon Bleu cook; both designed furniture for first-class hotels and worked for hotels in Paris. Now they run a sparkling B&B. Bedrooms are sunny and charming, more English than French with pastoral views, the family room is large and self-contained, Harriet's dinners are convivial and delicious, and sweet Mirepoix is just down the road.

Gratia

Luscious texture combinations of original floor tiles discovered virgin in the attic, stupendous carpentry: loving hands crafted Gratia in the 1790s; flair and hard work brought it back from ruin in the 1990s. Jean-Paul's motto 'less is more' informs the wonderful uncluttered bedrooms with their pretty beds and linens; Florence, chic and charming, will do physiotherapy in the great attic studio – mats, music, massage; the ethos is 'polished and cool', the attitude is determinedly green, breakfast is perfect. Chill out on the manicured lawn by the saltwater pool, converse delightfully, depart thoroughly renewed.

Ethical Collection: Food.
See page 410 for details.

Price	€50-€80.
Rooms	3: 1 double, 1 twin, 1 family suite with sitting room & kitchenette.
Meals	Dinner with wine, €30.
Closed	Rarely.
Directions	From Mirepoix D119 3km through Besset; after leaving Besset, 1st drive on left.

Price	€90-€120.
Rooms	4 doubles.
Meals	Restaurants nearby.
Closed	Mid-September to April.
Directions	From Toulouse A64 exit 28; at St Sulpice D19 for Foix/Vallée du Lèze; at Lézat sur Lèze left D19b for Esperce 200m; cross bridge over Lèze, small road opp.; Gratia at top of hill.

	Robert & Harriet Stow
	La Ferme de Boyer,
	09500 Coutens,
	Ariège
Tel	+33 (0)5 61 68 93 41
Mobile	+33 (0)6 22 04 05 84
Email	ferme.boyer@wanadoo.fr
Web	www.fermeboyer.iowners.net

	Florence Potey & Jean-Paul Wallaert
	Gratia,
	09210 Lézat sur Lèze,
	Ariège
Tel	+33 (0)5 61 68 64 47
Email	ferme.gratia@wanadoo.fr
Web	www.ariege.com/gratia

Midi - Pyrénées

Les Pesques

Surrounded by rolling farmland, at the end of a quiet lane, a gorgeous old manor house in a luxuriant garden – a happy place and home. Brigitte has decorated in peaceful good taste and all is charmingly cluttered, each country antique the right one. Bedrooms have white walls, vintage iron beds, fresh white linen and old terracotta floors; one has a wisteria-draped balcony; the newest smiles in soft nuances of colonial blue. A dreamy, comfortable, joyful house run by Brigitte, who concocts lovely fresh meals from vegetables from the potager and eggs from the hens. Great value. *Brocante on site.*

Price	€56.
Rooms	3: 1 twin, 1 family suite for 3; 1 double with separate shower.
Meals	Dinner with wine, €20.
Closed	Rarely.
Directions	From Toulouse E80/A64 for Tarbes; exit S D6 for Cazères; over Garonne, immed. right then 1st right D62; after camping, 2nd left; house set back on right, blue shutters.

Brigitte & Bruno Lebris
Les Pesques,
31220 Palaminy,
Haute-Garonne
Tel   +33 (0)5 61 97 59 28
Email   reserve@les-pesques.com
Web   www.les-pesques.com

Midi - Pyrénées

Le Moulin

In 2006 Ruth and John arrived at this remote mill with five children, a dog, a cat and a chinchilla in tow. Four years on, there are ducks paddling in the mill stream, chickens roaming and sheep grazing beyond. The organic garden provides veg for supper and there's a kitchenette for families on a budget. Cosy bedrooms are country traditional with beds in striped linen and wooden floors, but it's the outdoors that will soak up your time: the animals, the orchard, the ten acres of land. This couple's energy is contagious, what they've achieved is inspirational. Kids will adore it. *Minimum two nights June-September.*

Price	From €60.
Rooms	2: 1 double, 1 family room for 4.
Meals	Dinner with wine, €20. Guest kitchenette.
Closed	November-March.
Directions	From Toulouse A64 exit 21 to Boussens; D635 to Aurignac; right D8 for Alan 3km; left D8 to Montoulieu, cont. to Samouillan; left D96 follow signs to Le Moulin.

John & Ruth Temple
Le Moulin,
Samouillan, 31420 Aurignac,
Haute-Garonne
Tel   +33 (0)5 61 98 86 92
Email   john@moulin-vert.net
Web   www.moulin-vert.net

Midi - Pyrénées

Les Loges de St Sernin

Vast welcoming comfort lies in store behind those superb wooden doors in the heart of Toulouse – and no expense spared. Madame, living on the third floor, is a poppet: petite, delightful, up to speed with this vibrant town. Big peaceful guest bedrooms spread themselves across the floor below, each with warm colours, a huge bed, an antique mirror, luxurious linen. Breakfast is served on a balcony in good weather, as early or as late as you like it. Period detail abounds: inside shutters, marble fireplaces, sweeping parquet, tall windows beautifully dressed – Madame aims to please. Marvellous! *Min. two nights at weekends March-Oct.*

Price	€110–€125.
Rooms	4: 2 doubles, 2 twins.
Meals	Restaurants within walking distance.
Closed	Rarely.
Directions	In Toulouse for Église St Sernin. House in street between Place St Sernin & Bd de Strasboug. Easy parking Place St Sernin. Ask about special rate local car park.

Sylviane Tatin
Les Loges de St Sernin,
12 rue St Bernard,
31000 Toulouse, Haute-Garonne
Tel   +33 (0)5 61 24 44 44
Email logesaintsernin@live.fr
Web   www.dormiratoulouse.net

Entry 520   Map 14

Midi - Pyrénées

Anjali

Off a busy city road lies instant delight: welcoming red, cream and black Italian tiles run from front door to glass garden door, and lively, cultured Delphine leads you in. The big square empty bedrooms are strikingly styled in strong colours with superbly good big beds, the latest thing in bathrooms and a darling little bunk room for children. The garden, sheltered by typical Roman-style brick walls, holds trees, a small buddha and peace. Breakfast, served at a long communal table in the wood-heated conservatory, is mostly organic. And Toulouse is at your feet. *If you need open windows, book a peaceful garden room.*

Price	€90–€110.
Rooms	4: 2 doubles, 2 family rooms (one with bunkbeds).
Meals	Restaurant 50m.
Closed	Rarely.
Directions	In Toulouse centre, Place Palais du Parlement; Grande Rue St Michel leads off this square; house 500m on left. Metro: Palais de Justice.

Delphine Cizeau
Anjali,
86 Grande Rue St Michel,
31000 Toulouse, Haute-Garonne
Tel   +33 (0)9 54 22 42 93
Email contact@anjali.fr
Web   www.anjali.fr

Entry 521   Map 14

Midi - Pyrénées

Le Clos du Cèdre

Just 15 minutes from Toulouse city centre a grassy shrubby garden spreads its arms. Ideal for children to run, roll and hide in, it has two superb cedars and a curly pool with a quaint Hansel and Gretel pool house designed by Françoise. She welcomes you with energetic enthusiasm to her big 18th-century farmhouse, its family-elegant high-windowed drawing room, a grand gentleman farmer's double bedroom and a more cottagey twin room, both big, independent and comfortable. Her breakfast is the star turn: crêpes, cake or clafoutis, on a table decorated with flowers and imagination. And she's great fun. *Five minutes from airport.*

Price	€75-€85.
Rooms	2: 1 double, 1 twin.
Meals	Restaurant in village.
Closed	Rarely.
Directions	From Bd Périphérique for Auch/Colomiers then Tournefeuille; exit 'Armurié' A602 for metro & St Martin du Touch; left Chemin de Tournefeuille; house on right: high brick wall, black gates.

Françoise Martin
Le Clos du Cèdre,
130 chemin de Tournefeuille,
31000 Toulouse, Haute-Garonne

Tel	+33 (0)5 61 86 63 09
Email	closducedre@orange.fr
Web	closducedre.voila.net

Entry 522   Map 14

Midi - Pyrénées

La Ferme d'en Pécoul

Talented Élisabeth makes jams, jellies and liqueurs, pâté, confit and foie gras, keeps hens and is wonderfully kind. Almost-retired Noël gently tends the potager as well as the fields; wrap yourself in the natural warmth of their Lauragais farmhouse. The first floor is lined with new wood, there's an airy guest sitting room and two comfy bedrooms with tiny showers. Summer meals are outside, enjoyed with your hosts. One dog, two cats, fields as far as the eye can see – and exquisite medieval Caraman (once rich from the dye cocagne) just down the road. Great value. *Minimum two nights weekends & summer holidays.*

Ethical Collection: Food.
See page 410 for details.

Price	€46.
Rooms	2 doubles. Single child's room on request.
Meals	Dinner with wine, €17.
Closed	Rarely.
Directions	From Toulouse exit 17 Lasbordes to Castres; after approx. 20km, D1 to Caraman; D66 to Cambiac 3km, entrance on right.

Élisabeth & Noël Messal
La Ferme d'en Pécoul,
31460 Cambiac,
Haute-Garonne

Tel	+33 (0)5 61 83 16 13
Mobile	+33 (0)6 78 13 18 07
Email	enpecoul@wanadoo.fr
Web	pagesperso-orange.fr/enpecoul

Entry 523   Map 15

La Bousquétarié

Madame Sallier runs her family château with boundless energy and infectious joie de vivre, serves breakfast in her big kitchen in order to chat more easily to you (in French), loves everyone, especially children: she's a treasure. Charming bedrooms still have their original personality, one with rare 1850s wallpaper; turning walk-in cupboards into showers or loos was a brilliant stroke. Antique-filled sitting rooms are totally French; the little reading room holds hundreds of books; even the fresh roses are old-fashioned. It's all comfortably worn round the edges with a tennis court you're welcome to use. Don't miss.

Villa Les Pins

Madame's love of her home is infectious, and her 1903 house – built, intriguingly, in the Italian style – oozes history. Imagine high ceilings, tall windows, polished parquet and a staircase that brings you to wallpapered bedrooms, one with a balustraded balcony: huge charm. Early 20th-century antiques abound and bathrooms, spotless and light, are unquestionably dated. Lovely Madame, who winters in Paris, opens the house in summer and is proud of her great-value table d'hotes, hosted on a terrace with views to the Montagne Noire. The 'parc', a natural garden with roses by the house, conceals a super decked pool.

Price	€75.
Rooms	2 family suites.
Meals	Dinner with wine, €20-€24.
Closed	December-February.
Directions	From Revel D622 for Castres 9km; left D12 to Lempaut; right D46 for Lescout; house on left.

Price	€61-€84.
Rooms	2 twins/doubles.
Meals	Dinner, 4 courses with wine, €23.
Closed	November-April.
Directions	From Revel D622 for Castres 9km; left D12 to Lempaut; left D46 for Blan. House on left at end of village.

	Monique & Charles Sallier
	La Bousquétarié,
	81700 Lempaut,
	Tarn
Tel	+33 (0)5 63 75 51 09
Email	albisallier@aol.com
Web	www.chateau-bousquetarie.com

	Marie-Paule Delbreil
	Villa Les Pins,
	81700 Lempaut,
	Tarn
Tel	+33 (0)5 63 75 51 01
Mobile	+33 (0)6 18 13 65 06
Email	villa.les.pins@free.fr
Web	villa.les.pins.free.fr

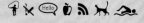

Entry 524   Map 15

Entry 525   Map 15

Midi - Pyrénées

La Villa de Mazamet & Le Petit Spa

A 'coup de foudre' caused Mark and Peter to buy this grand 1930s house in walled gardens, a few minutes' walk from the market town of Mazamet. Renovation revealed large light interiors of wood-panelled walls, parquet floors and sweeping windows. Furnished with modern elegance, the ground floor invites relaxation in comfy sofas or quiet corners. Bedrooms, with sumptuous beds and fine linen, are calmly luxurious; bathrooms are Art Deco gems. Your hosts are interesting, relaxed and well-travelled, meals in the restaurant are gastronomic. Ideal for Carcassonne, Albi and all those medieval villages. *Ask about speciality breaks.*

Price	€85–€150.
Rooms	5: 3 doubles, 2 twins/doubles.
Meals	Dinner €32.50. Wine list from €14.
Closed	Rarely.
Directions	A61 exit 23 to Mazamet; follow centre ville. Rue Pasteur opp. bandstand in Jardin de Promenade, 200m from railway station.

Peter Friend & Mark Barber
La Villa de Mazamet & Le Petit Spa,
4 rue Pasteur, 81200 Mazamet,
Tarn

Tel   +33 (0)5 63 97 90 33
Mobile +33 (0)6 25 50 56 91
Email   info@villademazamet.com
Web   www.villademazamet.com

Entry 526   Map 15

Midi - Pyrénées

Domaine d'en Naudet

Superb in every way, and such a sense of space! The domaine, surrounded by a patchwork-quilt countryside, was donated by Henri IV to a hunting crony in 1545 – and was in a parlous state when Eliane and Jean fell for it. They have achieved miracles. A converted barn/stable block reveals four vast and beautiful bedrooms (two with private wicker-chaired terraces), sensuous bathrooms and a stunning open-plan breakfast/sitting room. In the grounds, masses for children and energetic adults, while the slothful may bask by the pool. Markets, history and beauty surround you, and Eliane is a lovely hostess. *Minimum two nights.*

Price	€92.
Rooms	4: 2 doubles, 2 twins.
Meals	Guest kitchen. Restaurant 3km.
Closed	Rarely.
Directions	From Lavaur D112 to Castres; right D43 to Pratviel. House on left after 2km, signed.

Eliane Barcellini
Domaine d'en Naudet,
81220 Teyssode,
Tarn

Tel   +33 (0)5 63 70 50 59
Mobile +33 (0)6 07 17 66 08
Email   contact@domainenaudet.com
Web   www.domainenaudet.com

Entry 527   Map 15

Midi - Pyrénées

La Terrasse de Lautrec

Le Nôtre-designed gardens backing a graceful house, with terraces overhanging the village ramparts: the beauty and the peace are restorative. Seek out the secluded shady corners and roses, the box maze, the pond brimming with waterlilies, the pool that looks over the hills. As you swan through the frescoed dining room and the drawing room with its 1810 wallpaper you feel you've stepped back into another age. Dominique, warm and intelligent, treats you to the cooking of the region. Retire to a stunning drawing room, or a large, luminous bedroom filled with ochre and gilt. *Minimum two nights July/August.*

Price	€85–€120.
Rooms	4: 2 doubles, 1 twin, 1 suite.
Meals	Dinner with wine, €30.
Closed	November–March.
Directions	In Lautrec, take Rue Mercadial, cont. Rue de l'Église; past central square on right; cont. to Place du Monument; house opp. monument.

Dominique Ducoudray
La Terrasse de Lautrec,
Rue de L'Église,
81440 Lautrec, Tarn
Tel +33 (0)5 63 75 84 22
Mobile +33 (0)6 07 86 99 10
Email d.ducoudray@wanadoo.fr
Web www.laterrassedelautrec.com

Midi - Pyrénées

Borio Nove

Bubbly and well-travelled, Lu and Freddie are the perfect B&B hosts and their characterful house on the hillside has a pretty courtyard garden and stunning views. Inside you find a remarkably English style with a roaring fire, deep comfortable sofas, lamps in quiet corners, lovely paintings, fresh flowers and oodles of books. Bedrooms are dressed in soft creams with wooden floors, pleasant bathrooms, comfortable beds and antiques from all over the world; it's like staying with family friends. Meals are jolly affairs at flexible times round the big table – and Freddie knows his wines. *Minimum two nights.*

Price	€78–€90.
Rooms	2: 1 double, 1 twin/double.
Meals	Dinner with wine, €18–€30.
Closed	December–February.
Directions	From Réalmont D4 for Lombers 4.5km; D41 left 2km; left at sign for Borio Nove at top of hill. Large house on right, 2nd turning.

Freddie & Lu Wanklyn
Borio Nove,
Bouscayrens,
81120 Lombers, Tarn
Tel +33 (0)5 63 55 36 94
Email luwanklyn@aliceadsl.fr

Maison Puech Malou

The creeper-clad farmhouse in pretty wooded countryside is a friendly, calming home swimming in crisp light. It's a rustic yet immaculate restoration. Walls are stone or white plaster, floors terracotta or stripped pine, ceiling beams are of heavy oak. Rooms have generous beds and a romantic feel; the sitting room has two huge open fireplaces, the dining room, one big country table. There's teak on the terrace and the lawn leads to a lovely pool. Dutch Monique is friendly, hands-on, bakes her bread daily and cooks excellent dinners. *Min. three nights. Ask about cookery & golfing holidays. Sawday self-catering also.*

La Barthe

Your Anglo-French hosts in their converted farmhouse welcome guests as friends. The pastel-painted, stencilled rooms are smallish but beds are good, the hospitality is wonderful and it's a deliciously secluded place; take a dip in the raised pool or set off into the country on foot or by bike. The Wises grow their own vegetables and summer dinners are hosted on the terrace overlooking the lovely Tarn valley, in a largely undiscovered part of France where birds, bees and sheep serenade you. Watch the farmers milking for roquefort and don't miss Albi, with its huge and magnificent cathedral – it's no distance at all.

Price	From €90.
Rooms	2: 1 double, 1 twin.
Meals	Dinner with wine, €25.
Closed	Rarely.
Directions	A68 to Albi ring road, for Rodez/ Millau; D81 to Teillet. Left before pharmacy D138 for Alban; right to Terre Basse/Catalanie. House at top of road on right.

Price	€50.
Rooms	2: 1 double, 1 family room.
Meals	Dinner with wine, €22.
Closed	Rarely.
Directions	From Albi D999 for Millau 25km; at La Croix Blanche left to Cambon du Temple, up to La Barthe on D163; right; house on left.

Monique Moors
Maison Puech Malou,
81120 Teillet,
Tarn

Tel	+33 (0)5 63 55 79 04
Email	info@maisonpuechmalou.com
Web	www.maisonpuechmalou.com

Michèle & Michael Wise
La Barthe,
81430 Villefranche d'Albigeois,
Tarn

Tel	+33 (0)5 63 55 96 21
Email	labarthe@chezwise.com
Web	www.chezwise.com

Barbiel

You will settle quickly here. Tim and Tracy are relaxed and welcoming, all smiles and ease, the house is calming and there's a terrace for lazy breakfasts in the garden with stunning views over rolling hills. Independent ground-floor bedrooms are in the barn: aqua-washed walls, white cotton sheets, a cool mix of modern and antique furniture, zippy bathrooms with thick towels, even a tiny kitchenette for picnics or snacks. For gorgeous dinners at one big table you go to the main house where Tracy's sense of style is splashed all over a stunning art-filled sitting room. Albi is a must-see.

Price	€55–€60.
Rooms	2: 1 double, 1 twin/double.
Meals	Dinner with wine, €22. Light supper from €12. Guest kitchenette.
Closed	Rarely.
Directions	From Valence d'Albigeois D903 for Réquista 5km; D75 right for Albignac & Assac; D126 thro' Albignac; after 2.5km, left at blue Chambres d'Hôtes sign.

Tim & Tracy Bayly
Barbiel,
81340 Assac,
Tarn
Tel   +33 (0)5 63 56 97 12
Mobile   +33 (0)6 79 39 89 67
Email   ttbayly@gmail.com
Web   www.tranquiltarn.co.uk

Entry 532   Map 15

La Martco

Way off the beaten track but so delightful. Sylvie and Pierre have recreated the past in their brilliantly authentic restoration of a crumbled old farmhouse and Sylvie's kitchen is a poem: a cooking area in the farmer's old fireside bed, shelves groaning with goodies from Pierre's flowing garden. Pierre has a great sense of humour and loves to speak English: suppers are wonderful. They have put their hearts into this place – full of antique plates, dolls, bric-a-brac – and its sweetly rustic bedrooms with their armoires, Provençal prints, rush-seated chairs; and a terrace for the garden room. Glorious Albi is 30km.

Price	€50–€60.
Rooms	2: 1 triple. Garden: 1 double.
Meals	Dinner with wine, €20.
Closed	Rarely.
Directions	From Albi D903 to Valence d'Albigeois; left D53 for Tanus 5.5km; left for St Marcel 1.5km; Chambres d'Hôtes sign; opposite church (no bells!).

Sylvie & Pierre Dumetz-Manesse
La Martco,
St Marcel, Padiès,
81340 Valence d'Albigeois, Tarn
Tel   +33 (0)5 63 76 38 47
Email   lamartco@wanadoo.fr
Web   www.lamartco.com

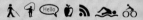

Entry 533   Map 15

8 place St Michel

Come for an absolutely fabulous French bourgeois experience: a wide stone staircase deeply worn, high ceilings, southern colours, plush carpets, loads of stairs, interesting *objets* at every turn. Add the owners' passion for Napoleon III furniture, oil paintings and ornate mirrors and the mood, more formal than family, is unmistakably French. Bedrooms, some with rooftop views, are traditional and very comfortable; breakfast is on the terrace overlooking the cathedral square. A treat to be in the heart of town, with utterly French people. Madame is a darling and it's excellent value for money.

Mas de Sudre

George and Pippa are ideal B&B folk – relaxed, good-natured, enthusiastic about their corner of France, generous-spirited and adding lots of extras to make you comfortable. Set in rolling vineyards and farmland, Sudre is a warm friendly house with beautiful furniture, shelves full of books, big inviting bedrooms and a very lovely garden full of sunny/shady fragrant corners in which you can sleep off delicious breakfast. The more energetic may leap to the pool, boules, bikes or several sorts of tennis and you are genuinely encouraged to treat the house as your own. French guests adore this very British B&B.

Price	€60.
Rooms	5: 3 doubles, 1 twin, 1 suite.
Meals	Restaurants 30m.
Closed	Rarely.
Directions	In centre of Gaillac, directly opposite St Michel abbey church as you come in across bridge from A68 Toulouse-Albi road.

Price	€80.
Rooms	3: 2 doubles, 1 twin.
Meals	Restaurants nearby.
Closed	Rarely.
Directions	From Gaillac for Cordes; over railway; left D964 for Caussade 1km; left D18 for Montauban 400m; right D4 2km; house on left (black gates) 200m beyond 1st turning on left.

Lucile Pinon
8 place St Michel,
81600 Gaillac,
Tarn
Tel +33 (0)5 63 57 61 48
Email lucile.pinon@wanadoo.fr
Web lucile.pinon.hotes81.monsite.wanadoo.fr

Pippa & George Richmond-Brown
Mas de Sudre,
81600 Gaillac,
Tarn
Tel +33 (0)5 63 41 01 32
Email masdesudre@wanadoo.fr
Web www.masdesudre.com

Entry 534   Map 15

Entry 535   Map 15

Midi - Pyrénées

Les Buis de St Martin

The dogs that greet you are as friendly as their owner, and the Tarn runs at the bottom of the garden: it's a dream place. Jacqueline has lived here for 30 years and is delighted to please you and practise her English. You will love the understated luxury of softest mushroom hues in bedrooms and bathrooms, the quilting on the excellent beds, the good paintings, the floaty muslin at the windows that look over the garden. Meals are served at one friendly table in the luminous white dining room – gleaming antiques on old terracotta tiles – or on the lovely teak-furnished patio. *Min. two nights in summer. Sawday self-catering also.*

Price	€100-€110.
Rooms	2 doubles.
Meals	Dinner with wine, €30.
Closed	Rarely.
Directions	From A68 exit 11 to Marssac; for Lagrave, right after level crossing; 2nd right Chemin du Rougé; 2nd right Rue St Martin; right at red transformer; left at fork, signed.

Jacqueline Romanet
Les Buis de St Martin,
Rue St Martin,
81150 Marssac sur Tarn, Tarn
Tel   +33 (0)5 63 55 41 23
Mobile   +33 (0)6 27 86 29 48
Email   jean.romanet@wanadoo.fr
Web   perso.wanadoo.fr/les-buis-de-saint-martin

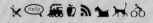

Entry 536   Map 15

Midi - Pyrénées

Domaine du Buc

Bright, smiling Brigitte is proud of her lovely 17th-century domaine, in the family for 100 years. An imposing stone stair leads to wonderful big bedrooms with original parquet and grand mirrors, period beds, subtle paint finishes and 19th-century papers, and quirky treasures discovered in the attic: sepia photographs, antique bonnets, vintage suitcases. Showers are top-range Italian and the old arched billiard room makes a perfect salon. It's unusually richly authentic, the breakfasts are locally sourced and delicious and you are eight miles from Albi, World Heritage Site. A huge treat. *Minimum two nights July/August.*

Price	€90-€110.
Rooms	3 twins/doubles.
Meals	Restaurant 1.5 km.
Closed	Rarely.
Directions	From Toulouse A68 exit 11 Marssac sur Tarn; left at stop sign, over motorway; left D22 for Lagrave & Cadalen; straight on at r'bout and x-roads. Entrance 200m on left.

Brigitte Lesage
Domaine du Buc,
Route de Lagrave,
81150 Marssac sur Tarn, Tarn
Tel   +33 (0)5 63 55 40 06
Email   contact@domainedubuc.com
Web   www.domainedubuc.com

Entry 537   Map 15

Midi - Pyrénées

Clos de Lacalm

Warmly generous, born to do B&B, Sally and Kirk have moved to a new lovely old place, a classic vigneron's house in a sweep of open countryside six minutes from hilltop Cordes sur Ciel. The guest suite is divine, thanks to crisp linen, curtains and calm colours, good books, pretty antiques and deep comfy chairs. Sally serves summer breakfasts of fruits, croissants, homemade cakes and jams on a beautiful terrace alongside sweet lavender and clipped box. Drop in on Gaillac's superb market (Fridays), spin off on a bike (they have two for guests), cool off by the pool: it's yours to adore.

Price	€95. €145 for 3.
Rooms	1 suite for 3.
Meals	Restaurant in Cestayrols, 3.5km.
Closed	Rarely.
Directions	From Gaillac D922 for Cordes sur Ciel 16km; right D25 for Noailles; over railway, up hill, right signed Lacalm. 500m, right 'Lacalm Haute'. House on right.

Kirk & Sally Ritchie
Clos de Lacalm,
Lacalm Haute,
81150 Cestayrols, Tarn
Tel   +33 (0)5 63 56 28 05
Email   info@closdelacalm.com
Web   www.closdelacalm.com

Entry 538   Map 15

Midi - Pyrénées

La Croix du Sud

Come here to tour the bastide towns – or just bask in the garden beneath stunning hilltop Castelnau. Catherine runs her B&B with sophistication and gentle humour: she wants you to love this place as much as she and Guillaume do. They welcome lots of hiking groups (hence the notices) and picnics can be arranged. Big immaculate bedrooms have pretty colours and scintillating bathrooms; dine before panoramic views on the terrace or in the bright dining room; the shared pool is discreet. Further afield are fascinating Albi, the Grésigne forest, great walks and a lake with all those water sports. Good for families.

Price	€84.
Rooms	3: 1 double, 1 twin, 1 family room for 4.
Meals	Occasional dinner with wine, €28. Guest kitchen.
Closed	Rarely.
Directions	From Gaillac D964 to Castelnau de Montmiral, right at bottom of village 100m; right at sign Croix du Sud; fork left for Mazars; on left.

Catherine & Guillaume Sordoillet
La Croix du Sud,
Mazars, 81140 Castelnau
de Montmiral, Tarn
Tel   +33 (0)5 63 33 18 46
Email   catherine@la-croix-du-sud.com
Web   www.la-croix-du-sud.com

Entry 539   Map 15

Midi - Pyrénées

Château de Mayragues

A paradise of history, culture, tranquillity and vines. Inside those stern walls you clamber up old stone stairs to the open sentry's gallery, enter your chamber and gasp at the loveliness of the room and the depth of the view. Beyond the fine old timbers and stonework, glowing floor, furniture and fabrics, your eyes flow out over luscious gardens, woods and vines. Alan is a softly-spoken Scot, Laurence a charming Parisienne; both are passionate about their prize-winning restoration, their musical evenings and, of course, their wonderful organic wines. Such a treat. *Min. two nights. Sawday self-catering also.*

Ethical Collection: Environment, Food & Community. See page 410 for details.

Price	€95–€100. Cottage €500–€600 per week.
Rooms	2 + 1: 1 double, 1 twin. Cottage for 4.
Meals	Restaurants within 4km.
Closed	December–February.
Directions	From Gaillac D964 for Castelnau de Montmiral; at junc. D15 to Château de Mayragues, signed.

Laurence & Alan Geddes
Château de Mayragues,
81140 Castelnau de Montmiral,
Tarn

Tel	+33 (0)5 63 33 94 08
Email	geddes@chateau-de-mayragues.com
Web	www.chateau-de-mayragues.com

Midi - Pyrénées

La Maison d'Hôtes Chez Delphine

You are perched high here, in an arty, medieval village with stunning views across wooded valleys. Delphine's big generous house has gardens with plenty of shady spots to sit in and a pool surrounded by roses to float in. Up wide stairs from the main hall find classic bedrooms with tiled floors or creaky floorboards, one with its own balcony, and a huge family suite with an open fireplace and a kitchenette should you prefer to do your own breakfast; small bathrooms are spotless and towel-filled. Wander the village, discover markets and restaurants, hike or bike, return to a squishy sofa: super. *Min. two nights July/August.*

Price	€62–€70. €75 for 3. €90 for 4.
Rooms	5: 2 doubles, 1 twin, 1 triple; 1 family suite for 5 & kitchenette.
Meals	Breakfast €8. Restaurants within walking distance.
Closed	December/January.
Directions	From Gaillac D964 to Castelnau de Montmiral; cont. D964 for Puycelsi & Larroque 20km; right D8 to Puycelsi. Park in square. House 150m on right.

Delphine de Laveleye
La Maison d'Hôtes Chez Delphine,
Au Bourg, 81140 Puycelsi,
Tarn

Tel	+33 (0)5 63 33 13 65
Email	delphine@chezdelphine.com
Web	www.chezdelphine.com

Aurifat

Good furniture, books and paintings are thoroughly at home in this multi-stepped, history-rich house (the watchtower is 13th-century) where all is serene and inviting. Each freshly decorated room has its own private entrance, the twin has a cosy sitting area, the double a terrace for sun-drenched views. Walking distance to everything, the house is on the southern slope of Cordes (borrow a torch for a night time stroll), the pool is delicious and there's a barbecue alongside the guest kitchen. Terrace breakfasts (spot the deer) are enchanting; nothing is too much trouble for these lovely hosts. *Minimum two nights.*

Monteillet-Sanvensa

A lovely old stone mini-hamlet next door to a working farm in the calm green Aveyron where there is just so much space. Two compact rooms, each with a nice little terrace, look out over a typical medieval château. One guest room is white and yellow with a walk-in shower, the other washed-pink and white, with a super bathroom and a small kitchenette; both are cool and airy. The garden is full of flowers, the rolling views stupendous, and Monique is fun, easy-going and eager to please. Relax in one of the many shady areas in summer with a drink or a book and enjoy the birdsong. *Well-behaved children & pets welcome.*

Price	€78.
Rooms	2: 1 double, 1 twin/double.
Meals	Kitchen & BBQ available. Restaurants within walking distance.
Closed	October-April.
Directions	From Albi D600 to Cordes; up Cité road on right of Tabarium/Maison de la Presse for 600m; fork left for Le Bouysset; 350m, left at hairpin bend Rte de St Jean; house 200m on right.

Price	€50.
Rooms	2 doubles, one with kitchenette.
Meals	Occasional dinner with wine, €22. Light suppers available, from €15.
Closed	2 weeks in September.
Directions	From Villefranche D922 for Albi; at entrance to Sanvensa, follow signs on right to Monteillet Chambres d'Hôtes.

Ian & Penelope Wanklyn
Aurifat,
81170 Cordes sur Ciel,
Tarn
Tel +33 (0)5 63 56 07 03
Email aurifat@gmail.com
Web www.aurifat.com

Monique Bateson
Monteillet-Sanvensa,
12200 Villefranche de Rouergue,
Aveyron
Tel +33 (0)5 65 29 81 01
Mobile +33 (0)6 89 28 60 76
Email monique.bateson@orange.fr

Entry 542   Map 15

Entry 543   Map 15

Midi - Pyrénées

Quiers - Ferme Auberge

Escape to vast pastures and sensational views. This is an outdoorsy place and is brilliant for families: canoe, climb, hang-glide, spot birds, hunt orchids. The farm feels rustic, charming and somewhat shambolic – but in the nicest way. Bedrooms, a short walk down a steepish track, sit snugly in the old 'bergerie'; expect shiny terracotta floors, old beams, freshly painted walls, simple pine beds. In the main house are tapestries and country antiques smelling of years of polish. Here, Véronique and her chef brother produce wonderful big meals of home-grown organic produce.

Price	€58.
Rooms	5: 2 doubles, 2 twins, 1 family room.
Meals	Dinner €20-€23. Wine list €10-€20. Restaurants in Millau.
Closed	November-April.
Directions	From Millau N9 N to Aguessac; on way out, D547 right to Compeyre; left in village, follow signs for Ferme Auberge, 3km.

	Véronique Lombard
	Quiers - Ferme Auberge,
	12520 Compeyre,
	Aveyron
Tel	+33 (0)5 65 59 85 10
Email	quiers@wanadoo.fr
Web	www.quiers.net

Entry 544 Map 15

Midi - Pyrénées

Montels

The rolling Languedoc hills are wild and ancient, and the views from the little garden are lovely… you can even watch paragliders launching from the cliff. It matters little that Madame speaks no English: she is so kind and welcoming. In this modern house she gives you two bedrooms, bright, sweet and spotless, and a very delightful third, just up the track in her daughter's house, complete with its own terrace and views. The family used to tend sheep and you can still enjoy Madame's 'lafloune', a sheep's-milk cake, at breakfast. Great value for money – and there's a lovely new conservatory for guests.

Price	€50. €65 for 3. €80 for 4.
Rooms	3: 1 triple, 1 family room for 4. House up track: 1 double.
Meals	Restaurants Millau, 3km.
Closed	Rarely.
Directions	From Millau D911 for Cahors; just after leaving city limits right after 'Auberge' x-roads. Signed. Follow small road for approx. 2km.

	Henriette Cassan
	Montels,
	12100 Millau,
	Aveyron
Tel	+33 (0)5 65 60 51 70

Entry 545 Map 15

Midi - Pyrénées

Chambres d'Hôtes Les Brunes

Swish through large wooden gates into a central courtyard and garden filled with birdsong to find lovely Monique and her 18th-century family home, complete with tower. Bedrooms are up the spiral stone tower staircase which oozes atmosphere; all are a good size (Le Clos is enormous) and filled with beautiful things. Antiques, beams, rugs, gilt mirrors and soft colours give an uncluttered, elegant feel; bathrooms are modern and bright, views from all are lovely. You breakfast on homemade cake, farm butter and fruit salad in the beautiful open kitchen with baker's oven. *Minimum two nights in school holidays preferred.*

Ethical Collection: Environment.
See page 410 for details.

Price	€92-€145.
Rooms	4: 1 double, 2 twins, 1 suite.
Meals	Guest kitchenette. Restaurant 5km.
Closed	Rarely.
Directions	D920 Espalion-Bozouls; D988 for Rodez. 3.5km on right after Bozouls.

Monique Philipponnat-David
Chambres d'Hôtes Les Brunes,
Hameau les Brunes,
12340 Bozouls, Aveyron

Tel	+33 (0)5 65 48 50 11
Mobile	+33 (0)6 80 07 95 96
Email	lesbrunes@wanadoo.fr
Web	www.lesbrunes.com

Entry 546   Map 10

Photo: Lesley Chalmers

Languedoc – Roussillon

Photo: www.istockphoto.com

Languedoc - Roussillon

La Maison de Marius

Fascinating Quézac is a pilgrimage 'street-village' with many cobbles and a lovely old bridge over the Tarn. The house sits prettily at its heart, all warm and lived-in with old stones and beams, nooks, crannies and stairs, and a light, fresh feel. The homely suite has artistic flourishes; the bathroom is super. Dany is a poppet, adores embellishing her home (country fabrics, hand-painted furniture) and spoiling her guests with gâteau de noix from her walnuts and delicacies from her impressive vegetable patch. Sit on the lovely terrace or rose garden where only birds, water and wind are to be heard.

Price	€85.
Rooms	1 family suite.
Meals	Dinner with wine, €25.
Closed	November-March.
Directions	From A75 exit 39 on N88 E for 25km; right N106 for Alès 25km; just before Ispagnac right to Quézac; signs in village.

Danièle Méjean
La Maison de Marius,
8 rue du Pontet,
48320 Quézac, Lozère
Tel   +33 (0)4 66 44 25 05
Email   dany.mejean@wanadoo.fr
Web   www.maisondemarius.fr

Entry 547   Map 15

Languedoc - Roussillon

Le Coupétadou

A five-hectare slice of tranquillity in the Cévennes National Park – a hiker's dream. This 18th-century terraced farmhouse blends beautifully with the land, delivering views south over wood-swathed hills burnished gold in autumn. Secluded terraces and rare butterflies in the garden, and a double hammock for siestas 'à deux'. Delightful bedrooms, one with a log fire, have exposed beams and stones, and exotic or antique pieces. Your foodie hosts cater for all diets and work enthusiastically to maintain their green credentials. A post-hammam skinny dip in the secret creek comes recommended! *Minimum two nights.*

Ethical Collection: Environment & Food.
See page 410 for details.

Price	€75-€85.
Rooms	5: 1 double, 2 twins/doubles, 1 family room for 3, 1 suite for 4.
Meals	Dinner with wine, €25. Restaurant 5km.
Closed	Rarely.
Directions	From Alès for Aubenas, left D906 for Génolhac 30km; left D52 at La Tavernole for Pont de M; thro' Ginestous, sharp right between rocks; thro' Figeirolles, right to house.

Stéphane Dupré
Le Coupétadou,
Souteyrannes,
48220 Vialas, Lozère
Tel   +33 (0)4 66 41 05 49
Email   coupetadou@orange.fr
Web   www.chambre-hote-cevennes.fr

Entry 548   Map 15

Languedoc - Roussillon

Château Massal

Flanking the road is the château façade; behind is the rambling, many-terraced garden – with views across river and red-roofed town. Up a stone spiral are big beautiful bedrooms with a château feel; walnut parquet and mosaic floors along with strong-coloured walls set off family furniture to perfection; one has a grand piano, another a bathroom in the tower; it's enchanting. Madame, one of an old French silk family who have been here for several generations, is as elegant and charming as her house; a fine cook, too. She will show you where to find really good walks, exciting canoeing, and wildlife.

Price	€68-€88.
Rooms	4 doubles. Child's bed available.
Meals	Dinner with wine, €28.
Closed	Mid-November to March.
Directions	From Millau S on N9 for 19km to La Cavalerie; left D7 for Le Vigan approx. 50km to Bez; before bridge, sign on left.

Françoise & Marie-Emmanuelle du Luc
Château Massal,
Bez et Esparon,
30120 Le Vigan, Gard
Tel   +33 (0)4 67 81 07 60
Email   francoiseduluc@gmail.com
Web   www.cevennes-massal.com

Entry 549   Map 15

Languedoc - Roussillon

Pont d'Ardèche

An ancestor built this fine fortified farmhouse 220 years ago: proudly worn, it still stands by the Ardèche with its own small beach. Inside, in sudden contrast, are a cavernous entrance hall, a stone staircase lined with portraits, and pale plain bedrooms above, saved from austerity by Ghislaine's painted furniture and friezes. There's no sitting room but a homely kitchen for good breakfast breads and jams. The squirrel'd park invites lingerers, and there's a delicious oval pool shared with gîte guests. Pierre can accompany you on canoe trips: this is a lovely sociable family who enjoy all their guests.

Price	€65. Triple €80.
Rooms	3: 1 double, 1 double with bunkbeds, 1 triple.
Meals	Dinner with wine, €25.
Closed	Rarely.
Directions	From A7 Bollène exit D994 to Pont St Esprit; D6086 for Bourg St Andéol; sign before bridge across river.

Ghislaine & Pierre de Verduzan
Pont d'Ardèche,
30130 Pont St Esprit,
Gard
Tel   +33 (0)4 66 39 29 80
Email   pontdardeche@aol.com
Web   www.pont-dardeche.com

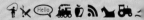

Entry 550   Map 16

Languedoc - Roussillon

Languedoc - Roussillon

Le pas de l'âne

Sheltering under umbrella pines, an ordinary house with an extraordinary welcome. Fun for food-lovers and families; even the parrot greets you with a merry 'bonjour'. Anne, ex-antique dealer in London, is chef; gregarious Dominique is host, both are intelligent, humorous Belgians. Dinners are fabulous affairs, full of joy and fresh delights: garden strawberries, home-laid eggs, homemade spiced oils. We like the upstairs bedrooms best; the double has its own terrace. Four cats, two dogs, a pool, a big garden – heaven for kids in summer. And all those gorges and southern markets to discover. *One night only? Dinner is a must.*

Les Marronniers

In love with their life and their 19th-century *maison de maître*, John and Michel welcome guests with exuberant gaiety. John is a joiner with a fine eye for interior design; Michel, quieter, takes care of beautiful breakfasts. From the classic tiles of the entrance hall to the art on the walls to the atmospheric lighting at night, every detail counts. Generous breakfast is elegantly served under the chestnut trees, after which you can wander off to join in lazy Provençal village life, or visit Avignon, Uzès, Lussan – your wonderful hosts know all the best places. *Heated pool May-Sept, weather permitting.*

Price	€60-€80. One night only: dinner is a must.
Rooms	3: 1 double, 1 twin/double, 1 twin.
Meals	Dinner with wine, €23.
Closed	Rarely.
Directions	From Bagnols sur Cèze D6 for Alès 4km; left to Combe; immed. into Chemin des Pelissiers, road 500m on left. 2nd house on left.

Price	€105-€120.
Rooms	4: 2 doubles, 2 twins.
Meals	Restaurant 5km.
Closed	Rarely.
Directions	From A9 exit 23 W to Uzès 19km; D979 N 7.5km; right D238 to La Bruguière. House on big square next to Mairie (vast micocoulier tree in front).

Anne Le Brun
Le pas de l'âne,
209 chemin du Pas de l'Âne, Combe,
30200 Sabran, Gard

Tel   +33 (0)4 66 33 14 09
Mobile   +33 (0)6 30 68 62 03
Email   pasdelane@wanadoo.fr
Web   www.pasdelane.com

John Karavias & Michel Comas
Les Marronniers,
Place de la Mairie,
30580 La Bruguière, Gard

Tel   +33 (0)4 66 72 84 77
Email   info@lesmarronniers.biz
Web   www.lesmarronniers.biz

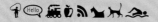

Languedoc - Roussillon

La Magnanerie

This happy, artistic, relaxed couple welcome guests to their light-filled former silk farm, splashed with Moroccan colour and ethnic *objets*. It has pretty ochre-coloured plates, a long wooden table on an uneven stone floor, an ancient sink, beams twisting, glimpses of age-old village rooftops, a ravishing court-yard, big, pretty, uncluttered bedrooms, a roof terrace looking over Provence. Michèle paints, manages tranquilly and adores cooking; Michel, passionately active in sustainable development, knows his wines and the local community; their talk is cultural and enriching. *Ask about art courses. Minimum two nights.*

Price	€60–€65.
Rooms	3: 2 doubles, 1 family suite for 4.
Meals	Dinner with wine, €23.
Closed	Rarely.
Directions	From Alès D6 E 27km; left D979 beyond Lussan for Barjac 1km; left D187 to Fons sur Lussan; right at fountain; up on left by church.

Michèle Dassonneville &
Michel Genvrin
La Magnanerie, Place de l'Horloge,
30580 Fons sur Lussan, Gard
Tel   +33 (0)4 66 72 81 72
Email   mimi.genvrin@orange.fr
Web   www.atelier-de-fons.com

Entry 553   Map 16

Languedoc - Roussillon

Mas Vacquières

Thomas and Miriam have restored these lovely 18th-century buildings with a pretty Dutch touch, white walls a perfect foil for southern-toned fabrics in bedrooms reached by steep stone stairs. Mulberry trees where silk worms once fed still flower; the little vaulted room is intimate and alcoved, the big soft salon a delight. Tables on the enchantingly flowered terrace under leafy trees and a lawn sloping down to the stream make blissful spots for silent gazing; and table d'hôtes is a delight. Share the pool, perfect in its roofless barn, with gîte guests and your charming hosts; it's all so relaxed you can stay all day.

Price	€85–€110.
Rooms	3: 2 doubles, 1 twin/double.
Meals	Dinner €25. Wine €6.50–€30.
Closed	Rarely.
Directions	From Alès D6 for 12km; right D7; in St Just, left for Vacquières, pink signs to house.

Thomas & Miriam van Dijke
Mas Vacquières,
Hameau de Vacquières,
30580 St Just & Vacquières, Gard
Tel   +33 (0)4 66 83 70 75
Email   info@masvac.com
Web   www.masvac.com

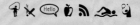

Entry 554   Map 16

Languedoc - Roussillon

Villa Virinn

Melons and cherries in season, homemade marmalade and fig jam – and proper porridge. Douglas, who's Scottish, is the chef, Geoff is the greeter and gardener, both are warm hosts loving the French life. Their house, new and spacious, private and peaceful, is a short stroll from the small hilltop town. Inside, all is fresh, comfortable, unflashy; beds have painted headboards and matching tables, walls are blue, soft green, pale honey; those off the garden have terraces. Bright flowers and striped loungers round the pool, an honesty bar, a vineyard view: the excursions are stunning but the temptation is to stay.

Price	€80.
Rooms	4: 3 doubles, 1 twin.
Meals	Dinner €25. Wine €8.
Closed	December-January.
Directions	On the Nîmes/Alès road D936, at foot of Vézénobres. Chemin de Bercaude next to Hôtel Relais du Sarrazin. Signed.

	Geoff Pople & Douglas Tulloch
	Villa Virinn,
	Chemin de Bercaude,
	30360 Vézénobres, Gard
Tel	+33 (0)4 66 83 27 30
Email	geoffanddoug@villavirinn.com
Web	www.villavirinn.com

Entry 555   Map 16

Languedoc - Roussillon

Mas Théotime

Once a barn on the edge of the village, on the shore of a sunflower sea, now a lovely house with a tasteful mix of old and new – and books galore to browse or borrow: your generous open-minded hostess is an editor, her husband has a garden studio. Enjoy fine modern paintings, rich colours, groovy furniture, red paintwork and subtly eye-catching ceramic *objets*. Split-level floors and clear lines provide bright, breezy 'studio' spaces, one reached from outside. Into the small, secluded garden for a bamboo-shaded splash pool, olive trees, six splendid cypresses, and designer chairs set on the lawn like sculptures.

Price	€80-€165.
Rooms	3: 2 suites for 2, 1 family room for 4 (2 with kitchenettes).
Meals	Restaurant 200m.
Closed	Rarely.
Directions	From Uzès for Alès on D981 for 6km; left into Serviers; cont. 200m following road to right, left down small street. House 50m.

	Monique Gourbeyre
	Mas Théotime,
	Chemin de la Fabrique,
	30700 Serviers, Gard
Tel	+33 (0)4 66 62 99 90
Email	monique@mastheotime.com
Web	www.mastheotime.com

Entry 556   Map 16

Languedoc - Roussillon

Les Bambous

Circles of delight, ten minutes from Avignon. Joël & Michèle love welcoming guests to their glowing little house in an unpretentious Provençal town, and the charming peaceful courtyard shaded by bamboo and bourgainvillea. He paints portraits and pastels, she cooks – linger over delicious food at the big mosaic table. In the courtyard studio is a delightful mix of soft limed walls and ethnic treasures from winter travels: a Peruvian wall hanging, an African sculpture. You get an inviting king-size bed, a pebble-floored shower, a bright kitchenette, a gently curving staircase to a bed-sitting area above. Such value!

Price	€65.
Rooms	Studio: 2 doubles & kitchenette.
Meals	Dinner with wine, €25.
Closed	Rarely.
Directions	From Avignon & Villeneuve N580 for Bagnols & Cèze; right on D377 & D177 to Pujaut. House opp. town hall; large metal door.

	Joël & Michèle Rousseau
	Les Bambous,
	Rue de la Mairie,
	30131 Pujaut, Gard
Tel	+33 (0)4 90 26 46 47
Mobile	+33 (0)6 82 93 06 68
Email	rousseau.michele@wanadoo.fr
Web	lesbambous.monsite.wanadoo.fr

Entry 557 Map 16

Languedoc - Roussillon

Les Écuries des Chartreux

Villeneuve is a mini Avignon without the crowds. In a stable block next to a 13th-century monastery you find these charmingly furnished, beautifully kempt guest quarters, smelling of beeswax. All is coolness, elegance and light: stone walls, terracotta floors, rustic beams, Provençal antiques. Two suites have mezzanines, all have perfect kitchenettes so you can self-cater if you prefer. No pool but a delectable courtyard garden. Pascale gives you breakfast in the main house and all the attention you require – including an aperitif before you head out for the evening. This is heaven. *Avignon ten-minute bus ride.*

Price	€85–€155.
Rooms	3 suites: 1 for 2, 1 for 3, 1 for 4, each with kitchenette.
Meals	Restaurants 50m.
Closed	Rarely.
Directions	From Avignon cross Rhône for Nîmes & Villeneuve lès Avignon. After bridge right for Villeneuve centre, Rue de la République. House next to monastery 'La Chartreuse'.

	Pascale Letellier
	Les Écuries des Chartreux,
	66 rue de la République,
	30400 Villeneuve lès Avignon, Gard
Tel	+33 (0)4 90 25 79 93
Email	ecuries-des-chartreux@orange.fr
Web	www.ecuries-des-chartreux.com

Entry 558 Map 16

Languedoc - Roussillon

Jardin de Bacchus

Care has been taken in this arty, relaxed house set against a rock. Park at roof level, walk down to the entrance, through the dining room and straight out onto the view-filled garden terrace. Simple bedrooms (one downstairs, two up) have good beds and colourful paintings and prints; bathrooms are white-tiled, one is open-plan behind the bed. It's all light and spacious, the salon has wicker chairs and stone floors, your sparkling hosts take food very seriously, run cookery courses and spoil you with delicious breakfasts and dinners at a convivial table in the open-plan kitchen. Lovely. *Minimum two nights; three July/August.*

Price	€90-€120.
Rooms	3 doubles.
Meals	Dinner with wine, €30.
Closed	Mid-December to mid-March.
Directions	From Avignon for Nîmes then Tavel. See website for map.

Christine Chapot
Jardin de Bacchus,
223 rue de Tourtouil,
30126 Tavel, Gard

Tel	+33 (0)4 66 90 28 62
Email	jardindebacchus@free.fr
Web	www.jardindebacchus.fr

Entry 559   Map 16

Languedoc - Roussillon

Mas d'Oléandre

Lovely, long stone buildings enfold the convivial two-tier courtyard, great trees shade the pool, the Cévennes hills march off beyond. It is enchanting. Your welcoming young Dutch hosts have created a beautiful unpretentious place to stay; the garden, the lawn round the pool, the glowing old furniture inside, the silvery weathered teak out. Bedrooms, each with its own piece of terrace, light and white with splashes of colour, feel separate from one another round the courtyard and Esther keeps it all utterly pristine. Gather your own picnic at glorious Uzès market and bring it back here. Breakfast and dinner are delicious.

Price	€75-€135.
Rooms	4: 2 suites; 2 doubles, each with separate shower.
Meals	Dinner €25. Wine €7.50-€25.
Closed	Mid-November to February.
Directions	From Uzès D981 to Montaren 6km; right into Montaren onto D337 to St Médiers; in village continue up & round to right. House on left with green shutters.

Léonard Robberts & Esther Küchler
Mas d'Oléandre,
Hameau St Médiers,
30700 Montaren & St Médiers, Gard

Tel	+33 (0)4 66 22 63 43
Email	info@masoleandre.com
Web	www.masoleandre.com

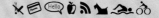

Entry 560   Map 16

Languedoc - Roussillon

La Maison

Old wood, old stone, new ideas. Christian's flair and human touch has revived the grand old stones with opulent Indonesian furniture and hangings, soft lighting and a gentle golden colour – he and Pierre are delighted with their Maison. Beneath the old village church of lovely Blauzac (daytime chimes), the lush walled garden and ancient tower look over wavy red rooftops to blue hills, bedrooms bask in ethnic fabrics and relaxed good taste, the stunning suite has its own roof terrace. Masses of books, a breakfast table by the fire, and good sofas in the sitting room. Charming. *Watch children near unfenced water.*

Price	€120-€205.
Rooms	5: 4 doubles, 1 suite for 4.
Meals	Bistros in village.
Closed	Mid-November to mid-March.
Directions	From Nîmes D979 for Blauzac, 16km; after Pont St Nicolas, left for Blauzac; into village, house behind church.

Christian Vaurie
La Maison,
Place de l'Église,
30700 Blauzac, Gard
Tel   +33 (0)4 66 81 25 15
Email   lamaisondeblauzac@wanadoo.fr
Web   www.chambres-provence.com

Languedoc - Roussillon

La Terre des Lauriers

Gérard has laid a path through the woods from the house to the river by the Pont du Gard; abuzz with wildlife, the setting is special. Inside, Marianick's decoration is warm and comfortable: good colours, new carpets, country furniture. Bedrooms are themed, fresh and spotless, one with a connecting room for bunk beds and soft toys; the sitting room has books, games for the children and a garden that slopes down to a pool with a heavenly view, shared with two gîtes. Your hosts are professionally committed to caring for guests and houses, and breakfasts have been described as "stupendous". *Sawday self-catering also.*

Price	€89-€150.
Rooms	5: 2 doubles, 2 twins, 1 suite.
Meals	Restaurants within 3km.
Closed	Rarely.
Directions	From Remoulins follow signs for Pont du Gard 'Rive Droite'. Sign on right.

Marianick & Gérard Langlois
La Terre des Lauriers,
Rive Droite - Pont du Gard,
30210 Remoulins, Gard
Tel   +33 (0)4 66 37 19 45
Email   langlois@laterredeslauriers.com
Web   www.laterredeslauriers.com

Languedoc - Roussillon

Mas de Barbut

Danielle's family home is stunning, imaginative, decorated with élan. Great travellers, the Gandons have gathered fascinating things in a strikingly harmonious way; bedrooms are Mexican, Mandarin or Provençal, outstanding bathrooms have fabulous tiles. Different food, a different table decoration every day: they love cosseting guests. The summer sitting room has a pebble floor, the stone bassin is overlooked by slatted oak loungers, there's a sweet spot for drinks by the river and the frond-shaded courtyard is bliss. Near the sea yet away from it all – and restaurants in lovely St Laurent. A treat from start to finish.

Price	€100-€120.
Rooms	4: 2 doubles, 2 triples.
Meals	Dinner with wine, €35.
Closed	Rarely.
Directions	From A9 exit 26 for Gallargues. D979 for Aigues Mortes 12.5km. Right at 7th r'bout for Le Vidourle 2km. House on right, B&B at further end.

	Danielle & Jean-Claude Gandon
	Mas de Barbut,
	30220 St Laurent d'Aigouze,
	Gard
Tel	+33 (0)4 66 88 12 09
Mobile	+33 (0)6 64 14 28 52
Email	contact@masdebarbut.com
Web	www.masdebarbut.com

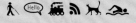

Languedoc - Roussillon

Burckel de Tell

An old townhouse in a little market town but step off the narrow street and you enter another world. First the courtyard, a source of light and greenery, then a living area for guests and a vaulted dining room for dinner (min. four guests). Up a spiral staircase lined with tapestries lie two tempting rooms and a lovely smell of wax-polished stone floors. Expect restored old doors, original chandeliers and windows that seem to frame pictures: it has tremendous visual appeal, you can tell that an artist and an art historian live here. Don't miss Calvisson's Sunday market. *Minimum two nights July/August.*

Price	€60-€65.
Rooms	2: 1 double, 1 suite.
Meals	Dinner with wine, €20. Restaurant in Calvisson.
Closed	Rarely.
Directions	A9 exit Gallargues; N113 for Nîmes; after Bas Rhône canal, D1 to Calvisson; in village, along main street, two doors from Mairie.

	Régis & Corinne Burckel de Tell
	Burckel de Tell,
	48 Grand'rue,
	30420 Calvisson, Gard
Tel	+33 (0)4 66 01 23 91
Email	burckeldetell@hotmail.fr
Web	www.bed-and-art.com

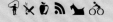

Languedoc - Roussillon

Hôtel de l'Orange

At his *hôtel particulier* (private mansion), Philippe receives with warm refinement. Each hushed room is in *maison de famille* style: polished floors, warm-painted walls, white bedcovers, a different and beautiful wall hanging over each bed; one room is an independent studio. The magic secluded terrace garden with gasping views over the roofs of the old town is where you swim; breakfast, which to Philippe is *the* moment of the day, is in the old-style dining room or at small tables in the courtyard. Walk into the old town: the river is a charming place. A touch of 'la vieille France'.

Price	€100–€160.
Rooms	5: 3 doubles, 1 twin, 1 triple.
Meals	Dinner with wine, €40.
Closed	Rarely.
Directions	From Nîmes D40 W 28km to Sommières; from town centre for 'centre historique'; from post office follow street up to château; signed.

Philippe de Frémont
Hôtel de l'Orange,
Chemin du Château Fort,
30250 Sommières, Gard

Tel	+33 (0)4 66 77 79 94
Email	hotel.delorange@free.fr
Web	hotel.delorange.free.fr

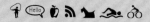

Entry 565   Map 16

Languedoc - Roussillon

Au Soleil

Catherine is as elegant and welcoming as her house. Once involved in theatre PR, she now devotes her energies to guests and house; it's a treat to stay in her town-centre *maison de maître*. Behind the front door, caressed by sweet jasmine, lie sunlight, space and simplicity, fine pieces of brocante and a sitting room with deep orange sofas. Bedrooms are peaceful and calm, with kilim rugs on glowing terracotta; windows overlook the rooftops or the lush inner courtyard where cat and dog doze. Simple Mediterranean food is served with pleasure… and on Sundays in summer the bulls race through town. *Beaches nearby.*

Price	€65–€75.
Rooms	3 doubles.
Meals	Dinner with wine, €22. Restaurant 100m.
Closed	Rarely.
Directions	A9 exit for Lunel; D34 to Marsillargues; in town centre after church, 1st right at square. Secure parking.

Catherine Maurel
Au Soleil,
9 rue Pierre Brossolette,
34590 Marsillargues, Hérault

Tel	+33 (0)4 67 83 90 00
Email	catherine.maurel@ausoleil.info
Web	www.ausoleil.info

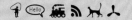

Entry 566   Map 16

Languedoc - Roussillon

Le Mas de l'Olivier

Silvi's bubbling enthusiasm for receiving and cooking – breakfast, lunch and dinner, all delicious – will inspire you to join in. Her arranging and decorating skills make the fine old wine-grower's house, now her family home (two children still at home), a generous and original B&B: big rooms, quiet colours and stunning old floor tiles in the first-floor 'apartment.' Lou Poustalou, the fireplaced and terraced garden room by the pool, is sheer delight if you like being a bit apart. In summer, the jumbly, bowery garden is ideal for cool evening drinks before convivial dinner outside. *Tennis free in village. Ask about massage & golf.*

Price	€80–€120.
Rooms	5: 2 doubles; 3 doubles sharing bath (2 rooms interconnect).
Meals	Lunch €20. Dinner €20–€25. Wine €15–€40.
Closed	Rarely.
Directions	From A9 exit 27 'Lunel' for Sommières; at r'bout 4th exit D34 to Vérargues. At wine-press r'bout, 2nd exit Rue du Laurier-tin. House 200m down on right.

	Silvi Leichtnam
	Le Mas de l'Olivier,
	Rue du Laurier-tin,
	34400 Vérargues, Hérault
Mobile	+33 (0)6 43 11 33 62
Web	www.lemasdelolivier.fr

Entry 567   Map 16

Languedoc - Roussillon

Castle's Cottage

On the edge of a wild, unspoilt forest, in a garden flooded with hibiscus and iris where 50 tortoises roam (no touching please)… it's hard to believe you're a bus ride from Montpellier. The house is recent, built with old materials, the vegetation lush, the saltwater pool set among atmospheric stone 'ruins'. You sleep in small but comfortable beds in pretty rooms full of family furniture and colour, sharing an excellent shower room and opening onto the terrace. Your hostess, who used to work in public relations, loves this place passionately. The garden is an oasis even in winter and the beach is nearby.

Ethical Collection: Environment. See page 410 for details.

Price	€86–€108.
Rooms	2 doubles, sharing shower & separate wc.
Meals	Restaurants in Montpellier, 3km.
Closed	Rarely.
Directions	From Mairie in Castelnau le Lez take Rue Jules Ferry; 5th left Chemin de la Rocheuse; last house on left.

	Dominique Carabin-Cailleau
	Castle's Cottage,
	289 chemin de la Rocheuse,
	34170 Castelnau le Lez, Hérault
Tel	+33 (0)4 67 72 63 08
Mobile	+33 (0)6 75 50 41 50
Email	castlecottage@free.fr
Web	castlecottage.free.fr

Entry 568   Map 15

Languedoc - Roussillon

Domaine de Pélican

Meals are eaten off local pottery, vignerons drop by for Monday tastings, cats and dogs doze. This superb, eco-leaning wine estate has a mulberry-lined drive and a real family atmosphere: come for peace, simplicity and fine bedrooms. Your hard-working hosts have four children of their own and share their saltwater pool. Guest rooms, in a separate building, have soft-coloured walls, some beds on mezzanines (no windows, just French doors), pretty shower rooms. Old honey-coloured beams protect the dining room – a dream that gives onto the terrace and rows of vines beyond: ideal for excellent authentic auberge food.

Price	€62-€72.
Rooms	4: 1 double, 1 suite for 4; 1 double, 1 twin, each with fold-out bed.
Meals	Dinner €24. Restaurant in village.
Closed	Rarely.
Directions	From Gignac centre for Montpellier; at edge of town, bus stop 'Pélican' on right; right & follow signs 3km.

	Isabelle & Baudouin Thillaye du Boullay Domaine de Pélican, 34150 Gignac, Hérault
Tel	+33 (0)4 67 57 68 92
Email	domaine-de-pelican@wanadoo.fr
Web	www.domainedepelican.fr

Entry 569   Map 15

Languedoc - Roussillon

The Village House

A great townhouse, unpretentious and spotless, run by unpushy hosts who live and work here. Tall and narrow, the oldest part of it is attached to the 14th-century ramparts of the sleepy market town which stands in a sea of Languedoc vineyards. Serene rooms are set round the charming first-floor guest terrace: the smaller room cool and light, with white floor tiles, the master room with its own elegant landing, big bathroom and balcony over the square. An excellent place to stay; inexpensive, stylish, discreet. Historic Pézenas has markets and boutiques galore, and the mountain bikes are free.

Price	€55-€60.
Rooms	2 doubles.
Meals	Restaurants 2km.
Closed	Rarely.
Directions	From Pézenas D13 for Bédarieux 15km. In Gabian centre, right for Montesquieu; 1st right to fountain. House on left.

	John Cook & Jean-Maurice Siu The Village House, 3 rue du Théron, 34320 Gabian, Hérault
Tel	+33 (0)4 67 24 77 27
Email	cdh@thevillagehouse.info
Web	www.thevillagehouse.info

Entry 570   Map 15

Languedoc - Roussillon

Château de Grézan

A 19th-century château built in a troubadour style, all towers, turrets and castellated walls. And a very big welcome from Marie-France – a remarkable, generous lady, a member of the champagne family who organises 'taste journeys'. Crystal chandeliers, original wallpapers, cavernous rooms, wonderful views… you'll forgive the odd imperfect corner. Bedrooms are big and absolutely château, bathrooms endearingly old-fashioned. The inner courtyard is lush with camellias and cyclamen, the gardens are lovely, the swimming pool lies beneath the palms. Breakfasts and dinners are enriching affairs. *Sawday self-catering also.*

Price	€98-€120.
Rooms	3: 2 doubles, 1 twin.
Meals	Restaurant in grounds.
Closed	Rarely.
Directions	From A9 exit 35 Béziers Est for Bédarieux; D909 for 20km, signs for château on right.

Marie-France Lanson
Château de Grézan,
Au Milieu des Vignes,
34480 Laurens, Hérault
Tel +33 (0)4 67 90 28 03
Email chateau-grezan.lanson@wanadoo.fr
Web www.grezan.com

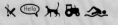

Languedoc - Roussillon

Château de Murviel

The château is perched on the pinnacle of the village, surveying mellow rooftops, sweeping vineyards and hills. Soft, plastered walls, honey-coloured floorboards, pale stone floors and bleached-linen bed curtains create a feeling of warmth, modernity and light – unexpected in such an old place. Lovely Michèle the housekeeper takes good care of you and serves breakfast in a cobbled, fountain'd courtyard dotted with lemon trees and oleander; there's a super guest kitchen, too. Whether you are interested in wine or the Cathars, this is an extremely charming place to lay your head. *Two nights high season preferred.*

Price	€80-€110. Whole house available.
Rooms	4: 1 double, 2 triples, 1 suite for 4.
Meals	Kitchen available. Restaurant 0.5km.
Closed	January.
Directions	From A9 exit 35 for centre ville; at 1st & 2nd r'bouts: for Bédarieux; 3rd r'bout: for Corneilhan & Murviel; in Murviel centre, next to Mairie.

Yves & Florence Cousquer
Château de Murviel,
1 place Georges Clémenceau,
34490 Murviel lès Béziers, Hérault
Tel +33 (0)4 67 32 35 45
Mobile +33 (0)6 89 88 10 41 / 07 42 47 08
Email chateaudemurviel@free.fr
Web www.murviel.com

Languedoc - Roussillon

Les Mimosas

The O'Rourkes love France, wine, food, their fine house in this enchanting old village and the dazzling countryside around. The door opens onto a high cool hall and old stone stairs lead to fresh, delicately decorated bedrooms with new shower rooms and art on the walls. Rooms at the back are south facing with views to the hills. You can walk, ride, climb rocks; swim, canoe in the river; visit the local markets and the unusual succulent garden. Then return for a superb, civilised meal on the terrace with your friendly hosts, he a retired architect and historian, she a creative cook. "A little slice of heaven," say readers.

Price	€70.
Rooms	5: 4 doubles; 1 studio & kitchenette.
Meals	Dinner with wine, €25-€35 (groups only). Restaurants in Roquebrun.
Closed	December/January.
Directions	From Béziers N112 W for St Pons 1/2km; right D14 through Maraussan, Cazouls lès Béziers, Cessenon to Roquebrun; signed in village.

	Martin & Jacqui O'Rourke
	Les Mimosas,
	Avenue des Orangers,
	34460 Roquebrun, Hérault
Tel	+33 (0)4 67 89 61 36
Mobile	+33 (0)6 42 33 96 63
Email	welcome.lesmimosas@wanadoo.fr
Web	www.lesmimosas.net

Entry 573   Map 15

Languedoc - Roussillon

La Métairie Basse

In these wild, pastoral surroundings with great walking and climbing trails, you bathe in simplicity, stream-babble and light. Your hosts, hard-working walnut and chestnut growers, have converted to 'bio' and sell delicious purées and jams. The guest barn is beautifully tended: country antiques, old lace curtains, new bedding and blue tones relax the eye; there's a fireplace and a full kitchen too. Monsieur has a big friendly handshake, Madame is gentle and welcoming, and breakfast on the shady terrace includes cheese or walnuts or honey. The wonderful Cathar city of Minerve is a 40-minute drive. Amazing value.

Ethical Collection: Food.
See page 410 for details.

Price	€54.
Rooms	2 doubles.
Meals	Guest kitchen. Restaurants 3km.
Closed	October-March, except by arrangement.
Directions	From A9 exit Béziers Ouest; D64 5km; D612 for Mazamet 47km; through St Pons de Thomières 5km; in Courniou, right to Prouilhe; farm on left.

	Éliane & Jean-Louis Lunes
	La Métairie Basse,
	Hameau de Prouilhe,
	34220 Courniou, Hérault
Tel	+33 (0)4 67 97 21 59
Email	info@metairie-basse.com
Web	www.metairie-basse.com

Entry 574   Map 15

Languedoc - Roussillon

Le Vieux Relais

Valerie and Mike have poured hearts and souls into this refurbished 18th-century coach house in Pepieux. Old door hinges gleam, tiled floors sweep across suites, spacious bathrooms are heaped with white towels, and ceiling fans keep you cool in big fresh-faced rooms. There's a cosy guest sitting room and a flower'd courtyard garden with – joy of joys – a pool; homemade cake for tea, fabulous dinners with local wines, and barbecues on a shady terrace. Your English hosts love their new life and have stacks of time for you; books for readers, maps for walkers, courses for artists and foodies. *Minimum two nights July/August.*

Languedoc - Roussillon

La Marelle

Full of energy for their new life, Sarah and Jean-Michel, who left busy city jobs for this peaceful Minervois village, are delighted with their handsome 16th-century house. In the pretty gardens: plenty of shady spots where you can take a drink or bury your nose in a novel; in the library: books and games for all. Big bedrooms have good bathrooms, florals and checks, nooks and crannies to explore. Sarah loves cooking, Jean-Michel will happily practise his (good) English over drinks and dinner, possibly by candlelight in the lovely courtyard. This couple thrive on looking after their guests: relax and enjoy it.

Price	€70-€80. €120 for 4.
Rooms	5: 1 triple, 2 family suites, 2 suites for 2.
Meals	Dinner with wine, from €25. Picnics available.
Closed	Rarely.
Directions	From Olonzac D115 to Pépieux. House on left as you enter village. Parking outside.

Price	€70.
Rooms	5: 4 doubles, 1 family room for 4.
Meals	Dinner with wine, €25. Restaurant 200m.
Closed	Rarely.
Directions	Exit A61 Carcassone Est dir. Narbonne; left at Trèbes for Marseillette, signed D610. Cont. 24km; left for La Redorte; after green bridge left 700m; house behind green railings on right.

	Valerie & Michael Slowther
	Le Vieux Relais,
	1 rue de l'Étang,
	11700 Pépieux, Aude
Tel	+33 (0)4 68 91 69 29
Email	mike@levieuxrelais.net
Web	www.levieuxrelais.net

	Jean-Michel Lemarechal
	La Marelle,
	19 avenue du Minervois,
	11700 La Redorte, Aude
Tel	+33 (0)4 68 91 59 30
Mobile	+33 (0)6 71 96 45 77
Email	reservations@chambres-lamarelle.com
Web	www.chambres-lamarelle.com

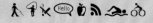

Entry 575   Map 15

Entry 576   Map 15

Languedoc - Roussillon

Le Domaine aux Quat'Saisons

Behind white wrought-iron gates in a lively wine-producing village is a little corner of paradise. The moment you enter this old *maison de maître*, elegantly furnished and charmingly run, you know you are in for a treat. The immaculately restored rooms, the beautiful antiques, the leisurely breakfasts taken on the terrace, the exceptional dinners produced from seasonal produce, the divine pool and the garden that is David's delight – all will inspire you to return. David and his team run an enchanting small hotel to which a trio of dachshunds – 'les Girls' – add the final delightful note. *Minimum two nights.*

Price	€95–€140.
Rooms	5: 4 doubles, 1 twin.
Meals	Dinner with wine, €39.
Closed	November-Easter, except Christmas & New Year.
Directions	From Rieux Minervois main street, house set back from road behind white wrought-iron gates, signed.

David Coles & Graeme McGlasson-West
Le Domaine aux Quat'Saisons,
26 avenue Georges Clémenceau,
11160 Rieux Minervois, Aude

Tel	+33 (0)4 68 24 49 73
Email	info@southoffrancehotel.com
Web	www.southoffrancehotel.com

Languedoc - Roussillon

L'Ancienne Boulangerie

In the history- and legend-laden north Minervois, Caunes is one of France's most beautiful walled villages. Quiet too, the twisting lanes making speed impossible. In a house that baked the abbey's bread from 1500 to 1988, you are sure of a charming Irish welcome from the owners of this tall, antique-furnished B&B: steep narrow stairs and characterful old floors, a galley kitchen in one suite, a tiny, pretty terrace for two others to enjoy summer breakfasts, a small library – and all those cobbled streets to explore. Plus, of course, Carcassonne, the oldest walled city in Europe, just down the road. *Minimum two nights.*

Price	€70. €88 for 3.
Rooms	5: 3 doubles, 1 triple, 1 family suite for 3.
Meals	Dinner with wine, €22. Restaurant opposite.
Closed	November to mid-March.
Directions	From Carcassonne D620 to Caunes Minervois; cross river & follow to Mairie; house behind Épicerie opp. Place de la Mairie & Hotel d'Alibert.

Gareth Armstrong
L'Ancienne Boulangerie,
20 rue St Gènes,
11160 Caunes Minervois, Aude

Tel	+33 (0)4 68 78 01 32
Email	ancienne.boulangerie@free.fr
Web	www.ancienneboulangerie.com

Languedoc - Roussillon

Domaine St Pierre de Trapel

Coming in from the magnificent gardens, catch the scent of herbs as you walk through the house. The delightful owners, lively, educated, well-travelled, moved here from east France for a more relaxing way of life and climate. Using exquisite taste, they have combined original 18th-century elegances with new necessities in big bedrooms and bathrooms of pure luxury, each with its own lovely colour scheme. Lovely in all seasons, with relaxing outdoor spots for all, a superb 150-year-old cedar, olive trees, a swimming pool surrounded by roses and a lovely covered terrace. A place of beauty, elegance and space.

Price	€85-€145.
Rooms	5: 1 twin, 3 doubles, 1 suite for 4.
Meals	Restaurants nearby.
Closed	November-March, except by arrangement.
Directions	From A61 exit 23 for Mazamet; at r'bout D620 for Villalier 1.5km; D201 for Villedubert; on right, thro' wrought-iron gates.

Christophe & Catherine Pariset
Domaine St Pierre de Trapel,
11620 Villemoustaussou,
Aude
Tel +33 (0)4 68 77 00 68
Email cpariset@trapel.com
Web www.trapel.com

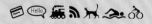

Entry 579   Map 15

Languedoc - Roussillon

Domaine des Castelles

There are space and air galore in this 19th-century gentleman-farmer's house. The freshly decorated bedrooms, each with its own entrance, are often huge, always charming; there are good mattresses, pine floors and a friendly feel; the 'parc' with canal fills a whole hectare. Madame, lively, artistic, open and welcoming, chats to guests over breakfast – on the terrace in fine weather – and enjoys their travellers' tales. You are in the country yet near the buzz of Carcassonne (and the airport!), while the dreamy Canal du Midi and the vineyards offer their seductively parallel alternatives. A gem.

Price	€70-€75. Extra bed €20.
Rooms	3: 1 double, 1 triple, 1 suite for 5.
Meals	Restaurants nearby.
Closed	Rarely.
Directions	On A61 exit Carcassonne-Ouest to Salvaza airport; stay on D119 for approx. 4 more km. Sign on left.

Isabelle Bretton
Domaine des Castelles,
11170 Caux et Sauzens,
Aude
Tel +33 (0)4 68 72 03 60

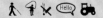

Entry 580   Map 15

Languedoc - Roussillon

Villelongue Côté Jardins

Painters, poets, nature-lovers love this place, where history and romance combine. Dark 16th-century passages and uneven stone floors open into heavily beamed rooms sympathetically revived. Bedrooms are big and simply refined in their white cotton and old armoires, the newest on the ground floor. Views are to the ancient trees of the park or the great courtyard and ruined Cistercian abbey. Sisters Renée and Claude, warm, knowledgeable, generous, were born here and provide convivial breakfasts and dinners. Wild gardens and duck ponds, lazy cats, retired horses, and lovely walking paths into the landscape. *No dinner July/August.*

Price	€60.
Rooms	3: 1 double, 1 twin, 1 family room for 3.
Meals	Dinner with wine, €22.
Closed	Christmas.
Directions	From A61 exit Bram; D4 thro' Bram & St Martin le Vieil; right on tiny D64 3km to Abbey. Caution: Go to Côté Jardins B&B not Abbey B&B next door.

	Claude Antoine & Renée Marcoul
	Villelongue Côté Jardins,
	11170 St Martin le Vieil,
	Aude
Tel	+33 (0)4 68 76 09 03
Email	villelongue11@yahoo.fr
Web	www.villelongue-cote-jardin.com

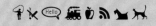

Entry 581   Map 15

Languedoc - Roussillon

La Rougeanne

Monique has endless energy and adores people, Paul-André is quiet and charming, together they promise you a wonderful stay. They bought the old wine-grower's estate on the edge of town in a most parlous state – but look at it now! The sitting room is stylish, restful, flooded with light and washed with pearl grey, the bedrooms are quietly luxurious; Monique has a way with interiors. Have breakfast by the lavender in summer, then discover hilltop bastides and the castles of the Cathars… monumental Carcassonne is up the road. Return to a garden within gardens and distant views, an orangery and a pool. Bliss.

Price	€72–€100.
Rooms	5: 3 doubles, 1 twin, 1 family room for 4.
Meals	Restaurants within walking distance
Closed	Rarely.
Directions	From Carcassonne D6113 for Toulouse. After Pezens D629 to Moussoulens. Left at r'bout; follow signs to La Rougeanne.

	Monique & Paul-André Glorieux
	La Rougeanne,
	8 allée du Parc,
	11170 Moussoulens, Aude
Tel	+33 (0)4 68 24 46 30
Email	info@larougeanne.com
Web	www.larougeanne.com

Entry 582   Map 15

Languedoc - Roussillon

Château de la Prade

Lost among the cool shadows of tall sunlit trees beside the languid waters of the Canal du Midi, here is a place of understated elegance and refinement. Sitting in 12 acres, the 19th-century house is more 'domaine' than 'château' – formal hedges, fine trees, ornamental railings – though the vineyards have long gone. Swiss Roland runs the B&B, Georges looks after the gardens: they are kind and discreetly attentive hosts. Dinner is served on pink cloths, breakfasts are a treat, bedrooms have tall windows, polished floors, an immaculate, uncluttered charm. Half a mile from the road to Carcassonne but so peaceful.

Price	€95–€115.
Rooms	4 twins/doubles.
Meals	Dinner €24. Wine €17.50–€23.
Closed	Mid-November to mid-March.
Directions	From A61 exit 22; thro' Bram 2.5km; left D6113 for Villepinte; house signed on left.

Roland Kurt
Château de la Prade,
11150 Bram,
Aude
Tel   +33 (0)4 68 78 03 99
Email chateaulaprade@wanadoo.fr
Web   www.chateaulaprade.eu

Entry 583   Map 15

Languedoc - Roussillon

Le Domaine de Puget

Janie and John are new to France, farming and B&B. The house, the space, the stars, the views that reach to the Pyrenees – let their gentle delight in it all rub off on you. The old mellow stone buildings are centred on an open courtyard, two guest rooms are in the main house, the suite has its own garden, and all are done in modern rustic style, with very pretty views. Outside are shady gardens and walking paths, orchard, lake and lovely pool. John is chef, treating you to regional, seasonal (often organic) food and a different wine to try each night; you can also visit the producers. *Minimum two nights July/August.*

Price	€75. Suite €120 for 2, €150 for 4.
Rooms	3: 2 doubles, 1 family suite for 2-4.
Meals	Dinner €35. Wine from €10. Restaurants 15-minute drive.
Closed	Rarely.
Directions	A6 exit 21 for Castelnaudary; D6 to Mirepoix for 15km; right D102 for Belpech; tiny 2nd right before bend. House on left.

Janie & John Haward
Le Domaine de Puget,
11270 Gaja La Selve,
Aude
Tel   +33 (0)4 68 60 26 30
Email john@lepuget.com
Web   www.lepuget.com

Entry 584   Map 15

Languedoc - Roussillon

Le Trésor

The most attractive house in the village, Le Trésor looks through green eyelids onto the sleepy town square. Inside, tall elegant windows and banistered stairs mix with white walls, crisp art and flamboyant chandeliers: ex-Londoners Will and Tilly have created a quirkily seductive B&B. Bedrooms, one with a roll top bath, have high ceilings, spare furnishings, masses of light. Tilly loves regional food so the treats continue at table, and breakfasts are superb. A hammock in the garden (kids love it!), L'Occitane oils by the shower, DVDs, snooker and super young hosts. Great for hiking or skiing or discovering Matisse's Collioure. *Minimum two nights.*

Price	€90-€120.
Rooms	4: 3 doubles, 1 suite.
Meals	Dinner, 3 courses, €28. Wine €10.
Closed	November-March.
Directions	From Carcassonne D118 to Limoux; D620 to Chalabre; D16 Sonnac, on main square, opp. church.

William & Tilly Howard
Le Trésor,
20 place de l'Église,
11230 Sonnac sur l'Hers, Aude

Tel	+33 (0)4 68 69 37 94
Email	contact@le-tresor.com
Web	www.le-tresor.com

Languedoc - Roussillon

Maison d'hôtes l'Orangerie

The most charming town with a tree-lined square for boules, a bustling market, lovely restaurants and interesting small shops... you stay in the heart of it all. Through huge green gates enter a pretty courtyard with flowering pots, the orange tree (as announced) and calm, relaxed Sylvie and Claude. A charming sitting room has a reading corner and comfy seating, the bright and inviting bedrooms are all a good size – one has a terrace – and the bathrooms are super. Breakfast on seasonal fresh fruit, cake and homemade jams in the dining room or the courtyard. Dinner can be served here too, in traditional French style.

Price	€65-€100.
Rooms	5: 3 doubles, 1 family room for 3, 1 suite for 2-4.
Meals	Dinner with wine, €27.
Closed	November.
Directions	A9 exit 41 Rivesaltes; at r'bout 1st right, D12 for Rivesaltes; D5, cross Pont Jacquet; 1st left after bridge; 1st right. House on right.

Sylvie & Claude Poussin
Maison d'hôtes l'Orangerie,
3T rue Ludovic Ville,
66600 Rivesaltes, Pyrénées-Orientales

Tel	+33 (0)4 68 73 74 41
Mobile	+33 (0)6 09 82 75 87
Email	maisonhoteslorangerie@wanadoo.fr
Web	maisonhoteslorangerie.com

Languedoc - Roussillon

El Pinyol d'Oliva

In March the valley is a sea of blossom: this is the peach capital of France. Views sweep from the roof terrace to the streets below and the snowy peaks of Mount Canigou beyond. Anne, active and delightful, loves her old house in the small square, a stone's throw from the church; its large, luminous rooms glow with good taste. Whitewashed walls rub shoulders with Catalan stonework, beams are high, cushions and curtains give bright bursts of colour, there's art on the walls and one of the shower rooms is triangular. Lovely old Perpignan is a 15-minute drive, the airport 20, and Spain just half an hour. Great food, too!

Price	€100.
Rooms	4: 1 double, 2 twins, 1 suite.
Meals	Dinner with wine, €25.
Closed	Rarely.
Directions	From Perpignan N116 for Andorra 2.5km; exit for Île sur Têt; Av Pasteur to centre; right for Montalba; follow ramparts on right 50m, right at El Pinyol d'Oliva sign, left, downhill to small square; knock on door No. 6.

	Anne Guthrie
	El Pinyol d'Oliva,
	10 petite place de l'Huile,
	66130 Île sur Têt, Pyrénées-Orientales
Tel	+33 (0)4 68 84 04 17
Email	web-enquiry@elpinyoldoliva.com
Web	www.elpinyoldoliva.com

Entry 587   Map 15

Languedoc - Roussillon

Castell Rose

A beautiful, pink marble, gentleman's house in its own parkland on the edge of a very pretty town between the sea and the mountains; the views are superb. Evelyne and Alex are both charming and give you large sumptuous bedrooms with thoughtful colour schemes, good linen, tip-top bathrooms and elegant antiques. After a good breakfast, wander through the flourishing garden with its ancient olive trees to find a spot beside the lily pond, or just float in the pool. It's a five-minute stroll to village life, or take the yellow train up the mountain from Villefranche for more amazing views.

Price	€79-€105. Family room €109-€129.
Rooms	5: 3 doubles, 1 twin, 1 family room.
Meals	Restaurant 500m.
Closed	Rarely.
Directions	From Perpignan N116 to Prades; for centre ville; thro' town on Av du Général de Gaulle; left at end & cont. Route de Ria; house signed 200m on left before Hôtel de Ville.

	Evelyne & Alex Waldvogel
	Castell Rose,
	Chemin de la Litera,
	66500 Prades, Pyrénées-Orientales
Tel	+33 (0)4 68 96 07 57
Email	castell.rose@wanadoo.fr
Web	www.castellrose-prades.com

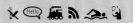

Entry 588   Map 15

Languedoc - Roussillon

Maison Prades

Informal, vibrant and fun is this peaceful townhouse with bright sunshiney rooms reflecting its artist owner. Angela has steeped herself in the culture of the charming market town of Prades and enjoys French as well as 'foreign' guests; meet them over breakfast (generous, delicious). There's a wonderful long garden with a sun-dappled terrace and a barbecue for summer – yours to borrow – a wood-burner for winter and comfort all year round; leave the car behind and Angela will scoop you up off the train. Stylish walk-in showers will delight you and quirky touches entertain you – not least the vintage frocks!

Price	€75-€100.
Rooms	3: 1 double, 1 twin, 1 triple.
Meals	Restaurants 5-minute walk.
Closed	Rarely.
Directions	From Perpignan N116 to Prades for centre ville, through town on narrow main street. House on left.

Angela Lanchester
Maison Prades,
51 av du Général de Gaulle,
66500 Prades, Pyrénées-Orientales
Tel   +33 (0)4 68 05 74 27
Mobile   +33 (0)6 19 01 27 86
Email   maisonprades@aol.com
Web   www.bed-breakfast-prades.com

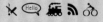

Entry 589   Map 15

Languedoc - Roussillon

Mas Pallarès

In a beautiful wooded valley five minutes from Céret is this ancient farmhouse with stepped gardens and a child-perfect stream. Birds sing, wisteria blooms, views sweep across the wooded valley and Lizzie has worked hard to ensure everyone has their own corner of calm; the B&B rooms have lovely big balconies. The mood is easy and the rooms are friendly: old floor tiles, inviting colours, country antiques, spotless showers. Lizzie's breakfasts are feasts and the fenced pool and summer kitchen are shared with apartment guests who self-cater. Céret's market is fantastic, Spain's peaceful bays are a hop away. *Minimum two nights.*

Price	€80-€180.
Rooms	2: 1 double, 1 suite & kitchenette.
Meals	Summer kitchen. Restaurant 1km.
Closed	Rarely.
Directions	From A9 exit 43 D115 to Céret; cont. 2km to Lepont; 1st left D15 to Reynes 800m; hairpin bend left for Coll. de Bousseilles. House on left after Allée du Mas Pallarès.

Lizzie Price
Mas Pallarès,
66400 Céret,
Pyrénées-Orientales
Tel   +33 (0)4 68 87 42 17
Email   lizzie@ceret-farmhouse-apartments.com
Web   www.ceret-farmhouse-apartments.com

Entry 590   Map 15

Languedoc - Roussillon

La Châtaigneraie

The Bethells have created a haven of Pyrenean-Scottish hospitality among some of Europe's wildest, remotest landscapes; in the wonderful lush garden are several intimate sitting areas where views dazzle up to snowy Canigou or down to the sea. Numerous steps lead to romantic rooms with comfy beds, original works of art and bright scatter cushions; the suite opens to a private terrace by the pool. Take breakfast out here, delivered by Kim or Gill — a mother and daughter team who look after guests beautifully. And for dinner, there's the famous Terrasse au Soleil in lively Céret — a good 15-minute walk away.

Price	€80-€170.
Rooms	4: 3 doubles, 1 twin/double, 1 family suite for 4 & kitchenette.
Meals	Restaurant 400m.
Closed	Rarely.
Directions	A9 for Spain, last exit before border; into Céret for centre ville then for Hôtel La Terrasse au Soleil. House 400m after hotel, on left.

Kim & Gill Bethell
La Châtaigneraie,
Route de Fontfrède,
66400 Céret, Pyrénées-Orientales
Tel   +33 (0)4 68 87 21 58
Email   kim@ceret.net
Web   www.ceret.net

Entry 591   Map 15

Photo: Lesley Chalmers

Rhône Valley – Alps

Photo: www.istockphoto.com

Rhône Valley - Alps

Le Couradou

Diana, bright and gifted, and Jos, a charming geologist, came from cool populous Belgium to empty rustic Ardèche and set about transforming this fine big silk-farm house into a warm home. Outside, vineyards and the distant Cévennes, inside, wonderful vaulted 15th-century ceilings, split-level living spaces and four big guest rooms creatively and luxuriously put together with the local gifts of stone walls, country antiques, Provençal patterns and wrought iron – there's even a sunken bath in one room. Gorgeous views from private terraces, beautiful garden and super pool. *Minimum five nights in high season.*

Price	€90-€130.
Rooms	4: 2 doubles, 2 triples.
Meals	Dinner with wine, €39.
Closed	October-April.
Directions	From N86 Bourg St Andéol; D4 to Vallon Pont d'Arc; D979 left for Barjac 4km; D217 left for Labastide.

Diana Little & Jos Vandervondelen
Le Couradou,
Le Chambon, 07150 Labastide de Virac,
Ardèche
Tel +33 (0)4 75 38 64 75
Email infos@lecouradou.com
Web www.lecouradou.com

Rhône Valley - Alps

Les Roudils

Breakfast like kings among the butterflies in an idyllic place. High up in the nature-rich regional park of Monts d'Ardèche the views are inspiring, the peace supreme. At the end of the long windy road, the house, built of stone and wood from the chestnut forests, has been lovingly restored to offer authentic bedrooms full of light and soft simplicity. Informal and fun, Marie makes heavenly preserves (apricot, rosemary), Gil makes aperitifs and honeys (chestnut, heather, raspberry). Come for sunshine and music, a great Cévenol fireplace and exceptionally warm hospitable people and their three cats. Paradise!

Ethical Collection: Environment & Food.
See page 410 for details.

Price	€65. Extra person €18.
Rooms	3: 2 doubles, 1 family suite for 4.
Meals	Kitchen available. Restaurant 4km.
Closed	November-March.
Directions	From Aubenas N102 for Le Puy 8.5km. At Lalevade, left to Jaujac centre. By Place St Bonnet, over river & follow signs 4km along narrow mountain road.

Marie & Gil Florence
Les Roudils,
07380 Jaujac,
Ardèche
Tel +33 (0)4 75 93 21 11
Email le-rucher-des-roudils@wanadoo.fr
Web www.lesroudils.com

L'Angelot

Come for the great outdoors! Ilsa and Fons have acres of chestnut forest around their stonebuilt 1797 farm, there's a circular walk to a medieval castle, and you can tackle the 15-minute uphill slog to the pretty village above. Return to large rustic rooms (an old door as a bedhead, a cupboard door from an armoire) and clean but dated bathrooms. The house is on many levels, with a cool pool for aching limbs, a tinkling stream below and plenty of tranquil corners to hide in with a book. Homemade jams and local honey for breakfast, hosts without a whiff of pretension: walkers adore it. *Minimum two nights.*

Price	€70-€90.
Rooms	3: 1 double, 1 twin, 1 triple.
Meals	Light supper with wine, €19.
Closed	Rarely.
Directions	A7 exit 16 Loriol; N304 to Aubenas, D578 to Antraigues, follow 'centre bourg'; left at Vival supermarket; 500m; follow Toutes Dir.; left after 1st house, over river, immed. right, signed.

	Ilse & Fons Jaspers
	L'Angelot,
	Ranc au Ranc, 07530 Antraigues
	sur Volane, Ardèche
Tel	+33 (0)4 75 88 24 55
Email	info@langelot.com
Web	www.langelot.com

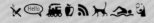

Entry 594 Map 11

Maison Hérold

Enjoy every bend through wild Ardèche to this elegant old bourgeois house, built on the remains of an ancient stronghold; feel the strength of the land; hear the untamed water piling past. You will be greeted by sweetly endearing people (teacher and nurse) who have renovated their family home with a fine eye, then be shown up the graceful curling staircase to a room with 19th-century antiques, modern bathroom and soul-cleansing views. A spring rises in the garden, delicious breakfast is in the pretty dining room. Writer Hérold received many literati and Ravel composed his 'Valse' here. Atmospheric and definitely special.

Price	€70.
Rooms	1 double.
Meals	Restaurant 200m.
Closed	Rarely.
Directions	A6 exit Valence to St Peray then D533 to Lamastre; D578 for Le Cheylard to Lapras; lane at entrance to village on left; immed. right.

	Joselyne & Patrick Moreau
	Maison Hérold,
	Lapras, 07270 St Basile,
	Ardèche
Tel	+33 (0)4 75 06 46 09
Email	contact@maisonherold.com
Web	www.maisonherold.com

Entry 595 Map 11

Rhône Valley - Alps

Myrtille

Remote, rural and with vast views of the volcanic Velay range, this sturdy farmhouse with its flower-hugged façade is ideal for a family holiday or a hiking sojourn. Like its owners, the décor is unpretentious and good-natured: wood-panelled rooms with honey-coloured floorboards; hand-painted bedheads with bows; blue and yellow colour schemes. Children will enjoy the log playhouse in the garden, the Tisseurs' own youngsters and the step-laddered bunks – or the balconied floor of the family room. You'll enjoy the peace, and the wholesome, organic dinners with your delightful hosts. André's passion is vintage cars.

Price	€45-€50.
Rooms	5: 2 doubles, 1 twin, 2 family rooms for 2-4.
Meals	Dinner with wine, €15. Restaurant 3km.
Closed	October-March (open Christmas).
Directions	A47 exit 16; N88 to Firminy; stt on to r'bout; D3 thro' St Maurice en Gourgois; D104 to Usson en Forez; D498 for Craponne s/Arzon 4km; left to Jouanzecq; signed.

Pascale Tisseur
Myrtille,
Jouanzecq,
42550 Usson en Forez, Loire
Tel   +33 (0)4 77 50 90 83
Email   chambre.myrtille@hotmail.fr
Web   chambre.myrtille.chez-alice.fr

Rhône Valley - Alps

Domaine du Fontenay

Huge care has been taken by these owners to make guests comfortable and well-informed. Simon's lifelong ambition was to become a wine-maker in France, now his wines are highly regarded; enjoy the tastings in the cellar. In a separate building are four super bedrooms with excellent mattresses, big showers, rugs on old terracotta tiles and astonishing views from this hilltop site; and each bedroom has an excellent folder with all the local info. In summer, breakfast is served at check-clothed tables on the big terrace. This is a great area for good-value gourmet restaurants so enjoy them – and ask about 'La Route Magique!'

Price	€68.
Rooms	4: 1 triple, 3 suites for 2.
Meals	Kitchen available. Restaurant in village.
Closed	Rarely.
Directions	From Roanne, Route de Villemontais via Faubourg Clermont; D53 for 10km; straight road until r'bout with wine press; left towards m'way; signed.

Simon & Isabelle Hawkins
Domaine du Fontenay,
Fontenay, 42155 Villemontais,
Loire
Tel   +33 (0)4 77 63 12 22
Email   info@domainedufontenay.com
Web   www.domainedufontenay.com

Domaine du Château de Marchangy

Down an avenue of oaks and through grand gates to a perfectly proportioned house. Light pours into intimate, immaculate guest rooms on the first and loft floors of the ivy-clad guest wing; expect big rugs on pale wood floors, harmonious colours, delightful armoires, stylish *objets*, gorgeous fabrics, garden flowers and, in the salon, a superb winter fire. Rise at your leisure for château breakfasts and fruits from the orchard, served by the pool in summer, in whinnying distance of the horses. Smiling Madame and her *gardienne* look after you wonderfully. *Minimum two nights July/August. Amma massage available.*

Price	€95-€115.
Rooms	3 suites.
Meals	Restaurants 10-minute drive.
Closed	Rarely.
Directions	From Roanne D482 north; 5km after Pouilly sous Charlieu right to St Pierre la Noaille. Signed.

	Marie-Colette Grandeau
	Domaine du Château de Marchangy,
	42190 St Pierre la Noaille,
	Loire
Tel	+33 (0)4 77 69 96 76
Email	contact@marchangy.com
Web	www.marchangy.com

Entry 598   Map 11

La Gloriette

Over a glass or two of the local beaujolais, discover what extremely good company your hosts are. Epic travellers (recently to Japan, China, Russia), they relish the simpler life. And a fine, simple B&B this is, cosy, friendly, and with good country food to match. A woodchip-burner fuels the central heating, the book-filled sitting room has a disarmingly uncoordinated air and guest bedrooms are simple, cheerful, airy and bright. Outside is a courtyard and a jungle of a garden, and 'la gloriette' — a delightful place to sit with long views over this almost-Tuscan countryside. Great value. *Parking in village square.*

Ethical Collection: Environment, Food & Community. See page 410 for details.

Price	€55.
Rooms	3: 1 double, 1 twin, 1 family room for 4-6. Cot available.
Meals	Dinner with wine, €22.
Closed	December-February.
Directions	From Mâcon N6 south; at Pontanevaux D95 right; through Les Paquelets; D17; D26 to Jullié. House off main square, signed.

	Antoinette & Jean-Luc Bazin
	La Gloriette,
	Le Bourg, 69840 Jullié,
	Rhône
Tel	+33 (0)4 74 06 70 95
Mobile	+33 (0)6 86 46 31 70
Email	lagloriette@lagloriette.fr
Web	www.lagloriette.fr

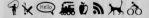

Entry 599   Map 11

La Croix de Saburin

To-die-for views soar over endless streaks of vines to Mounts Brouilly and, even, Blanc: a dream of a setting. Built in regional style against the hillside is this very French, contemporary-smart house. Sociable and perfectionist, Monique and Jean-Michel began B&B when they retired; bedrooms are pretty with chalky mango-wood tables and sparkling bathrooms. Guests are spoilt with the salon: tea-making kit and plenty of books. Rare birds, orchids and butterflies dwell in the valley below; cycling, wine tasting and Lyon are close by. Dine with the family on salade Lyonnaise and chicken in champagne. Intimate and stunning.

Price	€63. Extra person €17.
Rooms	2: 1 double, 1 family room for 3.
Meals	Dinner with wine, €25.
Closed	Rarely.
Directions	A6 exit Belleville sur Saône; D37 for Beaujeu; after Cercié, r'bout for St Etienne & Odenas; right to Saburin, 500m. Last house.

Jean-Michel & Monique Legat
La Croix de Saburin,
Saburin, 69430 Quincié en Beaujolais,
Rhône

Tel	+33 (0)4 74 69 02 82
Mobile	+33 (0)6 08 50 19 03
Email	jean-michel.legat@orange.fr
Web	lacroixdesaburin.free.fr

Entry 600   Map 11

Les Pasquiers

Come to meet Laurence, her daughter and two sweet cats in this beautiful home in a wine-country village setting. Oriental rugs and fine antiques rub shoulders with contemporary art, gorgeous books lie around for everyone to peruse, there's a grand piano in the drawing room, heaps of CDs, and a stunning spacious dayroom in the attic. Bedrooms are sunny, beds wear beautiful linen, bathrooms are fashionably screened, and the garden is divine – languid terraces, organic potager, summerhouse, pool. Delightful Laurence loves to cook and both breakfasts and dinners are scrumptious. One of the best!

Price	€85.
Rooms	4: 2 doubles, 2 twins.
Meals	Dinner with wine, €30.
Closed	Rarely.
Directions	From A6 exit Belleville to D306 for Mâcon 8km; left D9 for Courcelles en Beaujolais; right to Lancié D119; right D119E, right again after 100m to Les Pasquiers. Signed.

Laurence Adelé-Gandilhon
Les Pasquiers,
69220 Lancié,
Rhône

Tel	+33 (0)4 74 69 86 33
Mobile	+33 (0)6 83 42 86 60
Email	welcome@lespasquiers.com
Web	www.lespasquiers.com

Entry 601   Map 11

Rhône Valley - Alps

Domaine La Javernière

Through the huge wrought-iron gates into a courtyard lined with delectable roses and a house filled with history and soul. In the heart of Beaujolais country, this huge bourgeois residence is owned by wine distributor Thibault who treats guests as friends and runs it with an easy charm. Great Grandpapa's portrait hangs in the hall, there are books, photographs, art and sculpture everywhere, a piano if you wish, and space to roam: nowhere is out of bounds. Bedrooms are gracious, sunny and sprinkled with antiques, bathrooms range from swish Italian to cute and tiny under the eaves. Gastronomy and vineyards abound.

Price	€65–€130.
Rooms	4: 1 double, 2 twins, 1 suite for 4–5.
Meals	Restaurant 600m.
Closed	November–March.
Directions	A6 exit 30 Belleville; follow 'Autres Directions' for RN6, then for Villié Morgon; from Pizay to Morgon; D68 right; after 600m, signed on right.

Thibault Roux
Domaine La Javernière,
69910 Javernière,
Rhône

Mobile	+33 (0)6 66 05 90 52
Email	contact@la-javerniere.fr
Web	la-javerniere.fr

Entry 602 Map 11

Rhône Valley - Alps

Château de Longsard

Two Lebanon cedars in the grounds, wine from the estate, 17th-century beams to guard your sleep. Your Franco-American hosts, charming and well-travelled polyglots, share their enthusiasm for horticulture (founding a scheme allowing the public to visit private gardens while raising money for local charities); animal lovers too, they are the proud owners of a cluster of dogs and cats. Bedrooms and bathrooms, from faded pastel to those with the odd hint of modernity, are eclectically furnished; Olivier's brother is an antique dealer. You are just three minutes from the A6 to Villefranche.

Price	€130–€150.
Rooms	6: 3 doubles, 2 suites. Coach house: 1 suite.
Meals	Dinner with wine, €38.
Closed	Christmas & New Year.
Directions	A6 exit 31.1; over roundabout; through village; château on right after 1.5km.

Alexandra & Olivier du Mesnil
Château de Longsard,
69400 Arnas,
Rhône

Tel	+33 (0)4 74 65 55 12
Mobile	+33 (0)6 73 80 65 02
Email	longsard@gmail.com
Web	www.longsard.com

Entry 603 Map 11

Rhône Valley - Alps

Ancienne École du Chapuy

In the rural quiet of forests, lakes and unsung villages sits this old school house, peacefully by the road, classily converted by Marie-Christine and Alain. Up a winding staircase, petite pastel bedrooms with fine bedding and handsome bedsteads look out to lush pastures at the back. Bathrooms glitter in sea greens and have huge triangular bathtubs. Happy contrasts of bright fabrics and striking modern pieces mix with antiques in the sitting room; breakfasts are superb. Make the most of (flat) cycling, then tuck into those good old French clichés, frogs' legs and snails – local specialities! Intimate, charming. *17km from motorway.*

Price	€65-€130.
Rooms	2: 1 double, 1 family suite for 4.
Meals	Restaurant 2km.
Closed	November-March.
Directions	From Châtillon sur Chalaronne on D17 for Romans 2km to Les Bruyères; house on right.

Alain Privel & Marie-Christine Palaysi
Ancienne École du Chapuy,
Les Bruyères, Châtillon sur Chalaronne,
01400 Romans, Ain

Tel	+33 (0)4 74 55 63 30
Mobile	+33 (0)6 83 86 82 68
Email	ecoleduchapuy@hotmail.fr
Web	www.ecoleduchapuy.com

Rhône Valley - Alps

Manoir de Marmont

An amazing avenue of plane trees delivers you to an authentic experience – yet the people are the best part of it. Madame is a joy, laughing, enthusing, creating delicious cakes and jams for breakfast, her house as colourful as she is. Monsieur is quietly helpful. Up the grand stairs to a fine château room with Persian carpets, trompe-l'œil walls, antiques, books and fresh flowers. Madame pours tea from silver into porcelain and artfully moves the butter as the sun rises; at night she'll light your bedside lamp, leaving a book open at a chosen page for you to read after a game of (French) Scrabble. Step back in time…

Price	€95.
Rooms	2: 1 double, 1 family suite for 3-5.
Meals	Restaurant 3km.
Closed	Rarely.
Directions	From Bourg en Bresse N83 for Lyon. At Servas right D64 for Condeissiat 5km; left at sign Le Marmont: plane-tree avenue. Don't go to St André.

Geneviève & Henri Guido-Alhéritière
Manoir de Marmont,
2043 route de Condeissiat,
01960 St André sur Vieux Jonc, Ain

| Tel | +33 (0)4 74 52 79 74 |
| Web | www.chateau-marmont.info |

Rhône Valley - Alps

La Ferme du Champ Pelaz

Deeply rural is this gentle land where
distant peaks tantalise and three generations
of Smiths live in the big, creeper-smothered
19th-century farmhouse. Guests have their
quarters in the middle with Michael and
Linda at one end, daughter Katey and her
children at the other. The owners know all
about the area (Michael specialises in golf
breaks) and can guide you towards the best
alpine walks. Bedrooms are cosy and
pretty, pastel-painted, wooden floored, a
good size and ideal for all. There's a pool
for summer heat, and a big log fire and deep
sofas in the dayroom for cool nights.
Minimum two nights in summer.

Price	€70-€90.
Rooms	4: 2 doubles (shared wc on landing), 2 triples.
Meals	Restaurant 10-minute drive.
Closed	Rarely.
Directions	A41 exit 17 for Chambéry 2km; right N1508 for Bourg en Bresse 4km; D17 left to La Combe Silingy; D38 left for Thusy; through Pesey, right at top of hill. 1st house on left.

	Michael & Linda Smith
	La Ferme du Champ Pelaz,
	Le Pesey, 74150 Thusy,
	Haute-Savoie
Tel	+33 (0)4 50 69 25 15
Mobile	+33 (0)6 31 85 55 54
Email	champ-pelaz@wanadoo.fr
Web	www.champ-pelaz.com

Entry 606   Map 11

Rhône Valley - Alps

Chalet Châtelet

The lush Vallée d'Abondance envelops this
pretty new pine chalet whose owners fizz
with enthusiasm for the life they share with
guests. Oak floors, soft shapes, high ceilings
hug reclaimed furniture and works by
Pascal and Suzie's arty family. Warmth
comes from a Finnish stove and solar panels
– an eco-lover's dream but you still find
bliss in the spa. Expect cultured chat in the
intimate dining room and Suzie's range-
cooked organic meals, the ingredients
sourced from local farmers. Bedrooms have
stunning views and dreamy bathrooms; gaze
to mountains you climbed or skied that day.
A home from home in green tranquillity.

Ethical Collection: Environment & Food.
See page 410 for details.

Price	€90-€190.
Rooms	3: 1 double, 2 triples.
Meals	Dinner with wine, €30.
Closed	Rarely.
Directions	Thonon D902 for Morzine/Vallée d'Abondance. After 2nd tunnel, left at r'bout D22 for Vallée d'A. & Châtel. After La Solitude, right onto D32 Bonnevaux. At church fork left; chalet 300m on left.

	Pascal & Suzie Immediato
	Chalet Châtelet,
	Route d'Abondance,
	74360 Bonnevaux, Haute-Savoie
Tel	+33 (0)4 50 73 69 48
Email	p.s.immediato@orange.fr
Web	www.chalet-chatelet.com

Entry 607   Map 12

Rhône Valley - Alps

Alps in Style – Chalet Esprit & Chalet Exige

Energetic and charismatic, Toni and Jez moved to the Grand Massif to live the dream. Drop-offs, pick-ups, babysitting, children's teas... nothing is too much trouble. Near pretty Morillon find two super new chalets with cosy pine-clad bedrooms and big inviting sitting rooms. Sink into a hot tub beneath starry skies while your children lap up GameCubes and DVDs. It's sleek, stylish and heart-warming all at the same time, great for families and foodies: Jez's menus are delicious. Walks and woodland playgrounds in summer, skis and snowboots in winter, forest views all year round. *Lifts 500m. Min. two nights.*

Price	Winter: half-board from €475 p.p. Summer: s/c from €1,650. Apt from €465. Prices per week. B&B from €50 p/room p/night.
Rooms	Esprit: 2 twins, 2 triples, 2 family; s/c apt: 1 twin, 1 triple (summer). Exige: 2 triples, 1 family.
Meals	Winter: catered (half-board). Summer: self-catered.
Closed	Rarely.
Directions	Cluses-Taninges D902; D4 to Morillon; pass Kevin Sports, right at cross 400m; left opp. chapel. On right.

Toni & Jez Waite
Alps in Style – Chalet Esprit & Chalet Exige, Le Bois Lombard, 74440 Morillon, Haute-Savoie

Tel	+33 (0)4 50 90 31 10
Mobile	+33 (0)6 30 54 70 32
Email	info@alpsinstyle.com
Web	www.alpsinstyle.com

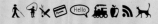

Entry 608   Map 12

Rhône Valley - Alps

Chalet Odysseus

The village has character; Chalet Odysseus has much besides. There's comfort in soft sofas, check curtains, bright rugs and open fire, and swishness in sauna and small gym; a French chef cooks for you once a week in winter, and your relaxed English hosts spoil you rotten (Kate, too, is a fine cook). They have the ground floor of this brand-new chalet; you live above. Cheerfully pretty bedrooms come with the requisite pine garb, two have balconies that catch the sun, the tiniest comes with bunk beds for kids. Marvellous for an active family break, whatever the season. *Minimum two nights.*

Price	€90. Half-board €100 p.p.
Rooms	5: 2 doubles, 2 twins, 1 family room.
Meals	Dinner with wine, €40.
Closed	Rarely.
Directions	From A40 exit 19 to Cuses; N205 for Sallanches; left D106. 2km before Les Carroz at red & white-shuttered chalet on left; signed.

Kate & Barry Joyce
Chalet Odysseus, 210 route de Lachat, 74300 Les Carroz d'Araches, Haute-Savoie

Tel	+33 (0)4 50 90 66 00
Email	chaletodysseus@wanadoo.fr
Web	www.chaletodysseuslachat.com

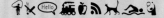

Entry 609   Map 12

Rhône Valley - Alps

La Ferme du Soleil

The hamlet of four old wooden houses (two chalets, two farm buildings) is high up, impossibly pretty, detached from the bustling world, with views to lift spirits and a deep silence in which to contemplate such beauty. In winter, you are a stroll from the top of a chair lift and a quick slide from the bottom of several, so you can stop skiing when you're ready for a blazing log fire and a delicious bite. In summer you can wander the mountains to enjoy the flowers and the bell-ringing cows. The word 'idyll' really does apply. Big, cosy, beautiful, open and convivial – another dream realised. *Minimum seven nights in winter.*

Price	Winter: half board €700-€865 p.p. Summer: self-catered (8) €1,440-€2,160; studio €720 for 2 (child €120). Prices per week.
Rooms	5: 2 doubles, 2 twins, 1 family studio for 3.
Meals	Winter: half-board. Summer: self-catered.
Closed	May-early June; Nov to early Dec.
Directions	La Clusaz-St Jean de Sixt on D909; D4 to La Chinaillon, then to La Côte; left at T-junc; 6th house.

	Veroni Gilbert La Ferme du Soleil, Les Gettiers, 74450 Le Grand Bornand, Haute-Savoie
Tel	+33 (0)9 52 76 34 01
Mobile	+44 (0)7789 947 024
Email	lafermedusoleil@hotmail.com
Web	www.lafermedusoleil.com

Entry 610 Map 12

Rhône Valley - Alps

Chalet Chovettaz

Join this outgoing family in their big high-mountain chalet, new-built for warmth and comfort. Chatty, gregarious, motherly Fiona serves real English tea with luscious brownies; a chef takes care of hearty meals in winter. Fancy fabrics and animal prints stand out among traditional English furniture and family ornaments; two wood-burners warm the generous living area. Kids can hide in the snug while you warm your toes in the hot tub or sauna. A wraparound balcony lets you drink in sunlight and alpine views: Mont Blanc is a mile as the crow flies. There's skiing a short hop away and hiking paths outside the door.

Price	€100-€120.
Rooms	5: 3 doubles, 2 twins/doubles.
Meals	Dinner with wine, €45. Packed lunch, €13.
Closed	Rarely.
Directions	A40 exit 22, D902 for Les Contamines; after La Tresse, right for Domaine Skiable; after 2nd bump, right Ch. de la Chovettaz d'en Haut; entrance on right by post box.

	Fiona Hopkinson Chalet Chovettaz, 30 chemin de La Chovettaz d'en Haut, 74170 Les Contamines Montjoie, Haute-Savoie
Tel	+33 (0)4 50 47 73 05
Mobile	+33 (0)6 27 39 02 70
Email	enquiries@skicontamines.com
Web	www.skicontamines.com

Entry 611 Map 12

Proveyroz

Madame has boundless energy, is a great walker, adores her mountain retreat in this lovely valley and cooks very well indeed. Her chalet rooms, all wood-clad of course, are bright and welcoming in blue, white and orange; they have unusually high ceilings, good storage and plenty of space. In the open-plan living area, huge windows open to a small sun-soaked terrace and a little garden while the mixture of old and modern furniture plus bits and pieces of all sorts gives the whole place a comfortable, family feel. Paragliding is the big thing round here, Annecy is close and Geneva an hour away.

La Touvière

Mountains march past Mont Blanc and over into Italy, cows graze in the foreground, the place is perfect for exploring this walkers' paradise. Myriam, bubbly and easy, adores having guests with everyone joining in the lively, light-hearted family atmosphere. In the typical old unsmart farmhouse, the cosy family room is the hub of life. Marcel is part-time home improver, part-time farmer (just a few cows now). One room has a properly snowy valley view, the other overlooks the owners' second chalet, let as a gîte; both are a decent size, simple but not basic, while shower rooms are spotless. Remarkable value.

Price	€52.
Rooms	2: 1 double; 1 triple with separate wc.
Meals	Dinner with wine, €20.
Closed	Rarely.
Directions	From Annecy D909 to Thônes; D12 for Serraval & D16 Manigod; 200m after 'Welcome to Manigod' sign, left at cross; chalet on left.

Price	€55.
Rooms	2 doubles.
Meals	Restaurant 3km.
Closed	Rarely.
Directions	From Albertville D1212 for Megève 21km; after Flumet, left at Panoramic Hotel; follow signs to La Touvière.

Josette Barbaud
Proveyroz,
74230 Manigod,
Haute-Savoie

Tel	+33 (0)4 50 44 95 25
Email	josette.barbaud@sfr.fr
Web	josette.barbaud.free.fr

Marcel & Myriam Marin-Cudraz
La Touvière,
73590 Flumet,
Savoie

Tel	+33 (0)4 79 31 70 11
Email	marcel.marin-cudraz@wanadoo.fr

Entry 612   Map 12

Entry 613   Map 12

Rhône Valley - Alps

Chalet Pecchio

Half way up the Tarentaise valley with peerless views, the new chalet in classic Savoie style is equally arresting inside: whole larch timbers limed white, heavenly beds covered in luxurious linen, smart rugs on terracotta, touches of gingham, perfect bathrooms. Reclaimed doors and armoires add to the rustic charm, wonderful in any season. Snowy slopes are a (free) ten-minute shuttle, tiny Le Miroir is as quaint as can be, Sainte Foy is just down the hill. Return to deep baths and Margaret's beautiful food served at the big table. Heart-warming, thanks to these delightful hosts, who live below. *Bike trails from the door.*

Price	€100–€150 (summer). Whole chalet available in winter.
Rooms	4: 2 doubles, 1 twin/double, 1 twin (2 rooms sharing shower).
Meals	Dinner with wine, €30.
Closed	B&B in summer, catered in winter.
Directions	From Albertville N90 to Moutiers & Bourg St Maurice; D902 to Ste Foy Tarantaise, thro' La Masure village, right to Le Miroir. Chalet on 2nd hairpin bend.

Margaret Margetts & Nick Kay
Chalet Pecchio,
Le Miroir,
73640 Ste Foy Tarentaise, Savoie

Tel	+33 (0)4 79 06 48 74
Mobile	+33 (0)6 10 52 53 21
Email	margaret@chalet-pecchio.com
Web	www.chalet-pecchio.com

Entry 614   Map 12

Rhône Valley - Alps

Maison Coutin

A year-round Alpine dream. In summer it's all flowers, birds and rushing streams, even a resident eagle. in winter you can ski cross-country, snow-walk or take the ski lift, 500m away, to the vast ski field of Les Arcs. La Plagne and Val d'Isère aren't far. Delicious, mostly organic, food is cooked in the wood-fired oven. Your friendly, dynamic young hosts cater for children: early suppers, three of their own as playmates, and Claude will babysit in the evening. View-filled bedrooms, a smallish comfortable dayroom with a fridge and a deeply eco-friendly ethos. *Discount on ski hire & passes.*

Ethical Collection: Environment & Food. See page 410 for details.

Price	€56–€62.
Rooms	3: 1 triple, 2 suites (1 for 4, 1 for 4-6).
Meals	Dinner with wine, €20. Child €7–€15. Restaurant 200m.
Closed	Rarely.
Directions	From Albertville N90 to Moutiers; on for Bourg St Maurice. Right D87E to Peisey Nancroix; left to Peisey centre; follow 3 green arrows; 9km from main road to house.

Claude Coutin & Franck Chenal
Maison Coutin,
Chemin de la Fruitière,
73210 Peisey Nancroix, Savoie

Tel	+33 (0)4 79 07 93 05
Mobile	+33 (0)6 14 11 54 65
Email	maison-coutin@orange.fr
Web	www.maison-coutin.fr

Entry 615   Map 12

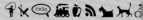

Rhône Valley - Alps

Chalet Colinn

Mylène and Elizabeth love the outdoors, hence their five-year fight to reincarnate a fallen ruin as a luxury mountain retreat. Join them for gourmet dinner under soaring, raftered ceilings in the grand living space which hovers above Tignes dam. Or soak in the terrace hot tub under the stars; there's a sauna too. Urban rusticity, mountain chic: the place reeks Italian style yet is impossibly hidden in this tiny hamlet. For daytime adventure: the slopes at Val d'Isère, or Tignes, or the Vanoise park. Just ask Elizabeth, off-piste skier extraordinaire. *Snow tyres/chains recommended in winter. Ask about ski lessons.*

Price	€90-€280.
Rooms	5: 3 twins/doubles, 2 triples.
Meals	Dinner €35. Wine from €13.
Closed	Rarely.
Directions	From Bourg St Maurice D102 for Val d'Isère; D902 past Barrage de Tignes; after 1st avalanche tunnel, left for Le Franchet. Chalet in hamlet up narrow path on right.

	Elizabeth Chabert & Mylène Charrière
	Chalet Colinn,
	Le Franchet de Tignes, BP 125,
	73150 Val d'Isère, Savoie
Tel	+33 (0)4 79 06 26 99
Email	contact@chaletcolinn.com
Web	www.chaletcolinn.com

Entry 616   Map 12

Rhône Valley - Alps

Le Traversoud

Rooms are named after painters; lovely 'Cézanne' lies under the eaves on the top floor. Nathalie, warm, bright and amusing, and attentive Pascal welcome you to their farmhouse, guide you up the outside stairs to colourful, comfortable bedrooms and spotless shower rooms (a sauna, too) and treat you to some of the best home cooking in France, served at a long table; even the brioche is homemade. The garden overflows with grass and trees, crickets chirrup, the Bernese Mountain dog bounds, the donkeys graze and the exuberant courtyard is a safe space for your children to join theirs. Wonderful, informal B&B.

Price	€56.
Rooms	3: 1 twin, 2 family rooms for 3.
Meals	Dinner with wine, €25.
Closed	Rarely.
Directions	A43 exit 9 at La Tour du Pin, thro' town D1516 left thro' St Clair de la Tour. At church left for Faverges 4km; left for Dolomieu; after 2km right at junc., signed.

	Nathalie & Pascal Deroi
	Le Traversoud,
	484 chemin Sous l'École,
	38110 Faverges de la Tour, Isère
Tel	+33 (0)4 74 83 90 40
Mobile	+33 (0)6 07 11 99 42
Email	deroi.traversoud@orange.fr
Web	www.le-traversoud.com

Entry 617   Map 11

Rhône Valley - Alps

Longeville

There is a gentle elegance about this house and the people who live in it, including three sleek cats and two friendly dogs. Of Scots and Irish origin, the Barrs have spent their adult years in France running a wooden toy business. Their love for this 1750s farmhouse shows in their artistic touch with decorating, their mix of old and modern furniture, their gorgeous big bedrooms, done in soft pale colours that leave space for the views that rush in from the hills. A high place of comfort and civilised contact where dinner in the airy white living room is a chance to get to know your kind, laid-back hosts more fully.

Price	€50–€80.
Rooms	2 twins/doubles.
Meals	Dinner with wine, €25.
Closed	Rarely.
Directions	From A43 exit 8; N85 through Nivolas; left D520 for Succieu 2km; left D56 thro' Succieu for St Victor 3km; sign for Longeville on right; farm at top of steep hill.

Mary & Greig Barr
Longeville,
5 Longeville,
38300 Succieu, Isère
Tel   +33 (0)4 74 27 94 07
Email   mary.barr@wanadoo.fr

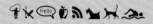

Rhône Valley - Alps

Domaine de Gorneton

The most caring of B&B owners: he, warmly humorous and humble about his excellent cooking; she, generous and outgoing. Built high on a hill as a fort in 1646, beside the spring that runs through the magnificent garden (a genuine Roman ruin, too), their superb old house is wrapped round a green-clad courtyard. Inside, levels change, vast timbers span the dining room, country antiques sprawl by the fire in the salon. In an outside single-storey building are traditional, rather sombre guest rooms with pristine bathrooms – and a bedhead from Hollywood in the best room. Family friendliness in deep country 15 minutes from Lyon.

Price	€120–€180.
Rooms	4: 3 doubles, 1 suite for 4.
Meals	Dinner with wine, €40.
Closed	Rarely.
Directions	From A7, A46 or A47 exit Chasse sur Rhône; through big Centre Commercial; left after Casino supermarket under railway; left then right for Trembas. (Will fax map or guide you to house.)

M & Mme Fleitou
Domaine de Gorneton,
712 chemin de Violans,
38670 Chasse sur Rhône, Isère
Tel   +33 (0)4 72 24 19 15
Email   gorneton@wanadoo.fr
Web   www.gorneton.com

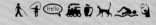

Rhône Valley - Alps

Château de Pâquier

Old, mighty, atmospheric – yet so homely. Hélène teaches cookery and Jacques spit-roasts poultry in the huge dining room fireplace, then they join you for dinner. Her modernised 17th-century tower kitchen (wood-fired range, stone sink, cobbled floor) is where she makes her bread, honey, jams and walnut aperitif. Wine is from the Rossis' own vineyard near Montpellier. Enormous rooms, high heavy-beamed ceilings, large windows with sensational valley views; terraced gardens and animals; bedrooms (handsome wardrobes, under-floor heating) up an ancient spiral staircase that sets the imagination reeling.

Ethical Collection: Food.
See page 410 for details.

Price	€70.
Rooms	5: 2 doubles, 2 twins, 1 family room.
Meals	Dinner with wine, €26.
Closed	Rarely.
Directions	From Grenoble A51 exit 12; D1075 for 11km; at r'bout left to St Martin de la Cluze; château signs in village.

Jacques & Hélène Rossi
Château de Pâquier,
Chemin du Château,
38650 St Martin de la Cluze, Isère
Tel   +33 (0)4 76 72 77 33
Email   chateau.de.paquier@free.fr
Web   chateau.de.paquier.free.fr

Entry 620   Map 11

Rhône Valley - Alps

Les Marais

Opt for the simple country life at this friendly farm, which has been in the family for over 100 years and has returned to organic methods. A couple of horses, a few hens, and, when there's a full house, beautiful meals of regional recipes served family-style, with homemade chestnut cake and 'vin de noix' aperitif. Monsieur collects old farming artefacts and Madame, although busy, always finds time for a chat. The bedrooms are in a separate wing with varnished ceilings, antique beds, some florals; baths are old-fashioned pink, new showers delight Americans. At the foot of the Vercors range, French charm, utter peace.

Ethical Collection: Environment & Food.
See page 410 for details.

Price	€50-€54.
Rooms	4: 1 double, 1 twin, 1 triple, 1 family room.
Meals	Dinner with wine, €17.
Closed	Rarely.
Directions	From Romans D538 for Chabeuil. Leaving Alixan left by Boulangerie for St Didier; left again, Chambres d'Hôtes St Didier signs for 3km; farm on left.

Christiane & Jean-Pierre Imbert
Les Marais,
26300 St Didier de Charpey,
Drôme
Tel   +33 (0)4 75 47 03 50
Mobile   +33 (0)6 27 32 23 65
Email   imbert.jean-pierre@wanadoo.fr
Web   pagesperso-orange.fr/les-marais

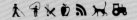

Entry 621   Map 11

Chambedeau

Madame's kindliness infuses her home, a double time warp that's coy about age and charms. Her eventful life has nourished a wicked sense of humour and she's a natural storyteller (she'll show you the pictures too). She may dislike housework but she's worth the detour. The fading carpets and small, old-tiled shower rooms become incidental after a while; enjoy, instead, her company, the cheap and cheerful value of the homely bedrooms, the terraces, the peace and birdlife of the leafy garden sheltering the house from the road, and breakfast (homemade jams and cake, cheese) where the table is a picture in itself. Simply unwind.

Les Péris

Here is the grandmother we all dream of, a woman who cossets her guests, puts flowers and sweets in the bedrooms and sends you off with walnuts from the farm. In the family for ten generations, the old stone house facing the mountains is a happy and delightful home. Join family, friends and guests round the long kitchen table for walnut cakes at breakfast and daughter Élisabeth's delicious *menu curieux* that uses forgotten vegetables. Roomy, old-fashioned bedrooms with armoires breathe a comfortable, informal air. Great for kids: a garden for wild flowers and a duck pond for splashing in.

Price	€57-€60.	Price	€50.
Rooms	2: 1 twin/double; 1 twin with separate shower.	Rooms	3 triples.
Meals	Restaurants 2km.	Meals	Dinner with wine, €17.
Closed	Rarely.	Closed	Rarely.
Directions	From A7 Valence Sud exit A49 for Grenoble; exit 33 right D538A for Beaumont, 2.6km; right at sign Chambres d'Hôtes & Chambedeau; 800m from main road on twisting track, 2nd house on right.	Directions	From A7 exit Valence Sud on D68 to Chabeuil. There, cross river; left on D154 for Combovin 5km; signed, on left.

Lina de Chivré-Dumond
Chambedeau,
26760 Beaumont lès Valence,
Drôme
Tel   +33 (0)4 75 59 71 70
Mobile   +33 (0)6 60 99 18 78
Email   linadechivredumond@yahoo.fr

Madeleine Cabanes
Les Péris,
D154 - Route de Combovin,
26120 Châteaudouble, Drôme
Tel   +33 (0)4 75 59 80 51

Rhône Valley - Alps

La Moutière

Surrounded by gorgeous gardens, the bastide sits large and square amid old outbuildings concealing perfectly converted gîtes. Bare stone façades and limestone trims under a Provençal roof set the tone for simple, fresh, uncluttered interiors: new limestone floors, white furniture, neutral tones and flashes of unexpected colour. Bedding is sumptuous, bathrooms fashionably funky, views from the beautiful pale blue pool glide pleasingly over rows of poplars and fields of lavender. Your wonderfully exuberant Belgian hostess gives convivial weekly dinner parties under the chestnut trees during high season. Divine.

Price	€100-€120.
Rooms	3 twins/doubles.
Meals	Dinner €30. Guest kitchen. Restaurant 3km.
Closed	Rarely.
Directions	A7 exit 18 to N7, 2km for Nyons; D133 & D547 for Grignan; D71 thro' Chamaret; D471 for Colonzelle; r'bout Montségur Richerenches 1.4 km; left, 300m house on left.

Françoise Lefebvre
La Moutière,
Quartier Moutière,
26230 Colonzelle, Drôme

Tel	+33 (0)4 75 46 26 88
Mobile	+33 (0)6 76 94 90 25
Email	lamoutiere@gmail.com
Web	www.lamoutiere.com

Entry 624   Map 16

Photo: Lesley Chalmers

Provence – Alps – Riviera

Photo: www.istockphoto.com

Provence - Alps - Riviera

Provence - Alps - Riviera

Le Château de Ribiers

History comes alive in this exquisitely restored 12th-century fortress, part of the town ramparts. The hospitality of artist Sally and wine consultant Frédéric includes her inspired cuisine from regional organic produce and his perfect wines from the cellar. Snug bedrooms leap with old beams, vaulted stone ceilings, luscious colours and fine hand-embroidered linens. All rooms face a riot of greenery, while the sun-drenched roof garden overlooks a wide sweep of Alps and village rooftops, all a-glitter at night. Food and wine evenings and tours, sports for all seasons – huge fun. *Min. two nights. Over 12s welcome.*

Mas St Joseph

Come for the view of row upon row of peaks fading into the distance, the walking, the welcome and the Slow Food. Hélène and Olivier bought the old *mas* on sloping terrain, restored it with love, then moved in and began taking guests. Olivier is the walker and knows all the trails; the countryside is spectacular. One bedroom has the old bread oven in the corner; another, in the stable, the old manger to prove it; all are rustic and charming. Delicious, delightful table d'hôtes is held on the terrace in warm weather or in the lovely old barn. Further treats: massage treatments, a hot tub and a pool. And oh, those views!

Price	€70–€100. Extra beds.
Rooms	4: 3 doubles, 1 twin/double.
Meals	Dinner with wine, €28. Packed lunch €10.
Closed	Rarely.
Directions	From Sisteron D948 to Ribiers; there, left at fountain into Rue du Château; continue straight into château courtyard.

Price	€63. Triple €82. Suites €101. Gypsy caravan €63.
Rooms	5: 1 double, 1 triple, 2 suites for 4, gypsy caravan for 2.
Meals	Dinner with wine, €22.
Closed	Mid-November to March.
Directions	From Châteauneuf Val St Donat for St Étienne les Orgues 1.5km; house on bend, on right above road; steep 100m drive to house.

Sally & Frédéric Feyler
Le Château de Ribiers,
5 cour du Château,
05300 Ribiers, Hautes-Alpes
Tel   +33 (0)9 62 28 01 25
Mobile   +33 (0)6 31 55 03 85
Email   bienvenue@chateauderibiers.com
Web   www.chateauderibiers.com

Hélène & Olivier Lenoir
Mas St Joseph,
04200 Châteauneuf Val St Donat,
Alpes-de-Haute-Provence
Tel   +33 (0)4 92 62 47 54
Email   contact@lemassaintjoseph.com
Web   www.lemassaintjoseph.com

Entry 625   Map 16

Entry 626   Map 16

Provence - Alps - Riviera

Le Jas du Bœuf

Here is Haute Provence bliss surrounded for miles by forests, vineyards and lavender and with stunning views of the Lubéron. Les and Wendy have restored the big 17th-century farmhouse to perfection and love having guests. Choose between traditional bedrooms in the house and two breathtakingly modern, wood and glass poolside bungalows that pull the outside in. Star attractions are Wendy's art and design courses, yet a multitude of sports, delightful villages, gardens and markets call you. Then chill out by the infinity pool or in the exotic sunken siesta house. Exquisitely minimalist, wonderfully welcoming. *Painting courses.*

Price	€80-€115. Bungalows €95-€130.
Rooms	5: 3 doubles, 2 bungalows for 2.
Meals	Dinner €25. Summer kitchen. Restaurants 3-8km.
Closed	Rarely.
Directions	From Apt N100 to Forcalquier; left D950/D12 to St Étienne les Orgues; D951 thro' Cruis, right fork leaving village 3km; signed track on left; 800m.

	Wendy & Les Watkins Le Jas du Bœuf, Lieu-dit Parrot, 04230 Cruis, Alpes-de-Haute-Provence
Tel	+33 (0)4 92 75 84 78
Email	jasduboeuf@googlemail.com
Web	www.colourdimensions.com

Entry 627 Map 16

Provence - Alps - Riviera

Ferme de Félines

Southern energies, wild evergreen hills and strong light push in through big architect's windows to meet the sober cool of northern design in a thrilling encounter. Small, wiry and full of laughter, Rita has a passion for this house, her land and the wildlife she fights to preserve. She may adorn your space of purity with one perfect flower in a glass cylinder, some fruit and a candle. Linen, beds, taps and towels are all top quality, her generosity is warm, her breakfasts (fruit smoothies, goat's cheese straight from the shepherd) make the heart sing, her vast living room is a treat. And you can swim in the lake. *Min. two nights.*

Price	€125-€150.
Rooms	3 doubles.
Meals	Restaurants in Moustiers.
Closed	Rarely.
Directions	From Aix A51 exit Manosque for Gréoux; D952 to Riez, Moustiers; D952 for Castellane, 6km of steep unmade track to black sign on right.

	Rita Lambrechts Ferme de Félines, Route des Gorges du Verdon, 04360 Moustiers Ste Marie, Alpes-de-Haute-Provence
Tel	+33 (0)4 92 74 64 19
Mobile	+33 (0)6 81 50 60 33
Email	ferme-de-felines@wanadoo.fr
Web	www.ferme-de-felines.com

Entry 628 Map 16

Provence - Alps - Riviera

La Belle Cour

The moment you enter the gorgeous big courtyard you feel at home. Angela and Rodney's welcome is second to none: cheerful and open, warm and humorous. On medieval foundations, the 18th-century house is all exposed stone and beams, its décor traditional/rustic; you'll love the embracing living rooms, the open fire, the cosy library with surround-sound music. Bedrooms overlook the courtyard and have private staircases; wallow in luscious fabrics and colours, an intriguing long wall map of London in 1647, exquisite Chinese silk paintings. Truly special, and in a friendly village with restaurants and a swimming pool.

L'École Buissonnière

A stone jewel set in southern lushness and miles of green vines and purple hills. Country furniture – a particularly seductive choice of Provençal chairs – is polished with wax and time; big whitewashed bedrooms are freshly sober; birds sing to the tune of the aviary outside. One balconied bedroom, in the mezzanined old barn, has a saddle and a herdsman's hat from a spell in the Camargue; ask about John's travels. He rightly calls himself a Provençal English-man, Monique is warmly welcoming too, theirs is a happy house, where German is also spoken. Wonderful Vaison la Romaine is four miles away.

Price	€75.
Rooms	2: 1 double, 1 triple.
Meals	Restaurants 200m.
Closed	November-March.
Directions	From Apt D900 (ex-N100) 18km to Céreste; right at small r'bout in village; immed. left Place Daniel Vigouroux; La Belle Cour on left when facing Boulangerie Barret.

Price	€58-€68.
Rooms	3: 2 doubles, 1 family room.
Meals	Guest kitchen. Restaurant in village, 1km.
Closed	Mid-November to March.
Directions	From A7 exit Bollène for Nyons D94; D20 right for Vaison & Buisson; cross River Aygues; left for Villedieu & Cave la Vigneronne, D51 & D75 for 2.2km.

Rodney & Angela Heath
La Belle Cour,
Place Daniel Vigouroux, 04280 Céreste,
Alpes-de-Haute-Provence
Tel +33 (0)4 92 72 48 76
Email angela.heath@wanadoo.fr
Web www.labellecour.com

Monique Alex & John Parsons
L'École Buissonnière,
D75, 84110 Buisson,
Vaucluse
Tel +33 (0)4 90 28 95 19
Email ecole.buissonniere@wanadoo.fr
Web www.buissonniere-provence.com

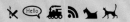

Entry 629   Map 16

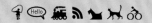

Entry 630   Map 16

L'Évêché

Narrow, cobbled streets lead to this fascinating and beautifully furnished house that was once part of the 17th-century Bishop's Palace. The Verdiers are charming, relaxed, cultured hosts – he an architect/builder, she a teacher. The white walls of the guest sitting room-library are lined with modern art and framed posters, and the cosy, quilted bedrooms, all whitewashed beams and terracotta floors, have a serene Provençal feel. Views fly over beautiful terracotta rooftops from the balconied suite, and handsome breakfasts are served on the terrace, complete with exceptional views to the Roman bridge.

Les Convenents

For the delightful Sarah, a refugee from spinning plates in London, welcoming visitors in her haven is as natural as breathing. Five former workers' cottages have become a relaxing Provençal *mas* where space and simplicity leave old stones and renovated timbers to glow and there's a typically lovely vine-shaded terrace. Small explosions of cushions and paintings bring fresh white walls and fabrics alive; more modernity in good clean bathrooms and fine finishes. Sarah, who was in catering, rules in the kitchen. She supports the local economy, uses the village shops, enjoys the community. *Sawday self-catering also.*

Price	€80–€88. Suite €110–€135.
Rooms	5: 3 twins/doubles, 2 suites for 2-3.
Meals	Restaurants nearby.
Closed	2 weeks in both November & December.
Directions	From Orange, D975 to Vaison. In town, follow Ville Médiévale & Castle signs.

Price	€90–€110.
Rooms	2 doubles.
Meals	Dinner with wine, €32.
Closed	November–March, except by arrangement.
Directions	From Orange D976 to Gap & Ste Cécile les Vignes; D11 left to Uchaux; through village, between Les Farjons & Rochegude, 3km. Les Covenents on left; signed.

	Aude & Jean-Loup Verdier
	L'Évêché,
	14 rue de l'Evêché, Cité Médiévale,
	84110 Vaison la Romaine, Vaucluse
Tel	+33 (0)4 90 36 13 46
Mobile	+33 (0)6 03 03 21 42
Email	eveche@aol.com
Web	www.eveche.com

	Sarah Banner
	Les Convenents,
	84100 Uchaux,
	Vaucluse
Tel	+33 (0)4 90 40 65 64
Email	sarahbanner@orange.fr
Web	www.lesconvenents.com

La Maison aux Volets Rouges B&B

Step off the street into the 'red-shuttered' house to be wrapped in its warm embrace. Rooms are big with tiled floors, beams and antiques; family photographs line the stairs; there's an open fire for cool days, a courtyard for warm ones. High-beamed bedrooms have good storage and individual touches – a brass bed, an arched window, a teddy bear on the baby's bed. Garden and pool are a three-minute walk, restaurants a short stroll. Borrow a bike, play tennis at the local club (no charge), drop in on the glories of Avignon and Aix. Delightful, energetic Brigitte has impeccable English and breakfasts are delicious.

La Ravigote

Madame and her house both smile gently. Hers a simple, authentic Provençal farmhouse that has escaped the vigorous renovator, its courtyard shaded by a lovely lime tree. Once a teacher in Africa and elegantly shy, Madame considers dinners with her guests, in dining room or courtyard, as the best part of B&B – her meals are showcases for local specialities. The interior is a bright version of traditional French country style with old family furniture and tiled floors. Set among vineyards below the Montmirail hills, it has soul-pleasing views across the surrounding unspoilt country. *Minimum two nights.*

Price	€65-€85.
Rooms	2: 1 double; 1 double with separate shower.
Meals	Restaurants within walking distance.
Closed	Rarely.
Directions	A7 exit 19 to Bollène; right at r'bout for Nyons 1km; left at x-roads for Nyons; cont. to small road on right D12 for Uchaux; 5km to Les Farjons; house on right.

Price	€52.
Rooms	4: 1 double, 2 twins, 1 family room.
Meals	Dinner with wine, €23.
Closed	Mid-October to March.
Directions	From Carpentras D7 N through Aubignan & Vacqueyras; fork right (still D7) for Sablet; right 500m after Cave Vignerons Gigondas; signed.

	Brigitte Woodward
	La Maison aux Volets Rouges B&B, Les Farjons, 84100 Uchaux, Vaucluse
Tel	+33 (0)4 90 40 62 18
Email	b.woodward@hotmail.fr
Web	www.lamaisonauxvoletsrouges.com

	Sylvette Gras
	La Ravigote, 84190 Gigondas, Vaucluse
Tel	+33 (0)4 90 65 87 55
Mobile	+33 (0)6 87 21 96 39
Email	info@laravigote.com
Web	www.laravigote.com

Provence - Alps - Riviera

Le Clos St Saourde

Indoors embraces out here, spectacularly: many walls, ceilings, even some furniture, are sculpted from solid rock. The décor is minimalist and luxurious with a flurry of natural materials but lots of quirky touches, too: the wrought-iron lamps and lanterns, the clever lighting, the solar pools. Indulge yourself in a private spa – exclusive to treehouse guests – or in a breathtaking grotto bathroom... enjoy an autumn aperitif by the fire in a spacious suite. This lovely young family will tell you about the wealth of activities in their exquisite area, with rock-climbing and massage on request. Dinners are superb.

Price	€170–€430.
Rooms	5: 2 doubles, 2 suites for 2-3 (with sofabeds), 1 treehouse for 2.
Meals	Dinner with wine, €40 (Friday only). Summer kitchen. Restaurant 2km.
Closed	Rarely.
Directions	A7 exit 23 Avignon N; D942 for Carpentras exit Sarrians, D31; thro' Beaumes de V to Rte de Caromb; right 200m after Domaine de la Pigeade entrance; 500m to Le Clos car park.

Jérôme & Géraldine Thuillier
Le Clos St Saourde,
Route de St Véran,
84190 Beaumes de Venise, Vaucluse
Tel   +33 (0)4 90 37 35 20
Email   contact@leclossaintsaourde.com
Web   www.leclossaintsaourde.com

Entry 635   Map 16

Provence - Alps - Riviera

Le Mas de la Pierre du Coq

What's especially nice about this 17th-century farmhouse is that it hasn't been over-prettified. Instead, it has the friendly, informal elegance of a house that's lived in and loved; grey-painted beams, soft stone walls, seductive bathrooms. The Lorenzes loved it the moment they saw it; it reminded gentle Stéphan of the house he grew up in. Bustling Martine starts your day with a terrific breakfast, Stéphan shows you the walks from the door. The gardens, sweet with roses, oleanders and lavender, are shaded by ancient trees and the pool and views are glorious. Stay for as long as you can: dinners are excellent, too.

Price	€120–€140. Suite €180.
Rooms	3: 1 double, 1 twin, 1 suite for 4.
Meals	Dinner with wine, €35.
Closed	August.
Directions	From Aubignan for Carpentras 2.5km; right at junction; immed. right Chemin de Loriol to Mazan; follow road, house up above on right after bridge.

Stéphan & Martine Lorenz
Le Mas de la Pierre du Coq,
434 chemin de Sauzette,
84810 Aubignan, Vaucluse
Tel   +33 (0)4 90 67 31 64
Mobile   +33 (0)6 76 81 95 09
Email   lorenz.stephane@wanadoo.fr
Web   www.masdelapierreducoq.com

Entry 636   Map 16

Provence - Alps - Riviera

Le Clos du Rempart

Outdoors drifts in so naturally, the lovely salon sweeping beyond the wide doors into a breathtaking suntrap courtyard. Relax among greenery galore with burbling fountain, wisteria-dripped pergola and Middle-Eastern niches. Or the cool of the salon, an oasis of white set off by rich reds, exotic touches, modern art. Attractive bedrooms – one large, one smaller – overlook the courtyard, where birdsong is balm to the soul: Aïda feeds the birds. Her origins and travels are reflected in her décor – and in the buzzing university neighbourhood within the old walls. Avignon's vast treasures are minutes away. *Minimum two nights.*

Price	€125–€150. Whole house available.
Rooms	2 doubles.
Meals	Restaurants nearby.
Closed	Rarely.
Directions	From A7 D225 for Avignon Centre along Rhône to ramparts; left to 3rd lights, thro' Porte St Lazare; immed. right along Rue du Rempart St Lazare; Rue Crémade 4th on left.

	Aïda Assad
	Le Clos du Rempart,
	35-37 rue Crémade,
	84000 Avignon, Vaucluse
Tel	+33 (0)4 90 86 39 14
Mobile	+33 (0)6 84 64 83 68
Email	aida@closdurempart.com
Web	www.closdurempart.com

Entry 637   Map 16

Provence - Alps - Riviera

Le Mas de Miejour

Fred and Emma are wonderful hosts, sommeliers with a passion for wine who have escaped their city pasts. The guest bedrooms of their delightful old *mas* are all different, all serene: one on the ground floor with a painted brass bed and a white appliquéd bedcover, another with Senegalese fabrics; the family suite spreads itself over two floors. The land here is flat with a high water table so the gardens, sheltered by trees and waving maize, are ever fresh and green. It's a beautiful, artistic place to relax, your littl'uns can play with theirs, the pool is delicious and the food a delight. *Sawday self-catering also.*

Price	€80–€115. €120–€180 for 3-4.
Rooms	3: 2 doubles, 1 family suite for 4.
Meals	Dinner €22. Wine €12.
Closed	November–March, except by arrangement.
Directions	From A7 exit 23 for Carpentras & Entraigues; 1st exit D6 to Vedène & St Saturnin lès Avignon; left D28 for Le Thor 2km; right Chemin du Trentin.

	Frédéric Westercamp &
	Emmanuelle Diemont
	Le Mas de Miejour, 117 chemin
	du Trentin, 84250 Le Thor, Vaucluse
Tel	+33 (0)4 90 02 13 79
Email	masdemiejour@orange.fr
Web	www.masdemiejour.com

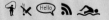

Entry 638   Map 16

Provence - Alps - Riviera

La Garance en Provence

Fields of maize wave in the sun, white canvas sails give shade by the pool: come for a slice of Provençal heaven. Régis from Paris and English Chantal share their deliciously renovated 'relais postal' with you; 17th-century beams are limewashed, new floors are tiled with old stone, antique pieces blend with ethnic touches, big bathrooms are rustic yet luxurious. Régis tells you where to go and what to do: antique fairs in Isle sur la Sorgues, opera in Avignon, bike rides from the door. Chantal concocts beautiful meals for the long table by the open fire... or under the awning in summer.

Price	€110-€125.
Rooms	5: 3 doubles, 1 twin, 1 triple.
Meals	Dinner with wine, €28.
Closed	Mid-November to mid-March.
Directions	A7 exit 23; right at r'bout for Carpentras; 1st exit to Vedène; D6 to St Saturnin lès Av.; left to Le Thor D28, 2.5km; right Route de St Saturnin 1km; Signed.

Chantal & Régis Sanglier
La Garance en Provence,
4010 route de St Saturnin lès Avignon,
84250 Le Thor, Vaucluse

Tel	+33 (0)4 90 33 72 78
Mobile	+33 (0)6 07 56 06 23
Email	contact@garance-provence.com
Web	www.garance-provence.com

Entry 639   Map 16

Provence - Alps - Riviera

La Nesquière

The gardens alone are worth the detour: trees and greenery galore, riots of roses, all flourishing in a huge many-terraced park by a river. The 18th-century farmhouse harbours a fine collection of antiques – one of Isabelle's passions – tastefully set off by lush indoor greenery and lovely old carpets on ancient tile floors. Softly old-elegant rooms have hand-embroidered fabrics and genuine old linens, including Provençal quilts – truly exquisite – with splashes of red, orange and beige against white backgrounds. Themed weekends, too (cookery, wine, embroidery), and a warm, gracious welcome from Isabelle and her family.

Price	€100-€130.
Rooms	5: 3 twin/doubles, 2 family suites.
Meals	Dinner with wine, €38.
Closed	Mid-December to mid-January.
Directions	A7 exit Avignon-Nord for Carpentras D942 5km. Just before bridge exit for Althen les Paluds D16 1.5km; left for Pernes les Fontaines D38 4.5km; La Nesquière on right.

Isabelle de Maintenant
La Nesquière,
5419 route d'Althen,
84210 Pernes les Fontaines, Vaucluse

Tel	+33 (0)4 90 62 00 16
Mobile	+33 (0)6 79 72 43 47
Email	lanesquiere@wanadoo.fr
Web	www.lanesquiere.com

Entry 640   Map 16

Provence - Alps - Riviera

Mas Pichony

Summer evenings are spent beneath the ancient spreading plane tree while sunset burnishes the vines beyond the slender cypresses and the old stones of the 17th-century *mas* breathe gold. Laetitia and Laurent have given the farmhouse style and charm, beautifying it with country antiques, books and vibrant colours. Two children, three horses (a corner of the hall is full of riding gear), a trio of cats and a lone dog complete the delightful picture. Laetitia serves good Provençal food at the big, convivial table; the terracotta-roofed area by the pool is a delicious place to sit and soak up daytime views.

Price	€88-€98.
Rooms	5: 3 doubles, 1 twin, 1 family room for 5.
Meals	Dinner with wine, €30.
Closed	November-March.
Directions	From Pernes les Fontaines D28 for St Didier. House on right, set back from road to St Didier.

Laetitia & Laurent Desbordes
Mas Pichony,
1454 route de St Didier,
84210 Pernes les Fontaines, Vaucluse
Tel   +33 (0)4 90 61 56 11
Email   mas-pichony@wanadoo.fr
Web   www.maspichony.com

Entry 641   Map 16

Provence - Alps - Riviera

Sous L'Olivier

Old stonework rules the scene, big arched openings have become dining-room windows, a stone hearth burns immense logs in winter, and all is set round a pretty courtyard. Charming young bon viveur Julien, apron-clad, started his career chez Paul Bocuse, a starred reference: breakfasts are sumptuous affairs and convivial dinners are worth a serious detour. Gentle Carole is behind the very fresh, Frenchly decorated bedrooms. Flat agricultural land spreads peacefully out around you; the big, child-friendly, saltwater pool is arched with canvas shading and surrounded by giant pots and plants. Lovely people, fabulous food.

Price	€90-€220.
Rooms	5: 3 doubles (2 with extra bed), 2 suites for 4.
Meals	Dinner with wine, €30.
Closed	Rarely.
Directions	A7 exit Avignon Sud; D900 for Apt, Digne, Sisteron 20km, do not turn off for Lagnes. 3km after Petit Palais turning, sign on right.

Carole, Julien, Hugo & Clovis Gouin
Sous L'Olivier,
Quartier le Petit Jonquier,
84800 Lagnes, Vaucluse
Tel   +33 (0)4 90 20 33 90
Email   souslolivier@orange.fr
Web   www.chambresdhotesprovence.com

Entry 642   Map 16

Villa La Lèbre

Well-travelled Charles speaks seven languages and is fascinating, Pierrette is a dear and both love doing B&B; come for an open-hearted welcome and a spotless guest bedroom. There's a big wall hanging from Bali over the bed, a private dressing room, a child's bed on the (steeply staired) mezzanine, air conditioning and a shower; you also have use of a fridge and may picnic in the garden, their passion, fabulous with roses, peonies and lavender. It's a modern house built of old stone in local style, surrounded by hills, woods and vineyards, and marvellous views towards Goult and the Lubéron. Great value for the area.

Price	€60. €70 for 3.
Rooms	1 triple.
Meals	Restaurants 5km.
Closed	Rarely.
Directions	From Avignon N7 for Marseille. At Caumont D973 for Gordes. At Imberts D207 & D148 to St Pantaléon; pass church (do not enter village); left after 100m; 3rd drive on right.

Pierrette & Charles Lawrence
Villa La Lèbre,
St Pantaléon,
84220 Gordes, Vaucluse
Tel   +33 (0)4 90 72 20 74
Email   jaclawrav@wanadoo.fr

Entry 643   Map 16

Le Mas del Sol

Wake to sumptuous views of hilltop villages, white-domed Mont Ventoux, medieval Bonnieux. Laze over breakfast fruits from the organic orchard before dipping into the pool and basking in the 360-degree panorama. This 18th-century stone farmhouse is a fresh, chilled, contemporary retreat. Ample bedrooms, nicely private, are simply furnished in sunny Provençal colours. Most have views, two have terraces, and there's a big bright sitting room for rainy days. The child-friendly owners may join you for excellent dinner or later on the terrace with its magical nightscape of twinkling lights – and festival fireworks!

Price	€85–€125.
Rooms	5: 1 double, 1 family room for 3, 2 family suites for 4, 1 suite for 2-4 (with sofabed).
Meals	Dinner with wine, €36.
Closed	December/January.
Directions	A7 exit 24 Avignon Sud for Apt; D900 right at r'bout D36 for Bonnieux 4km; right at sign; on for 1km, 2nd house on right.

Lucine & Richard Massol
Le Mas del Sol,
Le Pimbard,
84480 Bonnieux, Vaucluse
Tel   +33 (0)4 90 75 94 80
Email   lemasdelsol@gmail.fr
Web   www.mas-del-sol.com

Entry 644   Map 16

Mas de Bassette

A sophisticated simplicity reigns – you could be staying with friends. White walls and pale fabrics glow in the light filtering through the greenery outside: an ethereal picture of pure Provence. Your hosts are as charming and generous as their 15th-century *mas*, with its heavenly all-green and white garden where peacocks dally and a princely doberman keeps watch. Bedrooms are big and airy in whites and greys with old terracotta floors and touches of wicker. Philippe Starck chairs in the dining room, framed artists' letters in the handsome salon, an exquisite pool outside: it's worth every sou.

Mas des Tourterelles

Let the views wash over you. All around are peace and greenery, the little pool tucked into the garden; the beautiful, bustling centre of St Rémy is mere minutes away. The Aherns have thrown themselves into life in the Alpilles, Richard restoring the farmhouse with its honey-coloured stone, beams and tiles, Carrie adding the deceptively simple touches – pale walls, linen curtains, sisal carpets, splashes of colour. Bedrooms are restful spaces, utterly delightful. Cool off by the pool or under the vine-covered bower, look forward to dinner in town, a short stroll. *Min. two nights high season. Sawday self-catering also.*

Price	€130.
Rooms	2 doubles.
Meals	Restaurant 1km.
Closed	Rarely.
Directions	In Barbentane for Abbaye St Michel du Frigoulet; at windmill for tennis club; house entrance near club; signed.

Price	€90–€105.
Rooms	4: 3 doubles, 1 twin.
Meals	Restaurants within walking distance.
Closed	Rarely.
Directions	In St Rémy de Provence to Pl. de la République on one-way boulevard, exit right before school, past car park into Chemin de la Combette 400m; left up gravel track (after bins); sign by road.

Marie & François Veilleux
Mas de Bassette,
13750 Barbentane,
Bouches-du-Rhône
Tel   +33 (0)4 90 95 63 85
Email bassette2@wanadoo.fr
Web   www.masdebassette.com

Richard & Carrie Ahern
Mas des Tourterelles, 21 chemin
de la Combette, 13210 St Rémy
de Provence, Bouches-du-Rhône
Tel   +33 (0)4 32 60 19 93
Email richard.ahern@sfr.fr
Web   www.masdestourterelles.com

Entry 645   Map 16

Entry 646   Map 16

Mas Shamrock

A manicured farmhouse, its interior as southern cool as the welcome from its owners is sincerely Franco-Irish – John is relaxed and direct, Christiane is efficient and helpful. Natural stone, oak beams, terracotta floors and cool colours give a wonderfully fresh and open feel to the house, while bedrooms are light and airy with neat shower rooms. Outside, a delectable garden, centuries-old plane trees, a vine tunnel, three hectares of cypresses and a landscaped, secluded pool add to the magic. An oft-tinkled piano is there for you to play, and you can dine in lovely St Rémy. *Minimum two nights July/August. Massage.*

Price	€85–€115.
Rooms	5: 3 doubles, 1 twin, 1 family room for 3-4.
Meals	Restaurants in St Rémy.
Closed	November-Easter.
Directions	From St Rémy D571 for Avignon; over 2 r'bouts, left before 2nd bus stop (Lagoy), opp. 2nd yellow Portes Anciennes sign, Chemin des Lones; house 6th on right.

Christiane & John Walsh
Mas Shamrock, 1201 Chemin
des Lones et Velleron, 13210 St Rémy
de Provence, Bouches-du-Rhône

Tel	+33 (0)4 90 92 55 79
Email	mas.shamrock@orange.fr
Web	www.masshamrock.com

Entry 647   Map 16

Le Mas d'Arvieux

Carolyn and Alex, lovers of the outdoor life and well-travelled, have now put their elegant stamp on this generous manor house in beautiful Provence. Big bedrooms, one in the tower wing, one with a carved mezzanine, have beams and stone walls, fine old armoires, luxurious bathrooms, long views. There's a ground-floor room that's fine for wheelchair users and Arvieux' orchards drip with olives and luscious jam-worthy fruit. It's a great set-up for families in high season and for peace-loving couples out of it; cookery and art classes can be arranged. Marvellously close to Avignon's treasures. *Pool shared with gîte guests.*

Price	€85–€130.
Rooms	5: 2 doubles, 2 triples, 1 suite.
Meals	Occasional dinner with wine, €35. Restaurant 3km.
Closed	Rarely.
Directions	From Tarascon D970 for Avignon 5km; right at humpback bridge, signed before bridge.

Alex & Carolyn Miller
Le Mas d'Arvieux,
Route d'Avignon, 13150 Tarascon,
Bouches-du-Rhône

Tel	+33 (0)4 90 90 78 77
Mobile	+33 (0)6 28 74 20 65
Email	mas@arvieux-provence.com
Web	www.arvieux-provence.com

Entry 648   Map 16

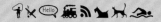

Le Mas d'Anez

A tree-lined drive and impressive wrought-iron gates lead to this impeccable 18th-century mansion. The Mantoux came here from Paris (a three-hour ride on the TGV, audibly close). He, knowledgeable and tri-lingual, swapped wine consultancy for olive oil; gentle Marie-Laure writes books on interior design and runs the odd course. The rooms are decorated with simple, assured elegance; the vast Provençal kitchen is a super place for breakfast. Beyond the stone wall that encloses house, garden and pool (reserved for the family at certain hours) stretch Thierry's olive groves. *Minimum two nights.*

24 rue du Château

On a medieval street near one of the finest castles in France, two *maisons de maître* are joined by an ochre-hued courtyard and a continuity of taste. It's an impeccable renovation that has kept all the soft patina of stone walls and tiles. No garden, but a courtyard for candlelit evenings and immaculate breakfasts. Calming, gracious bedrooms have fine old furniture and beams, perfect bathrooms, crisp linen. While you can be totally independent, your courteous hostess is relaxed and friendly and thoroughly enjoys her guests. Deeply atmospheric. *Minimum two nights.*

Price	€95–€110. Suite €190.
Rooms	3: 2 twin/doubles, 1 suite for 2-4.
Meals	Restaurant 1km.
Closed	Rarely.
Directions	From Avignon N570 for Tarascon; over Rognonas bridge, cont. for Tarascon; after Graveson r'bout D970 for Tarascon & Beaucaire 7km; entrance on right between trees and stone columns.

Price	€78–€95.
Rooms	4: 2 doubles, 2 twins.
Meals	Restaurants in town.
Closed	November-March.
Directions	In Tarascon centre take Rue du Château opposite château (well signed). No. 24 on right. Ask about parking.

Thierry & Marie-Laure Mantoux
Le Mas d'Anez,
Route d'Avignon, 13150 Tarascon,
Bouches-du-Rhône
Tel   +33 (0)4 90 91 73 98
Email   masdanez@wanadoo.fr
Web   www.masdanez.com

Martine Laraison
24 rue du Château,
13150 Tarascon, Bouches-du-Rhône
Tel   +33 (0)4 90 91 09 99
Email   ylaraison@gmail.com
Web   www.chambres-hotes.com

Mas de la Rabassière

Fanfares of lilies at the door, Haydn inside and 'mine host' smiling in his chef's apron. La Rabassière means 'where truffles are found' and dinners are a must. Vintage wines and a sculpted dancer grace the terrace table. Cookery classes with olive oil from his trees, jogging companionship, airport pick-up are all part of the elegant hospitality, aided by Thévi, Michael's serene assistant from Singapore. Big bedrooms and drawing room with roaring fire are comfortable in English country-house style: generous beds, erudite bookshelves, a tuned piano, Provençal antiques... and pool, tennis, croquet.

Ethical Collection: Environment & Food. See page 410 for details.

Price	€140.
Rooms	2 doubles.
Meals	Dinner with wine, €47.
Closed	Rarely.
Directions	A54 exit 13 to Grans on D19; right D16 to St Chamas; just before r'way bridge, left for Cornillon, up hill 2km; house on right before tennis court. Map sent on request.

Michael Frost
Mas de la Rabassière,
2137 chemin de la Rabassière,
13250 St Chamas, Bouches-du-Rhône
Tel   +33 (0)4 90 50 70 40
Email   michaelfrost@wanadoo.fr
Web   www.rabassiere.com

Entry 651   Map 16

Le Clos des Frères Gris

In through the gates of Hubert's exquisitely tended park and well-tree'd gardens; you'd never guess the centre of Aix en Provence was a seven-minute drive. Polyglot Caroline is a people person whose hospitality goes beyond her warm welcome. A passion for antiques is evident throughout her house, as is a talent with fabrics and colours; bedrooms combine comfort and cool elegance, fine linens, thick towels, special touches. Admire the rose and herb gardens on the way to boules or pool, then set off to discover the music and markets of Aix. A jewel of a bastide, a home from home and worth every sou. *Minimum two nights.*

Price	€110–€200.
Rooms	4 doubles.
Meals	Restaurant 1km.
Closed	31st October–1st April.
Directions	A8 exit 30 for Aix Pont de l'Arc/ Luynes. At r'bout, right D8, up hill 2.2km. Path on right, signed.

Caroline & Hubert Lecomte
Le Clos des Frères Gris, 2240 avenue
Fortune Ferrini, 13080 Luynes -
Aix en Provence, Bouches-du-Rhône
Tel   +33 (0)4 42 24 13 37
Email   freres.gris@free.fr
Web   freres.gris.free.fr

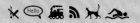

Entry 652   Map 16

Provence - Alps - Riviera

La Bartavelle

French Myriam and English Alastair, kind helpful hosts, live with exceptional views across the valley and sunrises framed by oak woods in their traditionally styled modern farmhouse, a testament to deft planning. Ground-floor bedrooms spread themselves round a lovely central pool and a walled terrace loaded with pot plants while an airy sitting room provides music, mod cons and reading space. Alastair knows the history of the region off by heart and every path and trail; trek up through the woods to the ridge-perched village of Mimet, with charming restaurants and views to Marseille and the sea.

Price	€70-€75.
Rooms	5: 2 doubles, 2 twins, 1 suite for 3.
Meals	Guest kitchen. Restaurant 3km.
Closed	Rarely.
Directions	Directions on booking.

	Myriam Boyd La Bartavelle, 348 Chemin des Amandiers, 13105 Mimet, Bouches-du-Rhône
Tel	+33 (0)4 42 58 85 90
Email	info@labartavelle.com
Web	www.labartavelle.com

Entry 653   Map 16

Provence - Alps - Riviera

Mas Ste Anne

On its hilltop on the edge of pretty Peynier, the old *mas* stands in glory before Cézanne's Montagne Sainte Victoire: pull the cowbell, pass the wooden doors and the red-shuttered farmhouse rises from beds of roses. Beautifully restored, it once belonged to the painter Vincent Roux and memories of his life live on, thanks to your gracious and very helpful hostess. The Roux room is the nicest, all beams, terracotta tiles, fantastic ochre/green bathroom down the hall and delicious garden view. The house has a wonderful old-fashioned patina and the gardens are perfectly kept. *Older children welcome. Min. two nights.*

Price	€90-€110.
Rooms	2: 1 double; 1 double with separate bath.
Meals	Summer kitchen. Restaurants in village.
Closed	1st three weeks in August.
Directions	From Aix on D6, 4km before Trets, right D57 to Peynier; up hill for Trets & Aubagne; left D908; right between Poste & Pharmacie. House 50m.

	Jacqueline Lambert Mas Ste Anne, 3 rue d'Auriol, 13790 Peynier, Bouches-du-Rhône
Tel	+33 (0)4 42 53 05 32
Email	stanpeynier@yahoo.fr
Web	www.stanpeynier.com

Entry 654   Map 16

La Royante

The Bishop of Marseille once resided in this delicious corner of paradise and you may sleep in the sacristy, wash by a stained-glass window, nip into the chapel/music room for a quick midnight pray. Your brilliant hosts, a cosmopolitan mix of talent, fantasy and joy, have got every detail right without a hint of pedantry. The stupendous big bedrooms throng with original features and Bernard's beloved antiques (the more old-fashioned St Wlodek is reached through its bathroom), leisurely breakfasts may come with apricots plucked from the tree. One of our absolute favourites. *Ask about gastronomic tours (min. 8).*

Ethical Collection: Environment.
See page 410 for details.

Price	€129–€159.
Rooms	4: 3 doubles, 1 triple.
Meals	Restaurant 1km.
Closed	Rarely.
Directions	Aix A8 for Nice; A52 Aubagne & Toulon, do not exit at Aubagne; A50 Marseille exit 5 La Valentine; keep right for Le Charrel 3km; after Légion Etrangère on left, 1st left D44a for Éourres; 1st right after bridge to La Royante; 800m.

	Xenia & Bernard Saltiel
	La Royante,
	Chemin de la Royante, 13400 Aubagne
	en Provence, Bouches-du-Rhône
Tel	+33 (0)4 42 03 83 42
Mobile	+33 (0)6 09 47 19 51
Email	contact@laroyante.com
Web	www.laroyante.com

Entry 655   Map 16

Le Clos de la Chèvre Sud

Carole's flair for design shows not only in the comfy, traditional décor but also in the wonderfully quirky touches such as the wok recycled as a bathroom basin. Colour-washed rooms are cosy and inviting, in beiges, ochres, reds, greys and blues. For summer, there's a broad sheltered terrace for breakfasting, dining, lazing and enjoying the views – the sea on one side, the forested hill on the other, a riot of flowering shrubs and trees in between. Patrice is a doctor and osteopath while Carole, a nurse, runs the spa and massage centre; both are charming and fun. Perfect – and there's a stunning pool.

Price	€85–€132.
Rooms	3: 2 doubles, 1 suite for 3.
Meals	Dinner €30. Wine list from €20.
Closed	Rarely.
Directions	From Marseille A50 exit 10 St Cyr for Bandol & Golf; left Chemin Naron; cont. past approx. 8 roads on left; left Chemin Pas Chèvre Sud; straight on.

	Patrice & Carole Zoro
	Le Clos de la Chèvre Sud,
	255 chemin du Pas de la Chèvre Sud,
	83740 La Cadière, Var
Tel	+33 (0)4 94 32 31 54
Mobile	+33 (0)6 83 98 98 48
Email	clochesud@wanadoo.fr
Web	www.closdelachevre.com

Entry 656   Map 16

Bastide Ste Trinide

You'll love the simple lines and bright, airy décor of this renovated 18th-century farmhouse that once belonged to Pascale's grandparents. Prepare to be seduced by reds, whites and chocolate touches, fine linens, exposed beams, a choice of terraces for cooling breezes. One delight is the captivating chapel across the courtyard, another is the vibrant art: walls throughout are splashed with the canvasses of a family friend. You'll also love the blissful quiet up here in the hills, though the beaches are minutes away. Walks, riding, golf, exotic gardens, zoo; let your charming young hosts help you explore.

45 boulevard des Pêcheurs

Looking from this perch past umbrella pines out over the town to the marina and the blue bay is a tonic served on your private terrace. The many-windowed space feels like a lookout tower, fittingly done in blue and white with a new parquet floor and good bathroom. Breakfast is served under the trumpet vine on the main terrace in the luxuriant garden with the pool. The sitting room, wide, welcoming and uncluttered, has nice old French furniture and ship's binoculars for the views, and it's a 15-minute walk to the centre. Claudine is active and attentive, Serge used to work in boats, both are helpful, unintrusive hosts.

Price	€70-€80.
Rooms	2: 1 double, 1 twin/double.
Meals	Restaurants nearby.
Closed	Rarely.
Directions	A50 exit 12 Bandol, Sanary; at r'bout 1st exit Le Castellet (Zoo); 1st right for Zoo; left Chemin Ste Trinide; straight 700m; right; immed. right into parking area.

Price	€75-€85.
Rooms	1 double.
Meals	Restaurants nearby.
Closed	Rarely.
Directions	From Toulon, at Lavandou r'bout St Glinglin 3rd exit 100m; left Rue Bois Notre Dame; left fork, right on 1st bend 500m; left Bd Gireliers; right at t-junc., Bd Pêcheurs.

Pascale Couture & Grégoire Debord
Bastide Ste Trinide,
1671 chemin Chapelle Ste Trinide,
83110 Sanary sur Mer, Var
Tel   +33 (0)4 94 34 57 75
Email   contact@bastidesaintetrinide.com
Web   www.bastidesaintetrinide.com

Claudine & Serge Draganja
45 boulevard des Pêcheurs,
Super-Lavandou,
83980 Le Lavandou, Var
Tel   +33 (0)4 94 71 46 02
Mobile   +33 (0)6 16 17 03 83
Email   draganja@orange.fr
Web   www.chambrehotes-draganja.com

Entry 657   Map 16

Entry 658   Map 16

La Maison de Rocbaron

You'll fall in love with this beautifully restored 19th-century stone bergerie set in a riot of greenery and flowers with terraces dotted about gardens and pool. Jeanne and Guy's welcome is warmly natural; he keeps guests happy over an aperitif, she produces a gourmet dinner not to be missed; it's one of those places where you feel you're part of the family. Various staircases lead to elegant and exquisite rooms where pinks, whites and floral prints reign. An early dip, a feast of a breakfast, and you're set up for the day's adventures. A magical place run by special people, in the heart of a lovely village.

La Cordeline

Owned by lawyers down the centuries, the fadingly elegant *hôtel particulier* stands in the quiet heart of the old town. Isabelle, a physiotherapist and keen cook, fell in love with it all, moved here in 2005 and now has a young family. One side looks over the street, the other over the walled garden (a fountained haven in the town centre) and you enter to warm old honeycomb tiles under a vaulted ceiling. The big bedrooms are being gradually updated, old-style charm giving way to a more modern take. In winter you can snuggle down by a log fire and read in peace. *Weekend packages include massage & beauty sessions.*

Price	€80–€125.
Rooms	5: 3 doubles, 2 suites.
Meals	Dinner with wine, €40.
Closed	Rarely.
Directions	A8 exit 35 Brignoles for Toulon; after Forcalqueiret D12 left to Rocbaron. House in centre of village, opp. Mairie.

Price	€70–€105.
Rooms	4: 3 doubles, 1 triple, all with separate wc.
Meals	Dinner with wine, €29.
Closed	Rarely.
Directions	From A8 exit 35 Brignoles; 2 r'bouts for Toulon; 3rd r'bout for Brignoles centre; right at lights Av Gustave Bret; 50m, car park on right, Rue des Cordeliers on left.

Jeanne Fischbach & Guy Laguilhemie
La Maison de Rocbaron,
3 rue St Sauveur,
83136 Rocbaron, Var

Tel   +33 (0)4 94 04 24 03
Email   contact@maisonderocbaron.com
Web   www.maisonderocbaron.com

Isabelle Konen-Pierantoni
La Cordeline,
14 rue des Cordeliers,
83170 Brignoles, Var

Tel   +33 (0)4 94 59 18 66
Email   lacordeline@wanadoo.fr
Web   www.lacordeline.com

La Grande Lauzade

This ancient monastery, bought at auction by Corine's great-grandfather, was a working wine estate. Now Corine and Thierry, extrovert musician, live here with their young family and pets, becoming ever more 'green' amid their wildish, well-tree'd grounds. Blues and whites predominate in big lofty rooms (some up twisty stairs) furnished with some exquisite and often fascinating pieces, such as the chicken-hatching box on legs, carved in fine wood. Distinct traffic hum from the terrace but so much to do on the spot: darts, table tennis, billiards, boules and pool… and convivial breakfasts each morning.

Un Air de Rien

Overlooking the plane-tree'd village square, this reverently renovated town hall is Provençal-perfect; bunting flutters, pétanque patonks, time slows to a sedate calm. Bedrooms are rustic chic – exposed brick, wrought-iron chandeliers, beamy ceilings – and bathrooms impress with solid marble basins, delicious smellies and sleek fixtures. Bright paintings add pools of colour. Both from Belgium, Lionel brings wine knowledge and humour, Caroline quietly cares for their guests and two small children. Their hospitality is reflected in beautiful breakfasts and the fine wine and tapas bistro. *Minimum two nights.*

Price	€95–€160.
Rooms	3: 1 double, 1 triple, 1 suite for 2-4.
Meals	Restaurants 1km.
Closed	Rarely.
Directions	A8 exit Le Luc; at r'bout D7 left for Toulon; at 4th 'Europe' r'bout, D97 left for Toulon; 2km after Le Luc, left at end of car park; road to La Grande Lauzade 'Le Prieuré'; park outside gates.

Price	€90–€105. Extra bed €15.
Rooms	2 doubles.
Meals	Tapas bar on site. Restaurants within walking distance.
Closed	December-February.
Directions	At Cuers, D14 through Pierrefeu du Var; in Collobrières, right into Place de la Libération.

Corine Varipatis
La Grande Lauzade,
83340 Le Luc en Provence,
Var
Tel +33 (0)4 94 60 74 35
Email contact@lagrandelauzade.com
Web www.lagrandelauzade.com

Lionel & Caroline Thomsin
Un Air de Rien,
3 place de la Libération,
83610 Collobrières, Var
Tel +33 (0)4 94 28 17 73
Email lionel@unairderien.com
Web www.unairderien.com

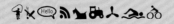

Entry 661   Map 16

Entry 662   Map 16

Provence - Alps - Riviera

Bastide des Hautes Moures

Colours rich with Mediterranean sunshine, a sure eye for stunning touches, a brilliant mix of furniture: this lovely house is a celebration of Catherine's love of colour, brocante and flawless workmanship. Delectable bathrooms by North African craftsmen are breathtaking. In the bedrooms there's space to waltz round the easy chairs, into and out of the walk-in wardrobe or through the blissful suite. Charming Angélique manages if needed, the chef does dinner, butterflies dance to the call of the cicadas beneath 300-year-old oaks. The wealth of Provence is here. *Children welcome for specific weeks. Sawday self-catering also.*

Price	€80–€150.
Rooms	4: 3 doubles, 1 suite for 3.
Meals	Dinner with wine, €34.
Closed	Rarely.
Directions	From A8 exit Le Luc & Le Cannet des Maures for Le Thoronet. Right on D84 for Vidauban 4.5km to Les Moures, right & 800m on to house.

	Catherine Debray
	Bastide des Hautes Moures,
	Quartier des Moures,
	83340 Le Thoronet, Var
Tel	+33 (0)4 94 60 13 36
Email	infos@bastidedesmoures.com
Web	www.bastidedesmoures.com

Entry 663   Map 16

Provence - Alps - Riviera

Domaine de la Blaque

The first and only property in the Var to be offically classified 'éco'! You are surrounded by nature at its best, and your lovely hosts have that artistic flair which puts the right things together naturally: palest pink-limed walls and white linen; old-stone courtyard walls with massed jasmine and honeysuckle; yoga groups and painters with wide open skies. Indeed, Jean-Luc is passionate about astronomy, Caroline is a photographer, they produce olives, truffles and timber, organise courses and love sharing their remote estate withlike-minded travellers. Each pretty, independent room has its own little terrace.

Ethical Collection: Environment.
See page 410 for details.

Price	€70–€90.
Rooms	2: 1 double, 1 twin, each with kitchenette.
Meals	Restaurants 2.5km.
Closed	Rarely.
Directions	A8 exit St Maximin; D560 before Barjols; at Brue Auriac D35 to Varages; sign on left leaving village for Tavernes; follow signs, partly unpaved track.

	Caroline & Jean-Luc Plouvier
	Domaine de la Blaque,
	83670 Varages, Var
Tel	+33 (0)4 94 77 86 91
Email	ploublaque@hotmail.com
Web	www.lablaque.com

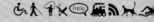

Entry 664   Map 16

Provence - Alps - Riviera

Domaine de St Ferréol

Readers write: "Armelle is wonderful". Breakfast is the highlight of her hospitality: she full of ideas for excursions, Monsieur happily sharing his knowledge of the area. They are a warm, lively and cultured couple, their working vineyard has a timeless feel, their wine tastings most civilised events. Glorious views to Pontevès castle from the first-class, authentically Provençal bedrooms; they and the breakfast room (with mini-kitchen) are in a separate wing but, weather permitting, breakfast is on the terrace. Peace and privacy in a beautiful old house, superb walking, an outdoor pool.

Price	€68-€80. Suite €98-€100.
Rooms	3: 2 twins/doubles, 1 suite for 4.
Meals	Kitchen available. Restaurant 1.5km.
Closed	Mid-November to February.
Directions	From A8 exit St Maximin la Ste Baume D560 to Barjols; D560 2km for Draguignan; entrance opp. D60 turning for Pontevès.

Guillaume & Armelle de Jerphanion
Domaine de St Ferréol,
83670 Pontevès,
Var

Tel	+33 (0)4 94 77 10 42
Email	saint-ferreol@wanadoo.fr
Web	www.domaine-de-saint-ferreol.fr

Entry 665   Map 16

Provence - Alps - Riviera

Domaine de Nestuby

Bravo, Nathalie! – in calm, friendly control of this gorgeous, well-restored 18th-century bastide. One whole wing is for guests: the light, airy, vineyard-view bedrooms, pastel-painted and Provençal-furnished with a happy mix of antique and modern (including WiFi), the big bourgeois sitting room (little used: it's too lovely outside), the new spa on the roof terrace and the great spring-fed tank for swims. Jean-François runs the vineyard, the tastings and the wine talk at dinner with sweet-natured ease. Utterly relaxing and very close to perfection. *Minimum three nights July/August.*

Price	€80.
Rooms	5: 1 double, 1 twin, 1 triple, 1 family room, 1 suite.
Meals	Dinner with wine, €27.
Closed	Mid-December to February.
Directions	From A8 Brignoles exit north D554 through Le Val; D22 through Montfort sur Argens for Cotignac. 5km along left; sign.

Nathalie & Jean-François Roubaud
Domaine de Nestuby,
83570 Cotignac,
Var

Tel	+33 (0)4 94 04 60 02
Email	nestuby@wanadoo.fr
Web	www.nestuby-provence.com

Entry 666   Map 16

Villa de Lorgues

Expect the unexpected in this stately 18th-century townhouse. From the basement spa to the traditional living rooms – level with the delicious garden and terrace – to the bedrooms at the top, all is pure enchantment. A red lantern here, zany birdcages there, four-posters, fireplaces and candles just where you least expect them. Bedrooms combine superb comfort with an elegant minimalist décor. Come evening, fairy lights wink along the wrought-iron balustrades from top to bottom. Claudie juggles a busy freelance career with talent, taste, a warm welcome and a fabulous sense of humour. *Minimum two nights July/August.*

Price	€100-€175.
Rooms	2 doubles.
Meals	Restaurants within walking distance.
Closed	January-March.
Directions	From Vidauban centre D48 to Lorgues; at r'bout on outskirts 3rd exit to Salernes; 1st right Rue du 8 mai. Park on street as high as possible; house straight ahead.

Claudie Cais
Villa de Lorgues,
7 rue de la Bourgade,
83510 Lorgues en Provence, Var
Tel   +33 (0)4 93 38 13 80
Email   cais.claudie@wanadoo.fr
Web   www.villadelorgues.com

Entry 667   Map 16

La Sarrazine

Sumptuous gardens on multiple levels, a wonderful variety of trees and flowers, and terraces for quiet moments: paradise at its best, with views thrown in. One spacious double is all creams, with white sheets beautifully embroidered; there are blues, reds and yellows elsewhere, and an uncluttered cosiness. Guests share a large, relaxed sitting/dining room with a fireplace and a terrace. Lively Hilary has won a seat on the village municipal council: looking after both guests and community comes easily to her. Tennis and boules here, and Lorgues' restaurants and weekly market a short walk. Delightful. *Minimum two nights.*

Price	€95-€125.
Rooms	3: 1 double, 2 twins/doubles.
Meals	Dinner €20-€30. Wine €15.
Closed	Rarely.
Directions	Directions on booking.

Hilary Smith
La Sarrazine,
375 chemin du Pendedi,
83510 Lorgues, Var
Tel   +33 (0)4 94 73 20 27
Mobile   +33 (0)6 77 15 63 24
Email   reservations@lasarrazine.com
Web   www.lasarrazine.com

Entry 668   Map 16

Les Trois Cyprès

What a view! Sit here, above surrounding villas, gazing past palms and pool to the plunging sea and enjoying Yvette's speciality of the day (apple tarts, fruit crumbles…). She is a wonderful woman, entertaining and endlessly caring; charming Guy collects the fresh breads and helps you plan your stay; they have travelled lots and simply love people. Pretty guest rooms lead off a bright, Moroccan-touched landing and have rugs on lovely honeycomb-tile floors. The biggest room is definitely the best; the one next door is ideal for children. You can catch the ferry to St Tropez twice a week. *Minimum two nights.*

L'Hirondelle Blanche

The beach is over the road, St Tropez a boat-trip away: charming out of season. Quite a character, Monsieur Georges enjoys painting, music, wine and old houses; he renovated this typical palmy 1900s Riviera villa himself. His paintings hang in the cosy sitting room, wines may appear for an evening tasting. Each room has a personal touch: a big red parasol over a bed, a fishing net on a wall; some have little balconies; bathrooms are basic with healthily rough eco-friendly, line-dried towels; breakfast is good. Despite the road, you don't need a car: fly in, train in, take a taxi or come by bike. *TGV station 10-minute walk.*

Price	€90–€120.
Rooms	2: 1 double, 1 twin.
Meals	Restaurants 500m.
Closed	October–May.
Directions	From Ste Maxime N98 E thro' San Peïre; left Av Belvédère; 2nd right Av de l'Ancien Petit Train des P; 50m, left Av de Coteaux; 3rd left Corniche Ligure to r'bout. Beige gate.

Price	€96–€176.
Rooms	6: 4 doubles, 1 twin/double, 1 family suite for 4.
Meals	Breakfast €4.50–€13. Restaurants 0.4km.
Closed	Mid-October to mid-February.
Directions	A8 exit 38 for St Raphaël town centre; from old port follow sea front towards Cannes (with sea on right) 900m; house after Casino de Jeux.

Yvette & Guy Pons
Les Trois Cyprès,
947 bd des Nymphes,
83380 Les Issambres, Var

Tel +33 (0)4 98 11 80 31
Mobile +33 (0)6 61 93 42 18
Email gyjpons@mac.com
Web homepage.mac.com/gyjpons/TOC.html

Georges & Florence Methout
L'Hirondelle Blanche,
533 bd du Général de Gaulle,
83700 St Raphaël, Var

Tel +33 (0)4 98 11 84 03
Email kussler-methout@wanadoo.fr
Web www.hirondelle-blanche.fr

Provence - Alps - Riviera

La Bégude du Pascouren

Monsieur Delambre runs a tight ship. Cool, stylish rooms have their own entrance terraces, ceramic lamps, pristine bathrooms and bursts of colour from modern art. A carefully planted garden is yours to enjoy; beyond the secure car park, shrubs and bamboo muffle daytime road noise. Thoughtful touches include a shared summer kitchen, a washing machine and pre-ordered breakfasts (apricot and basil jam a speciality) to avoid waste. Walk or cycle the forest trails that take off from behind the house… the handsome Pays de Fayence has stacks to offer, from music festivals to canyonning, and the coast is a 30-minute drive.

La Guillandonne

A very long drive, anticipation, then the house, the river, the cool forest. These lovely, civilised people, former teacher of English and architect, have treated their old house with delicacy and taste. Standing so Italianately red-ochre in its superb *parc* of great old trees and stream, it could have stepped out of a 19th-century novel. The interior speaks for your hosts' caring, imaginative approach (polished cement floors, rustic Salernes tiles). Bedrooms are full of personality, elegant and colourful; the living room is exquisite with vintage Italian hanging lamps and Le Corbusier chairs. *Sawday self-catering also.*

Price	€120-€183.
Rooms	3: 2 doubles, 1 suite.
Meals	Summer kitchen. Restaurant 2km.
Closed	Rarely.
Directions	From Grasse, D2562 then D562 for Draguignan; straight over at crossroads with D563 & D4; cont. 1.3km; signed, on right sharply off main road.

Price	€90.
Rooms	3: 2 doubles, 1 twin.
Meals	Restaurants 1.5km.
Closed	Rarely.
Directions	From A8 'Les Adrets' exit 39 for Fayence; left after lake, D562 for Fayence/Tourrettes; at Intermarché r'bout D19 to Fayence 2km; right D219 to Tourrettes; 200m black gate on right.

Philippe Delambre
La Bégude du Pascouren,
74 chemin de la Bane, Le Haut
Pascouren, 83440 Fayence, Var

Tel	+33 (0)4 94 68 63 03
Mobile	+33 (0)6 03 06 20 57
Email	labegudedupascouren@orange.fr
Web	www.chambres-hotes-labegudedupascouren.fr

Marie-Joëlle Salaün
La Guillandonne,
Chemin du Pavillon,
83440 Tourrettes, Var

Tel	+33 (0)4 94 76 04 71
Mobile	+33 (0)6 24 20 73 09
Email	guillandonne@wanadoo.fr

Entry 671   Map 16

Entry 672   Map 16

Provence - Alps - Riviera

Le Relais du Peyloubet

A hint of Tuscany seeps through this ancient farmhouse, its shutters and terracotta tiles, standing on a hillside wrapped in olive groves. Once growing flowers for Grasse perfumers, its delicious terraces and orchards are now tended by Roby while Xavier, a pâtissier, whisks up the fabulous breakfasts. Dinners are do-it-yourself in the summer kitchen overlooking the peaceful hills. Beamed and parquet-floored bedrooms, all with private terraces, are furnished in country Provençal style. There are shady seats in the woods, glorious views, boules, pool, and the coast 20 minutes. Blissfully calm, easy and welcoming.

Price	€70–€110.
Rooms	5 doubles.
Meals	Summer kitchen. Restaurant 3km.
Closed	Mid-November to mid-March.
Directions	From A8 exit 42 to Grasse. N85 last exit Grasse centre, then E.Leclerc, then St Jean, then Le Peyloubet.

Xavier Stoeckel
Le Relais du Peyloubet,
65 chemin de la Plâtrière,
06130 Grasse, Alpes-Maritimes
Email relais-peyloubet@wanadoo.fr
Web   www.relais-peyloubet.com.fr

Entry 673 Map 16

Provence - Alps - Riviera

Mas du Mûrier

The paradise of a garden, blending into the pine-clothed hillside, is a lesson in Mediterranean flora, aeons away from the potteries and madding fleshpots of nearby Vallauris. The Roncés restored this old building on a terraced vineyard: such peace. Make the most of the pool, relax to the sound of chirruping cicadas. The bedrooms in this multi-levelled house – one looking over the garden, one the pool – have in common modern paintings, stippled walls, bright textiles and old brocante. English-speaking Monsieur enjoys guests and breakfasts are basic. *Minimum three nights in summer.*

Price	€85–€90.
Rooms	2: 1 twin; 1 double with separate shower.
Meals	Bistro within walking distance.
Closed	Rarely.
Directions	From A8 Antibes exit 44 to Vallauris; Chemin St Bernard, then Chemin des Impiniers; right into Montée des Impiniers; left at Auberge du Gros Pin; sharp right into picnic area and right up track, signed.

M & Mme Roncé
Mas du Mûrier,
1407 route de Grasse,
06220 Vallauris, Alpes-Maritimes
Tel   +33 (0)4 93 64 52 32
Email fcwh-ronce@orange.fr
Web   www.guesthouse-cannes.com

Entry 674 Map 16

Le Clos de St Paul

A young Provençal house on a lushly planted and screened piece of land where boundary hedging is high. In a guest wing, each pretty bedroom has its own patio, and there's a wonderful summer kitchen for guests to share. Smiling Madame has furnished with great simple taste – anthracite greys, mellow yellows, painted chairs, the odd antique. She genuinely cares that you have the best, offers a welcome glass of rosé on her stunning shaded terrace and serves a very fresh breakfast in the garden. The lovely large mosaic'd pool is refreshingly discreet. Great value. *Minimum two nights.*

Lou Candelou

Terracotta roofs peep over lush foliage in this residential area to hills and the heavenly Mediterranean. A huge mimosa guards the small friendly house of local stone and blue shutters; arrive by narrow private road to a lovely welcome from young Boun. Fresh, charming rooms with ethnic cottons, painted furniture and spotless bathrooms lead to a potted terrace. Make your own picnic or barbecue in the kitchen by the guest sitting room; enjoy a feast of pastries, fresh fruit, exotic conserves on the big balcony with views; pull yourself away and hop on a train to the coast. *Children over 10 welcome. Summer +20% if one night only.*

Price	€75–€90.
Rooms	3 doubles.
Meals	Summer kitchen. Restaurant 1km.
Closed	Rarely.
Directions	A8 exit 48 for St Paul de Vence, 3km; after La Colle sur Loup cont. to St Paul. 1st right after r'bout; left at T-junc.; right, 1st house on left.

Price	€60–€80. Whole house available in winter.
Rooms	3 doubles.
Meals	Guest kitchen. Restaurant 1km.
Closed	Rarely.
Directions	A8 Nice to Cannes; exit 47 for Villeneuve Loubet & Grasse; after Le Rouret, over r'bout; Pré du Lac r'bout for Palais de Justice; 2nd exit at Les Roumégons r'bout, thro' tunnel to lights; house 1st on right.

	Béatrice Ronin Pillet
	Le Clos de St Paul, 71 chemin de la Rouguière, 06480 La Colle sur Loup, Alpes-Maritimes
Tel	+33 (0)4 93 32 56 81
Email	leclossaintpaul@hotmail.com
Web	www.leclossaintpaul.com

	Mme Bougie
	Lou Candelou, 57 avenue St Laurent, 06520 Magagnosc, Alpes-Maritimes
Tel	+33 (0)4 93 36 90 16
Mobile	+33 (0)6 03 86 45 58
Email	loucandelou@neuf.fr
Web	www.loucandelou.com

Entry 675   Map 16

Entry 676   Map 16

Les Coquelicots

Annick, charming, kind and well-travelled, is a former riding instructor, now more likely to be helping people into hammocks than onto horses. Take a siesta in her peaceful garden, a chaos of greenery and birdsong, its ancient olive trees dotted about the terraces and among the ponds and lush grasses. (Future plans include an extension with spaces for birds nests and bats.) The blue bedroom is charming with its own terrace, vast antique wardrobe, fine linen and old wooden bed. Breakfast outside, or among orchids on the greenhouse veranda. Then visit Vence for Matisse's final flourish. *Minimum three nights.*

Ethical Collection: Environment.
See page 410 for details.

Price	€60.
Rooms	1 double with kitchenette.
Meals	Restaurants in village.
Closed	November to mid-December & occasionally.
Directions	From Grasse D2085 to Le Rouret; thro' village, left D7 for La Colle sur Loup & Cagnes; on leaving village, hard right down steep track; house on right; call to meet Madame at Mairie.

Annick Le Guay
Les Coquelicots,
30 route de Roquefort,
06650 Le Rouret, Alpes-Maritimes
Tel +33 (0)4 93 77 40 04
Email annick.coquelicot@aliceadsl.fr

Entry 677 Map 16

The Frog's House

Quiet, green, frog-sung air, sight-lines over rooftops to mountains, valley and sea, a brand-new renovation done by a passionately committed young couple in an unspoilt village. Corinne, from La Réunion, and Benoît, a local boy, met in Australia. They will point (or take) you to fabulous hikes for all, from timid to trained; promote local produce and biodiversity; serve superb Provençal and Creole food; organise natural-wine tastings. And they know the local craftspeople. The atmosphere is all fresh simplicity with spotless white paint, new pine furniture – and friendship. A real place. *Guided tours. Cookery classes.*

Price	€74-€94. 3-day full-board stays available.
Rooms	6: 3 twins/doubles, 3 doubles.
Meals	Dinner €24-€34. Wine €12-€21. Restaurants in village.
Closed	Mid-November to mid-December; mid-January to mid-March.
Directions	Directions on booking.

Benoît & Corinne Couvreur
The Frog's House,
35 rue du Saumalier,
06640 St Jeannet, Alpes-Maritimes
Tel +33 (0)4 93 58 98 05
Email info@thefrogshouse.com
Web www.thefrogshouse.com

Entry 678 Map 16

La Locandiera

Built for holidays and for early 20th-century entertaining, this Côte d'Azur villa is a literal stone's throw from the fishing port and beach, and charming Madame Rizzardo has forsaken Venice to restore it. Her open-plan living room has an aura of witty conversation, dry cinzano and stylish cigarette holding (now a thing of the past, of course). Three of the cool, fresh, traditionally furnished bedrooms look straight out to sea over a walled garden whose jasmine-sweet corners are furnished for shaded retreat. Heaps of restaurants and smart places are reachable on foot. *Ask about massage & reflexology.*

Terrasses du Soleil

All the charm of a restored medieval hilltop village above the bustle and beach of Cagnes. The Bouvets' home was a 60s night club fashionable with celebrities, and traces remain: fine terrace breakfasts (home baking a speciality) happen next to the dance floor. Rooms are distributed up and down stairs and come in different styles: retro, Provençal, classic, each with a trim loggia or balcony and distant sea, mountain and rooftop views. Forget the car: Madame, a local expert, will help you negotiate excellent public transport links to Antibes, Monaco, Cannes and beyond. *Minimum two nights July/August.*

Price	€130-€150.
Rooms	4: 2 doubles, 1 twin, 1 suite for 2.
Meals	Restaurant 100m.
Closed	Last 2 weeks in November.
Directions	A8 exit 46 Bouches du Loup D241; follow signs for Cagnes sur Mer D6098; cont. Bd de la Plage; right Av Cap. de Frégate Vial.

Price	€105-€125.
Rooms	4: 2 doubles, 2 suites.
Meals	Restaurants 5-minute walk.
Closed	Mid-November to mid-December.
Directions	From Nice, A8 exit 48 for Cagnes sur Mer. Follow signs for Bourg Mediéval.

Daniela Rizzardo
La Locandiera,
9 av Capitaine de Frégate Vial,
06800 Cagnes sur Mer, Alpes-Maritimes
Tel   +33 (0)4 97 22 25 86
Mobile +33 (0)6 27 88 17 40
Email   daniela@lalocandieracagnes.com
Web   www.lalocandieracagnes.com

Catherine Bouvet
Terrasses du Soleil, Place Notre Dame
de la Protection, Le Haut de Cagnes,
06800 Cagnes sur Mer, Alpes-Maritime
Tel   +33 (0)4 93 73 26 56
Email   catherine.bouvet@terrassesdusoleil.com
Web   www.terrassesdusoleil.com

Provence - Alps - Riviera

Villa Kilauea

A grand Mediterranean villa that looks so settled in Nice's lush western hills you'd never guess it was a 21st-century creation. There are balustrade-edged terraces, an infinity pool and panoramic views of the open valley. Bedrooms have a zen-like calm: wrought-iron four-posters draped in muslin, teak floors, white walls; bright orchids and oriental silks hint at the exotic. The one in the main house is more traditional with lovely family antiques. Nathalie, the perfect host, kind, gentle and generous to a tee, delights in juggling a busy family life with her B&B venture. Nice is a ten-minute drive down the hill.

Price	€110-€140.
Rooms	3 doubles.
Meals	Restaurants in Nice.
Closed	Rarely.
Directions	From Nice Promenade des Anglais for Hôpital l'Archet, then for St Roman; follow Av. Bornala; Canta Galet, then Route de Bellet. At church in St Roman left; gates to house on right after 200m.

Nathalie Graffagnino
Villa Kilauea,
6 chemin du Candeu,
06200 Nice, Alpes-Maritimes
Tel   +33 (0)4 93 37 84 90
Email   villakilauea@orange.fr
Web   www.villakilauea.com

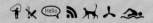

Entry 681   Map 16

Provence - Alps - Riviera

Villa L'Aimée

In one of the most authentic parts of Nice, a short bus ride from the city's rich culture (buses stop virtually at the gate), Villa L'Aimée was built in 1929 and is typical of its period. Toni's decoration has restored its wonderful shapes and details to their original opulence. Warm, cultured and much-travelled – one of her lives was in the art world – she has created delightful bedrooms in subtle colours with damasks and silks, fine linen, tulle canopies and beautiful furnishings, exuding an air of old luxury. The original parquet is breathtaking, the breakfasts are superb. *Babies & children over ten welcome.*

Price	€110-€135.
Rooms	3: 2 twins/doubles, 1 twin.
Meals	Restaurants within walking distance.
Closed	December-March.
Directions	A8 exit 54 for Nice centre ville; left Av du Ray; r'bout right; over 2nd r'bout; Pl Alex Médicin left; left Av Henry Durant; 1st left at Garage Auto Bilan; immed. right Vieux Ch de Gairaut; 1st right Av Piatti.

Toni Redding
Villa L'Aimée,
5 avenue Piatti,
06100 Nice, Alpes-Maritimes
Tel   +33 (0)4 93 52 34 13
Mobile +33 (0)6 71 82 67 72
Email   bookings@villa-aimee.co.uk
Web   www.villa-aimee.co.uk

Entry 682   Map 16

Provence - Alps - Riviera

La Tour Manda

Such engaging hosts – nothing is too much trouble. Set well back from the busy dual carriageway, the house is convenient for airport and town (a 15-minute drive). And, inside, what a classic Côte d'Azur setting: your delightful bedroom overlooks a charming garden with palms. Jean-Claude was born in this house; it is colourful, like its owners. Expect light, space and heaps of southern style – family antiques, sofas with throws, posters and paintings. Breakfast, on the pretty terrace in summer, is delicious – be sure to try Jean-Claude's scrambled eggs! *Open on request during carnival. Minimum two nights.*

Price	€110. €180 for 4. Extra bed €20.
Rooms	3: 2 doubles, 1 suite for 4.
Meals	Restaurant 1km.
Closed	Rarely.
Directions	From Nice airport D6202 for Digne Grenoble; past centre commercial Carrefour; right onto small road just before 'Cuisine Number 1'.

Jean-Claude & Brigitte Janer
La Tour Manda, 24 chemin de
St Roman, 682 route de Grenoble,
06200 Nice, Alpes-Maritimes

Tel	+33 (0)4 93 29 81 32
Mobile	+33 (0)6 19 02 43 13
Email	latourmanda@wanadoo.fr
Web	www.latourmanda.fr

Entry 683   Map 16

Provence - Alps - Riviera

Le Castel Enchanté

Way, way above Nice (the road up should not be tackled in the dark), drowned in bougainvillea, the old Italianate villa with 70s additions stands in a jungle of scented garden. Your hosts are extremely engaging and love meeting guests. Bedrooms – the biggest with a glassed-in veranda – are glossy with Provençal colours, fabric flounces, stippled walls and tiled floors; each has a fridge and a TV. On the sunny terrace with pretty views Madame's breakfast spreads offer cheese, cereals, pastries and fruit salads. A super pool above and a pretty puss complete the picture.

Price	€110. Suite €190.
Rooms	4: 2 doubles, 1 twin/double, 1 suite for 4.
Meals	Restaurants 2km.
Closed	Rarely.
Directions	From Nice, Pl St Philippe, under expressway, left Av Estienne d'Orves 600m, over level crossing, after sharp right-hand bend, hard back left, tricky track up to house.

Martine Ferrary
Le Castel Enchanté,
61 route de St Pierre de Féric,
06000 Nice, Alpes-Maritimes

Tel	+33 (0)4 93 97 02 08
Email	contact@castel-enchante.com
Web	www.castel-enchante.com

Entry 684   Map 16

Provence - Alps - Riviera

La Parare

Cradled in summer by cicada chant and the gentle wind, cocooned in winter in a romantic log-fired bedroom, you will be bewitched by the subtle mix of clean-cut modernity and fine oriental detail that your much-travelled polyglot hosts have achieved in this craggy old house. Breakfast in bed anyone? Bathtub for two? Elegant gourmet dinner? All of these and more: Karin from Sweden and French/Dutch Sydney love pampering people. The rough hills outside highlight the delicacy inside, the natural walled pool, the stunning bathrooms, the civilised conversation at dinner. Worth every centime. *Gourmet cookery courses in winter.*

Price	€130–€145.
Rooms	4 doubles.
Meals	Dinner €30–€45 (once or twice a week).
Closed	Rarely.
Directions	A8 exit 55, D2204 for Sospel 5km; fork left for Contes 5km; left D815 to Châteauneuf Villevieille. In village, right for church, 1st left, signed.

Karin & Sydney van Volen
La Parare, 67 Calade du Pastre,
06390 Châteauneuf Villevieille,
Alpes-Maritimes
Tel +33 (0)4 93 79 22 62
Email karin@laparare.com
Web www.laparare.com

Entry 685 Map 16

Provence - Alps - Riviera

Domaine du Paraïs

Walkers and birdwatchers are happy here, in the gentle isolation of private woodland, dramatic miles up from the hot Riviera. The slightly faded Italianate mansion is home to highly cultured, artistic, English-fluent people who have re-awakened its 19th-century magic. No clutter, either of mind or matter, here. Breakfast is in the atmospheric old kitchen or on the shady terrace in summer. White bedrooms have pretty fabrics, simple antiques and views of trees where birds burst their lungs and Monsieur Mayer's superb sculptures await you. Marie is multi-talented, too. Come for dreamy space, natural peace, intelligent conversation.

Price	€55–€70.
Rooms	2 doubles.
Meals	Restaurants in Sospel, 1km.
Closed	Rarely.
Directions	From Menton D2566 to Sospel; at entrance to village left for Col de Turini 1.9km; left at house 'miel' for 'La Vasta' & 'Campings'. Paraïs 1.3km along, hard back on right after ranch & sharp bend.

Marie Mayer
Domaine du Paraïs,
La Vasta Supérieure,
06380 Sospel, Alpes-Maritimes
Tel +33 (0)4 93 04 15 78
Email domaine.du.parais@wanadoo.fr
Web domaineduparais.monsite.wanadoo.fr

Entry 686 Map 16

Monaco

Villa Nyanga

Looking breath-takingly east over the yacht-studded bay, south over the onion domes of a *fin de siècle* Persian palace, here is a warmly human refuge from the fascinating excesses that are Monaco. Michèle's sober, white-painted flat is decorated with wood, marble and lots of contemporary art, her own and her friends'. Living room: arched doors, little fireplace, little breakfast table, wide balcony; guest room: white candlewick bedcover, big gilt-framed mirror, sea view; bathroom: gloriously old-fashioned beige. Space everywhere, and Michèle is as good a hostess as she is an artist.

Price	€110.
Rooms	1 twin/double.
Meals	Restaurants in Monaco.
Closed	Last 2 weeks in August.
Directions	From A8 exit 56 Monaco for centre (tunnel); past Jardin Exotique; on right-hand bend (pharmacy on corner) left; left at end Malbousquet; park opp. No. 26 to unload.

Michèle Rousseau
Villa Nyanga,
26 rue Malbousquet,
98000 Monaco

Tel	+377 93 50 32 81
Email	michelle.rousseau@mageos.com
Web	www.bbfrance.com/rousseau.html

Entry 687   Map 16

Photo: Lesley Chalmers

If you have any comments on entries in this guide, please tell us. If you have a favourite place or a new discovery, please let us know about it. You can return this form or visit www.sawdays.co.uk.

Existing entry

Property name: _____

Entry number: _____ Date of visit: _____

New recommendation

Property name: _____

Address: _____

_____

Tel/Email/Web: _____

Your comments

What did you like (or dislike) about this place? Were the people friendly? What was the location like? What sort of food did they serve?

_____

_____

_____

_____

Your details

Name: _____

Address: _____

_____

_____ Postcode: _____

Tel: _____ Email: _____

Please send completed form to:
FBB, Sawday's, The Old Farmyard, Yanley Lane, Long Ashton, Bristol BS41 9LR, UK

Many of you may want to stay in environmentally friendly places. You may be passionate about local, organic or home-grown food. Or perhaps you want to know that the place you are staying in contributes to the community? To help you we have launched our Ethical Collection, so you can find the right place to stay and also discover how each owner is addressing these issues.

The Collection is made up of places going the extra mile, and taking the steps that most people have not yet taken, in one or more of the following areas:

• **Environment** Those making great efforts to reduce the environmental impact of their Special Place. We expect more than energy-saving light bulbs and recycling – in this part of the Collection you will find owners who make their own natural cleaning products, properties with solar hot water and biomass boilers, the odd green roof and a good measure of green elbow grease.

• **Community** Given to owners who use their property to play a positive role in their local and wider community. For example, by making a contribution from every guest's bill to a local fund, or running pond-dipping courses for local school children on their farm.

• **Food** Awarded to owners who make a real effort to source local or organic food, or to grow their own. We look for those who have gone out of their way to strike up relationships with local producers or to seek out organic suppliers. It is easier for an owner on a farm to produce their own eggs than for someone in the middle of a city, so we take this into account.

Photo: Ecolodge des Chartrons, entry 399

How it works

To become part of our Ethical Collection owners choose whether to apply in one, two or all three categories, and fill in a detailed questionnaire asking demanding questions about their activities in the chosen areas.

You can download the questions here: http://www.sawdays.co.uk/ethical_collection/pdf/ethical_collection_English.pdf

We then review each questionnaire carefully before deciding whether or not to give the award(s). The final decision is subjective; it is based not only on whether an owner ticks 'yes' to a question but also on the detailed explanation that accompanies each 'yes' or 'no' answer. For example, an owner who has tried as hard as possible to install solar water-heating panels, but has failed because of strict conservation planning laws, will be given some credit for their effort (as long as they are doing other things in this area).

We have tried to be as rigorous as possible and have made sure the questions are demanding. We have not checked out the claims of owners before making our decisions, but we do trust them to be honest. We are only human, as are they, so please let us know if you think we have made any mistakes.

The Ethical Collection is still a relatively new initiative for us, and we'd love to know what you think about it – email us at ethicalcollection@sawdays.co.uk or write to us. And remember that because this is a relatively new scheme some owners have not yet completed their questionnaires – we're sure other places in the guide are working just as hard in these areas, but we don't yet know the full details.

Ethical Collection in this book

On the entry page of all places in the Collection we show which awards have been given.

Ethical Collection online

There is stacks more information on our website, www.sawdays.co.uk. You can read the answers each owner has given to our Ethical Collection questionnaire and get a more detailed idea of what they are doing in each area. You can also search for properties that have awards.

Photo: Pauliac, entry 436

Two and a half times the size of Great Britain and about the size of Texas, France offers rich rewards to the cyclist: plenty of space, a superb network of minor roads with little traffic, and a huge diversity of landscapes, terrains and smells (smell contributes so much to the pleasure of riding through the country-side). You can chose the leafy forests and undulating plains of the north, or the jagged glacier-topped mountains of the Alps. Pedal through wafts of fermenting grapes in Champagne, resinous pines in the Midi, or spring flowers in the Pyrenees. You can amble slowly, stopping in remote villages for delicious meals or a café au lait, or pit yourself against the toughest terrains and cycle furiously. Or you can plan to 'do' all the châteaux of the Loire, one after the other. Once you're in France, it is useful to know that, although the proper academic name for the "little queen", as fond users call it, is 'une bicyclette', it is always known as 'un vélo'.

You will be joining in a national sport: bicycling is an important part of French culture and thousands don their lycra and take to their bikes on summer weekends for a family ride or a serious race. The country comes to a virtual standstill during the three-week Tour de France bike race in July and cycling stars become national heroes with quasi-divine status. Their misdeeds and downfalls, physical or moral, are as important as those of Europe's royals and other objects of the celebrity cult.

When to go

Avoid July and August, if possible, as it's hot and the roads are at their busiest. The south is good from mid-March, though high ground may hold snow until the end of June. The north can be lovely from May onwards. Most other areas are suitable from April until October.

Getting bikes to and through France

You can get your bicycle to France prettily easily. Ferries carry bikes for nothing or for a small fee. On Eurostar, you should be able to store them in one of the guards' vans, just book ahead and 'buy your bike a ticket'.

Some mainline and most regional trains accept bikes, for a fee. Information on timetables is contradictory and ticket agents may not have up-to-date information so be certain, check up at the station the day before you set off. Insist on a ticket avec réservation d'un emplacement vélo. If you are two or more, make sure the booking is multiple. In the Paris area, you can take bikes on most trains except during rush hours.

Maps

The two big names are Michelin and the Institut Géographique National (IGN). For route-planning, IGN publishes a map of the whole of France showing mountain-biking and cycle tourism. The best on-the-road reference maps are Michelin's yellow 1:200,000 Series. IGN publishes a Green Series to the scale of 1:100,000. For larger scale maps, go for IGN's

excellent 1:25,000 Top 25 and Blue Series (which you will also use for walking).

A map of Paris showing bike routes, one-way streets, bus sharing lanes, long-term rental facilities (Maison Roue Libre), weekend pedestrian and bike-only streets is available at some bookshops. Order it on line: www.media-cartes.fr

Useful contacts

- Fédération Française de Cyclotourisme. For cyclists and mountain bikers. www.ffct.org
- Fédération Française de la Randonnée Pédestre (FFRP). Leading organisation for walkers and ramblers. Their guide books are useful for cyclists, too, and many of them have been translated into English. www.ffrp.asso.fr

Photo: Lesley Chalmers

- SNCF (French Railways) www.voyages-sncf.com

Bike hire

Consult the owners of the place you are staying at about local bike hire.

Cycling in French cities

Municipal hire schemes

- Paris: Velib' www.velib.paris.fr
  In 2007, the Paris council launched its bike rental scheme with 1,200 'stations', each holding a dozen solidly-built bikes for €1 per day, €5 per week, €29 per year, payable by credit card. The first half hour of each new rental period is included in the charge. Accessible to everyone over the age of 14.
- Many other French cities run bike-hire schemes: consult each city's website.

Quick reference indices

Cookery courses

For wine-lovers

Owner can organise wine
tasting/vineyard visits or
produces wine.

Quick reference indices

Quick reference indices

Child-friendly with a swimming pool

Pet-friendly

Pets are welcome and can sleep in your bedroom.

Places with a pool and a tennis court

Quick reference indices

Alastair Sawday has been publishing books for over twenty years, finding Special Places to Stay in Britain and abroad. All our properties are inspected by us and are chosen for their charm and individuality and, now, with twenty-four titles to choose from there are plenty of places to explore. You can buy any of our books at a reader discount of 35%* on the RRP.

List of titles:	RRP	Discount price
British Bed & Breakfast	£14.99	£9.74
British Bed & Breakfast for Garden Lovers	£14.99	£9.74
British Hotels and Inns	£14.99	£9.74
Pubs & Inns of England & Wales	£15.99	£10.39
Venues	£11.99	£7.79
Cotswolds	£9.99	£6.49
Devon & Cornwall	£9.99	£6.49
Wales	£9.99	£6.49
Ireland	£12.99	£8.44
French Bed & Breakfast	£15.99	£10.39
French Self-Catering	£14.99	£9.74
French Châteaux & Hotels	£14.99	£9.74
French Vineyards	£19.99	£12.99
Paris	£9.99	£6.49
Green Europe	£11.99	£7.79
Italy	£14.99	£9.74
Portugal	£11.99	£7.79
Spain	£14.99	£9.74
Morocco	£9.99	£6.49
India	£11.99	£7.79
Go Slow England & Wales	£19.99	£12.99
Go Slow France	£19.99	£12.99
Go Slow Italy	£19.99	£12.99
Eat Slow Britain	£19.99	£12.99

*postage and packaging is added to each order

How to order:

You can order online at: www.sawdays.co.uk/bookshop/

or call: +44(0)1275 395431

Becoming a member of Sawday's Travel Club opens up hundreds of discounts, treats and other offers at over 700 of our Special Places to Stay in Britain and Ireland, as well as 50% discount on all Sawday's books.

Offers range from money off your room price, to a bottle of wine, a basket of home-grown produce and champagne afternoon tea on arrival, just to name a few. For all the latest offers from participating places you can search online at www/sawdays/co.uk/travel_club or by searching for the 🧳 symbol at www.sawdays.co.uk/search.

Membership is only £25 per year. To join the Travel Club visit www.sawdays.co.uk/bookshop/travel_club.

The small print

Owners reserve the right to change the listed offer. You must mention that you are a Travel Club member when booking, and confirm that the offer is available. Your Travel Club card must be shown on arrival to claim the offer. Sawday's Travel Club cards are not transferable. If two cardholders share a room they can only claim the offer once. Some offers for Sawday's Travel Club members are subject to availability. Alastair Sawday Publishing cannot accept any responsibility if places fail to honour offers; neither can we accept responsibility if a place changes hands and drops out of the Travel Club.

Photos (from left): The Great House, Langar Hall, Moccas Court, all from our British Hotels & Inns guide

Your passport to a choice of Special Places to Stay in Britain

Sawday's Gift Cards can be used at a whole array of bed and breakfasts, hotels, self-catering places and pubs with rooms scattered across Britain. You may fancy a night in a country house which towers majestically over the River Usk, or perhaps a weekend in a splendid Georgian mansion in the Cotswolds. Stay in a garret above a legendary London coffee house or sample a stunning barn conversion in the depths of Northumberland.

Wherever you choose as a treat for yourself, friends or a loved one we know it will be fun, unusual, maybe even eccentric and definitely life affirming. A perfect present.

Gift cards are available in six denominations – £25, £50, £75, £100, £150 and £200, and come in attractive packaging, which includes a series of postcards and a printed booklet featuring all the participating places.

You can purchase Gift Cards at: www.sawdays.co.uk/gift-cards/ or you can order them by phone: +44(0)1275 395431.

You can also view the full list of participating places on our website www.sawdays.co.uk and search by this symbol: 🎁

Photo: Chalet Pecchio, entry 614

Photo: www.istockphoto.com

1 Poitou - Charentes

Little Meadows

2 An English rose and a country doctor have transformed a Charentaise farmhouse with talent and love: wine-red shutters against exposed stone, a pergola heaving with scented roses, potted plants happy in their lustrous jars on the terrace. Through the cathedral ceiling'd salon, new oak stairs lead to a salon/landing (make yourself a cuppa) beamed bedrooms; one baldaquin'd in sun-yellow, the other canopied in valentine-red with views on leafy fig and lemon trees. Cédric is a busy GP, Alison is charming, cultured and cooks divinely. You may be lucky and spot the owls and European buzzards in the barn. *French courses.*

4 Price	€65.	
5 Rooms	3: 1 double, 1 triple, 1 suite for 2-4.	
6 Meals	Lunch €20. Dinner with wine, €26-€35.	
7 Closed	Rarely.	
8 Directions	From Niort for St Jean d'Angely 25km; left at Tout Y Faut for Aulnay. 2nd left, last house on right. Red signs.	

Cédric & Alison Bergoend-Gaffyne
Little Meadows,
Rue des Petits Prés, 17330 La Croix
Comtesse, Charente-Maritime
Tel   +33 (0)5 46 32 24 32
Mobile   +33 (0)6 09 80 41 54
Email   alisonbergoendgaffyne@anglofrench.info
Web   www.anglofrench.info

9 ♿ ☆ ♀ ⚑ ✗ ☺ 🚚 ⓘ ➰ 🐖 ⚲

10 Entry 383   Map 9

Poitou - Charentes

Les Hortensias

Behind its modest, wisteria-covered mask, this 17th-century former wine-grower's house hides a charming interior – and a magnificent garden that flows through orchard to topiary, a delight in every season. Soft duck-egg colours and rich trimmings make this a warm and safe haven, light airy bedrooms are immaculate (one with its original stone sink, another with a pretty French pink décor), the bathrooms are luxurious, the walls burst with art and the welcome is gracious, warm and friendly. Superb value, scrumptious dinners and blackcurrants from the potager – Madame's sorbets are the best.

3 Ethical Collection: Environment & Food. See page 410 for details.

Price	€59-€66. Extra person €17.
Rooms	3: 2 doubles, 1 triple.
Meals	Dinner with wine, €24. Summer kitchen. Restaurant in village.
Closed	Rarely.
Directions	From A10 exit 34 on D739 to Tonnay Boutonne; left D114 to Archingeay; left for Les Nouillers; house just after turning, with hydrangea at door.

Marie-Thérèse Jacques
Les Hortensias,
16 rue des Sablières,
17380 Archingeay, Charente-Maritime
Tel   +33 (0)5 46 97 85 70
Email   jpmt.jacques@wanadoo.fr
Web   www.chambres-hotes-hortensias.com

♿ ☆ ♀ ⚑ ✗ ☺ 🚚 ⓘ 🏹 ⚬

Entry 384   Map 8